# Adolescence today

*Sex roles and the*
*search for identity*

The Dorsey Series in Psychology

Editor
HOWARD F. HUNT  *Columbia University*

# Adolescence today

## Sex roles and the search for identity

**DAVID R. MATTESON,** Ph.D.
Associate Professor of Psychology
Marietta College

 1975

**THE DORSEY PRESS**  Homewood, Illinois  60430
Irwin-Dorsey International  London, England  WC2H 9NJ
Irwin-Dorsey Limited  Georgetown, Ontario  L7G 4B3

*Cover photo courtesy of*
*Lew Yeager, Marietta College*

*First Printing, May 1975*

ISBN 0-256-01731-X
Library of Congress Catalog Card No. 74–27541
*Printed in the United States of America*

To MOTHER,

*who showed me that it is possible to affirm both realities.*

# Foreword

## Frameworks for understanding adolescence

THE TRADITIONAL psychoanalytic theory of adolescence focuses upon the issue of sexuality. According to this theory, adolescence is described as a crisis in personality balance that:

1. Reaches its peak during the first years after puberty,
2. Centers around the emergence of sexuality
3. Which precipitates conflict within the home, usually resulting in rebellion against the parents.
4. The crisis is resolved when the adolescent can reduce his attachments to his parents, and invest himself in a person of the opposite sex.
5. The resulting sexual stabilization allows the personality to function in a mature way; the individual can then carry out realistic work roles in adult society.

Without explicitly rejecting the psychoanalytic formulation, Erik Erikson has developed the view that the focal issue of adolescence is a crisis in identity. The adolescent struggles to determine who he is and who he shall be in adult society. Adolescence is a period of exploring alternatives, and a time of decision making. Erikson has helped us to see the adolescent period in the broad perspective of the individual in relation to the society. The emphasis in adolescent theory has shifted from the maintenance of a psycho-sexual balance within the individual personality, to a search for personal identity within the society. In Erikson's theory, points four and five become:

4. The crisis is resolved through a period of moratorium in which the individual partially disengages himself from society in order to find himself.
5. This eventually results in the confirmation of an identity. The individual can then reinvest himself with others and take a place in the adult society.

Such a summary cannot do justice to the richness of Erikson's thought. The reader will find references to him throughout the book.

Erikson has attempted to formulate a general theory of adolescence which is applicable to all cultures. The present work has more modest goals. I seek to use the identity theme developed by Erikson as a way of ordering the data from that group of adolescents about whom we have the most information, the white, middle and upper class educated Americans. What emerges from my own encounter with today's college students, and from my reading of the experimental data, is a view of adolescence which contrasts sharply with the psychoanalytic view. A comparison of the five points listed above with the five point summary of my view which follows will demonstrate the contrast.

1.  The critical period of identity crisis is late adolescence.
2.  The personal struggle is to accept both inner and outer reality, to admit the subjective and sensuous without rejecting the pragmatic.
3.  The major conflict is between self and society, precipitated by the move out of the home into the world.
4.  The quest for identity is best pursued through active involvement in society.
5.  The healthy resolution, functional for our pluralistic society, does not result in a final confirmation of identity, but in a new openness to experience.

Though the data impel me to sharply reject much of the classical view of adolescence, the relationship between my viewpoint and Erikson's is more difficult to define. The configuration of the data which emerges in this book grew out of Erikson's recognition that adolescence is a period of identity crisis. I am deeply indebted to Erikson's work, though my perspective differs in several respects from his. Our theoretical differences will become clearer in the course of the book.

One important similarity between Erikson's work and my own should be noted. Like Erikson's works, this one includes some value judgements. To define the healthy directions of adolescent growth, and thus to make sense of the maturation process, I have had to clarify what I consider "mature" and "healthy." I believe these value judgements have been stated openly, so that the reader will not confuse them with facts.

This book is the work of a psychologist trying to be scientific about the study of man; but it is also the work of a counselor who cannot lay down his claim to being human—an evaluating, personal animal. My hope is that students may find it not only useful academically, but an aid to their personal search for identity in a confusing but exciting world.

D. R. M.

# *Preface*

## *Empirical data and the style of the textbook*

During the many years in which I have been a student of psychology, and more recently as I have been teaching adolescent psychology, I have noted that three kinds of books dominate the field. Two of these are generally compiled by psychologists: the standard text, which attempts to survey vast amounts of research; and collections of readings, which illustrate the theories and experiments of experts in the field. A third type of book is the integrative essay. Books of this type tend to be written by clinicians and counselors, usually psychiatrists and social workers. These manuscripts are sometimes brilliant, and witness to a depth of personal insight untapped in the other types of texts. Furthermore, they appeal to students because they make sense in an integrated way and they are personal in style. Unfortunately, most of them show a lack of awareness of careful empirical research. They do not help the student to think carefully and objectively about the area, or to make use of the empirical evidence available.

I have chosen a different approach. I have attempted to formulate generalizations as clearly and sharply as possible. I have tried to present the relevant empirical material and have stressed the scientific methods of psychology. My hope is that the empirical material is concrete enough so that the reader will not lose sight of the complexity and ambiguity of the adolescent experience, and of the persons who are adolescents. In its emphasis upon empirical studies, this book is like the more traditional, standard texts in the field. However, like the integrative books written by clinicians, this book attempts to tell a coherent story. It is a book with a theme.

## *The theme*

Sex role identification has been chosen as the integrating theme for this study of adolescent identity. Adolescence is that period of development between childhood and adulthood, a phase of transition from the life established by and provided for by one's parents to the establishment of one's own style of life in the world. The split in the sex roles which has been described in these chapters is closely related to a discontinuity in development which is most noticeable during adolescence: the discontinuity between the warm, personal home in which the child is reared, and the tough, competitive, objective world into which he must go.

The search for identity during adolescence is interpreted in the light of this split in sex roles and this discontinuity in development.

## Acknowledgments

I am indebted to youth for my inspiration. Several classes of students at Marietta College and a number of youths from the University of Copenhagen have been influential in shaping the ideas and concerns expressed here. I especially want to thank Jeffrey Applebaum, Birthe Engelbrecht, John Fantuzzo, Howard Smith, Mary Lee Stocks, and Pierre Topaz.

I am grateful to the librarians of the Royal Danish School of Educational Studies, and of Marietta College, for their patience and help in securing sources and references.

Three colleagues in adolescent psychology have offered helpful comments on the manuscript: W. Andrew Collins, Victor B. Cline, and Dorsey's consulting editor in psychology, Howard F. Hunt.

A number of friends and colleagues at Marietta College and in the community have read and constructively criticized early forms of the manuscript. One of these, Martha Stegner, deserves mention by name. I thank her, both for her practical help, and for her continuous support over a three year period.

The most important source of support and strength was my wife, Sandy. She encouraged me during the early, exciting phases of writing, even when it meant she must assume more responsibility for the children. When the manuscript grew out of its early, expressive stage, and the tasks of shaping it up became tedious, hard work, Sandy was still beside me, as editor, typist, reference librarian, and at points, coauthor; and still she maintained her role as mother. My mother taught me to live in both the expressive and instrumental worlds. Now Sandy lives in both worlds with me, and was involved in both through the development of this book. For that I am deeply grateful.

*April 1975*                                                      DAVID R. MATTESON

# Contents

# *part one*

# Preparations for conflict

THE CONFLICT OF adolescence is the search for identity, the struggle to choose among many alternatives and affirm who one is in relation to the larger society. This attempt to establish an identity has its beginnings long before puberty, the official mark of the beginning of adolescence. The first five chapters of this book survey the preparations for the identity struggle of adolescence by describing the development of sex roles in American society.

The topic of sex roles may have sufficient interest for readers so that they will not question its use. Nonetheless, as the focal point for this study of the adolescent's search for identity, the choice needs some further justification. By centering upon sex roles to interpret the identity crisis of American adolescents, I do not intend to suggest that this is the only factor in the crisis. Erik Erikson has stressed the significance of vocational choice (at least for boys), and there is a body of relevant material on achievement motivation in the empirical literature. A focused presentation could have centered on this theme, or some other one. The multiplicity of factors must be recognized from the beginning to avoid the assumption that the identity crisis is caused by sex-role learning alone.

The choice is not arbitrary, however. Sex roles are a key factor in the identity crisis for two reasons. First, they are learned early and are closely related to how the individual defines himself. Ascription by sex is one of the few aspects of identity which is assigned at birth and remains unchanged throughout the individual's life.[1] Those areas of personality that are related to the cultural sex roles do not usually change during the individual's life. Since one's sex does not change, sex roles tend to be more stable than roles assigned according to other criteria. In American society, aspects of personality which are related to the sex-assigned roles are among the most stable characteristics of the individual personality.[2]

1

Second, the differences in our culture's sex roles parallel rather closely the differences in the two worlds between which the adolescent moves. The home, the world of child rearing, is closely linked with the warm, personal, "feminine" roles. Adolescents face a transition to a very different world when they seek to enter the adult society outside the home, which has a tougher, more objective, and predominantly "masculine" orientation.

In short, the sex-role issue provides the background for understanding the identity crisis because of the close connections between sex roles and the move from home to world. As stated before, sex roles are not the only factors in the adolescent identity crisis. But without an understanding of sex-role development, I doubt if it is possible to comprehend the identity crisis in today's youth.

## *Notes*

1. Sanford M. Dornbusch, "Afterword," in *The Development of Sex Differences*, ed. Eleanor E. Maccoby (Stanford: Stanford University Press, 1966), pp. 207–8.

2. Jerome Kagan and H. A. Moss, "The Stability of Passive and Dependent Behavior from Childhood through Adulthood," *Child Development*, 31 (1960): 577–91; Dorothy Rogers, "Persistence of Personality Traits," in *Issues in Adolescent Psychology* (New York: Appleton-Century-Crofts, 1972), p. 46.

# 1

## Sexuality and identifications

*And God created man in his own image*
*. . . male and female he created them.*
—Genesis 1:27

"I wish it was that simple," a college student might react. But "male and female" is no simple matter to today's youth, who are struggling to piece together their identity in this confusing world.

It is important to recognize that the term "sex roles" does not simply mean biologically defined categories. We are by nature male or female, but masculinity and femininity result from complex processes of socialization. The sex roles depend upon cultural definition and conditioning. Without the influence of society, people's sex would not define their identities or determine their personality styles. It is convenient to define adolescence as the period of life which begins when the individual's body becomes sexually mature, but biological maturation is only one aspect of the attainment of sexual identity.

In previous periods of history, cultural expectations for adult manhood and womanhood may have been so clearly defined that only one style seemed possible to a person in a particular status of society. Then a father might have said to his son, when the boy became physically mature, "Son, now you are a man." If a father were to say that today, the son might respond with something like, "Man, that's a heavy thing you're laying on me!" At least among youths who consciously struggle with identity issues, there is often a recognition that a traditional sex role may not fit for a particular individual.

The study of sex roles provides an important perspective for understanding the identity crisis of today's adolescents. The aim of these first five chapters is to clarify the developmental processes involved in

3

sex-role acquisition. Any discussion of the development of sex roles must include a presentation of the biological, psychological, and social factors involved. Since these chapters are preparatory to a study of the identity crisis, the focus will be upon psychological aspects. The psychological approach is concerned with how the norms and roles of society are learned by the individual and become incorporated into his style of life.

## Some questions

Some specific questions regarding the development of sex roles emerge from a recognition of the three aspects which influence their development: biological, psychological, and social. Questions to be considered in the chapters of this part include: What are the normative sex roles in our society, and what do they mean to the developing individual? (Chapter 2). To what extent are the sex roles a result of biological factors? (Chapter 3). What is the range of possibilities in sex-role development? How far can a culture's sex roles vary from those considered normal in our culture? (Chapter 3). Are sex roles learned, and thus subject to modification, in the same way as other learning tasks are? (Chapter 3). How are sex roles learned in our particular culture? (Chapter 4). What are the social and individual consequences of our culture's approach to sex-role learning? (Chapter 5).

In psychology today there is a multiplicity of viewpoints; no totally integrative theory exists. The most important approaches to understanding sex-role development include the psychophysiological viewpoint, social learning theory, and cognitive development.[1] In many areas these different viewpoints supplement one another. There are, however, situations in which they are not compatible, and it is necessary to weigh the data and choose among them, if, indeed, sufficient data exist for making such a decision.

## The wish for an integrative theory

Gaps in the data and conflicts between theories, plus data that in itself are ambiguous or inconsistent, may frustrate the reader's need for order and a sense of closure. Frequently the student of psychology wishes for the intellectual and personal satisfaction of embracing some overarching theory which might make sense of the whole field.

In the recent history of the social sciences there have been times in which a comprehensive and integrative theory of psychological development seemed possible. Sigmund Freud, in building his psychoanalytic theory, attempted such an integration. Even today psychoanalytic theory influences the thinking of many clinicians, and some of the researchers noted in this book have interpreted their data within the framework of that theory. It is useful, therefore, to become aware of the outlines of the story which provides the schema for the psychoanalytic interpretation of adolescence, the Greek myth of Oedipus. The myth also provides an illustration of some of the subjective characteristics of an integrative theory.

The Oedipus myth is the tragic story of a man who was abandoned in infancy because of an oracle's prediction that he would kill his father. Oedipus was adopted and raised by the King of Corinth. When he was grown he learned of the prediction and left Corinth, thinking he could thus prevent its fulfillment. In his travels, he fought and killed a stranger who treated him poorly. Later he solved the riddle of the Sphinx and thus saved Thebes from destruction. The king of Thebes had recently been killed, and Oedipus was crowned king. He married the dead king's wife, only to discover that the stranger he had killed was the former king and his real father, and the woman he had married was his mother. The truth destroyed him, and the tragedy ends with Oedipus blinding himself and wandering in exile.[2]

Freud used this myth to organize some observations about human development. He believed that, as part of the normal processes of development, children at about age three to six pass through a stage (he named it the oedipal stage) in which they repeat, in fantasy, much of the Oedipus myth. Freud thought that during these years the genital zone becomes highly erogenous and children desire intercourse with the person of the opposite sex they love the most—the parent. The little boy, for example, falls in love with his mother and sees his father as a rival for her affection. He wishes to possess his mother for himself and becomes jealous and hateful toward his father, wishing to get him out of the way. Since the father is more powerful and more acceptable to the mother, the boy eventually realizes that he cannot have the mother. Nevertheless, the boy fears that his aggressive wishes against his father will be retaliated. Having observed women and noted their lack of a penis, the boy assumes they have lost something; his fear of bodily harm from his father takes the form of fear that his father may avenge his love of his mother by castrating him. These forces lead the boy to seek a compromise; he resolves the oedipal complex by channeling his energies into emulating his father, while introjecting the father's prohibitions against sexuality. Since he cannot take his father's place, the boy accepts second best; he can become like his father. By doing so he overcomes his fear of his father's revenge (this defense is called identification with the aggressor) and resecures his mother's love by becoming the kind of person she loves—becoming like his father.

Most psychologists today are highly critical of Freud's elaborate and speculative theory. As a description of childhood development, this theory strikes many as preposterous. But Freud was an astute observer who had a profound understanding of humanity. It is not wise to dismiss the theory too quickly.

It seems to me helpful to discriminate between the power of the Oedipus story as a myth and its power as a psychological theory. As myth, the story is touching as an expression of the depth of human tragedy. There is a recognition, both in the myth and in Freud's writings, that much of human destiny lies outside our own abilities to understand and change our own behaviors. The Greek play and the theory instill both a passion to know and a fear of the tragic consequences of our passions. We see in Oedipus a hero who has the courage to do what feels right. In the end, following his own feelings leads him to a truth he is unable to tolerate; he is blinded, never again to see the truth.[3]

It is my opinion that much of the continued influence of the Freudian system is due not to strictly scientific considerations but to the power of the system to function as an integrative myth. The term "myth" is not used derogatorily. Sensitive youth, grappling with life issues, respond to integrative systems ( Freud's, Jung's, Adler's, and others) because they sense in them a grappling with the issues of life values. Thus the depth psychologies are appealing not so much because of the descriptive power of their systems but because of their expressiveness.

Throughout this book the reader will be asked to discriminate between descriptive statements, which can and should be subjected to empirical investigation, and value judgments, which are of critical importance to the identity struggle but cannot be tested empirically. The problem, in this time when psychology functions without an integrative theory, is that psychologists attempt to write without making value judgments. Their texts are frequently seen by students as factually correct but irrelevant. The tack in this text is not to proceed without making judgments but to clarify when the statements made express the author's values and when they are propositions subject to empirical test.

On the descriptive level, Freud's use of the story of Oedipus makes at least three important points about human development which, in modified form, still hold today. Freud believed that:

1.  During the oedipal period, about age three to six, the patterns for relationships with the opposite sex are established.
2.  The learning of these patterns is mostly unconscious.
3.  The love for the parent of the opposite sex is denied, but the child is led to identify with the same-sex parent and to incorporate the value system of that parent.

Each of these propositions from Freud's theory will be briefly examined in the light of contemporary research, and then some fundamental areas of agreement between Freudian theory and present-day understandings of sex-role development will be summarized.

## Childhood roots of adult sex roles

In the Victorian era it was commonly assumed that adult sexuality emerges as a new event at puberty. In contrast, Freud theorized that the human is highly sexual from birth and that sexuality is focused in different areas of the body at various developmental stages. He called this concept "childhood sexuality" and spoke of the progression of "erogenous zones" from the mouth (infancy, the oral stage) to the anus (during the toilet training period), to the genitals. According to Freud, for the three- to six-year-old the sexual zone of importance is the genital area. Freud called this the phallic period and stated that the focus for both boys and girls is the male penis.

Freud was correct in observing that children show a pleasurable interest in their genitals long before puberty. Genital manipulation is common in young boys, except where it has been inhibited by punishment. It is less common in girls, probably due to the less easily manipulatable character of female genitalia. In that sense, Freud was correct in noting the penis as central (though his belief that little girls were terribly concerned with penises does not follow). However, Freud's belief that the genital zone emerges as a new area of interest and first becomes erogenous at age three is clearly wrong. The genital area is pleasurable for children of both sexes even in infancy,[4] and genital manipulation is common in childhood before age three and does not appear to increase at that time.[5]

Though Freud was apparently wrong about the reasons, he appears to have been correct in observing that the period from age three to six is the most crucial stage for the development of sex roles. Freud observed that boys and girls make their first identifications with mother, for it is mother who provides the bodily pleasures around which early learning occurs. This first identification figure cannot accurately be considered a sexual model, since the child has not yet discriminated between the sexes. Experimental studies since Freud's time suggest that this discrimination is generally made between age two and three. The child also becomes aware of his own gender during those years; usually by age three the boy knows "I'm a boy," and the girl consistently labels herself a girl.[6] The most relevant data regarding sex identification come from studies which have concentrated on the oedipal period and have used the method of comparing children from intact families to children who have an absent parent. After an extensive review of child development research, Leon J. Yarrow reached this conclusion:

> The limited evidence on father absence supports dynamic and learning theories in indicating that appropriate sex role identification is hindered by the lack of a role model of the same sex. . . . The theoretical discussion and research of father absence has concentrated on the Oedipal period, and it is likely that this period is a particularly vulnerable one for boys with regard to father-absence. Early adolescence might be an equally critical period, although no direct data are available.[7]

Further supportive data come from a study of children whose biological characteristics were neither clearly male nor clearly female. Some of these hermaphrodite children were assigned a sex at birth based upon the appearance of the external genitalia; later it was discovered that their internal sexual organs were more like those of the opposite sex. Thus a family which had been raising a child as a boy switched to treating the offspring as a girl, or vice versa. The study suggests that if the switch had been made before the child was three or four, the child's later sexual adjustment was normal. If the change in gender was made after age four, real maladjustment seemed to result.[8]

A rather ingenious study has provided further data on this issue. The experimenter reasoned that if any age period were especially important in learning sex roles, the loss of a parent during this period should result in less certainty about sexual identity later.[9] Groups of high school and college girls who had lost either their fathers or mothers during the pre-oedipal, oedipal, latency, and adolescent periods were compared to girls whose parents were still living. Sexual diffusion was measured, using projective tests. When the scores were plotted in terms of the children's ages at the time the loss occurred, the results were striking (see Figure 1).

This study suggests that the conclusions cited previously for boys apply to girls as well. Since the general slopes of the graphs are downward, it appears that the earlier the loss occurs (i.e., the longer the period of childhood spent without one parent), the greater the effect. More important for the present analysis are the two peaks on each graph. The study provides evidence that both the oedipal and the adolescent periods are of special importance in the learning of sex roles. It is not surprising that the sex-role learning should be of special importance during adolescence, when adult genitality is emerging. It is not so obvious why the earlier childhood period should be so important. Again, Freud must be given credit for his accurate observation, but we need not accept his conclusion that this period of childhood is critical

## FIGURE 1
### Psychosexual conflict and age at loss of parent

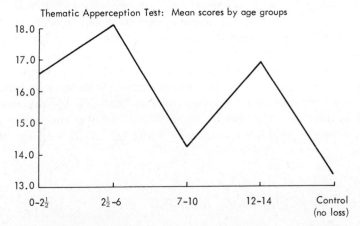

Thematic Apperception Test: Mean scores by age groups

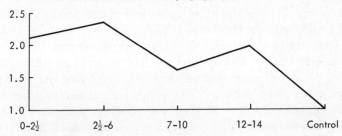

Cole Animal Test: Mean scores by age groups

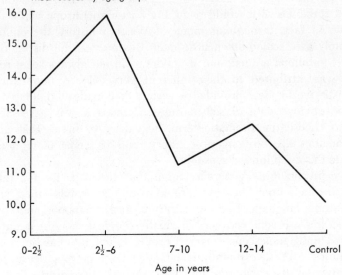

Draw A Person (sexual differentiation scale):
Mean scores by age groups

Age in years

Source: Adapted from Henry T. Grayson, "Psychosexual Conflict in Adolescent Girls Who Experience Early Parental Loss by Death" (Ph.D. diss., Boston University, 1967), *Dissertation Abstracts* No. 67-13, 327.

because the genital zone becomes especially erogenous. It is more parsimonious to assume that the learning occurs at this age because the
child now has accurate-enough perceptions to discriminate between the
sexes and to differentiate sex roles.[10] The recognition of the importance
of this discrimination should not be taken to imply full acceptance of a
perceptual or cognitive position. Undoubtably much sex-role learning
goes on as simple behavior shaping (operant conditioning) prior to the
child's learning of verbal gender labels. It is clear from the studies presented, however, that sex-role identity is not confirmed until age three
or four.

## The nature of childhood learning

Though it does not seem possible, on the basis of the experimental
data, to accept Freud's theory of erogenous zones, there is a sense in
which Freud's belief in childhood sexuality was well founded. An illustration from the oral period will clarify. An unmarried friend of my
wife's came to visit us shortly after we had adopted an infant. During
her stay, while we were visiting in the living room, our young son
squawled incessantly until my wife popped a pacifier into his mouth.
In a few minutes he was sucking with obvious delight. The friend,
observing this sensuous pleasure, was horrified and asked in alarm, "Do
you let him do that in *public?*"

One has only to look at an infant to recognize how sensuous life
is at that stage. Or so it would seem, but Victorian Europe had a different view. In fact, throughout much of Western history the child was
seen simply as a scaled-down little man. Reason was the distinguishing
mark of the human animal, and if children did not always seem reasonable, it was attributed to their inherent perversity. A moralistic and
rationalistic world view provided a gestalt that made it difficult to observe the obvious data of sensuousness. Perhaps it was necessary for
Freud to choose the dramatic term "sexuality" to break that gestalt.
The dramatics are no longer necessary, and it seems more accurate
to refer to this as childhood sensuality.

Today psychologists generally agree that the capacity for rational
thought depends upon learning how to symbolize events—most specifically, learning language. Like most learning tasks, symbolic and concep-
tual processes are achieved very gradually. Logical thought is not fully
developed until adolescence; early learning is not rational but sensual.
The infant's earliest explorations include developing a sense of his
own body and its capacities for pleasure and discomfort. The body
is important to all early learning as the center of pleasurable experiences, which are the primary reinforcers. Since rational thought has
not yet developed, early learning is a highly emotive process. The pri-

mary content of early learning is not thoughts or ideas, but total, molar responses.

It would be false to give the impression that psychologists today are in agreement about the nature of childhood learning. This is an

"Clarissa knows better names for all the parts of our body than we do."

Source: *The Family Circus,* by Bil Keane, reprinted courtesy The Register and Tribune Syndicate.

area of extensive research activity and much debate. The central figures in the debate are the behaviorists and the cognitive theorists. Both of these schools of thought, in common with the Freudian view, recognize the importance of bodily pleasure and physical activity in early learning. Kohlberg, a cognitive theorist, states that "childhood sex role concepts are essentially defined in . . . physical or body terms."[11] The behaviorists emphasize the importance of physical pleasure as a "reinforcer" (reward).[12] Without getting into the very important differences between these viewpoints, it is noteworthy that there is agreement throughout the field of phychology that early learning does not take place through the rational, logical process which is generally implied by the commonly accepted sense of the term "learning."

## Sex-role learning and the internalization of values

Freud's third important observation noted above was that the consolidation of sex roles at the end of the oedipal period results in the internalization of values. In psychoanalytic theory, the process is referred to as the introjection of the parental superego. It is as if the child swallows whole the parent's conscience like one big unchewed apple, which remains in the child but is not really digested and assimilated by him. The image of swallowing in one gulp and the term "introjection" are extremely expressive, but we can accept them only as metaphorical.[13] We must turn to more recent psychological work to clarify the nature of this learning process (Chapter 4). What we learn from Freud is that when the child labels himself as to gender, he not only accepts the sexual roles which his parents inculcate; along with these roles, he also accepts certain value orientations. For example, in studies of boys' father identification it has been shown that the same years in which father identification is increasing (age four to seven), development is characterized by internalization of moral judgements and increased behavioral control.[14] These internalized values are not conscious learnings. We do not assume that the child thinks them through, yet they become a part of him.

## Summary

Though the focus of this book is the psychological study of adolescent identity, I shall first undertake a description of the development of sex roles in childhood, in order to provide a background in understanding of the adolescent identity quest. Comprehension of the development of sex roles demands a presentation of biological and cultural information, as well as psychological data.

The Freudian theory is no longer functional as an integrative theory for contemporary scientific data. Nonetheless, some of the fundamental observations of Freud remain valid and provide a good starting point for understanding sex-role development. Freud recognized that early in life important learning which affects adult sexuality takes place, that learning in the childhood years is an uncritical sensual process, and that this learning is closely connected with the internalization of values. These three observations can be accepted today and can be stated as propositions, without reference to the psychoanalytic framework:

1.  Sex-role learning takes place throughout the childhood years, with the period from three to six being of special importance.

2. This learning does not take place through the rational, logical processes referred to in the commonsense use of the term "learning." Bodily pleasure is important as a reinforcement, and thought patterns, where involved, are very concrete and primitive.

3. The learning of sex roles is intricately bound up with the acceptance of sex-typed value orientations.

In the next chapter the sex roles that typify American culture, and their associated value orientations, will be described.

## Notes

1. For a summary of each of the major perspectives for viewing sex-role acquisition, see B. G. Rosenberg and Brian Sutton-Smith, *Sex and Identity* (New York: Holt, Rinehart & Winston, 1972).

2. Edith Hamilton, *Mythology* (New York: Mentor Books, 1940), pp. 256–61.

3. Rollo May, *Existence* (New York: Basic Books, 1958).

4. Alfred Kinsey, Wardell B. Pomeroy, and Clyde E. Martin, *Sexual Behavior in the Human Male* (Philadelphia: W. B. Saunders Co., 1948).

5. See Wardell B. Pomeroy, *Boys and Sex* (New York: Delacorte Press, 1968), chap. 3, "Sex Play before Adolescence." Though masturbation and orgasm are possible as early as six months of age, the endocrinal base for adult responses is not present until puberty. There is no evidence that sexual sensation during the oedipal period is any different than it is during any other preadolescent period.

6. Lawrence Kohlberg, "A Cognitive-Developmental Analysis of Children's Sex-role Concepts and Attitudes" in *The Development of Sex Differences*, ed. Eleanor E. Maccoby (Stanford, Calif.: Stanford University Press, 1966), pp. 883–89. See Lenore A. DeLucia, "Some Determinants of Sex-Role Identification in Young Children" (Master's thesis, Brown University, 1961).

7. Leon J. Yarrow, "Separation from Parents during Early Childhood," in *Review of Child Development Research,* ed. Martin L. Hoffman and Lois Hoffman (New York: © 1964 Russell Sage Foundation), vol. 1, pp. 135–36. Further evidence for this period's importance in sex-role learning can be found in Pauline S. Sears, "Doll Play Aggression in Normal Young Children: Influence of Sex, Age, Sibling Status, Father's Absence," *Psychological Monographs* No. 6, 65 (1951): 42; in a review of research in Gene R. Medinnus and Ronald C. Johnson, *Child and Adolescent Psychology: Behavior and Development* (New York: John Wiley & Sons, 1969), pp. 347–49; and in Rosenberg and Sutton-Smith, *Sex and Identity.*

8. J. Money, Joan G. Hampson, and J. L. Hampson, "Imprinting and the Establishment of Gender Role," *Archives of Neurology and Psychiatry,* 77 (1957): 333–36.

9. Henry T. Grayson, "Psychosexual Conflict in Adolescent Girls Who Experience Early Parental Loss by Death" (Ph.D. diss., Boston University, 1967), *Dissertation Abstracts* No. 67-13, 327.

10. Kohlberg, "Cognitive-Developmental Analysis," pp. 83–137.

11. Ibid., p. 83.

12. Sidney W. Bijou and Donald M. Baer, *Child Development,* vol. 2, *Universal Stage of Infancy* (New York: Appleton-Century-Crofts, 1965), pp. 40–51.

13. The metaphor "internalized but not digested" may be interpreted to mean that the responses are no longer dependent upon the parent's being present (in behavioral terms, the person originally imitated is no longer a necessary discriminative stimulus for the response), but the responses have not become symbolized and are not consciously integrated into one's self-image.

14. Lawrence Kohlberg, "Moral Development and Identification," in *Child Psychology: Sixty-second Yearbook of the National Society for the Study of Education*, ed. H. W. Stevenson (Chicago: University of Chicago Press, 1963).

# 2

# *Stereotypes of femininity and masculinity*

**The myth of the woman as womb**
  Inner and outer space
  The expressive orientation
**The myth of the male**
  The strong one
  The rational one
  The instrumental orientation: The effective one
  A dangerous perception: The cruel one
**Summary**

THE COMPLEX PROCESS OF establishing one's own sexual identity takes place in the context of the cultural expectations regarding male and female roles. Since this learning begins early in childhood and is fairly well crystalized by age four, it is not surprising that it involves gross generalizations about masculinity and femininity. Most of the person's sexual identity is confirmed before highly differentiated concepts have emerged. Further, since childhood learning is highly personalized and subjective, it is not surprising that the generalizations the child develops are heavily value loaded. It can be said, then, that early sex-role learning involves undifferentiated and value-laden concepts; in other words, the child pieces together stereotypes.

In spite of the many individual differences in the roles American parents play, there appears to be "a remarkable consensus among young children in their conceptions of differences between mother and father roles as revealed by the studies of parent stereotypes."[1] Three important dimensions of gender role emerge from studies of these conceptions: power and prestige, aggression and exposure to danger, and nurturance and child care. There is some evidence that the development of sex-role stereotypes in children is not simply derived from observation of their own parents; children's role conceptions appear somewhat similar despite differences in their home backgrounds.[2] The task of figuring out what masculinity and femininity mean is in part a matter of making generalizations from the males and females the child observes.

In this chapter we are concerned with the generalizations that can be made about masculinity and femininity in our society and the sex-role stereotypes that are developed by most American children. The process of sex-role learning will be discussed in Chapter 4; the focus here is on the content of the learning. Two portraits make up the substance of this chapter: the child's images of manhood and womanhood. I shall refer to these portraits as myths. Like the myth of Oedipus introduced in the last chapter, which transmits the classical Greek perception of reality, the myths of manhood and womanhood are expressions of our cultural viewpoint which they help to perpetuate and transmit. These myths differ from scientific descriptions in several ways. They are emotive expressions. They fail to take into account the huge individual variations in behavior within each sex; they fail to note the large overlap between male and female behavior. Most importantly, the sterotypic roles tend to carry with them a sense of destiny and righteousness.

As a social scientist, I wish to avoid any claim that men and women, through some biological predisposition, are destined to behave in any prescribed fashion. (We will examine possible biological determinants in the next chapter.) Neither do I wish to suggest that men and women should define their roles in this manner. I only argue that these myths must be taken seriously, for they approximate the perceptions our children have of the adult world. These myths mold and shape the minds and personalities which develop within our culture. The first to be communicated to the child is the myth of womanhood.

## The myth of the woman as womb

When adult women were asked to describe themselves on adjective checklists, they frequently chose the words "emotional, affectionate, pleasant, and temperamental."[3] Similarly, female college students drawn from a cross section of American colleges, as compared to males, more often favored the words "affectionate, dreamy, generous, honest, softhearted, sympathetic, tactful, well-mannered."[4]

These and other studies suggest that adult women in our society, as a rule, accept the stereotyped view that women are more emotional, warmer, and more nurturant than their male counterparts.[5] College men as well as women share this stereotype of feminity. For both sexes, over 75 percent of the sample in one study described women as expressing tender feelings, aware of the feelings of others, and gentle, but having a strong need for security (among other traits).[6] Both sexes seemed to believe that women are naturally warmer and more nurturant.

Longitudinal studies of the stability of personality traits throughout childhood and adult life show that traits supported by the culturally acceptable roles of masculinity and femininity are among the most stable.[7] The tendency to practice sex-typed behavior is very stable for both men and women; in fact, these behaviors show greater stability from childhood through adulthood than almost any other personality traits psychologists have studied.[8] According to Jerome Kagan, "The data on sex differences in passivity and dependency are less consistent than those for aggression, but there are more studies reporting greater dependency, conformity and social passivity for females than for males at all ages."[9]

The stereotypes children form of male and female roles thus have some correspondence to the society they observe. Both objective measurements and self-descriptions present a picture of women in our culture as the weaker sex, but the warmer and more nurturant one. The same pattern occurs when children are asked for their perceptions of mother. There are, of course, individual differences in the way children perceive sex roles, but a summary of research on children's perceptions of parents shows that most children see mother as loving, more nurturant, and more likely the use psychological methods of control (in contrast to physical punishment).[10] As might be expected, children of both sexes view women as more nurturant than men.[11]

Although most of the studies have drawn their populations from average and above average socioeconomic statuses, similar patterns occur with children from the working class. A study of children in grades four through eight in five working-class schools showed that these children generally saw mother as more accepting than father and using more psychological control, while fathers were seen as exerting "firmer" control.[12]

Child care is recognized as a feminine function very early by most American children, usually by age five.[13] Associated with this is a general differentiation of maternal, inside-the-home functions from paternal, outside-the-home functions.[14] This distinction between male and female functions and orientations has been elaborated by Erik Erikson in his concepts of inner and outer space.

### Inner and outer space

The central thing that distinguishes a woman from a man, according to Erikson, is that she holds within herself a womb. It is in the womb that we begin our lives, and the womb becomes the primary symbol for our image of womanliness. The essence of femininity, Erikson claims, is the awareness of inner space. The identity formation of woman differs from man's "by dint of the fact that her somatic design harbors an 'inner space' destined to bear offspring of chosen men, and with it a biological, psychological, and ethical commitment to take care of human infancy."[15]

Psychoanalytic theory advanced prior to Erikson had failed to develop an adequate understanding of womanhood partly because it saw female development simply as a counterpart of male development. Freud's choice of the phallus as the essential organ around which male and female sexual identification occurs was typical of this male-centered attitude. In Freud's view, the dynamics of womanhood center around compensation for what she is missing, that is, around her envy of the male penis. Erikson made a major break with Freud on this point and attempted to rebuild the theory on the foundation of what is unique to the female rather than what she is missing. He focused, however, not on the breasts and the nursing role but on the presence of internal organs. Erikson chose the womb as the most expressive image for female psychological development: Woman is unique in that she possesses an inner space, a womb.

Erikson believes this somatic design predisposes a particularly female use of life space, presumably because of some type of kinesthetic experience.[16] Erikson's empirical data are limited to his own inadequately controlled study, which compares constructions made by 10- to 12-year-old children from blocks and toys. The differences Erikson finds between boys' and girls' use of space may be attributed to social influences rather than revealing some somatic design, as Erikson infers. What is interesting, regardless of interpretation, is the sensitive expression of the psychological differences that typify girls' play configurations; they emphasize enclosures, with static, peaceful interiors. Sometimes these are intruded upon or invaded from the outside. The girls are concerned with what takes place within the home or within themselves, and "seem to have taken it for granted that the outer world space belongs to men."[17]

The particular characteristic of femininity, then, is a special "sense of vital inner potential." Erikson uses the biological structure for productivity, the womb, as a metaphor for the special emotional creativity he attributes to women, maintaining that their orientation toward inner space provides them with a special potential for psychological creativity and richness.

As a result of their inner orientation, Erikson believes, women may develop a special propensity for experiencing the world of emotions and feelings, the subjective world. With the pubescent experience of menstruation comes the "ability to stand pain as a meaningful aspect of human experience."[18] Their somatic design encourages a turn inward that involves pain as well as pleasure, loneliness as well as creativity. "The very existence of the inner productive space," Erikson says, "exposes women early to a specific sense of loneliness, to a fear of being left empty or deprived of treasures, of remaining unfulfilled and of drying up.[19] This inward orientation contrasts to the more masculine goal directedness. Erikson notes that even those functions not peculiarly feminine are often performed by women in a beautifully feminine way. For example, some college girls, more easily than boys, seem able to engage in the pursuit of knowledge for its own sake, with less concern for practical or applied results. Erikson aptly describes women's carrying out of these functions as "aesthetic phenomena which almost seem to transcend all goals and purposes and therefore come to symbolize the self-containment of pure being."[20] This calls to mind the quiet, static quality of girls' play constructions. Pure being, rather than striving after goals, seems essential to womanhood.

Erikson's view contains a depth of insight which sharpens our portrait of the feminine myth, though many of the interpretations and connections he makes are hard for the social scientist to accept. In the loose, emotive associations between body plan and social destiny, we begin to understand the sex roles in somewhat the way the child, in his vague attempt to make connections, must experience them. The little girl senses that in some mysterious way her body defines her as a girl, and predestines that she will be motherly—warm, nurturant, and emotive. Somehow inside-the-home functions belong to her.[21]

### The expressive orientation

The sociological theory of Talcott Parsons helps clarify the central themes that differentiate the masculine and feminine sex roles which parents transmit to their childern. Similar to Erikson's contrast between the quiet, inner orientation and the active, outer orientation is Parsons' contrast between the "expressive" quality of femininity and the "instrumental" orientation of masculinity.

The crux of Parsons's distinction between expressive and instrumental roles has been described by M. M. Johnson as a different focus in personal interactions. The male instrumental role is oriented toward goals that transcend the immediate interaction, whereas the female role receives rewards from the interaction itself. Parsons sees the woman as an expressive role player who "is oriented toward the relationships among the actors within a system. [She] is primarily oriented to the attitudes and feelings of those actors toward each other . . . . By being solicitous, appealing, and 'understanding' a woman seeks to get a pleasurable response by giving pleasure."[22] The woman's focus is personal; the interpersonal interactions are ends in themselves rather than means to an end. This involves sensitivity to the immediate feelings and emotions, rather than concern for long-term consequences.

An attempt has been made to operationalize Parsons's terms "expressive" and "instrumental" for testing purposes. Four clinical psychologists were asked to choose from the adjectives in the Adjective Check List those that fit the orientations "expressive" and "instrumental." There was 93 percent agreement among the psychologists, and the list of adjectives chosen provides us with a good consensual description of the meaning of expressive orientation:

> Adaptable, appreciative, artistic, attractive, contented, emotional, excitable, fearful, outgoing, pleasant, praising, relaxed, reliable, self-pitying, sentimental, sincere, sympathetic, understanding, warm, wholesome.[23]

The term "expressive" clarifies the concept that the inwardness of femininity cannot remain self-contained. The woman's being must be communicated interpersonally to avoid becoming stagnant. In vernacular terms, if the "mothering instinct" is frustrated, the woman becomes a "bitch."[24]

There is considerable evidence in counseling psychology that a deep awareness of one's inward resources leads to a more accepting mode of interaction with others.[25] If femininity involves an inner strength, it makes sense that it might be expressed interpersonally as sensitivity and warmth or, to use Erikson's term, as "caring." If we combine the themes of Erikson and Parsons, we get a good sense of the feminine ideal in our culture: an inwardness sensitively expressed.

This expression of inner warmth is the essence of ideal mothering. For the infant, mother is the primary source of pleasure—the very sensuous pleasures of breast and body warmth and tactile stimulation. Babies love anything soft and warm and cuddly (as was widely recognized from experience before experimental psychology took the trouble to prove it through surrogate mother experiments).[26] The archetypal mother, for the infant, is warm and soft. At the earliest level, the feminine is experienced as sensual.

In childhood some separation develops, and mother and child are not as totally united as in infancy. With the growing autonomy of the child, the mother may not be experienced quite so directly and sensuously. But even when physical contact is not desired, mother continues to stand for warmth and emotionality, and the emotions imply directness (psychological, if not physical). Emotionality is associated with open expression, spontaneity, and freedom. The playfulness of childhood is in part a reflection of the spontaneity of the emotive atmosphere.

This is not to suggest that the American mother is always nurturant or that home is always warm and joyful. But it is these characteristics (however partially they are experienced in an individual's life) that come to signify what our culture idealizes in womanhood.

It is the task of the mother to transmit her special sensitivity to the child. Erikson says, "She creates in each child the somatic (sensual and sensory) basis for his physical, cultural, and individual identity.

This mission, once a child is conceived, must be completed. It is the woman's unique job."[27] At least, it is the job that the American home has assigned to mother.

It is significant that in American culture the word "emotional" has a double meaning. That which is hidden, inner, or personal often carries innuendos of danger; the word "emotional" signifies both sensitivity and instability. As the objective world enters the child's perceptions (at first as father represents the outside world to the child, and later as the child experiences it directly), inner space is called into question.

## The myth of the male

The essence of femininity is personal; the core of femininity revolves around the home and the mothering role. Masculinity finds its center not at home but in the world. The male role is less personal than the female role and appears to be learned in a less personal way. In our culture it is the male image, not a man's personality, that is transmitted. Generally the sex identification of a male child is not firmly rooted in his relationship with his father as a person. Rather, masculinity is based upon learning the social role expected of men in the outside world.[28] By age five or six, the distinction between inside-the-home and outside-the-home functions is clear, and most children associate father with the latter.[29]

Since the masculine image centers on a social role rather than a total personal identity, it is appropriate that sociological theory be relied on for its explication. In Talcott Parsons's sociological theory of sex roles, the male role is described as instrumental-adaptive. The male takes responsibility for the social system (in this case, the family); he is concerned with its objective needs and goals. The instrumental role focuses upon goal achievement in the outside world.[30] Functioning in the instrumental role, in contrast to the expressive orientation, involves treating interpersonal interactions primarily as means toward goals. According to Alfred Heilbrun, "The instrumental-role-player cannot be primarily oriented to the immediate emotional responses of others to him. Rather than soliciting positive responses from others, like the expressive person, instrumental-role-playing requires an ability to tolerate the hostility it will very likely elicit."[31] In sum, the instrumental orientation is pragmatic, goal directed, and focused on the relations between the social unit and the outside world, rather than relationships within the social unit.[32]

The meaning of the instrumental role can also be clarified by the consensus obtained on applicable words from the Adjective Check List.[33] I have organized these words in content groups:

1. *Strong:* aggressive, forceful, robust, steady, stern, tough, unaffected.
2. *Rational:* factfinding, foresighted, frank, logical, inventive, reliable, sharpwitted, shrewd.
3. *Effective:* deliberate, enterprising, resourceful, opportunistic, unscrupulous, progressive.
4. *Cruel:* hardheaded, vindictive, reckless.

### The strong one

If the earliest infant experience of mother is sensual, probably the childs' earliest view of father is as "the strong one." Father may be seen as strong partly because of his relationship to the child as protector. This is one of the earliest distinctions in sexual roles among primates. Protection can be seen as movement into outer space, as in Erikson's illustration drawn from the social organization of baboon troops:

> The whole wandering troop in search of food over a certain territory is so organized as to keep within a safe inner space the females who bear future offspring within their bodies or carry their growing young. They are protectively surrounded by powerful males who, in turn, keep their eyes on the horizon, guiding the troop toward available food and guarding it from potential danger. In peacetime the strong males also protect the "inner circle" of pregnant and nursing females against the encroachments of the relatively weaker and definitely more importunate males. Once danger is spotted, the whole wandering configuration stops and consolidates into an inner space of safety and an outer space of combat. In the center sit the pregnant females and mothers with their newborns. At the periphery are the males best equipped to fight or scare off predators. . . .
>
> Whatever the morphological differences between the female and the male baboons' bony structures, postures, and behaviors, they are adapted to their respective tasks of harboring and defending the concentric circles, from the procreative womb to the limits of the defensible territory.[34]

Strength is considered a masculine trait by both men and women in our culture. In both male and female college samples, over 75 percent of the students rated the following adjectives (among others) as typical of men: aggressive, dominant, not easily influenced, active, self-confident, not dependent.[35] In another study, male college students were more likely than females to describe themselves as "rugged and self-confident."[36] Suppression of fear was found to be a primary attribute of the male in still another study.[37]

That the male image, for Americans, seems centered around the issue of strength is reflected in children's perceptions of father. Children almost always describe father as "stronger" and "more powerful" than mother; often father is described as "fearless."[38] According to Lawrence

Kohlberg, "It appears likely . . . that children's stereotypes of masculine dominance or social power develop largely out of . . . body-stereotyping of size-age and competence."[39] Whatever their roots, the perception of father as the strong one is nearly universal in American culture.

### The rational one

Rationality is the second aspect of the instrumental role and may be the second view of father to develop in the child's perception. At first the child responds to persons in an immediate and physical way: mother as warm, father as strong. As his perception becomes more differentiated, the child notes more subtle differences: mother is associated with the emotional, father with the rational.

The contrast intended here is between a spontaneous, expressive thinking style (associated with femininity), and a deliberating and objective rational style (associated with masculinity). Expressive thought serves to symbolize one's subjective experience, both to one's self and to others. The purpose of rational thought, however, is to order, to understand, and to manipulate the objective world.

In our society, adult males, more often than females, think of themselves as "deliberate, logical, and realistic."[40] They frequently emphasize rationality in contrast to expressiveness, and value the "capacity to control expression of strong emotion in time of stress."[41] Similarly, college males view themselves as "shrewd and wise" more often than do females.[42] College subjects of both sexes considered the following traits descriptive of males: unemotional, objective, independent, logical, never cries, feelings not easily hurt, able to separate feelings from ideas.[43]

In reality, tremendous individual differences in thinking styles exist among members of the same sex. Where male-female differences do exist, there is a wide area of overlap. Despite these reservations, the childhood stereotypes do have some basis in reality. The relevant experiments use J. P. Guilford's terms "convergent" (focused, goal-directed) thinking and "divergent" (open, creative) thinking,[44] which are parallel to the rational and expressive modes. Girls generally seem to use more divergent thinking; they produce a greater variety of ideas in response to a verbally presented problem. It is well known that girls generally outperform boys in tasks involving verbal skills, but when confronted with a task which demands restructuring (an analytic skill), boys excel.[45] It can be said that male thinking is characteristically convergent thinking; it is more rational. Research shows that males perform better than females on some measures of analytic ability, from the early school years on. If analytic ability is defined as "the ability to respond to one aspect of a stimulus situation without being greatly influenced by the background or field in which it is presented,"[46] four- and five-year-old boys and girls perform about equally, but school-age boys score consistently and substantially higher than girls.[47]

Analytic ability has also been operationally defined as a mode of grouping objects together on the basis of some selected element that they have in common. Tested in this way, boys more commonly use analytic groupings than do girls, at least by the time they are in the second grade.[48]

The observed differences in male and female cognitive styles are most likely the results of cultural training. As is the case in each of the sex-typed traits discussed, a cycle exists which perpetuates the myth. Children are subtly taught that boys can think more analytically and therefore can become, for example, better scientists. Children's closer day-to-day involvement with mother makes them more aware of the emotive aspects of her thinking style. Since father's interactions with children are much more restricted, they are likely to be less colored by emotional responses. If father's more sustained involvements on the job lead to emotional thinking, this occurs out of the child's sight. Thus the myth of sex differences in thinking fits the child's experience, affects the training he or she gets, and is consequently fulfilled, at least partially, in the adult who develops, completing the cycle.

It is important to note that both expressive and rational styles of thinking serve important personal and social functions. Expressive symbolization may be helpful in close personal communication, in creative thought, and in certain phases of problem solving, though clearly more goal-directed thought is needed in decision making and implementation. Two aspects that differentiate rational from expressive thought are directly related to the instrumental role in society:

1. Rational thought involves consensus; it is highly socialized and publically agreed upon. Emotive thought, by way of contrast, retains its personal roots in highly individual forms.
2. Rational thought is goal oriented; it seeks to move to a specific end result, to solve a problem. The goal, rather than the pleasure of the process, defines the task. For expressive symbolization, the joy of self-expression is at least as important as the communicative aspect, and neither is specifically goal-oriented.

### The instrumental orientation: The effective one

"Children agree earliest and most completely that fathers are bigger and stronger than mothers, next that they are smarter than mothers, and next that they have more social power or are the boss in the family."[49] Children also perceive fathers as more instrumentally competent than mothers.

The child's stereotype of masculinity, as with other traits, is supported by the self-perception of males in our society. Adult males think of themselves as "resourceful, mature, adventurous, efficient."[50] Male college students, more often than females, view themselves as "ambitious and independent."[51] Students of both sexes consider as masculine the following traits: knows the way of the world, direct, skilled in business, worldly, competitive, adventurous, makes decisions easily, ambitious. The only trait attributed to women which could be construed as instrumental is "neat in habits."[52]

Both the strength of the male and his more objective cognitive orientation contribute to the instrumental role that Parsons and Erikson view as the essence of masculinity. The central thrust of this orientation is described by the cluster of adjectives I have called "effective"; these include deliberate, enterprising, resourceful, and opportunistic. The trait of competence epitomizes the picture of father as the one who comes from the outside world. As Erikson summarizes it: "The dominant male identity is based on a fondness for 'what works' and for what man can make, whether it helps to build or to destroy."[53]

The ethical ambiguity of "what works" has been beautifully expressed in one sequence in Stanley Kubrik's film "2001: A Space Odessey." Two colonies of primitive ape-men are fighting over a pool of water. One individual (our mythology claims it was a male) looks down, spots a bone, and seizes it as a weapon. The film sequence which follows flashes between using the bone as a tool and as a weapon. Thus we are reminded that every extension of man's instrumental power has potential for good and evil; every creation of man can be an instrument of creativity or of destruction; every tool is also a weapon.

As "the effective one," man joins objectivity and strength in industry. The instrumental mode, with strength channeled into objective and effective goal striving, can result in man as the feelingless manipulator of his world and can reach frightening extremes of depersonalization. It is interesting that the cluster of words including "cruel" is associated with the instrumental orientation.

## A dangerous perception: The cruel one

P. W. Jackson has described the cultural standard for masculinity as "aggressive and punitive."[54] Unlike motherhood, fatherhood tends to be seen as a social obligation rather than as

> . . . a state having biological roots and involving psychological satisfaction. Since society does not recognize fatherliness as a male counterpart of motherliness, the father who shows tenderness and nurturance towards his children is regarded as effeminate; regarding child care as emasculating, the father is handicapped in achieving a proper relationship with his children.[55]

I believe it is an exaggeration to speak of masculinity as "aggressive and punitive" and to claim that nurturant fathers are "regarded as effeminate." However, a number of studies that have interviewed children (both boys and girls) to explore their perceptions of their fathers have shown that many children—about 40 percent—wish their fathers would show more love.[56] One of the terms the children frequently used to describe their fathers was "bossy."[57] Kagan concluded from interviews with more than 200 six- to ten-year-olds that both boys and girls found fathers to be less friendly, more dominant, more punitive, and more threatening than mothers.[58] In a later study, children six to eight described father as stronger than mother, but also "darker, more dirty, and more dangerous." Children in this study tended to characterize aggressive animals (tigers, alligators) as male, while thinking of rabbits, birds, and other such animals as female.[59] Other studies found that if children are asked which parent is more dangerous or punitive, both boys and girls agree that father is more aggressive than mother,[60] and fathers are perceived as stricter, more prone to use physical punishment, and more fear arousing.[61]

Fathers' self-perceptions do not match children's on this cluster of traits; adult males do not describe themselves as punitive, dangerous, and cruel. Male college students, do, however, describe themselves as "aggressive, ambitious, independent, pleasure seeking, and rugged"[62]—a combination of traits which could easily lead to asocial behavior. Students of both sexes describe males as competitive and ambitious. Perhaps more telling are the results of a study of college males in which it was discovered that high scores on masculinity scales were negatively correlated with friendliness.[63] There is considerable evidence that cruelty is part of the stereotype of masculinity that boys learn. According to Kagan, "It is difficult to find a sound study of preschool or school-age children in which aggressive behavior was not more frequent among boys than among girls. . . . This difference is also present in the make-believe themes children tell to dolls or to pictures."[64] Even in homes where parents report no use of physical punishment, boys frequently include violence in their "discipline" of dolls or puppets.[65]

It is important to remember that what is being described here is the stereotypic male image, the social role which the child incorporates as an understanding of masculinity. The point is not that men are hard and cruel in all their relationships. There is evidence that in the primary husband-wife relationship, men do interact in an expressive way and are not constrained to the instrumental role (although it is usually the wives who initiate expressive interaction).[66] The generalization to be recognized is that children do not perceive masculinity in terms of the father as a person. Instead they learn a role—father functions as a representative of a social role.[67] The role appears to be perceived by the child as strong, rational, effective, and cruel.

Of course such an image of man is not inevitable. It should be possible for the strong, muscular male to be firm without being punitive and cruel. It should be possible for the logical thinker to manipulate ideas carefully without abandoning his care for humans. It should be possible to competently and bravely tackle the outside world without denying the riches of the inner world.

## Summary

"The circle is complete, with both children and adults expecting and receiving more dependence, passivity, and nurturance from females, more aggression from males."[68] Kagan's extensive summary of the research on sex-role typing concludes by supporting the descriptive power of Parsons's dichotomy of masculine and feminine roles into instrumental versus expressive.

> The cluster of covert attributes that are closely linked to the concept of female in our culture include the ability to gratify a love object and the ability to elicit sexual arousal in a male; the desire to be a wife and mother and the correlated desires to give nurturance to one's child and affection to a love object; and the capacity for emotion. For males, the primary covert attributes include a pragmatic attitude, ability to gratify a love object, suppression of fear, and a capacity to control expression of strong emotion in time of stress.[69] There are fewer systematic data in support of these covert attributes than there are for the overt behaviors listed earlier. However clinical studies[70] and self-ratings by adults[71] agree with these statements.
>
> In sum, females are supposed to inhibit aggression and open display of sexual urges, to be passive with men, to be nurturant to others, to cultivate attractiveness, and to maintain an effective, socially poised, and friendly posture with others. Males are urged to be aggressive in the face of attack, independent in problem situations, sexually aggressive, in control of aggressive urges, and suppressive of strong emotion, especially anxiety . . .
>
> This list may strike readers as old fashioned or unrealistically traditional, and not representative of contemporary values. Existing data on children indicate that despite a common adult assumption that sex role standards are changing at a rapid rate, children continue to believe that aggression, dominance, and independence are more appropriate for males; passivity, nurturance, and affect more appropriate for females.[72]

Certainly the myth of masculinity and feminity is an effective and powerful one. The concepts of inner and outer space, of expressive versus instrumental roles, are descriptive of much of human behavior and, as myths, effectively shape that behavior. To what extent do these myths reflect a biological destiny? We shall seek to answer that question in the next chapter.

## Notes

1. Lawrence Kohlberg, "A Cognitive-Developmental Analysis of Children's Sex-role Concepts and Attitudes," in *The Development of Sex Differences*, ed. Eleanor E. Maccoby (Stanford, Calif.: Stanford U. Press, 1966), pp. 83–89.

2. Ibid., pp. 99–100. Kohlberg argues that the sex-role stereotypes are nearly the same regardless of socioeconomic class or subcultural differences (e.g., white vs. Negro). Other research indicates that traditional sex roles are strongest in the middle class, and more mixing of roles occurs in lower and upper classes. The quality and direction of sex stereotypes appear similar throughout our culture, though the magnitude of differences is not constant.

3. Ruth Wylie, *The Self Concept* (Lincoln: University of Nebraska Press, 1961).

4. A. C. Sherriffs and J. P. McKee, "Qualitative Aspects of Beliefs about Men and Women," *Journal of Consulting Psychology*, 13 (1957): 169.

5. E. M. Bennett and L. R. Cohen, "Men and Women: Personality Patterns and Contrasts," *Genetic Psychology Monographs*, 60 (1959): 101–53.

6. B. G. Rosenberg and Brian Sutton-Smith, *Sex and Identity* (New York: Holt, Rinehart & Winston, 1972), 83.

7. Jerome Kagan and H. A. Moss, "The Stability of Passive and Dependent Behavior from Childhood through Adulthood," *Child Development*, 31 (1960): 577–91; Arlene Skolnick, "Stability and Interrelations of Thematic Test Imagery over Twenty Years," *Child Development*, 37 (1966): 389–96.

8. Dorothy Rogers, *Issues in Adolescent Psychology*, 2d. ed. (New York: Appleton-Century-Crafts, 1972), pp. 45–67.

9. Jerome Kagan, "Acquisition and Significance of Sex Typing and Sex Role Identity," in *Review of Child Development Research*, ed. Martin L. Hoffman and Lois W. Hoffman. (New York: Russell Sage Foundation, © 1964), vol. 1, 137–68.

10. Wesley C. Becker, "Consequences of Different Kinds of Parental Discipline," in *Review of Child Development Research*, vol. 1, ed. Hoffman and Hoffman, pp. 169–208. See especially p. 172.

11. E. M. Bennett and L. R. Cohen, "Men and Women," pp. 101–53.

12. James A. Armentrout and Gary K. Burger, "Children's Reports of Parental Child-Rearing Behavior at Five Grade Levels," *Developmental Psychology*, 7 (1972): 44–48.

13. Kohlberg, "Cognitive-Developmental Analysis," pp. 82–172. Note especially pp. 100–102.

14. D. Lindskoog, "Children's Differentiation of Instrumental and Expressive Parent Roles" (Master's thesis, University of Chicago, 1964).

15. Reprinted from *Identity: Youth and Crisis* by Erik H. Erikson. By permission of W. W. Norton & Company, Inc. Copyright © 1968 by W. W. Norton, Inc. Austen Riggs Monograph No. 7.

16. Ibid., pp. 261–77. For a critique of Erikson's view, see Chapter 3.

17. Ibid., p. 274.

18. Ibid., p. 275.

19. Ibid., p. 277.

20. Ibid., p. 283.

21. Lindskoog, "Instrumental and Expressive Parent Roles."

22. M. M. Johnson, "Sex Role Learning in the Nuclear Family," *Child Development,* 34 (1963): 320–21.

23. Alfred B. Heilbrun, "An Empirical Test of the Modeling Theory of Sex-Role Learning," *Child Development,* 36 (1965): 790.

24. Elizabeth Janeway, *Man's World, Woman's Place: A Study in Social Mythology* (New York: Morrow, 1971). Elizabeth Janeway argues that woman's propensity to use power personally—to bitch—results from being deprived of other spheres of power. We will return to this argument in Chapter 5.

25. E. Sheerer, "An Analysis of the Relationship between Acceptance of and Respect for Self and Acceptance of and Respect for Others in Ten Counseling Cases," *Journal of Consulting Psychology,* 13 (1949): 169; E. Berger, "The Relation between Expressed Acceptance of Self and Expressed Acceptance of Others," *Journal of Abnormal Psychology,* 47 (1952): 778; K. Omwake, "The Relation between Acceptance of Self and Acceptance of Others Shown by Three Personality Inventories," *Journal of Consulting Psychology,* 18 (1954): 443.

26. See Harry F. Harlow, "The Nature of Love," *American Psychologist,* 13 (1958): 673–85.

27. Reprinted from *Identity: Youth and Crisis* by Erik H. Erikson. By permission of W. W. Norton & Company, Inc., Copyright © 1968 by W. W. Norton, Inc. Austen Riggs Monograph No. 7.

28. Evidence for these assertions is presented in Chapter 4.

29. Jerome Kagan, "The Child's Perception of the Parent," *Journal of Abnormal and Social Psychology,* 53 (1956): 257–58.

30. Talcott Parsons, *Social Structure and Personality* (London: Free Press, 1964), Chap. 2, "The Father Symbol."

31. Heilbrun, "Empirical Test of Modeling Theory," p. 790.

32. Rosenberg and Sutton-Smith, *Sex and Identity,* p. 59.

33. Heilbrun, "Empirical Test of Modeling Theory," p. 794. I have added the headings "rational" and "effective," which do not appear in the Adjective Check List.

34. Erikson, *Identity: Youth and Crisis,* pp. 279–80.

35. Paul Rosenkrantz et al., "Sex-Role Stereotypes and Self-concepts in College Students," *Journal of Counseling and Clinical Psychology,* 32 (1968): 287–95.

36. Sherriffs and McKee, "Beliefs about Men and Women," pp. 451–64.

37. Kagan, "Sex Typing and Sex Role Identity."

38. Jerome Kagan, B. Hosken, and S. Watson, "Child's Symbolic Conceptualization of Parents," *Child Development,* 32 (1961): 625–36.

39. Kohlberg, "Cognitive-Development Analysis."

40. Wylie, *The Self Concept.*

41. Kagan, "Sex Typing and Sex Role Identity."

42. Sherriffs and McKee, "Beliefs about Men and Women."

43. Rosenkrantz et al., "Sex-Role Stereotypes and Self-concepts."

44.   J. P. Guilford, "Potentiality for Creativity and Its Measurement," in *Proceedings of the 1962 Invitational Conference on Testing Problems* (Princeton, N.J.: Educational Testing Service, 1962), pp. 31–39.

45.   H. J. Klausmeier and William Wiersma, "Relationship of Sex, Grade Level, and Locale to Performance of High I.Q. Students on Divergent Thinking Tests," *Journal of Educational Psychology,* 55 (1964):114–19.

46.   Eleanor E. Maccoby, "Sex Differences in Intellectual Functioning," in *Development of Sex Differences,* ed. Maccoby, pp. 25–55.

47.   H. A. Wilkin et al., *Personality through Perception* (New York: Harper & Row, Publishers, 1954), p. 28; I. E. Sigel, P. Jarman, and H. Hanesian, "Styles of Categorization and Their Perceptual, Intellectual, and Personality Correlates in Young Children" (paper, Merrill-Palmer Institute, 1963), cited in *Development of Sex Differences,* ed. Maccoby, p. 46; Eleanor Maccoby et al., "Activity Level and Intellectual Functioning in Normal Preschool Children," *Child Development,* 36 (1965): 761–70.

48.   Sigel et al., "Styles of Categorization," p. 46; Jerome Kagan, H. A. Moss, and I. E. Sigel, "The Psychological Significance of Styles of Conceptualization" *Monographs of the Society for Research in Child Development,* 28 (1963): 73–111.

49.   Jerome Kagan and Judith Lemkin, "The Child's Differential Perception of Parental Attributes," *Journal of Abnormal and Social Psychology,* 61 (1960): 446–47; citing Charles E. Smith, "The Effect of Father-Absence in the Development of Sex-Role Attitudes in Boys" (Ph.D. diss., University of Chicago, 1969).

50.   Wylie, *The Self Concept.*

51.   Sherriffs and McKee, "Beliefs about Men and Women."

52.   Rosenkrantz et al., "Sex-role Stereotypes and Self-Concepts," p. 291.

53.   Erikson, *Identity: Youth and Crisis,* p. 262.

54.   P. W. Jackson, "Verbal Solutions to Parent-child Problems," *Child Development,* 27 (1956): 339–51.

55.   Irene M. Josselyn, "Cultural Forces, Motherliness and Fatherliness," *American Journal of Orthopsychiatry,* vol. 26, No. 2 (1956): 264–71. Copyright 1956, The American Orthopsychiatric Association, Inc. Reproduced by permission.

56.   See L. P. Gardner, "Analysis of Children's Attitudes to Fathers," *Journal of Genetic Psychology,* 70 (1947): 3–38.

57.   L. P. Gardner, "A Survey of the Attitudes and Activities of Fathers," *Journal of Genetic Psychology,* 63 (1943): 15–53.

58   Kagan, "Child's Perception of the Parent," pp. 257–58.

59.   Kagan, Hosken, and Watson, "Child's Symbolic Conceptualization of Parents," pp. 625–36.

60.   W. Emmerich, "Young Children's Discriminations of Parent and Child Roles," *Child Development,* 30 (1959): 403–419.

61.   Becker, "Different Kinds of Parental Discipline."

62.   Sherriffs and McKee, "Beliefs about Men and Women."

63.   Robert C. Pace, "College Environments," in *Encyclopedia of Educational Research* (Toronto: Macmillan Publishing Co., 1969), p. 172.

64.   Kagan, "Sex Typing and Sex Role Identity."

65.   Pauline Sears, "Child Rearing Factors Related to the Playing of Sex-Typed Roles," *American Psychologist,* 8 (1953): 431.

66.   George Levinger, "Task and Social Behavior in Marriage," *Sociometry*, 27 (1964): 433–48.

67.   Evidence for this generalization is presented in Chapter 4.

68.   Kagan, "Sex Typing and Sex Role Identity."

69.   Kagan and Lemkin, "Differential Perception of Parental Attributes."

70.   Irving Bieber et al., *Homosexuality* (New York: Basic Books, 1962).

71.   Bennett and Cohen, "Men and Women," pp. 101–53.

72.   Kagan, "Sex Typing and Sex Role Identity."

# 3

# Determinants of sex roles

## Biological factors

To WHAT EXTENT does biology determine the sex roles? In discussing the stereotypic sex roles of American culture, it was noted that the stereotypes have some basis in reality. American men do tend to be more instrumental and women more expressive in their orientations. Are there biological differences in men and women that lead them toward these roles, or do they simply result from cultural learning?

### Body and environment

The nature-nurture controversy has a long history in the field of psychology and is not subject to easy resolution. Some general statements about unraveling the role of biology and of learning in any particular personality trait are in order before turning to the sexually linked traits in particular. Simply because certain traits are passed down within a family, it cannot be assumed that they are genetically inherited. To illustrate, it was generally assumed some decades ago that retarded couples who had retarded children were passing on lower intelligence in their genes. Subsequent studies showed that cultural changes and better education were able to raise the IQ's of many such children to within normal range.[1] These families were passing on low intelligence by their failure to provide adequate stimulation in infancy, their lack of verbal interaction when the children were small, and other environmental variables. Even though a man's father was a cabinetmaker and he also became a cabinetmaker, and the trade was passed on from father to son for six generations, we still would not assume that cabinetry is an inherited trade. Rather, in this case the family and social setting encouraged learning the trade. Similarly, if the females in a family (or in a culture) have been found to be quiet and "ladylike" for generations, while the men have been dominant and rowdy, it cannot be assumed that these roles are biological. Similarities within a family or a culture do not prove biological causation.

One method for assessing biological factors is to study individual differences in the reactions of newborn and very young infants, because cultural and learning factors would not be expected to have played a substantial role in the first weeks of life. Most parents, nurses, pediatricians, and others who work with infants have observed that infants have very different personalities, even in the first weeks of their lives. It is not enough for the psychologist to note that infants differ; he also needs to know if these differences are stable. If the infant is very active at three weeks of age, is he more likely than other infants to be also very active in childhood and adulthood? A number of physiological responses have been shown to be stable through infancy and appear to be inherited. Identical twins are more alike than ordinary siblings on such autonomic responses as pulse, respiration, salivation, and blood pressure.[2] Other biological responses that appear to be stable in infancy are: sensory thresholds,[3] quality and intensity of emotional tone,[4] and electroencephalographic waves.[5] Theodore Millon notes that "despite the value of [the findings reported above] as evidence of stability in infantile functioning, it remains unclear as to which biological measures are likely to be pertinent to later personality."[6]

The inability of psychology at present to determine the effects of these biological differences on personality traits leads to consideration of behavior differences in infancy. Extensive studies surveyed by Millon showed that each infant in his first weeks of life has a recognizable and distinctive way of behaving that persists through early childhood.

Although infants can be differentiated on a number of dimensions of behavior, Millon noted that

> . . . one descriptive term seemed to summarize or tie together a number of the characteristics which were felt to be especially relevant, if not crucial, to later development: the infant's *activity* pattern. Marked differ-

ences in vigor, tempo, smoothness, and rhythm colored the infant's style and frequency of relating to his environment, and influenced the character of responses he evoked from others. Of course, all children displayed both active and passive tendencies, but in most one pattern predominated.[7]

There is some evidence that the differences that do exist in the style of the infant's responding tend to be amplified because they evoke different types of responses from the persons involved with the infant.

> Although early patterns were modified only slightly from infancy to childhood, . . . this continuity could not be attributed entirely to the persistence of the infant's innate endowment. Subsequent experiences tend to reinforce characteristics which the infant displayed in early life. The impact of the infant's initial behavior transforms his environment in ways that intensify and accentuate these behaviors.[8]

It may be that the biological differences themselves are not particularly significant but become so as the interaction accentuates them. It was noted in the preceding chapter that sex-role-related personality traits are among the most stable, probably because they continue to receive cultural reinforcement. So far, the discussion of biological differences has not dealt with male-female differences.[9] But if a boy were born with a higher activity rate than his sister, these differences might become accentuated as the family interacted. It might treat the children differently, accepting the more active behavior of the boy and reinforcing it, but if the girl showed signs of a higher activity rate, the parents might expect her to be quiet: "If your brother can sit still, surely you can." The point is that differences in nature would more likely be amplified if they fit in with the cultural sex-role expectations; differences that did not fit in might be minimized.

### Sex differences in early childhood

In turning from studies of infants to research on children, it must be kept in mind that interaction styles of boys and girls may have been exaggerated by the social interaction of the parents. Jerome Kagan provides a good illustration of such differences:

> Some of the sex differences seen in adults can be observed very early in development. Young girls are more likely than boys to stay close to their mothers when they are either apprehensive or bored. This writer has observed two-year-old boys and girls with their mothers in a large room decorated as a living room. Initially, the children were left in the room to become accustomed to the new situation. The girls stayed in closer physical contact with their mothers than the boys. Several toys were then brought into the room and the children were allowed

to play for half an hour. Most of the children left their mothers immediately and began to play. However, after twenty minutes many children became bored and restless. The girls drifted back toward their mothers and the boys wandered around the room. . . . The boys were [different in the style of their play, as well; they were] more likely to use their body as an object of play.[10]

**1921522**

These findings are consistent with those reported in the preceding chapter supporting the more aggressive masculine role. Certainly they reflect the parents' reactions, for, as Patricia Sexton has noted, ". . . parents feel that aggression is more normal in boys, so they are more tolerant of it. They also think boys can take more verbal and physical punishment, and deserve more."[11] Yet, if broad generalizations are made, sex differences in activity and aggression can be noted right after birth. Studies of infants have shown greater activity and aggression among boys, and evidence about their greater capacity of energy suggests that they may be born that way.[12]

Kagan points out the similarity of the results in his study of children with their mothers to observations of other primates:

The rhesus monkey and baboon . . . show sex differences resembling those observed in this study with children. Infant female monkeys stay closer to their mothers than do male monkeys. Moreover, display of threatening gestures and body-contact play is more frequent among young male than female monkeys, whereas passive withdrawal to stress is more common among females. These similarities force us to consider the possibility that some of the psychological differences between men and women may not be the product of experience alone but derivative of subtle biological differences between the sexes.[13]

Male chimpanzees tend to be more active, restless, and aggressive than the females; they walk before females do. The females sit more and use their hands more and are more sociable. We find these same differences in human children:

Though girls develop faster, boys are at all ages more active. The Gesell studies of infants show that boys begin to creep, stand, and use their muscles about a month before girls. The girls are less active, sit longer, engage in more sedentary work, and are more able to use finer hand motions. Girls sleep more and boys are more restless.[14]

The similarity between human and other primate development suggests that males may be predisposed by constitutional variables toward activity and dominance, while females are predisposed toward passivity.[15] Boys generally have an advantage over girls in strength and energy.[16] Experiments in which androgens were administered to pregnant female monkeys resulted in "masculinized female offspring which exhibited behavior more typical of males: threatening, initiating activity, and rough-

and-tumble play."[17] These researchers found that the biological effects of the androgen may be both direct and indirect; that is, it may affect musculature and energy patterns, but it may also make large muscle movements more gratifying and thus more likely to be repeated.

A parallel analysis can be made of anxiety and fear as inhibitors of activity in females. When nursery school children are subjected to fear situations, girls exhibit more fearful, withdrawing behavior than boys do.[18] As early as the first year of life, when girl infants are put down on the floor in a strange room, they cling to their mother's legs longer before crawling away to explore objects. They are also more upset than boys when placed behind a barrier so that they can see the mother but cannot get to her.[19]

Males tend to exhibit greater motor activity than girls at each period of development that has been tested. Similarly, girls seem to show greater anxiety and more fearful behaviors at each stage of life. A review of 26 studies showed "strong evidence for greater anxiety in girls when anxiety is measured with paper and pencil tests"; 14 reported that girls scored higher on anxiety, while the other 12 found no differences. However, the tendency for girls to score higher in anxiety on these tests may simply reflect the greater willingness of women in our culture to admit such feelings; it is not conclusive evidence that a more basic difference exists.[20]

No research has directly studied the relationship between fear responses and female hormones. Two studies do exist which measured physiological reactions to stress. In both, females were found to have greater autonomic reactivity.[21] The subjects in these studies were all at least 12 years old, so the possibility that these reactions, though physiological, are learned cannot be excluded.

Further evidence of a physiological base for female fear reactions comes from the experiments already cited in which pregnant animals were given male hormones. Not only did the female offspring exhibit more rough and tumble play, but their tendency to withdraw from the approaches and threats of others was decreased.[22] Possibly the higher activity levels of males and the more inhibited, withdrawing behavior of females are two aspects of the same dimension. In any case, it can be said that "the argument from the chromosomal-hormonal position is that inherent sexuality provides a built-in bias influencing the way an individual interacts with his environment."[23]

### From "predispositions" to sexual stereotypes

It is a long leap from the possibility of a built-in sexual bias on the dimension of activity levels to the assumption that males are predisposed to an instrumental role and females to an expressive one. Before such inferences are warranted, much more research is necessary. In reviewing the available research, the areas in which, statistically speaking, male-female differences in personality might conceivably have a biological base must be kept clearly in mind: the higher activity levels of males and the more inhibited, withdrawing behavior of females. Do higher activity rates lead to the instrumental role of masculinity described in Chapter 2 as strong, rational, effective, and cruel? And do inhibition and withdrawal lead to the expressive feminine role—the concern with vital inner potential and the interpersonal orientation?

Recent experimental and theoretical work has focused upon the importance of activation levels in predicting behavior. At first blush, this would suggest that the males' generally higher activity levels must be significant for later personality development. However, the most sophisticated activation theories treat "orientation toward internal or external sources of stimulation" as a separate dimension from level of activation.[24] This suggests the impossibility of an easy move from data on activity levels to Erik Erikson's inferences regarding internal and external spatial orientations, a suggestion that is reinforced by the fact that activation theory has not found it important to note sex differences. No conclusion can be reached from this information alone, however. The focus of activation theory is on stimulation input, while activity levels and Erikson's spatial orientations emphasize motor output. It is not possible to make direct inferences from one to the other. Further, activation research is a relatively new area of psychological investigation, and though it may prove fruitful in answering some of the nature-nurture questions that have been raised, it has not yet led to the sort of longitudinal investigation which would provide clarifying data.

What is needed is longitudinal research on both sexes which measures activity rates at birth and throughout infancy and childhood and later compares the sex-typed personality and behavioral traits of high-activity boys, low-activity boys, high-activity girls, and low-activity girls. If it is the activity level itself (in contrast to the socialization effects) which leads to instrumental, outward-directed behavior, we should see the effects of high-activity in both sexes.

### Physical structures and predispositions to sex roles

*Muscular strength, manipulation, and the instrumental role.* Lacking this and other more conclusive evidence, an effort must be made to think clearly about what data are available. First, apart from the question of the relationship between activity levels and the instrumental orientation, it is at least possible that the common childhood perception of the father as "strong" has to do with the superior physical strength of the male. The strong shoulders and more developed fighting equipment of the male primate suggest morphological adaptation for the protective role. And certainly the roles of protector and defender were important instrumental roles in earlier periods of history, as with Erikson's image of concentric circles of baboons in which the males faced outward. The problem of the image, of course, is that it allows us to slip uncritically from the concept of physical strength and defense to Erikson's outward orientation—to instrumentality in the 20th-century sense of the word. Physical strength and activity are of minor importance today; the instrumental orientation has more to do with manipulation than with defense. Effectiveness in manipulating objects and in treating the world realistically is the focus of Talcott Parsons's and Erikson's concepts of masculinity, not defensive strength.

If we are to draw upon phylogenetic history, however, we must remember that instrumental capacities were greatly advanced in certain primates by the opposable thumb, which made it possible to grasp and manipulate objects. Manipulation, as the etymology of the word suggests, has to do with manual dexterity—and in this realm it is the female who is generally superior! In an earlier period of history the male superiority in strength and in large motor tasks may have equipped him to take the instrumental role, but human manipulations have become increasingly refined. Today, if we are to argue at all from built-in sexual biases to personality orientations, it would seem cogent to argue that girls have the edge of instrumentality, since their hand coordination is finer and develops earlier.[25]

To summarize, the argument that higher levels of activity in boys leads to the instrumental role seems appropriate only as concerns aspects of physical strength and defensiveness, which are no longer of central importance to the instrumental orientation.

*Genital structure and personality differences.*   Some personality theories place a great deal of importance on the differences in the structure of the male and female genitalia. Erikson's emphasis on the womb in his description of femininity was noted in Chapter 2. His belief that a woman's somatic design predisposes a particularly female use of life space assumes that a woman's kinesthetic experience of her internal organs influences her behavior.[26] Studies of hermaphroditic individuals provide empirical evidence to the contrary; the presence of female internal organs did not affect the roles and behaviors of children with these characteristics who were raised as boys.[27] Erikson's use of the phrase "somatic design" cannot be accepted as scientific description.

Another argument for built-in sexual biases resulting from physical structure ascribes certain sex-role differences to characteristics of the male genitalia. The fact that the male genitals, instead of being hidden, are visible and easily accessible may be an important factor in the earlier arousal of purely sexual feelings and experimentation in the adolescent boy, in contrast to the generalized romantic view of sex in the girl. Doubtless these physical differences contribute to the earlier occurrence and much greater frequency of masturbation among males, but do they have broad ramifications for personality which relate to the instrumental and expressive roles? Some psychoanalytic theorists have argued that the male's experience of masturbation contributes to the more objective, goal-directed male view. By contrast, the female view of sex as mysterious and highly personal stems from her possession of more hidden, secret sexual organs.

It is difficult to obtain data pertinent to such speculations; some evidence seems to point to the opposite conclusion. Male masturbation appears to encourage a more active fantasy life, at least among middle- and upper-class boys for whom heterosexual gratification is delayed for several years. For these males, sexuality in the early adolescent years tends to be privatistic, and this experience encourages an increase in fantasy. Thus some psychologists attribute to the structure of male sexual organs an inclination toward subjective, personal, and imaginative pursuits, in direct opposition to the argument that these organs predispose the boy to objective, goal-oriented pursuits. It is true that middle-class boys catch up to and surpass girls in academic achievement and creativity during adolescence. But these changes could better be explained by the cultural expectations that males should be preparing for work or college (in the earlier school years, academic pursuits are seen as feminine, but in the last years of public school males, more than females, are pushed to achieve). Arguments attributing either objective or subjective personality traits to the genital structure are at best highly speculative and cannot be taken as evidence for biological predisposition.

***Breasts and the nurturant role.*** There is one structural difference between men and women that historically has had an important influence on sex-role differentiation. Before the advent of the baby bottle, the role of nursing the infant was necessarily the woman's; thus the breasts, more than the presence of inner space, have influenced the sex-typing of the nurturant role for nontechnological societies throughout history. Because her anatomy forced the female to take the nurturant role, it may have encouraged women more than men to develop nurturant, person-oriented feelings and behaviors. The male had to cope with the more external problems of food, shelter, and defense. In societies where the technology of the baby bottle and laborsaving machines does not exist, it might be expected that man's muscles and woman's breasts would predispose sex roles to some degree (though, as will be seen in the last section of this chapter, the types are much more various than the American expressive-instrumental mythology would suggest).

### Conclusions regarding biological factors

The biological characteristics that are most easily lumped into male and female categories are largely structural characteristics. Present-day technology makes these largely irrelevant as predisposing factors for the sex roles. The only built-in sexual bias of significance to personality appears to be an endocrinal-based continuum of activity levels. The fact that boys are generally more active does not go very far in explaining the total constellation sex typed as male, the instrumental orientation.

I am not trying to argue that the person is totally shaped by his environment. However, Freud's dictum that "anatomy is destiny" seems historically dated. It is not that biological factors do not matter, but the biological factors that have the greatest influence on personality development are not anatomical. Individual differences in activity rates, neurological structures, and so on which provide the biological base for understanding personality development are not neatly lumped into two categories, male and female.

## Cultural factors

Having limited the degree to which sex-role differences can be attributed to biological factors, the next step is to look at the nature-nurture issue from the other side. The data from cross-cultural and anthropological studies illustrate the range of possibilities for defining sex roles within the human race.

### Tests of masculinity and femininity

The whole cluster of traits normally associated with masculinity and femininity is a cluster not because of biological destiny but because our culture reinforces these responses differently for males than for females. Other societies may label different behaviors masculine or feminine. The clearest experimental illustration of this point concerns the collection of questions used in the psychological tests to indicate degree of masculinity or femininity (psychologists refer to these as M–F scales.) Each of the items on these scales differentiates between the sexes in America. That is, if the test is given to a large group of Americans, on some items most of the boys will agree and most of the girls disagree; on others the reverse will be true. All items seem to be sex related in the United States. But when the same questions are posed in another culture (even in a technologically advanced nation such as Holland) the same pattern of responses does not occur. Only a few of the many questions which differentiate sexes in America will do the same in Holland.[28]

Sex roles are not universal entities; they are the result of individual learning histories and of the histories of the various cultures. A similarity of behavior for a particular sex within a culture only indicates similar training for members of that sex. The similarities in sex roles that exist between cultures also may be indications of a similar history. What is impressive when considering other cultures is the wide range of sex-role possibilities.

## History and a general pattern

It has been suggested that the division of sex roles may have its historic roots in the division of labor that grew out of the woman's biological role of bearing and nursing children and the greater muscular strength of men. This is the common division of labor in nonliterate cultures, though I have argued that it is not a necessary division in modern technological society. G. P. Murdock reviewed data from 225 nonliterate tribes and found that, in general, men gravitate toward warfare, metalwork, hunting, mining, quarrying, and boat building—that is, toward work requiring muscular strength—while women usually perform occupations centering around home and children—basketry, gathering fruits and nuts, water carrying, grain grinding, potterymaking, and clothes manufacture and repair.[29] Certainly many of the activities that societies see as masculine or feminine could be equally well done by the opposite sex. Though the initial division of labor may have been established upon generalities about sexual differences, the roles have extended far beyond their biological base. Once the division of labor is established, however, Ernest Hilgard notes, "complex regulation by social pressure sets in, and familiar ways of doing things are enforced by taboo, ritual, superstition, prejudice, and other forms of social control."[30]

## A wide range of possibilities

In our own culture we tend to think it is natural for the male to carry out the instrumental role, the female the expressive role. But it has been demonstrated that these roles are far removed from the hormonal and structural differences in the sexes. Anthropological studies reveal that there are societies in which the sex roles are markedly different from our own. There is a wide range of possibilities available to a culture.

While our own society assigns rather different personality traits and sex roles to men and women, this was not the case in some of the New Guinea tribes studied by Margaret Mead.

In a mountain-dwelling tribe known as the Arapesh, men and women were more alike than in our culture. Their similarity lay in their passivity, gentleness, mildness, and domesticity. . . . Men and women shared the care of the children and other home duties with less division of labor than that with which we are familiar.[31]

In Arapesh culture both men and women are raised in a way which we would call feminine. Other cultures train both men and women to be masculine by our standards. For example, in another New Guinea tribe, the Mundugumor, men and women are also more nearly alike than in our own culture, but among these river-dwelling people "both sexes tended to be ruthless, aggressive and violent."[32]

Some societies believe, as we do, that certain traits and activities are natural for men and others for women, but the specific traits are nearly the opposite of our own. A third New Guinea tribe, the lake-dwelling Tchambuli,

. . . offer the most dramatic contrast to our culture. While the sexes had dissimilar roles . . . the pattern was largely reversed. The Tchambuli woman was the aggressive partner, the manager of business affairs. The man was emotionally responsive to the feelings of his children, and he was subordinate to and dependent upon his mate. The psychological reversal was so real that the Tchambuli interpreted it as biologically natural—even to the extent that the man went into confinement and suffered while his wife had the baby.[33]

These few examples illustrate the extremely malleable character of humanity. B. G. Rosenberg and Brian Sutton-Smith found that "the overlap in behavior between the sexes is so extensive and human malleability so great that both sexes are capable of exhibiting most forms of human behavior. At this time there are few behaviors that may be viewed as solely within the province of one sex."[34] Technological innovations, and the fact that highly literate societies are able to consciously consider possibilities and reshape themselves, mean that even more possibilities are open to us today. The kibbutzim in Israel offer an example of a deliberate attempt on the part of a modern society to reshape sex roles and child rearing. In the kibbutz,

. . . the emphasis is on equality of the genders, with no sexual division of labor. Women spend part of their time driving the tractors and toiling in the field, while men, on their part, help with the laundry and kitchen work. One might conclude that almost any cultural patterning that emphasizes sex similarities or differences appears workable.[35]

### Patterns directly related to sexual behavior

The evidence for cultural variation in the extended sex roles is rather persuasive. But what about behaviors more closely linked to sexuality itself? Aren't these biologically determined? According to our cultural standards, the petite, narrow-waisted woman endowed with full bust and well-rounded hips is a feminine sex symbol. But our culture's view of sexual beauty is not shared by some societies. A review of European art history will demonstrate that, even within Western society, the standards of feminine beauty have changed.[36] Anthropological data show that in a number of cultures "a beautiful woman should be relatively tall and powerfully built."[37] In other cultures, the larger a woman is, the more beautiful she is considered. A massive figure, powerful limbs, and strength are the desired traits of femininity.[38]

It is not difficult to understand how standards of beauty can be learned and thus can be culturally determined. But there is a tendency to see the courting and mating behavior as directly under the control of hormones. It is generally recognized that specific courting customs have changed, but in our culture we often assume that the male naturally takes the sexual initiative, although we allow that the female may do so in subtle ways.

The view that male initiative is the norm is projected to our perceptions of the sexual behavior of other animals, but this does not jibe with data collected in objective studies. Studies with chimpanzees, in which initiative may be operationally defined as "the tendency of one animal to enter the other's living cage as soon as the connecting door was raised," found that the female took the initiative in 85 percent of all matings when she was in estrus and 65 percent of the time during other stages of her sex cycle.[39] This example has been chosen because chimpanzees are among the higher primates, those closest to man phylogenetically. The illustration is not atypical; Clellan Ford and Frank Beach conclude their survey of animal sexual behavior with this statement: "So far as we have been able to ascertain, there is no mammalian species in which sexual initiative rests solely with either the male or the female."[40] They note that:

> There is a widespread belief that male animals of most species always assume complete command of the mating situation and inevitably play the more active role in precoital courtship. Nothing could be further from the truth. Distribution of initiative varies from species to species, but in the main the relationship is a reciprocal one in which both partners are sexually aggressive and each contributes to the complete arousal of the other. The relative sexual readiness of the male and female frequently determines which individual will solicit and which will respond.[41]

To return to the human species, in the majority of societies on which information is available, the male is expected to assume the more active role in sexual advances, as he is in our own culture. However, this is by no means the only way in which all human societies have been organized. In a few societies, the girl generally begins all love affairs. Among the Kwoma tribe of New Guinea, the girl makes the first advances; the boy is afraid to do so because the girl's relatives might be angered. And in the Maori tribe of New Zealand, women are considered more amorous than men and attempt to attract their attention by slyly pinching or scratching their hands.[42] In a number of societies women are not so subtle in the manner in which they take sexual initiative. An almost universal form of sexual invitation throughout the mammalian class is for the receptive female to expose her genitals to the male. It is an acceptable custom in some human societies for the female to take the initiative in this same manner. In these cultures "deliberate exposure by a woman of her genitalia to a man's gaze is a common form of sexual invitation."[43] The assumption that sexual initiative is naturally a male prerogative clearly does not fit the data.

Thus in some societies initiative is customarily left to the male; in others, to the female. Other societies make little or no distinction between the sexes in the matter of initiating sexual affairs. Either the boy or the girl is permitted by custom to take the first steps in soliciting intercourse. In the Trobriander and Lesu societies of Melanesia and the Kurtatchi society of the Solomon Islands, for example, love making is said to be as spontaneous on the part of one sex as of the other.[44] Ford and Beach conclude that "From the cross-cultural evidence it seems clear that unless specific pressures are brought to bear against such behavior [as in our society], women initiate sexual advances as often as do men."[45]

The variation between societies in their expectations of male and female sex roles suggests that no particular behavior can be appropriately termed natural or unnatural. However, the different socializing methods do have consequences beyond their immediate intent. It is not surprising that women who are inhibited in sexual activity throughout childhood and adolescence are much less able to achieve sexual satisfaction, even when it is permissible in adult life. According to Ford and Beach:

> Social learning and experience powerfully affect the extent to which a man or woman adopts and enjoys a passive or an active role in the sexual relationship. We have pointed out that in every infra-human species the distribution of sexual initiative is bilateral. Both the male and the female may extend the sexual invitation and both have an active share in the continuation of the relationship until coitus is completed. The wide divergence between different human societies in this regard is probably due, not to biological differences between males and females, but to the lifelong effects of early training.
>
> The societies that severely restrict adolescent and preadolescent sex play, those that enjoin girls to be modest, retiring, and submissive, appear to produce adult women who are incapable of or at least unwill-

ing to be sexually aggressive. The feminine products of such cultural training are likely to remain relatively inactive even during marital intercourse. And, quite often, they do not experience clearcut sexual orgasm. In contrast, the societies which permit or encourage early sex play usually allow females a greater degree of freedom in seeking sexual contacts. Under such circumstances the sexual performance of the mature women seems to be characterized by a certain degree of aggression, to include definite and vigorous activity, and to result regularly in complete and satisfactory orgasm.[46]

The data from other cultures makes it clear that there is a very wide range of possibilities of sex roles behaviors. Being created male or female defines very little of what people in a particular culture term masculine or feminine. The argument I am presenting here, then, is that most of what we tend to think of as natural for boys, or for girls, is actually culturally transmitted behavior.

## Sex roles as social learning

The implication of the biological and anthropological data which have been presented is that sex-assigned personality traits are learned. Laboratory psychological experiments provide clear evidence that this is the case. I have chosen to illustrate this by reviewing the evidence for the social learning of aggression, in keeping with the conclusion reached at the end of the survey of biological factors in the first part of this chapter. There it was suggested that the physiological trait that appears most important in a biological explanation of sex differences is the generally higher activity of male infants. It does not seem possible to argue that their higher activity level predisposes males to an instrumental orientation. But is a more limited argument possible? Does their activity level predispose males to more aggression?

It would be difficult to design a research strategy which could give a definitive answer to that question. It is possible, however, to demonstrate the degree to which social reinforcers can change levels of aggression. Albert Bandura, a leading advocate of social learning theory, conducted a series of laboratory experiments in which preschool children were exposed to aggressive models.[47] They viewed films of adults acting aggressively, punching and kicking a man-sized Bobo doll, for example. In the early experiments, Bandura and his associates found that after seeing models of aggression, boys tended to perform more imitative aggression than girls did. A new variable was added in a later experiment. After seeing the sequence of films in which an adult displayed aggression, the children saw a second film sequence. Some children saw a sequence in which another person entered the scene and rewarded the model with praise and candy. Others saw a different film in which the model was punished. For a third group, the film ended without any indication of the consequences of aggression. Following the films, the children who had viewed the punishment ending performed significantly fewer acts of aggression in a play setting than the children who saw the other film sequences. Clearly the models do not simply elicit some "innate" aggression in the children; children react in terms of the consequences of aggression they are led to expect.

In the last phase of the experiment, and this is the most interesting for present purposes, all three groups of children were offered rewards if they imitated the adult in the film. In this phase, the three groups performed nearly the same! This showed they had learned the aggressive responses, but some (due to the punishment ending) were inhibited from performing them. The offering of rewards for imitating can be seen as disinhibiting the children. And the results showed that, once disinhibited, girls demonstrated nearly the same amount of aggression as boys.[48]

Whatever biological differences exist between the sexes, it is clear that social consequences have the power to increase or decrease aggression, and where earlier inhibitions are removed, sex differences are practically eliminated.[49]

Learning theorists point out that a person can be very aggressive in some circumstances and nonaggressive in others. A field study by Bandura which illustrated the effects of child-rearing methods demonstrated that aggression is not a unitary trait. Many of the boys in the study, described by school officials as "highly aggressive," were found to be nonaggressive in their homes. Their parents punished aggression at home but were frequently aggressive themselves; besides setting an example in the homes, the parents verbally encouraged their sons to be aggressive with their peers. Thus the boys learned to be aggressive but to express aggression only in situations where their parents would reward it.[50]

Both under laboratory control and in the real-life situation, aggression appears to be largely a result of the rewards and social expectations of the society. These studies suggest that sex roles are learned and are subject to modification in the same way as other learning tasks.[51] The process by which they are normally learned in American society will be explored in Chapter 4.

## History and change in sex roles

The survey of cross-cultural data makes it clear that there is a wide range of possibilities for sexual roles. The data strongly suggest that the determining factors in sex-role definitions are cultural. Cultures which have developed distinctive sex roles have often extended such distinctions to behaviors remote from the sexual differences themselves. This extension may have been perpetuated because such a division of labor was efficient in previous societies. To draw an example from Western society, by centering woman's work around the home the society had to educate only the male half of the population for life in the larger world.

But once a society has stressed the values of individual fulfillment and claimed that government of the society is the responsibility of all its citizens, the efficiency of this division of labor comes into question. Our society has insisted that public education is necessary for females as well as males, and it has extended the vote to women. Certainly it is not necessary that women's place be in the home or that males be instrumental and females expressive, and each be discouraged from developing the other behaviors. If these roles are no longer necessary we must ask if it is wise for our society to continue to perpetuate them.

Some students of contemporary events argue that the sex roles are already undergoing fast change. Surely that is the impression given by the mass media, but it has not as yet been validated by careful empirical research, so it is hard to assess how deep such trends may be and whether they apply to more than a small educated subculture. The impressions of social scientists have not been consistent. Sexton argues that the American man is becoming "feminized."[52] Alice Rossi, on the other hand, believes that mothers are becoming increasingly more instrumental but fathers are not increasing in their expressiveness.[53] The area of greatest consensus is that if male and female roles are changing, they are changing in the direction of becoming more similar.[54]

Whatever changes may be occurring, it is still the case that most Americans are fully acculturated into the stereotypic sex roles, as the data in Chapter 2 demonstrated. At least for the present, they are the norm. The next chapter will show more specifically how these norms are learned in our society and some of the effects of this socialization process.

## Summary

Boys generally show higher activity rates; girls exhibit higher anxiety. These may have a physiological base, but they are clearly amplified by social interactions. These differences do not directly suggest the cultural roles of the expressive and instrumental orientations.

Responses to psychological tests indicate that the constellation of traits considered sex typed in American society does not have this implication in some other Western societies. In more primitive societies, sex roles are frequently based on men's muscular strength and women's infant care. The roles have extended far beyond their biological bases, and societies exist in which they are diametrically opposite those of our society. Standards for sexual beauty, prescriptions as to which sex should take the initiative, and related cultural norms indicate a very wide range of possibilities. Our culture's particular role definitions are not predetermined biologically.

Social-psychological studies indicate that such sex-typed behaviors as aggression can be learned. Once disinhibited, girls show nearly the same amount of aggression as boys.

## Notes

1. Anne Anastasi, *Individual Differences* (New York: John Wiley & Sons, 1965), pp. 195–236.

2. See Theodore Millon, *Modern Psychopathology* (Philadelphia: W. B. Saunders & Co., 1969), p. 127. Even studies of twins do not establish that the differences are inherited; it is likely that the parents' reactions to twins are more similar than they are to other siblings.

3. P. Bergman and S. Escalona, "Unusual Sensitivities in Very Young Children," in *Psychoanalytic Study of the Child* (New York: International Universities Press, 1949), vols. 3–4.

4. R. Meili, "A Longitudinal Study of Personality Development," in *Dynamic Psychopathology of Childhood* (ed. L. Jessner and E. Pavenstedt (New York: Grune & Stratton, 1959).

5. G. Walter, "Electroencephalographic Development of Children," in *Discussions on Child Development* ed. J. M. Tanner and Barbel Inhelder (New York: International Universities Press, 1953).

6. Millon, *Modern Psychopathology*, p. 127.

7. Ibid., p. 128.

8. Ibid., p. 128.

9. From a physiological perspective, there are important male-female differences in hormone production. Unfortunately, little is known about the influences of hormones on behavior and personality in humans. Extensive research has been done to understand hormonal influences on behavior in animals. Results indicate that the interactions are highly species-specific; that is, it is impossible to apply results from one type of animal to another. Consequently, the animal research provides little help in understanding hormonal influences in man.

10. From *Understanding Children* by Jerome Kagan, © 1971 by Harcourt Brace Jovanovich, Inc. and reprinted with their permission.

11. Patricia Sexton, *The Feminized Male: Classrooms, White Collars, and the Decline of Manliness* (New York: Vintage Press, 1969), p. 127.

12. F. L. Goodenough, *Anger in Young Children,* Institute of Child Welfare Monograph Ser. 9 (Minneapolis: University of Minnesota Press, 1931), pp. xiii and 278.

13. Kagan, *Understanding Children*, p. 23.

14.   Sexton, *Feminized Male*, p. 106, citing Arnold Gesell, *The First Five Years of Life: A Guide to the Study of the Preschool Child* (New York: Harper Bros., 1940).

15.   I. Devore and P. Jap, "Mother-Infant Relations in Baboons and Langurs," in *Maternal Behavior in Mammals*, ed. Harriet L. Rheingold (New York: John Wiley & Sons, 1963); Harry Harlow and R. R. Zimmerman, "Affectional Responses in the Infant Monkey," *Science*, 130 (1959): 421–32; D. O. Hebb, "Behavioral Differences between Male and Female Chimpanzees," *Bulletin of the Canadian Psychological Association*, 6 (1946): 56–68.

16.   Sexton, *Feminized Male*, p. 104.

17.   D. A. Hamburg and D. T. Lunde, "Sex Hormones in the Development of Sex Differences in Human Behavior," in *The Development of Sex Differences* ed. Eleanor E. Maccoby (Stanford, Calif.: Stanford University Press, 1966), pp. 1–24.

18.   Eleanor E. Maccoby, "Sex Differences in Intellectual Functioning." In Maccoby, ed., *Development of Sex Differences*.

19.   Ibid., p. 48. Maccoby cites unpublished research by Jerome Kagan, "Sex Differences in Intellectual Functioning" (1967).

20.   Maccoby, "Sex Differences in Intellectual Functioning," p. 48.

21.   L. W. Sontag, "Physiological Factors and Personality in Children," *Child Development*, 18 (1947): 185–89; J. L. Berry and B. Martin, "GSR Reactivity as a Function of Anxiety, Instructions and Sex," *Journal of Abnormal and Social Psychology*, 54 (1957): 9–12.

22.   Hamburg and Lunde, "Sex Hormones in Sex Differences."

23.   B. G. Rosenberg and Brian Sutton-Smith, *Sex and Identity* (New York: Holt, Rinehart & Winston, 1972), p. 31.

24.   Salvatore R. Maddi, *Personality Theories: A Comparative Analysis* (Homewood, Ill.: Dorsey Press, 1972), p. 369.

25.   Sexton, *Feminized Male*, p. 27, pp. 105–6.

26.   Erik H. Erikson, *Identity: Youth and Crisis* (New York: W. W. Norton & Company, 1968).

27.   J. Money, Joan G. Hampson, and J. L. Hampson, "Imprinting and the Establishment of Gender Role," *Archives of Neurology and Psychology*, 77 (1957): 333–36.

28.   Walter Mischel, "A Social-Learning View of Sex Differences in Behavior," *Development of Sex Differences*, ed. Maccoby, pp. 56–81.

29.   G. P. Murdock, "Comparative Data on the Division of Labor by Sex," *Social Forces*, 15 (1937): 551–53. Also see Rosenberg and Sutton-Smith, *Sex and Identity*, p. 75.

30.   Ernest Hilgard and Richard C. Atkinson, *Introduction to Psychology*, 4th ed. (New York: Harcourt, Brace & World, 1967), p. 106.

31.   Ibid., p. 106. Hilgard cites Margaret Mead, *Sex and Temperament in Three Primitive Societies* (New York: William Morrow, 1935).

32.   Ibid.

33.   Ibid. This practice, which anthropologists call "couvade," is common in a large number of societies spread throughout the world. Malinowski reports it among certain Trobiand Island tribes—Bronislaw Malinowski, *Argonauts of the Western Pacific* (New York: E. P. Dutton & Co., 1961; originally published, 1922). It has also been observed in certain African cultures and in parts of South America (personal discussions with Dr. Stephen Nourse, anthropologist, Marietta College, Ohio, October 1972.

34.  Rosenberg and Sutton-Smith, *Sex and Identity,* p. 88.

35.  B. G. Rosenberg and Brian Sutton-Smith, *Sex and Identity,* p. 72, citing M. E. Spiro, *Kibbutz: Venure in Utopia* (Cambridge: Harvard University Press, 1956).

36.  See, for example, H. W. Janson, *History of Art* (Englewood Cliffs, N.J.: Prentice-Hall, 1971). Compare colorplates 41 and 42 to black and white photo 558, colorplate 62, plate 737, and 756.

37.  Clellan S. Ford and Frank A. Beach, *Patterns of Sexual Behavior* (New York: Harper & Row Publishers, 1951), p. 86. The cultures noted are the Chukchee, Hidatsa, Pukapukans, and Thonga.

38.  Ibid., p. 87(the Wageo culture).

39.  R. M. Yerkes and J. H. Elder, "Oestrus, Receptivity, and Mating in the Chimpanzee," *Comparative Psychological Monograph,* 13 (1936): 1–39.

40.  Ford and Beach, *Patterns of Sexual Behavior,* p. 103.

41.  Ibid., p. 102.

42.  Ibid., p. 102.

43.  Ibid., pp. 93 and 95.

44.  Ibid., p. 102.

45.  Ibid. p. 105.

46.  Ibid., pp. 265–66

47.  Albert Bandura, and R. H. Walters, *Social Learning and Personality Development* (New York: Holt, Rhinehart & Winston, 1963); Albert Bandura, "Influence of Model's Reinforcement Contingencies on the Acquisition of Imitative Responses," *Journal of Personality and Social Psychology,* 1 (1965): 589–95.

48.  Bandura, "Acquisition of Imitative Responses."

49.  Mischel, "Social-Learning View of Sex Differences."

50.  Albert Bandura, "Relationships of Family Patterns to Child Behavior Disorders" (progress report, U.S. Public Health Service Research Grant M-1734, Stanford Universtiy, 1960).

51.  This does not imply a particular learning theory, nor is it meant to deny the comparative stability of gender identity noted in Chapter 1.

52.  Sexton, *Feminized Male.*

53.  Alice Rossi, "Transition to Parenthood," *Journal of Marriage and Family,* 30 (1968): 26–39.

54.  Rosenberg and Sutton-Smith, *Sex and Identity,* pp. 83 and 89.

# 4

# *Sex-role learning in American society*

## *The learning process*

IT IS COMMONLY BELIEVED that the boy learns to become a man by identifying with his father, and the girl does so through identifying with her mother. The term "identification" was given its special psychological meaning by Sigmund Freud, who considered this the mechanism by which the child successfully concludes the oedipal period. But Freud's image of the child "swallowing whole" the parent is rather inadequate as scientific description.

In order to understand how a particular masculine or feminine behavior develops in an individual, it is useful to distinguish two aspects

51

of the learning process: the initial occurrence of the behavior, and the perpetuation of the behavior once it has occurred. Once a particular behavior has occurred, if it gets reinforced (rewarded), it will continue to occur. The most simplistic learning theory would explain the learning of sexual roles through this single concept—reinforcement. Masculine and feminine behavior occur in both boys and girls. In a boy, for example, when a masculine behavior occurs it is likely to be rewarded; thus a boy will emit more and more masculine behaviors. When a boy does something that those around him consider feminine, it is less likely to be positively reinforced; such behaviors will drop out or be suppressed.

Operant learning theory is very helpful for a scientific understanding of learning in general, and it applies to sex-role learning in particular.[1] It is unlikely, however, that the complexity of sex-role behavior can be wholly explained in terms of the reinforcement of specific behaviors. The initial occurrence of a behavior is frequently the result of the child's imitation of one of his parents.[2] If this new behavior is reinforced, it will reoccur. If the behavior imitated is considered sex specific, it probably will be reinforced only if the child is imitating the parent of the same sex. Gradually the child will learn a "set" for imitating only the same-sexed parent on sex-typed behaviors. It seems that an adequate theory of sex-role learning demands, in addition to the concept of reinforcement, the process of imitation learning and the discrimination of appropriate models. How, for example, does the boy discriminate which behaviors are sex-typed and which are not and thus are safe to learn by imitating mother? The child appears to develop a concept of masculinity and femininity which goes beyond his immediate family, a discrimination based upon experience with persons in addition to his parents. A full account of the learning process may need to include the process of self-labeling and the development of social stereotypes, not just parental identifications.

Evidence on self-labeling suggests the following progression of learning: By about age three the child learns to call himself a boy or a girl and to be consistent in this gender label. Probably the child recognizes the constancy of his own gender first and then learns that sex identification is constant for others as well. The understanding of the constancy or "conservation" of many physical things is learned during these years of childhood from age three upward; gender constancy appears to be simply another part of the same type of learning. By about age five or six the child has understood the rule of gender constancy: he recognizes that boys cannot change into girls, and vice versa. Boys will grow up to be men, and girls to be women.[3]

Research data are scant, so this progression from increasing consistency in labeling self as to gender to a generalized concept of gender constancy must be taken as tentative.[4] Regardless of the exact sequence, the importance of cognitive factors in gender identity is suggested by two kinds of data. Developmental data, particularly the studies of hermaphrodites, indicate the difficulty of changing gender after age four.[5] The stability of sex identity is also indicated, at least for girls, by experimental data showing resistance to change in gender identity even when reinforcements are given for making sex-typed responses.[6] More adequate research is needed to directly test the role of cognitive variables in sex-role development.[7]

## Who teaches the sex roles? Three theories

At this point another important distinction must be made—one that is all too frequently missing in psychological research on identification. It is one thing to become like the parent of the same sex, as, for example, when the girl imitates the mother. It is another thing for the girl to become feminine and to learn the behaviors this society sees as appropriate for women. It is perfectly possible for the girl to have a close relationship with her mother and effectively learn to imitate her and yet not have a "normal" sex-role identification—if her mother is an atypical model (that is, if the mother does not fit the culturally accepted standard). D. B. Lynn has suggested that we use separate terms for these two constructs: parental identification, and sex-role identification.[8] According to Lynn, parental identification involves "the internalization of personality characteristics of one's own parent," or behaving in ways similar to either parent. Sex-role identification, on the other hand, is defined as "the internalization of the role typical of a given sex in a particular culture"; that is, behaving in ways characteristic of that role.

This distinction should be kept in mind in considering the question of who teaches the sex roles. There are essentially three views on this issue. The first and most common is an outgrowth of Freud's theory which maintains that sex roles are learned through identification with the same-sex parent. This is the simplest position if one holds that imitative learning is important.

The second view considers father the primary trainer of sex roles. This position grows out of the sociological theories of Talcott Parsons.[9] The important influence of mother on other aspects of the child's personality is not minimized, but her influence is not considered the most important factor in sex-role learning. Both boys and girls make an initial identification with mother, but this identification is not sex-typed.[10] In Parsons's theory, the essence of masculinity and femininity is a difference in instrumental and expressive orientations, as noted in Chapter 2. The implications of this theory for sex-role learning have been extrapolated as follows: The early relationship of both boys and girls is with mother, from whom both learn expressive behavior. Later father reinforces the expressive behavior in his daughter but teaches a new orientation, the instrumental role, to the son. Thus the sex-role differentiation is learned by both girls and boys through an interaction with the father, who differentially reinforces masculine and feminine behavior.[11]

However, it is possible that sex roles may be learned through different processes by girls and by boys. This is the third view, represented by Lynn. Lynn argues that since the American child spends most of his waking hours with mother, mother bears the burden of responsibility for teaching sexual roles to boys as well as girls. Since the girl has mother available as an appropriate model, she develops her style of femininity mainly through imitation. Direct imitation of father is not as possible for the boy, since father is not so available as a model. A masculine role is scantily spelled out for the boy by his mother and his teachers (who are mainly female), and the boy is left to trial and error, shaped up by the culture's system of rewards and punishments. The process of learning is imitative for the girl, but for the boy it has more to do with reinforcements administered by mother. In short, both boys and girls are taught sex roles by mother, but through different processes.

Again it must be said that some combination of these three views may best account for sex-role learning. Before turning to data regarding the role of each parent in typical sex-role training, one point of agreement among the three positions is worth noting. All three assume the importance of mother as the main identification figure in the first years of life, for children of both sexes. Despite this congruence the effect of mother identification in the American home has been underestimated in most studies of adolescence. It is important that we recognize the significance of this early identification with mother if we are to understand today's adolescents.

## The mother in me

I would like to ask a personal question: Are you more like your mother or your father? When asked this question, college boys will generally insist that they are most like their fathers. Girls, too, tend to answer that they are like the same-sexed parent (their mothers), although not infrequently they will reject their similarity to mother during their adolescent years and reaffirm it later in life. Though many persons think of themselves as more similar to their fathers and experience them as the primary identification figure, the evidence is that both males and females in actuality identify more closely with mother.

Studies show that perceived similarities to parents are not very accurate measures of the similarities that actually exist. Rather than relying on how the adolescent perceives his parents, it is better to actually measure such things as attitudes and values in both the parents and the children, and compare the two. This procedure gives an empirical measurement of identification; that is, it indicates whether the child is most like mother or father. It is also important (following the distinction between parental identification and sex-role identifications presented above) to use scales that measure personality variables which are not clearly sex-typed. Research based on these procedures has consistently shown that boys as well as girls are more like their mothers than their fathers.[12]

One example of a well-designed study assessing parental identification was conducted by Susan W. Gray and Rupert Klaus.[13] The subjects were male and female students in a southern college, and their mothers and fathers. The personality test used was the *Study of Values* (AVL), an instrument which does not include items that are obviously sex-typed. Nonetheless, the pattern of scores for males contrasts to the one for females. Each student was asked to take the test three times: once to obtain the student's own value scores, once to respond as the student believed his or her mother would answer each question, and once as his or her father would respond. The parents of these students simply took the test to obtain their actual responses.

Collecting the data in this way allowed the experimenters to determine how much a daughter, for example, perceived herself as like each of her parents. These perceived similarities could then be compared to actual similarities. Thus the experiment helps answer the question of which parent the son or daughter *thinks* he or she is more identified with, and which the youth is actually more like (on these personality traits).

The results for daughters are exactly what would be expected from the viewpoint of identification with the parent of the same sex (mother, in this case). Daughters saw themselves as more like their mothers than their fathers, and the comparison of daughters' scores to parents' showed that perception to be correct. Daughters actually were more like their mothers than like their fathers.

The results for sons were not what would be predicted from the theory of identification with the same-sexed parents. Though sons perceived themselves as more like their fathers than like their mothers, a comparison of actual scores showed them to be wrong. This does not mean that the sons were as influenced by the mother as the daughters were; they were not. Nor does it mean the daughters were as similar to their fathers as the sons were. Sons were more like fathers than daughters were—but even so, they were no more like their fathers than like their mothers, even though they themselves thought they would be.

Though the subjects used in the Gray and Klaus experiment cannot be considered representative of American youth, the results of this experiment appear to be consistent with those of every experiment I am aware of in which care has been taken to separate parental identification from sex-role identification and to gather data on actual similarities as well as perceived similarities.[14] They point to the fact that children in our society, regardless of sex, are raised primarily by mother. This does not mean father is not, or could not be, important in child rearing (a point which will be discussed later). In the present chapter the purpose is to describe what actually happens, as a general rule, in the development of sex roles in our culture. The first step in understanding this is to recognize the pervasive role of females in the development of children of both sexes.

Nearly all schools of psychological development have recognized that the earliest identification of the child is with the mother. But most psychology has been written by men, and, following Freud, psychologists have tended to construct a picture of the man wearing the pants in the family and predominating as the authority in the child's life at least from the age of three on. The center of Freud's developmental theory was the oedipal period, age three to six, when father was clearly the dominant figure. Perhaps this picture was accurate at the time Freud was living; it does not seem accurate today. The picture for our age seems best expressed in the words of G. Gorer: "Most boys reach and pass through adolescence under almost undiluted female authority."[15]

The recognition that parts of American society are matriarchal began more than two decades ago. White psychologists somewhat condescendingly referred to black culture as being matriarchal and blamed many of the black man's difficulties upon his odyssey from his mother-dominated home. Later it was recognized that a female-based household is normative throughout lower-class urban society and is not restricted to urban black families.[16] The mother-dominated home appeared throughout the literature on male adolescent deviance—juvenile delinquency, boys who showed evidence of sex-role conflict, and so on.[17] In each case, the etiology included mother domination and inadequate parental care.

Middle-class professionals have been able to see the effects of the female-dominated home in minority subcultures, but only recently have they begun to recognize that their own culture is matriarchal. B. O. Rubenstein and M. Levitt were among the early social scientists to recognize the American home as matricentric. It is a "cultural expectation that the American male will delegate all parental responsibility to the mother" constricting his role to material provision, they stated.[18] There is some evidence (too limited to be conclusive) that the nurturant role is more strictly defined as maternal in middle-class white families than in middle-class black families.[19] (This finding, if replicated, would indicate that social scientists have been able to see the problems in black society while ignoring even bigger problems in their own.)

Even among well-educated parents, where sex roles are least differentiated, this expectation is apparent. I recently attended a birthday party

By Charles M. Schultz. © 1972 United Feature Syndicate, Inc.

for another faculty member's daughter. Once the ice cream and cake were consumed, the men (mostly college professors) gravitated to their own corner, leaving the preschool children to the mothers to entertain. Fathers with above-average education and socioeconomic status appear to have ample time to do a lot of fathering; studies show, however, that as a rule they do not make use of this opportunity. They do not take a major role in the rearing of their children.[20]

Further evidence related to the father's role in child rearing comes from children themselves. In a study of children aged 10 to 12 which attempted to measure the comparative attachment of the children to each parent, 32 percent showed a preference for mother over father, while only 14 percent preferred father; 35 percent thought mother was more understanding, while only 9 percent thought so of father.[21]

Another source of data is observations of children's play. While girls, even in early childhood, identify with the mother role and imitate domes-

tic roles in their play, boys are frequently unable to visualize any meaningful masculine role; they very rarely identify masculinity with the
father's role of child-rearing in their play. This does not mean sex-typing
never occurs in boys; in fact, boys appear to make "sex-appropriate
choices" earlier and more consistently than girls do.[22] This learning seems
to occur in some way other than through direct observation and imitation.

During much of the period he is growing up, the young boy in our
society is expected to stay with girls and women, while the men are
off working somewhere else. H. Elkin has claimed that the development
of the male in American society is "less distinct from that of young
girls than in any other country."[23]

In a fairly complete review of relevant research, John Nash concludes
that "the weight of informed opinion would seem to regard our culture
as matricentric, rather than giving equal importance to the two parents
in their contribution to the psychological well-being of children; it certainly cannot be called patricentric as regards child-rearing. . . ."[24] Nash
suggests that the father's role may be more important than these authorities recognize, but most of the data he presents argues that it is the
father's failure to be involved that is important. That children would
benefit by an expanded paternal role seems clear, but there is little
indication that any substantial percentage of American fathers presently
take a major role in the rearing of their children.

It is historically understandable that child rearing in the American
home is largely left to mother. The modern mother, freed by timesaving
housework devices and raising a smaller family, has more time to devote
to each child. The same technology that makes mom more available
to the children takes dad out of the home. When father was a farmer
or craftsman, his industry had its locus around the house, where the
son could model it. But with the mushrooming of factories during the
Industrial Revolution, man left the home to work in the factory. The
Industrial Revolution eventually resulted in shorter working hours, but
for the most part these leisure hours were consumed commuting from
home to work and in recreational pursuits to make up for the lack
of satisfaction in the job. So far there is little empirical evidence that
fathers have reassumed any major role in child rearing.

These historical events are too well known to need elaboration, but
their psychological significance must be stressed. Mother is not just the
first identification figure for the child; she remains the primary identification figure throughout childhood and into adolescence. The traditional
view of male adolescence as a rebellion against the father fails to recognize the depth of the adolescent bonds with mother. Not just the deviants
and those from lower economic groups, but most Americans, come from
female-dominated homes. Mother identification is stronger than father
identification for most of us.

To rework the metaphor applied to Freud's theory of introjection in Chapter 1, it must now be said that regardless of our sex, the first apple we swallow whole is our image of mother. Despite sex-specific identifications, the primary personal identification, the one most fully internalized, is that of mother. As the adolescent begins the search for his own identity, it should not surprise him if he discovers that "at the very heart of me there is some of Mom."

## Differences in male and female learning

Now that the importance of the primary personal identification with mother has been established, it is possible to return to the question of who teaches the sex roles and to begin to answer this question separately for males and females.

For the girl, it is not particularly important to distinguish between parental identification and the learning of sex roles; the initial learning for both takes place by way of an immediately available model. Since mother dominates the home, the daughter can learn directly from the lessons mother teaches. Though the imitation of mother is probably confirmed through reinforcement from father and other representatives of society, the fact that mother is the central figure in child rearing makes it highly probable that the daughter learns the role primarily from her.

The learning of masculinity is not so simple and direct. The male child must turn away from his primary identification with mother, at least in areas of sex-specific behavior. The boy must learn the masculine role through some other means than direct imitation of mother. The three major theories of sex-role learning discussed above have different views of the way the boy learns of the male role.

Freud assumed that the boy learns the male role primarily through direct personal involvement and identification with his father. Though this may have been the usual case in Freud's culture, it is doubtful that the father's minimal involvement in early child care allows this to take place today.

Parsons and his followers believe that the mother teaches both male and female children much of their behavior, but the father provides the model for sex-specific behavior for both sons and daughters. In this theory, father is the primary reinforcer of the behavior that differentiates male and female roles in children. Some interpreters of Parsons believe father is not only the dispenser of differential reinforcement for both male and female roles but acts as the model for *both* roles. They argue that because the father learned the expressive role (through his primary identification with mother) and then the instrumental role, he is capable of acting as a model for both orientations. The father accents the expressive role in his interactions with his daughter and the instrumental role in his relationships with his son.

If this theory is correct, both roles (male and female) would be expected to reflect selected aspects of the father's personality. Sex behaviors are learned as specific roles rather than as total personal identifications.

Lynn's position stresses the role of negative learning, rather than direct personal modeling, in the boys' acquisition of the masculine role. He argues that the male learns the masculine role because he is punished for feminine behavior; he is forced to solve the problem of piecing together masculine behavior by trial and error, since father is not present enough to present a clear model.

## Additional related research

Abundant evidence that mother dominates the child rearing of both sons and daughters has been presented and provides the context for interpreting some additional research data. Direct tests of the different theories are nearly impossible; the data available are insufficient to permit discarding one theory and accepting another in any final way. Not only is the evidence scanty, but much of the research fails to include in its design the important distinctions between perceived and tested similarities of parent and child and between sex-role learning and parental identifications.

The distinction between parental identification and sex-role learning is especially relevant to an understanding of male development. Mother's presence expresses a person; the teacher is personal and the content of the learning is personalized. But father plays a role; he enters the home as the representative of the male world.[25]

The relative absence of father from the home is important, as will be shown. But I am not arguing for his total absence or lack of importance. The point is that since father spends much of the child's day away from home, in a foreign, outside world, when he returns home he is received as a representative of a different world. His coming is important and effective; but his presence is not pervasive enough to be fully personal. Instead, he represents and teaches a role, the role of the male.

In this section two areas of research will be reviewed:

1. Evidence that boys have a more difficult time than girls in learning sex roles.
2. The effects of father-absence on sex-role development.

### Sex-role development—more difficult for males

Data have been presented showing that personal identification with the same-sex parent is weaker for boys than for girls. The distinction has been made between parent identification and sex-role identification. There is considerable evidence, albeit indirect, that males also have greater difficulty achieving a firm, nondefensive sexual identity.[26]

Males more often than females fail to achieve same-sex identification and consequently make the opposite-sex identification (as evidenced in certain types of homosexuality).[27] More importantly, the majority of men, even though they have overtly achieved the culturally acceptable identification, show more anxiety in regard to sex roles than women do in our culture.[28] This anxiety may reflect the fact that our society imposes greater censorship upon males than upon females if they exhibit the opposite-sex behavior. The male role is esteemed by our culture as the preferred role, and deviation from it is thus more a threat to our cultural values.[29] Lynn notes that:

> Males are more likely than females to be ridiculed or punished for adopting aspects of the opposite-sex role. For a girl to be a tomboy does not involve the censure that results when a boy is a sissy. Girls may wear masculine clothing (shirts and trousers), but boys may not wear feminine clothing (skirts and dresses). Girls may play with toys typically associated with boys (cars, trucks, erector sets, and guns), but boys are discouraged from playing with feminine toys (dolls and tea sets).[30]

Direct evidence that males have greater difficulty achieving sex-role identity than females do comes from a study of five- and six-year-old children who were tested to determine the effects of verbal reinforcement on choices of masculine or feminine toys. The amount and direction of change from pretest to posttest suggested that the sexual identity of girls is more stable than that of boys in this age range. Boys were unable to maintain their initial sex-role preference scores unless they received a reward for correct responses followed by punishment for incorrect ones, or unless a female experimenter rewarded them.[31] The necessity of punishment in boys' learning in this experiment is suggestive of the way in which the boys originally learn their sex roles and indicates the tenuousness of the masculine identity.

At least four reasons can be given for the greater difficulty that males experience:

1. Males have to switch identifications, while females retain the primary identification with mother.
2. The male figure (father) is less available as a model.

3. The learning of male identity occurs concurrently with the unlearn-
   ing of the prior feminine identification; consequently more negative
   reinforcement is used, resulting in conflict.
4. The male role in our society is more complex.

### The effects of father-absence on sex-role development

The role of father in child rearing has received far less attention
in psychological theory and research than has the mother role. Nonetheless, considerable evidence exists that the loss of father from the nuclear
family has significant effects upon children, particularly if it occurs during the first six years of their lives.

Most of the studies have investigated the effect of father-absence
on the development of sons. An early study found that college men
whose fathers were absent from the home scored significantly lower
on measures of sexual adjustment and maturity than those from intact
homes. Surprisingly, the absence of mother produced no effect, perhaps
because the lost mother is almost always replaced by another mothering
figure.[32]

Martin L. Hoffman studied the effect of father-absence on conscience
development of both sons and daughters.[33] Levels of moral development
for girls whose fathers were absent were not significantly different from
those for girls raised in intact homes. Father-absent boys, however, scored
considerably lower on six of the eight measures of moral maturity than
did boys from a matched control group. It might be assumed that the
boy is handicapped in his personal development because father is not
available as a model. It is also possible that, with the father absent,
mother treats the son differently. Hoffman found that at least part of the
effect of father-absence on boys is due to the mothers' reaction. When
a girl loses her father, the mother tends to overcompensate for the father's
absence by giving her daughter increased amounts of affection. But boys
in father-absent homes report even less maternal care and affection than
boys in intact homes. Perhaps the mothers become fearful of feminizing
the boys and withdraw their attention.

Reports of some studies do not differentiate the effects in terms of
the sex of the children but give the impression that both sons and daughters are adversely affected. Portia Holman found among 5- to 15-year-old
children referred to guidance clinics that permanent early separation
from father had as adverse effects as mother separation.[34] Even temporary separation seems to be harmful. One study involved children who
were separated from their fathers during the early years of their lives
because their fathers were in active military service. Even after their
fathers returned, the war-separated children, when observed in social
and projective play situations, appeared less independent and showed

more serious behavior problems, more fears, and more overt tensions than controls.[35]

*Reactions of daughters to father-absence.* Where studies have reported differences in the effects of father-absence for sons and daughters, sons seem to have been affected on such variables as moral development and dependency, while daughters have not. This should not lead to the conclusion that the loss of father is not so significant for the daughter. Though there is less research on girls, most of the research reported shows that they are also adversely affected by the absent father, particularly in the area of sexual roles. A study of girls who had lost a parent (reported in Chapter 1) showed that the greatest sexual diffusion resulted if the loss occurred during the oedipal or adolescent periods.[36] (The data were not analyzed to reveal differences between loss of mother or loss of father.) A variety of evidence suggests that as the girl becomes closer to her father during middle childhood her feminine values and identification are consolidated, not weakened.[37] It may be that the father's expectations concerning femininity facilitate the girl's identification with her own role, in line with Parsons' theory. Some data have been so interpreted.[38] The tendency for identification with the opposite-sex parent to strengthen the child's own sexual identity appears stronger for girls than for boys.[39]

It might be helpful if more research distinguished two aspects of girls' sexual identity: possessing the personality traits which are considered feminine, and relating to the opposite sex in the ways considered appropriate. When the boy is deprived of a father, he is deprived of a model for masculine personality traits and understandably may develop effeminate traits. The girl still has the model for the development of feminine traits but does not have the experience of relating to a man. It is not surprising that studies which have concentrated on personality traits of young girls have failed to show the effects of father loss. But when measurements of female sexual identity are made during adolescence, particularly when the area of relationships between the sexes is investigated, the data demonstrate that girls raised without fathers do have sex-role problems.

A very interesting study in this regard, used firstborn daughters of lower- and middle-class parents, with the sample limited to girls who had no brothers.[40] In the control group, the father was the only male in the family. The two other groups consisted of families in which the father had died and families in which the parents had divorced and the children had minimal contact with the father; in both these groups the mother had remained unmarried; thus there were no males in these households. The personality inventory and the projective instruments used showed that all groups of girls had "adopted normal sex roles and interests."

However, when the girls were interviewed by men, the three groups differed markedly in their nonverbal communication. Seating arrangements and postures were objectively recorded, with half of each group interviewed by women and half by men. The scene was the same for all the girls:

> A laboratory assistant ushered the young girl into the interview room. The person behind the desk looked up from his work and asked the girl to pick a chair and be seated. There were three empty chairs in the room: one chair was at the end of the desk adjacent to the interviewer; the second was directly across the desk facing the interviewer; the third was across and about three feet down from the interviewer. . . . There was little difference between girls from the various family groups in their gestures, posture or seat selection when the interviewer was female. Three quarters of the girls chose the middle seat. There were significant differences in the behavior of the girls when the interviewer was male; eight of the twelve girls whose parents lived together chose the middle seat. . . ; eight of the twelve girls whose parents were divorced chose the chair closest to the interviewer. . . ; ten of the twelve girls whose fathers had died chose the chair farthest from the interviewer. . . .[41]

Both groups of girls who were raised without male models in the home showed inappropriate behavior in relating to men. The daughters of divorcees might be described as "precocious and provocative with men," while daughters of widows seemed to shy away from and avoid men.

These results suggest two types of pathology in girls which may arise from father-absence: a phobic avoidance of males, and a counterphobic pseudocloseness to males. Much more research on female development is needed before conclusions can be reached.

*Reactions of sons to father-absence.* Developmental factors contributing to pathology in male youth have been the subject of much research. Two types of problem behavior seem especially related to father-absence; aggressive acting out, and overdependent effeminate behavior. These types parallel the two reactions reviewed in girls; one reaction is a moving away or withdrawal, and the other is an aggressive moving toward. For girls the effects of father-absence are limited to relations with males; for boys, the effects include more general personality traits.

Overdependency and effeminate behavior in boys seems to be related to a lack of interaction with father. In the study of temporary father separation due to military service cited above, the fathers complained of their sons' unmasculine behavior. Similarly, sons of Norwegian seamen who were absent from the home for extended periods were found, in three separate studies, to be dependent and immature and to have problems of identification.[42]

Using projective play techniques, Pauline S. Sears found that boys whose fathers were absent differed less from girls than from the male control group in frequency of aggression shown. In play with dolls these boys (up to age five) also emphasized less the differences between male and female dolls. (Girls from father-absent homes showed no differences from the controls.)[43]

A study of lower-middle-class children ages six to ten found that father-absence results in an idealistic and feminine fantasy picture of father.[44] Another study asked social workers for their descriptions of boys; boys from fatherless families were judged to be more anxious about sex and more effeminate than boys with fathers.[45]

It has been suggested that the period of development from three to six years is very important. However, it is misleading to term this span a "critical period" if this is taken to mean that damages cannot later be ameliorated. Nash conducted a study which compared boys in female-run orphanages to boys raised in normal homes. On a battery of tests, the institutionalized boys scored more in the direction of the feminine role than did the control subjects. When these boys were moved to cottages with male figures present, the scores became significantly more masculine (though they still remained below the norms).[46]

It does not seem surprising that the absence of a male figure in the home should result in poor masculine identifications, except in the light of Lynn's view that the male role is learned chiefly by reinforcements administered by women, who dominate child rearing. Though Lynn's viewpoint is important, it is not the whole story. The data on father-absence support the view that the male sex role is learned, at least in part, from father.

To complete the picture of the effects of father-absence on sons, another behavior pattern which superficially seems the opposite of the one just described must be noted. Father-absence also seems to play an important role in aggressive, acting-out disturbances, a contention supported by studies of juvenile delinquent behavior. In one study, 94 of 305 delinquent boys were found to come from homes in which the father was dead; and 48 from homes in which the mother was dead.[47] Another researcher statistically analyzed data from clinical referrals involving the absence or inadequacies of both fathers and mothers and concluded that the father is at least as important in the etiology of maladjustment, particularly in regard to conduct disorders (in contrast to neurotic disorders).[48]

A study of male college freshmen compared the relative frequency of antisocial activities. Students in the experimental group, whose fathers were in the armed forces during the students' early childhoods, ranked significantly higher in antisocial behavior than did students in the control group, whose fathers were at home.[49] In Hoffman's study of moral devel-

opment in boys and girls cited above, it was found that boys who had
had no male living in the home scored significantly lower on indices
of moral maturity than a matched control group. This moral immaturity
manifested itself behaviorally; teachers rated these boys as more
aggressive.[50]

Thus far the studies reported have dealt solely with the physical
absence of father from home. It is important to note that the correlations
between father-absence and pathology do not prove direct causation.
The loss of the father may affect the child indirectly through the emotional loss experienced by the mother and the economic instability the
family suffers with the loss of the father's income.[51] The effect of these
confounding variables is lessened in a culture where father-absence is
both common and acceptable. It is interesting, therefore, that a study
of boys in Barbados, where these conditions exist, found evidence of
greater feminine identification among father-absent boys than in the
control group.[52] These results do not, of course, eliminate the possibility
that some of the effects of father loss are indirect.

In spite of these problems of interpretation, it is striking that father-
absence results in pathology so clearly related to the masculine role.
Such a relationship would seem unlikely if the effect were totally an
indirect one. This impression is reinforced by the results of research
on subjects for whom father is not physically absent from the home
but seems to be psychologically absent.

In homes in which the father is passive or ineffectual, or for other
reasons poor identification is made, the same two behavioral pathologies
seem to emerge. First, the studies strongly suggest that poor identification with father may result in the son adopting feminine behavior.[53]
Second, the psychological absence of father can also produce the opposite result, the defensively supermasculine role. A number of observers
of lower class cultures have noted "the compulsive rejection by boys
of what they consider feminine, as they move out of the female-based
household."[54]

The evidence is strongest in studies of juvenile delinquency. Studies
of juvenile gangs in 1927[55] and in 1951[56] showed poor paternal relationships among members of delinquent groups as compared to members
of socialized, constructive gangs. Perhaps the best experimental study
is R. G. Andry's comparison of 80 delinquent boys and their parents
with matched control groups. He found that the delinquents' relationships with mother were "decidedly more satisfactory that the relationships between them and their fathers." Paternal rejection and a failure
to identify with father were characteristic among delinquents.[57]

It appears that when the father is physically or psychologically removed from child rearing, two kinds of disturbances occur more frequently: behavior that is perceived as feminine, and behavior that might

be termed supermasculine. An obvious interpretation (which pervades the literature) is that the aggressive behavior is pseudomasculine and occurs as a denial of a weak masculine identification and a defense against a threatening feminine identification.

*Implications of data on father-absence for a theory of male sex-role learning.* The evidence that extreme father deprivation is an etiological factor in pathology, particularly in the pathologies related to the masculine role, seems overwhelming. This data, plus the experimental data on the relinquishment of child rearing to mother presented earlier in this chapter, lead to a position on male identification that integrates the contrasting views of Lynn and Parsons.

Unfortunately, in many if not most American homes, father does not play a major role in child rearing. As noted above, the matriarchal structure of family life in lower-class society has been fully documented. Though the educated professional male tends to hold a less stereotyped view of masculinity and might be more open to child-rearing tasks, there is little evidence that he actually spends much time interacting with his children (especially as compared to mother).[58] The image of father may be changing—he is increasingly pictured as an active, sharing helper. But his actual behavior appears to fall short of this ideal, as noted above.

When father is minimally present, it seems likely that his personal effect will be diminished and that his role as representative of a social image will have the predominant influence. Father's instrumental role can affect the socialization of the child both directly, through his concrete interactions with the child, and indirectly, through the family's esteem for his work.[59] Since the American father is not particularly involved in the child-rearing tasks, direct interactions with the children are minimized and his effect lies primarily in his symbolic function, his role as representative of the outside world. Unfortunately, this leaves many males with an impersonal and unrealistic view of masculinity. It has been noted that children separated from their fathers tend to have an idealistic fantasy picture of them. "We may assume," to quote Nash, "that partially father deprived children also experience some difficulty in identifying with him."[60]

## Conclusions

The conclusions which follow attempt to summarize and integrate the data that have been presented. The reader is reminded that these conclusions are generalizations. I do not wish to obscure the fact that tremendous individual differences exist for both sexes. Nonetheless, some patterns do emerge in our society. As generalizations, the conclusions stated apply across broad populations; they do not apply to every individual.

## Conclusions for male sex-role learning

*Conclusion 1: There is a split between sex-role learning and personal identification.* In order to understand the learning of the masculine sex role, it is important to distinguish between parental identification and sex-role identification. Much of the positive learning of sex role that the boy experiences is less personal than for the girl; he learns a social image, the instrumental role, through sex-role identification more than through personal identification with father.

*Conclusion 2: The minimal presence of father encourages stereotypes.* Frequently, father is present in the American home more as a representative of a role than as a person with whom the child can interact deeply and identify. This minimal presence does contribute to the learning of the masculine role, but the role is learned in a stereotypic way without the humanizing aspects of personal identification. Consequently, sex typing tends to be more rigid among boys than girls.[61]

Experimental evidence suggests that, despite the minimal presence of father in the home, some male role learning does occur through imitation.[62] Lynn's negative learning theory is not the whole picture. However boys are frequently forced to rely on the imitation of other males they observe, in addition to father. Some experimental evidence suggests that boys imitate strange males (rather than females) even before they make a preference for father over mother.[63]

*Conclusion 3: Negative learning may have negative effects.* As a consequence of the minimal presence of father in the home, much sex-role learning is left to mother, teachers, and peers, reinforcing the stereotypic and depersonalized aspects of the learning and increasing the likelihood that punishment will be used to suppress feminine responses. This negative (punitive) aspect of the learning of sex roles for boys commonly results in the rejection of femininity.[64]

*Conclusion 4: Boys need fathers' involvement in child rearing.* The need for greater participation of the father in the child rearing process is a recurring theme throughout the rest of this book. It is important to state the argument now in the context of the views of male sex-role learning presented in this chapter. Lynn has argued that, in our society, masculinity is learned mainly by negative responses to the boy's feminine behavior as given by mother and the others (mostly women) who surround him during the early years. The conclusions I have drawn regarding male sex-role learning amount to a modified version of Lynn's view. Generally father is involved enough in child rearing to present a male image, but not a personal identification, for the child.

In addition to the negative evidence already given, there is considerable positive evidence that warm, interested, nurturant fathers make better models for solid masculine identification. Sears and her associates have found that father's discipline is more effective if father is warm toward children. Though children can be inhibited by punishment from father, they are not likely to obey his admonishments when he is not present unless a nurturant relationship has been established prior to the punishing experience.[65] The inference is that in order for the child not just to fear the punishment, but to internalize the father's values in the situation, the child must view father as a positive figure.

This inference is supported by the finding that children more readily imitate more-nurturant adult models. The strengths of the masculine role are more adequately learned by children if their fathers show real interest in them and can be nurturant as well as masculine.[66] Other studies have shown that boys who report stronger affectional ties to their fathers show more masculine traits than boys whose fathers have not taken much part in their rearing. These more masculine boys were "better adjusted, more contented, more relaxed, more exuberant, happier, calmer, and smoother in social functioning" than the less masculine group.[67]

The evidence for boys is clear; masculinity can best be learned through personal identification with a warm male figure. Unfortunately, father is not generally involved enough for this personal identification to occur.

### Conclusions for female sex-role learning

Far less experimental data exist regarding sex-role learning in girls. The evidence that mother is the central figure in child rearing makes it highly probable that daughters will identify with her and learn her style of femininity, whether or not that style represents the cultural stereotype.

*Conclusion 5: Mother serves as model.* Girls benefit from the presence of the same-sex parent in the home in that they have a personal model for sex-role learning. The presence of father in the home probably helps the girl to discriminate which behaviors are considered sex-typed. Though selective reinforcement from the father may be important to the maintenance of feminine role behavior in the daughter, it seems likely that the behaviors considered feminine are at first elicited through imitation of the mother.

*Conclusion 6: Girls need fathers' involvement in child rearing.* Father's presence is especially important in order for the daughter to learn how to relate appropriately with men. Girls can learn feminine personality traits in a personal way through imitation of mother, but they generally need a male figure in the home if they are to become comfortable with men.

Unlike boys, girls probably do not suffer from too much negative (punitive) learning in the process of sex identification. They acquire their roles through the positive learning processes of imitation and reward. However, two negative effects of the mother-dominated child-rearing pattern arise. First, because their identification is so completely tied to the home, they may be more likely than boys to have a narrow, provincial view of the world. Secondly, since father is minimally present, it is easy for girls to develop an idealized image of him and of the male role. Thus they may tend to envy the male role, even though their identification with the female role is secure. For these reasons, it appears that girls would benefit if father were more involved in the child-rearing process.

## Summary

The American home is very maternal. Even though the family has relinquished many responsibilities to larger society, the society that surrounds the growing child is largely female. Girls establish a reasonably secure feminine identity through modeling after their mothers, with whom they can personally identify. Unfortunately, that identity is frequently a constricted one. Boys also become close to their mothers, but they then have to solve the puzzle of male identity without adequate personal models. Father's minimal involvement in child rearing and the negative and impersonal way in which masculinity is taught have serious consequences, to be explored further in the next chapter.

## Notes

1. Walter Mischel, "A Social-Learning View of Sex Differences in Behavior," in *The Development of Sex Differences*, ed. Eleanor E. Maccoby (Stanford, Calif.: Stanford University Press, 1966), pp. 56–81.

2. Albert Bandura, "Influence of Models' Reinforcement Contingencies on the Acquisition of Imitative Responses," *Journal of Personality and Social Psychology*, 1 (1965): 589–95.

3. Lawrence Kohlberg, "A Cognitive-Developmental Analysis of Children's Sex-Role Concepts and Attitudes," in *The Development of Sex Differences*, ed. E. Maccoby, pp. 82–172. Kohlberg states that the "stabilization of gender identity concepts is only one aspect of the general stabilization of physical objects that takes place between the years three and seven." This gives the false impression that all constancy issues are mastered at about age seven. The child in our culture usually masters the conservation of discontinuous quantity and substance at six or seven, but conservation of weight

is not usually learned till nine or ten, and conservation of volume is seldom understood until age eleven or twelve.

4. One study has validated this sequence: Aimee Dorr Leifer, "The Relationship between Cognitive Awareness in Selected Areas and Differential Imitation of a Same-Sex Model" (Master's thesis, Stanford University, 1966).

5. These studies are reviewed in Chapter 1, in the section entitled "Childhood Roots of Adult Sex Roles."

6. Lenore A. DeLucia, "Some Determinants of Sex-Role Identification in Young Children," (Master's thesis, Brown University, 1961).

7. To date, the only research I have found which attempts to test the importance of self-labeling in sex-role development has been designed to test other aspects of Kohlberg's theory as well. A brief review of two important studies, and of my own position, may clarify the precise questions not yet answered by available research data. Leifer, in "Relationship between Cognitive Awareness and Differential Imitation," (cited above) failed to find a relationship between the development of gender identity and a tendency to imitate same-sex peer models. Alice R. Gold and M. Carol St. Ange, in "Development of Sex Role Stereotypes in Black and White Elementary School Girls," *Developmental Psychology*, 10 (1974): 461, found that third-grade girls show more stereotyped sex roles in regard to peers than in regard to adults.

Though these findings, if replicated, appear to refute portions of Kohlberg's theory, they do not disprove the importance of self-labeling in sex-role development. That issue can be tested only after the other data on the process of sex-role learning for each sex are analyzed and formulated. (My attempt to do this makes up the rest of this chapter.)

If one concludes, as I do, that males in our society do not learn the sex roles primarily through imitation, then the effect of self-labeling in boys must be operationalized in some manner other than imitative responses. For that reason, Leifer's data do not refute the assumption that cognitive factors are important in male sex-role development. They only refute the theory that the cognitive factors operate through the process of imitation.

If one concludes also that females achieve their own sex-role identity through imitation of mother as a personal model, the Leifer study fails because it tests only imitation of peers. A study using imitation of same-sexed adults as a test would be more relevant. The Gold and St. Ange data are certainly not inconsistent with my viewpoint. If girls have a more personalized perception of adult females, those generalizations that girls make about sex roles might be more evident in regard to peers than to adults.

The thesis of this book and the thrust of this chapter do not stand or fall on the issue of whether or not cognitive factors are crucial to the learning of sex roles. I simply wish to point out that the lack of support for Kohlberg's specific theory does not settle the issue. Cognitive factors help us to account for the observed stability of sex roles.

8. David B. Lynn, "The Process of Learning Parental and Sex-Role Identification," *Journal of Marriage and the Family*, 18 (1966): 466–70.

9. Talcott Parsons, *Social Structure and Personality* (London: Free Press, 1964).

10. Alfred B. Heilbrun, "An Empirical Test of the Modeling Theory of Sex-Role Learning," *Child Development*, 36 (1965): 789–99.

11. M. M. Johnson, "Sex Role Learning in the Nuclear Family," *Child Development*, 34 (1963): 320–32.

12. Lynn, "Parental and Sex-Role Identification"; James Bieri and Robin Lobeck,

"Acceptance of Authority and Parental Identification," *Journal of Personality*, 27 (1959): 76–79; Andrew H. Souerwine, "Relationships between Parents and Sons in Authoritarianism," *Dissertation Abstracts*, 15 (1955): 157.

13. Susan W. Gray and Rupert Klaus, "The Assessment of Parental Identification," *Genetic Psychology Monographs*, 54 (1956): 87–114.

14. Hans Sebald, "Parent-Peer Control and Masculine-Marital Role Perceptions of Adolescent Boys," *Social Science Quarterly*, 49 (1968): 229–36, found that "Boys resemble their fathers in personality and attitudes much less than girls resemble their mothers." Also Susan W. Gray, "Masculinity and Femininity in Relation to Anxiety and Social Acceptance," *Child Development*, 28 (1957): 203–14; and Lionel W. Lasowick, "On the Nature of Identification," *Journal of Abnormal and Social Psychology*, 51 (1955): 175–83.

15. Geoffrey Gorer, *The American People: A Study of National Character* (New York: W. W. Norton & Co., 1948).

16. Walter B. Miller, "Lower Class Culture as a Generating Milieu of Gang Delinquency," *Journal of Social Issues*, 143 (1958).

17. See J. H. Rohrer and M. S. Edmondson, *The Eighth Generation* (New York: Harper & Row, Publishers, 1960).

18. B. O. Rubenstein and M. Levitt, "Some Observations Regarding the Role of Fathers in Child Psychotherapy," *Bulletin Menniger Clinic*, 21 (1957): 16–27.

19. Gold and St. Ange, "Sex Role Stereotypes in Elementary School Girls."

20. L. P. Gardner, "A Survey of the Attitudes and Activities of Fathers," *Journal of Genetic Psychology*, 63 (1943): 15–53; Cantril Hadley, ed., *Public Opinion 1935–46* (Princeton, N.J.: Princeton University Press, 1951); J. M. Mogey, "A Century of Declining Paternal Authority," *Marriage and Family Living*, 1957, p. 238.

21. L. P. Gardner, "Analysis of Children's Attitudes to Fathers," *Journal of Genetic Psychology*, 70 (1947): 3–38.

22. Josef E. Garai and Amram Scheinfeld, "Sex Differences in Mental and Behavioral Traits," *Genetic Psychology Monographs*, 77 (1968): 169–299; R. E. Hartley, L. K. Frank, and R. M. Goldenson, *Understanding Children's Play* (New York: Columbia University Press, 1952).

23. H. Elkin, "Aggressive and Erotic Tendencies in Army Life," *American Jour- of Sociology*, 51 (1946): 408–13.

24. John Nash, "The Father in Contemporary Culture and Current Psychological Literature," *Child Development*, 36 (1965): 261–97.

25. Kohlberg, "Cognitive-Developmental Analysis."

26. This is in contrast to the Freudian position, as described, for example, in Otto Fenichel, *The Psychoanalytic Theory of Neurosis* (New York: W. W. Norton & Co., 1945), pp. 89–99.

27. D. B. Lynn, "Sex Differences in Identification Development," *Sociometry*, 24 (1961): 372–84.

28. Lynn, "Parental and Sex-role Identification," p. 470.

29. R. E. L. Faris, *Social Psychology* (New York: Ronald Press Co., 1952).

30. Lynn, "Parental and Sex role Identification."

31. DeLucia, "Sex-Role Identification in Young Children."

32. R. Winch, "Some Data Bearing on the Oedipal Hypothesis," *Journal of Abnormal and Social Psychology*, 45 (1950): 481–89.

33. Martin L. Hoffman, "Father Absence and Conscience Development," *Developmental Psychology*, 4 (1971): 400–406.

34. Portia Holman, "The Etiology of Maladjustment in Children," *Journal of Mental Science,* 99 (1959): 654–88.

35. L. M. Stolz et al., *Father Relations of War-Born Children* (Stanford, Calif.: Stanford University Press, 1954).

36. Henry T. Grayson, "Psychosexual Conflict in Adolescent Girls who Experience Early Parental Loss by Death" (Ph.D. diss., Boston University, 1967), *Dissertation Abstracts* No. 67-13, 327.

37. See Kohlberg, "Cognitive-Developmental Analysis."

38. G. H. Mead, *Mind, Self and Society* (Chicago: University of Chicago Press, 1932); Thomas Colley, "The Nature and Origins of Psychological Sexual Identity," *Psychological Review,* 66 (1959): 165–77; Johnson, "Sex Role Learning in the Nuclear Family."

39. Kohlberg, "Cognitive-Developmental Analysis."

40. E. Mavis Hetherington, "The Effects of Father Absence on Personality Development in Adolescent Daughters," *Developmental Psychology,* 7 (1972): 313–26.

41. E. Mavis Hetherington, "Girls without Fathers," *Psychology Today* Magazine, 6 (February 1973): 47. Copyright © Ziff-Davis Publishing Company.

42. E. Gronsetti, "The Impact of Father-Absence in Sailor Families upon the Personality Structure and Social Adjustment of Adult Sailor Sons," Part I, in *Studies of the Family,* ed. N. Anderson (Gottingen, Norway: Vanderhoeck and Ruprecht, 1957), vol. 2, pp. 97–114.

43. Pauline S. Sears, "Doll Play Aggression in Normal Young Children: Influence of Sex, Age, Sibling Status, Father's Absence," *Psychological Monographs* no. 6, 65 (1951).

44. G. R. Bach, "Father-Fantasies and Father-Typing in Father-Separated Children," *Child Development,* 17 (1946): 63–80.

45. W. N. Stephens, "Judgments by Social Workers of Boys and Mothers in Fatherless Families," *Journal of Genetic Psychology,* 99 (1961): 53–64.

46. Nash, "Father in Contemporary Culture."

47. W. L. Chinn, "A Brief Survey of Nearly 1000 Delinquents," *British Journal of Educational Psychology,* 8 (1938): 78–58.

48. W. Warren, "Conduct Disorders in Children," *British Journal of Delinquency,* 1 (1957): 164.

49. Aron W. Seigman, "Father Absence during Early Childhood and Antisocial Behavior," *Journal of Abnormal Psychology,* 71 (1966): 71–74.

50. Hoffman, "Father Absence and Conscience Development."

51. John Bowlby, *Maternal Care and Mental Health* (Geneva: World Health Organization, 1951, vol. 2).

52. Roger V. Burton, "Cross-Sex Identity in Barbados," *Developmental Psychology,* 6 (1972): 365–74.

53. P. Mussen, "Some Antecedents and Consequences of Masculine Sex-Typing in Adolescent Boys," *Psychological Monographs,* no. 2, 75 (1961). There is considerable evidence that a lack of warm affectionate relationships with father is a factor in the development of male homosexuality—Nash, "Father in Contemporary Culture," and D. G. Brown, "The Development of Sex-Role Inversion and Homosexuality," *American Journal of Orthopsychiatry,* 50 (1957): 613–19. Homosexuality must not be identified with effeminate personality characteristics nor with taking a female role in sexual relationships, however. Thus homosexuality is not necessarily an instance of feminine behavior.

54.  Lee Rainwater, "Crucible of Identity: The Negro Lower-Class Family," *Daedalus*, 95 (1966): 1.

55.  F. M. Thrasher, *The Gang* (Chicago: University of Chicago Press, 1927).

56.  A. R. Crane, "A Note on Preadolescent Gangs," *Australian Journal of Psychology*, 3 (1951): 43–46.

57.  R. G. Andry, "Faulty Paternal and Maternal Child Relationships, Affection and Delinquency," *British Journal of Delinquency*, 97 (1960): 329–40.

58.  Gardner, "Attitudes and Activities of Fathers"; Gardner, "Children's Attitudes to Fathers."

59.  Parsons, *Social Structure and Personality*, p. 49.

60.  Nash, "Father in Contemporary Culture."

61.  Lorraine Nadelman, "Sex Identity in American Children: Memory, Knowledge, and Preference Tests," *Developmental Psychology*, 10 (1974): 413–17.

62.  R. Epstein and S. Leverant, "Verbal Conditioning and Sex-Role Identification in Children," *Child Development*, 34 (1963): 99–106; H. W. Stevenson, "Social Reinforcement of Children's Behavior," in *Advances in Child Development*, ed. C. Spiker, (New York: Academic Press, 1965), vol. 2.

63.  Kohlberg, "Cognitive-Developmental Analysis."

64.  This rejection is the topic of Chapter 5.

65.  Sears, "Doll Play Aggression."

66.  Albert Bandura and A. C. Huston, "Identification as a Process of Incidental Learning," *Journal of Abnormal and Social Psychology*, 63 (1961): 311–18.

67.  P. H. Mussen and L. M. Distler, "Child-Rearing Antecedents of Masculine Identification in Kindergarten Boys," *Child Development*, 31 (1960): 89–100. Also see Mussen, "Masculine Sex-Typing in Adolescent Boys."

# 5

## A consequence of sex-role learning in America: The desecration of the feminine

Male development and the rejection of the feminine
  Roots
  The defensive character of masculinity
The conflict of women: Envy and fear of the masculine
Continuing the argument for greater paternal involvement
The vicious cycle
Family and culture
Summary

In early childhood, mother is the central nurturant figure for both boys and girls. The warm home is the center of the child's perspective; father is seen as the one who comes from the outside world. The children may be glad to see him, but they do not think much about the world from which he comes.

As children of both sexes gradually become more interested in the outside world, however, the characteristics represented by father begin to be held in more esteem. For children of age three to four father is not awarded more prestige than mother, but a study of gender stereotypes indicates that by age five or six, children award greater power, strength, and competence (and consequently more status) to the male.[1] Gradually there is a shift of focus in evaluation from the home to the world; increasingly the child's values are influenced by the society beyond the home. Thus, for late childhood it is more accurate to turn the image around; father is seen as the one who goes out into the world. The prestige accorded father for his work makes it clear that, though what he does is unknown and mysterious, it is nonetheless his work in the world that really counts.

Increasingly the child becomes aware of the social values of others outside his own family. Older children (age five to eight) move away from the assumption that something is best because it is like self ("egocentric self-projective modes of valuing"), and begin to make their evalu-

ations in terms of place in the social order.[2] With their growing awareness of the occupational order, of economic functions and powers, there
comes an increase in attribution of power and competence to the masculine role.[3]

This trend continues through later childhood, a period Erik Erikson
associates with the attainment of "industry." Though Erikson considers
this shift without regard for sex, it is obvious that this involves an increased evaluation of the masculine world, a world concerned "with
things rather than people."[4]

American culture is dominated by values that favor the male. Consequently males and females are differently affected by developmental
changes in their roles as they move out of the family and into the
wide world. In the preceding chapter it was noted that, in our mother-
dominated society the masculine sex role is the more difficult one to
achieve. But once the child moves into the world, the tables are turned
and males have the advantage. With increasing age, males become relatively more firmly identified with the masculine role.[5] By the first years
of high school, boys are considerably more positive about the male role
than girls are about the female role.[6]

During late childhood sexual stereotypes reach their peak and often
become associated with moral values. As Lawrence Kohlberg states,
children often "view same-sex behavior as morally required and express
punitive sentiments to children who deviate from sex-typed behavior."[7]
At this period children often hold more rigid stereotypes than their
parents.[8] Thus, at the same time boys and girls are attributing more
status to the male role, they are also insisting that girls must be girls
and boys must be boys. Though it takes different forms, for both boys and
girls this moralization of roles may mean the debasement of femininity.

## Male development and the rejection of the feminine

Though male identification is weaker in childhood years, during the
period of adolescence and young adulthood males increase in "ego suffi-
ciency and complexity" (as measured by Thematic Apperception Test
stories), while females show a significant decrease.[9] Males also improve
in intellectual and manipulative skills as they move into the masculine
world; females do not. But as males become more firmly identified with
the masculine role, they also become more rejecting of the feminine
one. Masculinity appears to be bought at the cost of a hostility toward
females which continues into adulthood.[10]

### Roots

Why is the rejection of the feminine so closely connected with the
boy's affirmation of masculinity? At least three factors are apparent.

The first two have to do with the negative way in which masculinity is learned. It has been stated that the boy learns masculine behavior in part by being punished for any display of feminine behavior. Playing with girls' toys or doing things considered "sissy" result in ridicule. Punishment often leads to dislike of the activity that has been punished, even when that activity is being engaged in by someone else. Thus the behaviors the boy is taught to reject in himself come to be rejected in others. Second, in the absence of father, much of the punishment is inflicted on the boy by women. Since the learning is a negative experience, he rejects the teachers who provided him with that experience. The boy is led to reject not only the behavior that is punished but the punishers—and in both cases this is a rejection of the feminine. According to D. B. Lynn, boys can be expected to "generalize and consequently develop hostility toward all females as representatives of this disliked role."[11]

The third reason why rejection of the feminine is allied to affirmation of masculinity in boys is that it is characteristic of avoidance learning that the feared behavior is not actually eliminated. The punished behavior is not extinguished, but suppressed.[12] Since the male identification is built upon a prior feminine identification, there is always a risk that the feminine behaviors will again come to the surface. This risk is sensed by both the boy, who feels insecure about his grasp of the male role, and by his parents, who punish inappropriate sex-role behavior more harshly in sons than in daughters, in an attempt to suppress it fully. The feminine aspects of the boy's personality have been learned through long and constant association with mother. Since the American mother spends so much time with her children, strong dependency is also well established. The negative training and punishment cannot undo the previous feminine identification and dependency; these feminine traits are merely driven underground.[13] In sum, the training of masculinity in our culture yields "practically the perfect combination for inducing anxiety—the demand that the child do something which is not clearly defined to him, based on reasons he cannot possibly appreciate, and enforced with threats, punishments, and anger by those who are close to him."[14]

## The defensive character of masculinity

Masculinity is maintained as a precarious balance, a defensive shell against a softer interior.[15] The boy's insecurity can easily result in his being defensively masculine. To paraphrase Talcott Parsons, exaggerated and distorted masculinity may be a reaction formation to a component of feminine identification resulting from incomplete identification with a stable father figure. This is shown in a need to impress and gain control over women."[16]

This defensive masculinity and rejection of feminine identifications by males has been termed the masculine protest. The antisocial character of defensive masculinity is built into the training process. Parsons notes: "When he revolts against identification with his mother in the name of masculinity, it is not surprising that a boy unconsciously identifies 'goodness' with femininity and that being a 'bad boy' becomes a positive goal."[17] As stated in the preceding chapter, a number of studies of boys where fathers were absent during some part of childhood and who thus "grew up close to their mothers . . . revealed . . . aggressive protest against social rules."[18]

The hypothetical link between exaggerated masculinity and feminine identification has been tested in a more recent study by Charles C. Harrington. Rather than beginning with broken homes, he chose a population of deviant boys. Some were deviant in the direction of exaggeratedly masculine behavior; others exhibited characteristically feminine behavior. He found that boys of both types more often had greater "unconscious feminine identity" than a control group matched for social class and body construction.[19]

The defensive character of masculinity is not limited to deviant juveniles. The normal boy begins his sex-role learning in a less personal way than the girl, since he has fewer opportunities to model the same-sex parent at home or in school. When a boy moves into the peer group, he continues a less intimate style of relating; rather than a few friendships, the boy typically becomes part of a gang of boys. This gang adds to the stereotypic quality of the male role. In their pooled ignorance of genuine male personality, the boys glorify the male image. A series of interviews with 8- and 11-year-old boys revealed that they frequently express "hostility toward anything even hinting at 'femininity' including females themselves."[20]

Exaggerated masculinity appears to be typical of normal adult males as well. Ruth E. Hartley observed that most males show anxiety about masculinity.[21] The most common social manifestation of this anxiety is the continued need to dominate the female. Despite two centuries of American democracy, men fear allowing women equality in decision making in the real world of business and government. As Erikson notes, this defensiveness on the parts of men results not only in a failure to recognize and accept the contribution women have to make in the outer world, but an impoverishment of the interpersonal relationhips between men and women as well.[22]

Thus, as the male begins to experience closeness and warmth in heterosexual relationships, he frequently feels threatened. He becomes aware of his own warmth and sensitivity but fears a regression. Then, "doubting his potency and to avoid ridicule and danger, he becomes obsessionally heterosexual and competitive."[23] The first price the individual and society pay for man's rejection of the feminine is in the area of heterosexual relations. On the interpersonal level, these relations are impoverished by man's resorting to power and domination in his fear of his own tenderness. On the social level, contributions both sexes might make to the world are lost as energy is channeled into competition between the sexes.

In the Greek myth, Oedipus unwittingly kills his own father. The classical view of adolescence is that the son's aggression is rebelliously displayed against the father. However, in our society, the male feels hostile toward the feminine. Seldom is the anger overtly displayed against mother. Instead, there is a general degradation of femininity. The Greek myth ends with Oedipus cutting out his own eyes; he is unable to tolerate the objective truth. The American male, by contrast, rejects the subjective and cuts himself off from his own feelings. Rejecting the roots of his own development, he tries to kill the mother inside himself. In addition to the interpersonal and social costs, the rejection of femininity often leaves men barren in their personal lives—the most tragic cost of all.

In man's defensive affirmation of the male role, the strong overcomes the tender, the rational masks the emotive, and the focus on goal achievement results in a failure to experience life as it is happening, "to live in the now" (to use the argot of today's youth). Charles Reich illustrates how this failure affects the way in which father portrays the world to his son. If a young boy asks his father, "What do you do, Daddy?" the father is likely to answer: "I am a lawyer. I help people and businesses to solve their problems. I help everybody to know the rules that we all have to live by, and to get along according to these rules."[24] The son is given a glorified image of the work world. If the father were really aware of the process of his life, he might answer instead:

> "I struggle with crowds, traffic jams, and parking problems for about one hour. I dictate to a secretary and then proofread what she types. I have all sorts of meetings with people I don't know very well or like very much. I eat lunch in a big hurry and can't taste or remember what I've eaten. I hurry, hurry, hurry. I spend my time in very functional offices with very functional furniture, and I never look at the weather or sky or people passing by. I talk, but I don't sing or dance or touch people. I spend the last hour, all alone, struggling with crowds, traffic, and parking. . . ." We are taught to be an instrumental people; we think of the purposes or goals of some activity rather than of the activity itself. . . .[25]

By focusing on future goals, man is not really aware of his own boredom and misery, but he also loses the excitement and beauty of the here and now. To succeed in a machine age, he becomes a machine. The instrumental role alone is simply not sufficient for full humanness.

## The conflict for women:
## Envy and fear of the masculine

The process of personal learning of sex-role behavior in girls, started through identification with mother, is continued in the wider society, since the girl usually has female teachers. In the preadolescent period, girls tend to develop close friendships with a few girl friends, in contrast to boys' preference for being part of the gang. Perhaps it is the continuation of a personal style of relationships which protects the girl from more severe psychological damages when she confronts man's world.

Girls, too, are affected by the shift of emphasis to the world outside the home. Though girls continue to state a desire to be like mother, they generally perceive father as wiser and stronger.[26] Their sex-role identification and their personal identification are securely female, but their sex-role preference is often masculine. It is not a question of role confusion: they know who they are, but nevertheless they often wish for the status and perogatives of the male. This preference should not be equated with sex-typing. It has been found that "Females prefer to be males more than males prefer to be females, but this does not indicate that these unhappy females are unable to engage in behavior appropriate to their sex.[27]

From age five on, girls make fewer judgements than boys that their own sex is better, and they are less apt to prefer only girls' activities or only girls as friends.[28] As girls grow older, their preferential evaluations of their own sex continue to decline.[29] They wish, far more frequently than boys do, that they were members of the opposite sex.[30] As women move toward adulthood, they value their own role less and less.[31]

Though girls have the advantage of a continuing identification with an available and personal model, they eventually sense that they are expected to be persons in a very restricted world. They learn that the more important world, the outside world, is man's world. For males sex-role training in our society leads to repression of the expressive; their most personal self is lost. For females, the sex roles lead to resentment; the richness of personal feeling is not allowed effective expression in the real world. Though women are allowed to express their emotions, they are not expected to execute significant activities that will put their feelings into action. Boys are depersonalized, but girls are restricted.

Though female-dominated child rearing may allow girls a richer, more expressive, and individuated identification with mother, it often does so at the expense of real movement into the world. This theme will be amplified in other parts of this book as the girl's development is traced through adolescence, revealing her fear of achievement (Chapter

10) and her dissatisfactions with adult roles (Chapter 16). But even before adolescence, in the school years, the negative effects of her over-identification with stereotypic femininity are apparent. While the feminine stereotype encourages dependency, it is the more independent girls who do better intellectually. H. A. Moss and Jerome Kagan found that for girls, "the crucial factor in the development of I.Q. appears to be relative freedom from maternal restriction—freedom to wander and explore."[32] Greater aggressiveness and impulsivity appear to facilitate intellectual development in girls.

The opposite factors are involved for boys, according to Moss and Kagan: "Maternal protection and warmth during the early years of life are positively related to high I.Q. in later years for boys."[33] Most boys seem to have been taught too much aggressiveness and impulsiveness. These traits in boys have the opposite effect than they do in girls: they decrease some aspects of boys' intellectual development. Lynn's observations that the mother is involved in the boy's child rearing, but in a more negative way than for the girl, have been noted. Dominating mothers may respond punitively to aggression, which only increases aggression in other situations.[34] Permissive mothers may fail to give boys sufficient training in channeling their energies productively. Either response hampers the boy's intellectual development. The boy needs warmth and protection which does not foster aggression and impulsiveness. The girl needs greater encouragement toward exploration and independence.

## Continuing the argument for greater paternal involvement

The apparent contrasts in the factors which facilitate greater intellectual development for girls and for boys are easily reconciled; boys need less of the traits associated with stereotypic masculinity, and girls need less of the restrictiveness associated with femininity. Boys need the kind of maternal warmth we take for granted in raising girls. Girls need to be allowed the kind of freedom to explore we encourage in boys. In short, a better blending of the positive qualities associated with each of the sex roles might facilitate intellectual development in both sexes.

The benefits of cross-sex identification became particularly clear in a study of the biographies of outstanding women mathematicians; there was evidence in each of these women of a strong attachment to and identification with their fathers.[35] Further evidence comes from a more careful experimental study which related sex typing to performance on a test of analytical perception (an embedded-figures test). Men who scored high on this test revealed high identification with their mothers on the semantic differential. High-scoring women, by contrast, showed high levels of identification with their fathers.[36] A thorough review of the relevant research indicates that, with few exceptions, "analytic thinking, creativity, and high general intelligence are associated with cross-sex-typing."[37]

The material in the preceding chapter on the learning of sex roles suggested that an integration of the positive aspects of each role might occur if father were more involved in child rearing. Of course, it is not just more time with father that is needed, but a particular quality of relationship: a warm personal involvement which helps the child cope realistically with the objective world without rejecting the expressive and subjective. The data suggest that greater paternal involvement of this type would not only aid sex-role learning but would have positive benefits in the cognitive domain. In addition, adolescent and adult males who have good personal identifications with their fathers, suggesting positive personal relationships with their fathers during childhood, exhibit low neuroticism, high peer reputation, and high adjustment. The positive factor cannot be attributed to a presumed adaptiveness resulting from masculine sex-typing; "consistent correlations between masculine sex-typing and measures of adjustment have not been found."[38] Apparently it is personal identification with father, not sex-typing, which fosters better mental and social adjustment for males.

As usual, the evidence regarding female development is less abundant. The available data suggest that increased father identification strengthens the girl's feminine values and characteristics. It is not clear whether father identification fosters mental and social adjustment in girls or merely strengthens female sex-typing. We would predict the latter if father is only available to teach roles but is not involved enough in child rearing to be experienced as an individual. The present data do not allow us to decide between these alternatives; they simply indicate that the girl's feminine values are consolidated by father identification.

## The vicious cycle

The impression given thus far is that the rejection of femininity is largely a consequence of the negative methods women use in teaching masculinity in the absence of male models. Consideration of the consequences of the cultural sex-typing for females indicates that women may also teach the rejection of the feminine in a more direct manner, to both sons and daughters. This more direct derogation of femininity stems from the mother's unresolved conflict about her own femininity.

Often mother places much esteem on father's role as worker in the world. If this esteem were an outgrowth of her satisfaction with her own role and her positive recognition of the importance of the complementary role of her husband, it might have a positive effect upon the child's growth. But because of the high values our male-dominated culture places upon competitive, achieving aspects of masculinity, the housewife is likely to feel that she is not accomplishing anything. Thus her esteem for her husband's role is frequently tinged with envy and disappointment stemming from her own wish to be out of the home and working in the world. Because of her identification with her own mother, she may value deeply the expressive aspects of child rearing and honestly desire the maternal role. But she also wishes for the social reinforcements and the sense of fulfillment of personal abilities and competence which our society grants mainly to those who work outside the home. Thus the woman is trapped between her own need for expressiveness and the overvaluation of the male role and devaluation of femininity which she learns from society. Many women handle their role ambivalence by accepting behaviorally the stereotyped woman's role, but they resent the limitations of the role and unwittingly teach that resentment to their children. Through their unresolved conflict, they directly contribute to the child's devaluation of femininity.

Similarly, children may get cues from their father that he degrades femininity. Though it is true (as Parsons's theory states) that the father has lived through both feminine and masculine identifications, it is doubtful that the earlier feminine identification is accessible to him. As has been noted, the male in our culture has usually suppressed the expressive role in himself. Thus, as a model for his children, he is all the more alert not to reveal his feminine side. Men gossip among themselves, and to their children, about not understanding their wives. Comic strips repeatedly portray men as baffled by the foolish logic of women, while the women wilefully and seductively succeed in understanding male psychology. There is some truth in this portrayal. Though man has the potential for a deep and sensitive understanding of womanhood because of his early identification with mother, the repressions resulting from child rearing and the culture have rendered it inoperative. The negative learning of the male role puts the father in a poor position to be a model. The children are left to model a man who has rejected a part of himself: "The sins of the fathers are visited upon the children even unto the fourth generation" (Deuteronomy 5:9). Thus the father participates in the rejection of the feminine.

## Family and culture

When father's work was removed from home by the Industrial Revolution, the home became a smaller place, both physically and psychologically. If a woman's place was in the home in preindustrial Western society, that home was a large and extensive territory, for it included the extended family of grandparents, aunts, uncles, and cousins, and it was a center of social and economic life. With the move to the factory, home and world became geographically and psychologically separated. The home gradually shrunk to today's 50 by 150-foot plot, with its five-room house for the nuclear family.[39] Child rearing became increasingly alike for boys and girls, and more and more dominated by females.

The historical paradox that results is that boys and girls are being reared in the same place by the same people, but for two different worlds. On the surface child rearing for boys and girls is alike—yet the split between home and world, between expressive and instrumental aspects of our culture is wider than ever. The strength we identify with masculinity is of positive value, except when it loses touch with the personal. The emotionality and warmth of femininity is corrupt only when it is restricted and thus becomes possessive and turns relationships into closed, stagnant systems.

The sex-role confusion of our times is not simply due to the rapid change in sex roles, but to the fact that our child-rearing is not attuned to our society, and our society, wedded to the machine, is out of touch with its human roots. The error is not that we have begun to raise boys and girls similarly, but that we have not healed the split between expressive and instrumental roles. We have kept children at home with mother while allowing home and world to become isolated from each other. Consequently too many of our youth become depersonalized men and resentful women.

I have argued that the family would benefit if father were more personally involved in child rearing. Now, in view of the cultural side of the process, the mirror argument must be made. Women must move out of the home and influence the work world, if the more humanized male is to survive. Erikson makes this point in his discussion of the contribution women could make in man's work world:

> It is as yet unpredictable what the tasks and roles, opportunities and job specifications will be once women are not merely adapted to male jobs in economics and politics but learn to adapt jobs to themselves. Such a revolutionary reappraisal may even lead to the insight that jobs now called masculine force men, too, into inhumane adjustments.[40]

It is premature to speculate further about how to bring our child rearing and our culture into more humane alignment. In the next section the focus is upon the adolescent's search for identity; after I have described how adolescents struggle with the split between home and world, between expressive and instrumental roles, I will return (in Part three) to some resolutions.

## Summary

Gradually children award increasing status to father and become more concerned about the world outside the home. The larger society is dominated by values that favor the male. Though the masculine role is the more difficult one to achieve, it is awarded more prestige in adulthood. The feminine identification is rejected by the male, often resulting in a defensively masculine character. Females increasingly envy the male role and devalue their own. Yet they fear moving into the masculine world, and restrict their own development. It would be beneficial if fathers were more involved in child rearing and mothers were more involved outside the home.

## Notes

1. Lawrence Kohlberg, "A Cognitive-Developmental Analysis of Children's Sex-Role Concepts and Attitudes," in *The Development of Sex Differences,* ed. Eleanore E. Maccoby (Stanford, Calif.: Stanford University Press, 1966), p. 102.

2. Ibid.

3. Jean Piaget, *The Psychology of Intelligence* (London: Routledge & Kegan Paul, 1947), cited in Kohlberg, "Cognitive-Developmental Analysis."

4. Reprinted from *Identity: Youth and Crisis* by Erik H. Erikson. By permission of W. W. Norton & Company, Inc. Copyright © 1968 by W. W. Norton & Company, Inc. Austen Riggs Monograph No. 7.

5. David B. Lynn, "The Process of Learning Parental and Sex-Role Identification," *Journal of Marriage and the Family,* 18 (1966): 466–70.

6. Arthur J. Rudy, "Sex-Role Perceptions in Early Adolescence," *Adolescence,* 3 (1968): 453–70, especially p. 459.

7. Kohlberg, "Cognitive-Developmental Aanalysis," p. 142.

8. See Maccoby, ed., *Development of Sex Differences,* p. 123.

9. M. M. Nawas, "Changes in Efficiency of Ego Functioning and Complexity from Adolescence to Young Adulthood," *Developmental Psychology,* 4 (1971): 412–15.

10. David B. Lynn, "Divergent Feedback and Sex-Role Identification in boys and Men," *Merrill-Palmer,* 10 (1964): 17–23.

11. Lynn, "Parental and Sex-role Identification."

12. Albert Bandura, *Principles of Behavior Modification* (New York: Holt, Rinehart & Winston, 1969), chap. 8, "Aversive Counterconditioning."

13. By now it should be obvious why we cannot trust the self-perceptions of adolescents when studying their parental identifications. If males repress a large portion of early childhood memories, there is no need to invoke the incest taboo to explain it (as Freud did); the negative training of masculinity should be reason enough.

14. Ruth E. Hartley, "Sex-Role Pressure and the Socialization of the Male Child," *Pscyhological Reports,* 5 (1959): 457–68.

15.  Talcott Parsons, *Social Structure and Personality* (London: Free Press, 1964), p. 169. Jerome Kagan reports empirical evidence that dependency is no longer a stable personality trait in males after age seven—Jerome Kagan and Howard A. Moss, "The Stability of Passive and Dependent Behavior from Childhood through Adolescence," *Child Development,* 31 (1960): 577–91. McCandless found differences in styles of dependency between boys and girls as early as age four. These differences are related to the instrumental and expressive roles; boys limit their expression of dependency to where it aids in achieving a goal—Boyd R. McCandless, C. B. Bilous, and H. D. Bennett, "Peer Popularity and Dependence on Adults in Pre-school Age Socialization," *Child Development,* 32 (1961): 511–18.

16.  Parsons, *Social Structure and Personality,* p. 53.

17.  Ibid.

18.  J. W. Whiting, R. Kluckholn, and A. Anthony, "The Function of Male Initiation Ceremonies at Puberty," in *Readings in Social Psychology,* ed. Eleanore Maccoby, T. M. Newcomb, and E. L. Hartley (New York: Holt, Rinehart & Winston, 1958).

19.  Charles C. Harrington, *Errors in Sex-Role Behavior in Teen-Age Boys* (New York: Teachers College Press, 1970).

20.  Hartley, "Sex-Role Pressures and Socialization."

21.  Ibid.

22.  Erikson, *Identity: Youth and Crisis,* p. 290.

23.  Paul Goodman, *Growing up Absurd* (New York: Vintage Books, 1956), p. 42.

24.  Charles A. Reich, *The Greening of America* (New York: Random House, 1970), p. 166.

25.  Ibid., pp. 166–67.

26.  Jerome Kagan and Judith Lemkin, "The Child's Differential Perception of Parental Attributes," *Journal of Abnormal and Social Psychology,* 61 (1960): 446–47.

27.  D. S. Brown, "Sex-Role Development in a Changing Culture," *Psychological Bulletin,* 55 (1958): 232–42; see also Sanford M. Dornbusch, "Afterword," in *Development of Sex Differences,* ed. Maccoby.

28.  R. E. Hartley and F. Hardesty, "Children's Perception and Expression of Sex Preferences," *Child Development,* 33 (1962): 221–27; Patricia Minuchin, "Children's Sex-Role Concepts as a Function of School and Home Environments" (paper presented at the American Orthopsychiatric Association Meeting, March 1964); Kohlberg, "Cognitive-Developmental Analysis."

29.  S. Smith, "Age and Sex Differences in Children's Opinions Concerning Sex Differences," *Journal of Genetic Psychology,* 54 (1939): 17–25; Kohlberg, "Cognitive-Developmental Analysis."

30.  Sibylla E. Clautour and T. W. Moore, "Attitudes of Twelve-Year-Old Children to Present and Future Life Roles," *Human Development,* 12 (1969): 221–38. See especially p. 231.

31.  Lynn, "Divergent Feedback and Sex-Role Identification"; Lynn, "Parental and Sex-Role Identification."

32.  H. A. Moss and Jerome Kagan, unpublished manuscript (1962), cited in Eleanor E. Maccoby, "Sex Differences in Intellectual Functioning," in *The Development of Sex Differences,* ed. Maccoby.

33.  Moss and Kagan, unpublished manuscript.

34.  Albert Bandura, "Relationships of Family Patterns to Child Behavior Dis-

orders" (progress report, U.S. Public Health Service Research Grant M-1734, Stanford University, 1960). See last section of Chapter 3 above.

35. Emma H. Plank and R. Plank, "Emotional Components in Arithmetic Learning as Seen through Autobiographies," in *The Psychoanalytic Study of the Child,* ed. R. S. Eissler, et al. (New York: International Universities Press, 1954), vol. 9.

36. James Bieri, "Parental Identification, Acceptance of Authority, and Within-Sex Differences in Cognitive Behavior," *Journal of Abnormal and Social Psychology,* 60 (1960): 69–79.

37. Maccoby, "Sex Differences in Intellectual Functioning," p. 35.

38. Kohlberg, "Cognitive-Developmental Analysis."

39. Elizabeth Janeway, *Man's World, Woman's Place: A Study in Social Mythology* (New York: William Morrow & Co., 1971).

40. Erikson, *Identity: Youth and Crisis,* p. 290.

# Conclusions to part one

In the first section of this book, I have sought to establish that sex roles and their related values are learned early in childhood (Chapter 1) and that in our society these roles involve a splitting of inner and outer life, of expressive and instrumental orientations (Chapter 2). This split may once have been functional but is no longer necessary (Chapter 3). For most males, the way in which these roles are learned involves a rejection of the inner world and the putting on of a defensively masculine armor as the boy seeks to meet the outer world. For females the masculine world is held up as enviable but out of reach (Chapter 4). The child, male or female, moves from a world in which the feminine role is central, to a world in which it is considered inferior and is desecrated. Too frequently, the split between home and world, between expressive and instrumental roles, results in depersonalized men and restricted women (Chapter 5). I will turn now to a survey of adolescence, the developmental period in which the move from home to world is most dramatic.

*part two*

# Where the battle is waged

THE FOCUS OF Part two is the move from childhood into adulthood, the move from the home into the world. The image of the outside world that children gain through their fathers is often seductively positive. The world is portrayed as one of challenge and opportunity, a place where their growing competence can be geared with the grand issues of real life.

Once adolescents make that crucial step over the threshold, they are indeed in a different world; they have moved from the female-dominated world of childhood to the male-dominated society. But instead of the world of their dreams, they face the reality of a hard, often cold, and depersonalized world. The effect of this confrontation with reality has been expressively portrayed by Charles Reich:

> The youngster of earlier generations discovered reality by exploring outside his own front door. He encountered the world of the farm or of city streets, tested it, and found out about horses, cows, and pumpkins, other youngsters, stores and traffic; the knowledge he gained did not play him false. Perhaps in old age, retelling his experiences, he turned them into myths, but they were myths that were fashioned out of his own reality.
>
> With the child of (today), the process is reversed. Our society insists that children first be taught the prescribed mythology, in school, in films, and earliest and most universally, on television. The television world is what our society claims itself to be, what it demands that we believe. But when the television child finally encounters the real world, he does not find families like Ozzie, Harriet, David and Ricky, "Father Knows Best," or "My Three Sons." He does not find the clean suburbs of television but the sordid slums of reality. He does not find the high-minded statesmen of the screen, but politicians who are mediocre, small-minded, and corrupt. He does not find perpetual smiles or the effervescent high spirits of a Coke ad, but anxieties and monotony. And when he stops believing in this mythic world, the breach in his credulity is irreparable.[1]

It is doubtful that television would be as effective as Reich suggests if the male image were not reinforced in the home. But the contrast Reich draws between learning an image and learning reality is an important one. Even the active involvement with reality for which the adolescent hungers often turns out to be an illusion. Much of real life, both on the job and in the university, proves to be busy work—Mickey Mouse stuff. Rather than an active participation in society's decisions, the young person increasingly recognizes that he is a spectator. Often he finds himself in passive and obsequious roles, carrying out the decisions of someone else. Indeed, no thoughtful decisions may be made at all, as the impersonal direction of technocracy takes over (as Reich claims). The adult world, so mysterious when viewed in fantasy, turns out to be a drag, and the adolescent finds himself wishing to return to the world of fantasy and feeling, the playful world of childhood with Mom.

The problems of today's adolescents are not simply the normal struggles of growth into adulthood. Nor are they merely the difficulties of growing up in an absurd society. In addition to each of these, there is the struggle of transition from one world to another, for the outside world is clearly a different environment from that in which the child was raised.

## Note

1.   Charles Reich, *The Greening of America: The Coming of a New Consciousness and the Rebirth of a Future* (New York: Random House, 1970), pp. 220–21.

# 6

## *Is there a crisis?*

**Are adolescents rebellious?**
  Sex differences
  Geographic differences
**Restating the question**
**Summary**

THE TERM "CRISIS" is commonly interpreted to mean a period of severe turmoil and trauma. G. Stanley Hall, one of America's earliest students of adolescent psychology, likened adolescence to the theme of *Sturm und Drang* (storm and stress) in 18th-century literature.[1] This view of adolescence has been perpetuated by Freudian psychologists, who have argued that the upsurge of libidinal energy resulting from sexual maturation threatens the ego, increases anxiety, and results in defensiveness so extreme as to make normal adolescence appear pathological.[2]

According to Freudian theory, rebellion against the parents is a necessary and inevitable part of normal adolescence. The emergence of sexuality in adolescence brings with it a renewal of the oedipal complex. Since the adolescent is unable to reject the new sexuality, he defensively rejects his own parents. The theory states two reasons for this rebellion against the parents: it is a defensive pushing away of those who tempt him sexually, and, secondly, it is an external expression of something he rejects within himself—his childhood conscience—which is largely the product of parental prohibitions.

Another influential view has also characterized adolescence as a period of rebellion against parents but has attributed this to social factors, most importantly the "generation gap" and the influence of the peer culture. Kingsley Davis has argued that it is probably inevitable that there will be some generation gap in a fast-changing society, for child rearing tends to develop out of the experiences of the parents' own childhood and is therefore bound to be outdated:

> The content which the parent acquired at the stage where the child now is, was a different content from that which the child [needs for life in today's world]. . . . Since the parent is supposed to be socializing the child, he tends to apply the erstwhile but now inappropriate content. He makes this mistake, and cannot remedy it, because, due to the

logic of personality growth, his basic orientation was formed by the experiences of his own childhood.[3]

Because of the time interval between generations, parents habitually prepare children for a society of the past. The gap that youths experience is not simply a problem of communication with their own parents but a result of the changes that have occurred in the interval between generations. Youths accurately sense that much of the wisdom of the past generation will not be helpful in the future world they will inhabit; as Bob Dylan puts it, "The times, they are a 'changin'." Not that youths have clear premonitions of the future. But parents necessarily speak from the integration they have achieved from their own past, while children are increasingly aware, as they move into the peer group and the wider world, of differing standards and competing authorities. They realize that they must achieve their own synthesis of this pluralism to prepare for the world they will live in. The wisdom of the older generation is, for youth, an outdated synthesis.

Another aspect of this social viewpoint is that the peer group becomes an adolescent culture, with values and norms which are distinct from the larger adult culture. James S. Coleman puts it this way:

> With his fellows, the child of high school age comes to constitute a small society, one that has most of its important interactions within itself, and maintains only a few threads of connection with the outside adult society. . . . The adolescent lives more and more in a society of his own; he finds the family a less and less satisfying psychological home. As a consequence, the home has less and less ability to mold him.[4]

Whether the turmoil is attributed to intrapsychic factors, such as the defense against the reemergence of the oedipal complex, or to social factors, such as the generation gap and the peer group, early adolescence is commonly portrayed in psychological literature as a time of trauma centering around rebellion against parents. Recently, however, a number of social scientists have attacked this stereotype of a stormy and rebellious adolescence, stressing the evidence which shows agreement between the adolescent and his parents.[5]

## Are adolescents rebellious?

### Sex differences

A problem with almost all adolescent theory to date is that it has centered upon male development. There is considerable evidence that storm and stress as a description of early adolescence does not generally apply to girls. Rather, the data indicate that girls show considerable conformity to parents throughout adolescence.[6] F. Ivan Nye's study of adolescent's adjustment to parents found no change in the relation between parents and adolescent girls in eighth through eleventh grades.[7] Dale B. Harris and Sing Chu Tseng studied students from grades four through twelve and found that girls actually became more positive in their attitude toward parents during the adolescent years.[8] Clay V. Brittain, in a study of high school girls in Alabama and Georgia, used descriptions of situations in which the young person portrayed had to make a decision between following parental advice or the opinions of peers. The same situations were repeated in a retest, but with the parental and peer advice attributed to the opposite source. The results showed a greater overall incidence of conformity to parents than to peers.[9]

In none of the empirical data surveyed do girls appear to increase in negative attitudes toward their parents. One psychoanalytic interpretation is that this positive response is merely a defense against unconscious rebellion. A study by John V. Liccione used projective techniques in an attempt to tap a deeper layer of personality. Subjects were administered the Thematic Apperception Test, in which they were asked to tell a story in response to ambiguous pictures. Themes of stories involving older female characters were catagorized as showing either conflict or tranquility. The responses showed a high percentage of conflict themes around mother and father "projections"; in fact, themes showing conflict outnumbered tranquil themes five to one.[10]

The use of projective instruments deserves comment, since it is possible that the other studies showing a low parental conflict simply reflect a social desirability factor. Unfortunately, a problem of apparatus factors arises with the use of projective techniques to test attitudes toward parents: the Thematic Apperception Test, for example, uses pictures of authority figures as the projective stimuli, on the assumption that attitudes evoked by these stimuli are a projection from unconscious attitudes toward parents. It is equally possible to assume that one may feel hostile toward the objective authorities in the impersonal world and feel quite differently toward one's own parents. My own studies, to be reported later, revealed a marked difference in attitudes toward one's parents and attitudes toward other authority figures.[11] There seems to be no unambiguous way to interpret projective tests; consequently it may be impossible to devise an instrument to measure feelings toward parents that will not be influenced or colored by social desirability factors. Thus, the supposition that girls harbor repressed rebellious attitudes toward their parents remains simply a supposition.

## Geographic differences

Not only do adolescent girls generally fail to fit the storm and stress caricature, but this view of adolescence seems invalid for most rural adolescents, male as well as female. R. C. Bealer, F. K. Willits, and P. R. Maida have argued persuasively that youth in rural areas continue to respect and conform to their parents' views.[12] Rural high school students in two studies were asked which was the most important reference point in their lives: family, school chums, or someone else; over three fourths indicated parents, while less than 10 percent indicated school chums.[13] In another study, the Minnesota Multiphasic Personality Inventory was administered to 15,000 ninth-graders in Minnesota. The results showed considerably less conflict with authority and resistance to social norms among the rural students than among the urban students.[14] A similar study in Michigan found that urban teen-agers scored higher on dominance, aggressiveness, and radicalism.[15] Rural adolescents and preadolescents in Minnesota, responding to a sentence completion test, showed only a small percentage of negative attitudes toward mother or father.[16] Studies of high school sophomores in rural Pennsylvania in 1947 and in 1960 gathered opinions on the acceptability of drinking, smoking, school failure, makeup, dancing, dating, use of money, church attendance, and similar behavior. Youths in both studies were more likely to evaluate their parents' attitudes on these subjects as "sensible" than as "too critical" or "not critical enough." As they increased their involvement in school functions, the proportion of "sensible" responses went up, not down, suggesting that peer group involvement does not necessarily weaken adolescent respect for parental attitudes.[17] If the identity crisis stems in part from a breakdown of traditional familial and vocational patterns, it is not surprising that crisis is not evident in rural youth, since in these areas patterns have not been so severely ruptured.

It should be noted that all of the cited studies that showed differences between rural and urban youth used subjects from the Midwest. Brittain's study of a southern population, cited above, found no rural-urban differences, though finding differences might have been more likely had his study included urban boys, who generally report more negative attitudes.

Although there may be reservations concerning the rigor of some of these studies and their interpretations, the data do suggest that the picture of the rebellious adolescent is a stereotype which should not be applied generally to adolescent girls or to rural adolescents, at least at the level of conscious attitudes. There are, of course, individual exceptions to these generalizations.

It is now appropriate to ask if the storm and stress view applies at all to contemporary American adolescents. In an influential article entitled "The Stormy Decade: Fact or Fiction," Albert Bandura argued that the view of normal adolescence as a period of rebellion is a fiction. He claimed that by the time the boys in his study had reached adolescence, they had internalized their parents' values and standards to such a large degree that the parents were highly trustful of them and no longer felt that externally imposed limits were necessary.[18] His conclusions seem to be based on the control group of an earlier study of aggressive adolescents by Bandura with Richard H. Walters. School staff were instructed to identify aggressive adolescents as the experimental group for this study and to select as a control group students who were "neither markedly aggressive nor markedly withdrawn."[19] Thus the sampling appears from the beginning to have been biased against the storm and stress hypothesis.

Bandura drew upon an earlier article by Frederick Elkin and William Westley which questioned not only the storm and stress view but the assumption that participation in youth culture constitutes a widespread pattern among adolescents.[20] The population studied included 40 adolescents and their parents, drawn from suburban professional and business families. The authors noted that in the families studied "ties are close and the degree of basic family consensus is high." Few sharp conflicts between parents and children were reported, and no serious problems seemed to arise from the children's developing choices of occupation or growing emancipation from the parents. However, Elkin and Westley were more cautious than Bandura in interpreting their data, stating that: "The empirical data do not deny that there are psychological tensions and distinctive interests in adolescents; they do suggest that, for the middle class, the current model [of storm and stress] is an erroneous conception."[21] The point is well taken. Clearly the storm and stress model of adolescence has been uncritically accepted and overgeneralized.

## Restating the question

Rather than arguing whether or not early adolescence is a time of conflict, I will put the issue into quantitative form. In this procedure three questions emerge, each involving comparative measures:

1. Do children express more negative attitudes toward their parents as adolescents than they did when they were younger?
2. Do they feel more negative toward parents than toward peers?
3. Do they feel more negative toward parents than toward other authority figures?

Implied in these questions is the important distinction between attitudes toward parents and attitudes toward other authorities. Only those studies that have made this distinction are reported below.[22] The studies by Nye and by Harris and Tseng cited above found no increased conflict with parents for girls in grades 4 through 12. For boys the data are less clear. Nye reports a deterioration in the relationship between adolescent boys and their parents during adolesence.[23] Harris and Tseng, using a sentence completion test, found an increase in the number of boys who expressed negative feelings but no increase in the percentage of negative feelings expressed.[24] A number of studies in other countries have reported increased rebelliousness and parental alienation in boys of high school age.[25]

Though these data suggest that boys' negative attitudes toward their parents increase during the high school years, all the above studies share a methodological weakness. Instead of using the longitudinal method (following the same subjects through a period of time), these studies have compared cohort groups (subjects of different ages tested at the same time). It is possible that the differences reported are due to sampling biases rather than developmental changes. For example, it is likely that some students have dropped out of school before reaching the more advanced classes. Since these students will not be present in the older age group tested, a comparison of the scores of the different classes confounds age differences with academic achievement, motivation, and other variables involved with continuing in school. Higher negative scores in the upper classes may simply reflect the greater critical ability of those students who continue in school.[26]

This confounding of variables is avoided when the same subjects are studied over a period of time. The Berkeley longitudinal project,[27] although dated, provides a valuable model in two respects. First, since data regarding attitudes toward authority were gathered in several different settings, it is possible to discriminate between attitudes toward parents and attitudes toward nonparental authorities, such as school teachers. Second, the data were not limited to responses to questionnaires, which are often subject to social desirability effects. Ratings of the subjects' behavior were made by other persons (teachers, peers), thus providing a variety of data. The results for girls were consistent with the findings already cited; girls increased in their acceptance of authority (on all ratings) between 14 and 16 years of age. Boys also tended to increase in their acceptance of parental authority, though the data were less consistent. At school, however, boys became less conforming to nonparental authority as they grew older.[28] The subjects in this study were adolescents in the mid-1940s.

A more recent longitudinal study suggests that boys today maintain essentially positive relations with their parents throughout the high school years.[29] The study was limited to normal boys in a suburban area; psychiatric assessments of the subjects were made over the four-year high school period. Typically the boys felt closer to mother than father at age 14, but claimed to be more intimate with father than mother at 18. Throughout the high school years they appeared to like and admire their parents.

When these subjects were interviewed in their second or third years after high school, the majority continued to respect their parents, to want to be like them, and to believe that their parents understood them.[30] These subjects indicated that their relationships with their parents were as harmonious as they had been previously or were even better during the post-high-school years. Most of the parents, responding to questionnaires, revealed satisfaction with their sons' performances. A significant minority of these subjects did express annoyance with their parents, particularly during the first two post-high-school years. Parental advice or questionning was sometimes regarded by the boys as interference with their autonomy. The authors concluded that, though the subjects were shifting away from dependence upon parents, they were not in open rebellion and did not discard their parents' basic values. When ambivalent feelings toward parents emerged, they usually were found to "infect trivial matters that neither subject nor parent allows to spiral out of control."[31] A continuity of styles of coping, rather than strong fluctuations, was revealed in the seven years of development studied.

Regarding Question 1 above, it appears that girls' attitudes toward their parents do not become more negative during adolescence. The data for boys are conflicting; no generalization is possible.

In answer to Question 2, the relative importance of peers in adolescence has been widely debated. Many observers of adolescents have claimed that a separate adolescent subculture exists.[32] This view gained credence with the publication of Coleman's landmark study *The Adolescent Society*, quoted from above. Based on data from students in high schools in several types of communities, Coleman concluded that the adolescent peer group constitutes a separate and distinctive society, centered around the high school students and having its own set of norms and values. Loyalty to peers was so strong in these subjects that they were almost equally divided as to which would be worse, breaking with a friend or disappointing a parent.[33]

There is general agreement that as the child grows older the peer group becomes increasingly important to him, and dependence upon parental guidance decreases. A comparison of students in grades four through ten supports this view.[34] By tenth grade three times as many students preferred to spend their time with friends rather than with family. Tenth-graders agreed with their peers on 50 percent of the value items tested, as compared to 30 percent agreement with parents. In both these areas there were steady increases in peer influence with age. Nonetheless, an assessment of identifications[35] showed twice as many tenth-graders with a family orientation as with a peer orientation. This calls into question "whether adolescents really live in a separate world of their own."[36]

Despite the increase in peer interaction, much of the evidence suggests parents continue to wield considerable influence on adolescents.[37] One study asked senior high school students:

> Which things would make you most unhappy?
> 1.  If my parents did not like what I did.
> 2.  If my favorite teacher did not like what I did.
> 3.  If my best friend did not like what I did.

Over 80 percent of boys and girls alike replied that they would be most concerned over parental disapproval. The disapproval of a best friend would be most important to 18 percent of the girls and 16 percent of the boys.[38]

Brittain's study of southern high school girls cited above provides more experimental evidence concerning the relationship of parental and peer influence. As noted, the study showed a greater incidence of conformity toward parents than toward peers. Adolescents tended to turn to their parents in making decisions they considered difficult or as having long-term consequences. It should be noted, however, that there were some issues on which these same adolescents were more influenced by their peers; they appeared anxious to conform to peers on highly visible issues such as dress and on decisions related to being with their friends, such as the choice of which courses to take. Further, when adolescents faced decisions that involved cross-pressures between peers and parents, the evidence suggests that they handled this problem by avoiding communication with their parents.[39] Brittain concluded that conformity to parents or peers varies as a function of the type of choice to be made by the adolescent.

Further evidence of this comes from a Purdue Opinion Poll which involved a representative sampling of all the nation's high schools.[40] Adults were found to be more influential than peers on issues such as political feelings, attitudes toward race and nationality, how to spend money, and personal problems. But peers were more influential on matters of personal grooming and dress, what clubs to join, and how to act with the gang. The areas of conflict reported were different for the sexes: boys had disagreements with parents over the use of the car and how they spent the money they earned; girls disagreed over their choices of friends, strictness on dates, and feelings of favoritism given their brothers. It is noteworthy that this study showed no evidence of intense conflict with parents during the high school years; the highest level of complaints on any single question was about 5 percent.

Pursuing the view that conflict with parents varies depending upon the type of choices to be made by the adolescent, Elizabeth Douvan and Joseph Adelson found that specific areas of disagreement in girls changed with age. Personal grooming and issues about clothes caused disagreements in early adolescence, but social activities were the chief contention in middle adolescence (ages 14–16). Later, differences occurred over beliefs and attitudes.[41]

Even in those areas in which peers are influential, they do not necessarily wield more power than parents. On the issue of how to act with the gang, 62 percent of the adolescents questioned in one study would "take the ideas of their parents"; only 23 percent would "take the ideas of people their own age." On joining clubs, the figures showed that 47 percent state they would follow parents' advice and 34 percent would follow peers. On personal grooming, 45 percent would pay attention to parents and 30 percent to peers.[42]

A comparative study of parent-adolescent relationships in the United States and Denmark by Denise Kandel and Gerald Lesser attempted a direct test of Coleman's hypothesis of a distinct peer culture.[43] It improved on the methodology of the previously cited studies by gathering data directly from parents and teachers, rather than depending solely on adolescent perceptions. The American sample included secondary students in rural, regional, and urban schools, forming a population "representative of the majority of American adolescents."[44] Adolescents in both countries were found to have close ties with their parents. The data did not support Coleman's prediction that family involvement is inversely related to intensity of peer involvement. It was also found that, "contrary to Coleman's assumption, adolescents and adults do not form two distinct societies with consistently different values and attitudes."[45] Only on concerns which might be characterized as "the fun of adolescence" are youth values different from parental values; this exception holds for both countries. On fundamental issues—general life values, future goals, and the means to such goals—the answers of parents and youth in each culture were very similar. Kandel and Lesser note that, overall, "there appears to be much less conflict between the two generations than has been suggested by Coleman and other investigators."[46]

Although Bandura, Bealer, and others have made their case that there is no explosive rebellion against parents during the high school years, it appears that a number of areas of conflict do emerge, but these are handled gradually and in succession. There is some evidence that the adolescent phase is experienced as more conflictual than earlier periods. In spite of this, the relationship with parents generally continues to exert a strong influence on the adolescent. The nature of the conflict and its effects on parent-adolescent interactions are explored in Chapter 7.

Question 3 above concerns authority figures other than parents. Negative attitudes toward nonparental authority do seem to increase during the adolescent years, though this is not generally the case for attitudes toward the parents themselves. The evidence from projective studies, frequently interpreted as hostility displaced from the parents,[47] might equally well be interpreted as evidence of negative feelings toward impersonal authority figures. The Berkeley longitudinal study cited above found a decrease in acceptance of authority as boys moved through early adolescence, yet no consistent change in attitudes toward the parents.[48]

Further evidence that adolescents are more negative toward impersonal authority than toward their own parents comes from a comparison of responses to items on a sentence completion test I used in two separate longitudinal studies.[49] The test consisted of 12 items having to do with nonparental authority figures.[50] An additional item, "My father . . ." was added for the purpose of comparison. In the second study, the item "My mother . . ." was also included.

This test was given in both studies to students before their entrance into college and during their freshman year. The first population consisted of the entering class of a state college, largely students of lower-middle-class economic backgrounds. The second study was done at a private liberal arts college with students from upper-middle-class and upper-class homes. Samplings from these two rather different populations had similar results, as shown in Table 1.

TABLE 1

Responses to parental and nonparental authority from percentage and freshman students (percentage of sentence completions)

|  | State college students | | Liberal arts students | |
| --- | --- | --- | --- | --- |
|  | Precollege | Freshmen | Precollege | Freshmen |
| Liking responses: | | | | |
| Mother . . . . . . . . . . . . . . . . . . . |  |  | 57% | 61% |
| Father . . . . . . . . . . . . . . . . . . . | 50% | 60% | 48 | 49 |
| Other authorities . . . . . . . . . . . . | 23 | 25 | 19 | 20 |
| Disliking responses: | | | | |
| Mother . . . . . . . . . . . . . . . . . . . |  |  | 14 | 14 |
| Father . . . . . . . . . . . . . . . . . . . | 5 | 5 | 10 | 8 |
| Other authorities . . . . . . . . . . . . | 16 | 17 | 22 | 24 |
| Submissive or fearful responses: | | | | |
| Mother . . . . . . . . . . . . . . . . . . . |  |  | 1 | 1 |
| Father . . . . . . . . . . . . . . . . . . . | 1 | 1 | 1 | 1 |
| Other authorities . . . . . . . . . . . . | 16 | 15 | 14 | 14 |

Source: David B. Matteson, "Changes in Attitudes toward Authority Figures in Selected College Freshmen" (Ph.d. diss., Boston University, 1968), and "Changes in Attitudes toward Authority Figures with the Move to College: Three Experiments," *Developmental Psychology*, 4 (1974): 340–47.

Note: Percentages, based on the total number of responses placed in six categories, do not total 100 percent because only three of the six categories of responses are reported.

For both populations, both before and after entering college, the positive responses were two or three times as frequent in relation to the parents as in relation to nonparental authorities. Negative and avoidant responses were considerably less frequent for parents as compared to those for nonparental authorities. It should be noted that the test was not designed to test hypotheses contrasting attitudes toward parents with those toward nonparental authority. The data are suggestive, however. Perhaps the more critical area of conflict for adolescents is impersonal authority outside the home, rather than the parents. This thesis is explored further in Chapter 12.

## Summary

A review of the research data allows four tentative conclusions:

1. There may be an increase in parent-child conflict during early and middle adolescence, at least for boys. Nonetheless, parent-child relationships in adolescence generally are more positive than negative and continue to wield a major influence in the adolescent's life.

2. The conflicts that do occur tend to be specific rather than pervasive. A succession of issues are dealt with, allowing the differences to be handled gradually.

3. Similarly, peer conformity tends to be limited to specific areas of judgment in which adolescents perceive the peers to be more adequate guides. During the high school years, issues of grooming and dress and, later, issues involving choice of peer groups and friends predominate.

4. Though adolescents do not generally experience intense conflicts with parents, they do hold increasingly negative attitudes toward nonparental authority.

These tentative conclusions are generalizations. There are, of course, individual adolescents whose lives and experiences do not fit this picture. Some adolescents do experience intense conflict with parents in early adolescence; others have their greatest difficulties in relating to peers. In both cases, the experienced conflicts may not be pathological and can lead to useful personal growth.[51] The reader is cautioned against interpreting individual differences as "bad."

## Notes

1. G. Stanley Hall, *Adolescence*, 2 vols. (New York: Appleton-Century-Crofts, 1916).

2. Peter Blos, *On Adolescence: A Psychoanalytic Interpretation* (New York: Free Press, 1962); Irene Josselyn, *The Adolescent and His World* (New York: Family Service Association of America, 1952).

3. Kingsley Davis, "The Sociology of Parent-Youth Conflict," *American Sociological Review*, 5 (1940): 524. Davis's argument assumes, as he realizes, that personality style is "fixed" at childhood. The present view, that identity is much in flux during adolescence, suggests that this is an ideal time for training in parenting.

4. James S. Coleman, *The Adolescent Society: The Social Life of the Teenager and Its Impact on Education* (New York: Free Press, 1961), pp. 3 and 312.

5. Albert Bandura, "The Stormy Decade: Fact or Fiction?" *Psychology in the School,* 1 (1964): 224–31; R. C. Bealer, F. K. Willits, and P. R. Maida, "The Rebellious Youth Subculture—A Myth," *Children,* 11 (1964): 43–48.

6. One contradictory finding has been reported. Freshmen girls at a midwestern university reported more conflict with parents during their high school years than did the boys studied—Graham C. Kinloch, "Parent-Youth Conflict at Home: An Investigation among University Freshmen," *American Journal of Orthopsychiatry,* 40 (1970): 658–64. This was a lower- and middle-class sample. Since a smaller percentage of girls attend college than boys, especially in these lower classes, those girls who attend may be the most achievement oriented, yet their families may not support autonomy in adolescent girls. Thus these girls may experience more conflict with their parents than is typical for girls.

7. Francis Ivan Nye, "Adolescents' Adjustment to Parents," *Microfilm Abstracts,* 10 (1950): 302.

8. Dale B. Harris and Sing Chu Tseng, "Children's Attitudes toward Peers and Parents as Revealed by Sentence Completions," *Child Development,* 28 (1957): 401–11.

9. Clay V. Brittain, "Adolescent Choices and Parent-Peer Cross-Pressures," *American Sociological Review,* 28 (1963): 385–91.

10. John V. Liccione, "The Changing Family Relationship of Adolescent Girls," *Journal of Abnormal and Social Psychology,* 51 (1955): 421–26.

11. David R. Matteson, "Changes in Attitudes toward Authority Figures in Selected College Freshmen" (Ph.D. diss., Boston University, 1968), and "Changes in Attitudes toward Authority Figures with the Move to College: Three Experiments," *Developmental Psychology,* 4 (1974): 34–47.

12. Bealer, Willits, and Maida, "Rebellious Youth Subculture."

13. Arnold M. Rose, "Reference Groups of Rural High School Youth," *Child Development,* 27 (1956): 351–63; Leonard A. Ostlund, "Environment-Personality Relationships," *Rural Sociology* 22 (1957): 31–39. Subjects for these studies came from Minnesota and Oklahoma, respectively.

14. S. R. Hathaway and E. D. Monachesi, *Adolescent Personality and Behavior* (Minneapolis: University of Minnesota Press, 1963).

15. A. O. Haller and Carole Ellis Wolff, "Personality Orientations of Farm, Village, and Urban Boys," *Rural Sociology,* 27 (1962): 275–93.

16. Harris and Tseng, "Children's Attitudes toward Peers and Parents."

17. Bealer, Willits, and Maida, "Rebellious Youth Subculture."

18. Bandura, "Stormy Decade."

19. Albert Bandura and Richard H. Walters, *Adolescent Aggression* (New York: Ronald Press Co., 1959), pp. 8–9.

20. Frederick Elkin and William A. Westley, "Myth of Adolescent Culture," *American Sociological Review,* 20 (1955): 680–84.

21. Ibid.

22. The importance of this distinction will be clarified later in this chapter and in Chapter 12.

23. Nye, "Adolescents' Adjustment to Parents."

24. Harris and Tseng, "Children's Attitudes toward Peers and Parents." Note that this study used a rural population, so less negative attitudes would be likely.

25.  A. Yahoda and T. Kuse, "The Psychological Study of Parent-Adolescent Relationships," *Bulletin of Faculty Education*, Nagaya University, 3 (1957): 100–127; Marcello Lostia, "*Atteggiamento dei Geovani nei Confronti della Autorita*" ["Attitudes of Adolescents when Confronted with Authority"]. *Rivista di Psicologia Sociale, e Archivio Italiano di Psicologia Generale, e Del Lavoro*, April–September 1966, pp. 217–64.

26.  The problems of cohort sampling are discussed in Harold Webster, "Some Quantitative Results," in *The American College: A Psychological and Social Interpretation of the Higher Learning*, ed. Nevitt Sanford (New York: John Wiley & Sons, 1962), pp. 822–23.

27.  Elias Tuma and Norman Livson, "Family Socioeconomic Status and Adolescent Attitudes to Authority," *Child Development*, 31 (1960): 387–99.

28.  Ibid., Figure 1, p. 391.

29.  Daniel Offer, M. Sabshin, and David Marcus, "Clinical Evaluation of Normal Adolescence," *American Journal of Psychiatry*, 121 (1965): 864–72.

30.  Daniel Offer, David Marcus, and Judith L. Offer, "A Longitudinal Study of Normal Adolescent Boys," *American Journal of Psychiatry*, 126 (1970): 917–24.

31.  Ibid.

32.  Davis, "Sociology of Parent-Youth Conflict"; Talcott Parsons, "Age and Sex in the Social Structure of the United States," in *Essays in Sociological Theory, Pure and Applied* (Glencoe, Ill.: Free Press, 1949); J. M. Yinger, "Contraculture and Subculture," *American Sociological Review*, 25 (1960): 625–35.

33.  Coleman, *Adolescent Society*. Note that the wording of the choices in the question was not parallel, which might have influenced the results. The item read, "Which one of these things would be hardest for you to take—your parents' disapproval, your teacher's disapproval, or breaking with your friend?" Some criticisms of this study are noted in Chapter 9.

34.  Charles E. Bowerman and John W. Kinch, "Changes in Family and Peer Orientations of Children between the Fourth and Tenth Grades," *Social Forces*, 37 (1959): 206–11.

35.  To measure identification, subjects were asked two questions: (1) which group, family or friends, understood them better, and (2) when they grew up, whether they would rather be the kind of persons their parents are or the kind they thought their friends would be. Regarding values, subjects were asked (1) whose ideas were most like theirs regarding right and wrong, things that were fun to do, the importance of school, and (2) what would they do if one group wanted to do something of which the other did not approve. Ibid., p. 206.

36.  Denise Kandel and Gerald S. Lesser, *Youth in Two Worlds: United States and Denmark* (San Francisco: Jossey-Bass, Publishers, 1972).

37.  There is some evidence that the peer group plays an earlier and more significant role in lower-class adolescence, both because of inadequate communication with parents—H. S. Maas, "Some Social Class Differences in the Family Systems and Group Relations of Pre- and Early Adolescents," *Child Development*, 22 (1951): 145–52—and as a support for rejection of unobtainable middle-class goals—H. Phelps and J. E. Horrocks, "Factors Influencing Informal Groups of Adolescents," *Child Development*, 29 (1958): 69–86. These results are in contrast to a study which found no relationship between an indicator of class status and the frequency and type of conflict—R. Connor, T. Johannes and J. Walters, "Parent-Adolescent Relationships: I. Parent-Adolescent Conflicts," *Journal of Home Economics*, 46 (154): 183–86. Also see E. V Kohrs, "The Disadvantaged and Lower Class Adolescent," in *Under-*

*standing Adolescence: Current Developments in Adolescent Psychology,* ed. James F. Adams (Boston: Allyn & Bacon, 1968), pp. 287–317.

38. Mollie S. Smart and Russell C. Smart, *Adolescents: Development and Relationships* (New York: Macmillan Publishing Co., 1973), p. 128, citing D. C. Epperson, "A Reassessment of Indices of Parental Influence in the Adolescent Society," *American Sociological Review,* 29 (1964): 93–96.

39. This pattern of avoidance is also common between parents and adolescents on the subject of sexual behavior. See Chapters 7 and 9, below.

40. H. H. Remmers and D. H. Radler, *The American Teenager* (Indianapolis: Bobbs-Merrill Co., 1962).

41. Elizabeth Douvan and Joseph Adelson, *The Adolescent Experience* (New York: John Wiley & Sons, 1966).

42. Survey Research Center, *A Study of Adolescent Boys* (Ann Arbor: University of Michigan Press, 1956). Note that these results contrast with Brittain's data, in which peers were found to have more influence than parents on some issues. The methodologies of the two studies are different.

43. Kandel and Lesser, *Youth in Two Worlds.*

44. Ibid., p. 13.

45. Ibid., pp. 111–12.

46. Ibid., p. 112.

47. Liccione, "Changing Family Relationship of Adolescent Girls."

48. Tuma and Livson, "Family Socioeconomic Status."

49. Matteson, "Attitudes toward Authority in College Freshmen," and "Changes in Attitudes with the Move to College." The data reported here have not previously been published. See Chapter 12 for a fuller description.

50. Test items were derived from Henry Clay Lindgren, and Robert Sallery, "Arab Attitudes toward Authority: A Cross-Cultural Study," *Journal of Social Psychology,* 69 (1966): 27–31.

51. Evidence that some experiences of turmoil in adolescence lead to greater sensitivity and maturity can be found in Chapters 8, 13, and 14.

# 7

## *The nature of the crises: To do it my way*

> Two roads diverged in a yellow wood,
> And sorry I could not travel both
> And be one traveler, long I stood
> And looked down one as far as I could
> To where it bent in the undergrowth;
>
> Then took the other, just as fair,
> And having perhaps the better claim,
> Because it was grassy and wanted wear;
> Though as for that the passing there
> Had worn them really about the same,
>
> And both that morning equally lay
> In leaves no step had trodden black.
> Oh, I kept the first for another day!
> Yet knowing how way leads on to way,
> I doubted if I should ever come back.
>
> I shall be telling this with a sigh
> Somewhere ages and ages hence;
> Two roads diverged in a wood, and I—
> I took the one less traveled by,
> And that has made all the difference.[1]

TODAY'S ADOLESCENT faces not two, but dozens of possibilities in choosing his way of life. In previous centuries, the "most traveled road" was to follow in the footsteps of one's parents, both vocationally and in lifestyle. Many of today's adolescents continue to make progress on the most traveled road. Though it is unlikely a contemporary adolescent boy can learn a trade as an apprentice to his father, many adolescents are able to accept with little question the expectations their parents have for them. But others are uncertain. They need to pause for awhile at the intersection to look down the roads. They search longingly, often impatiently, to determine where there is a path that will be their way.

Generally speaking, the adolescent period is not one of open rebellion against the parents. It is, however, a period of sorting out one's own way, a period of individuation.[2] In that sense, adolescence is a period of crisis: the crisis of choosing what kind of person one will become. Erik Erikson has made a major contribution to the theory of adolescence by making it clear that the central issue of adolescence is the search for identity.

The search for identity involves sorting, sifting, and blending the experiences of the past. According to Erikson, "Identity formation . . . begins where the usefulness of identification ends. It arises from the selective repudiation and mutual assimilation of childhood identifications, and their absorption in a new configuration."[3] Decision making always involves accepting and rejecting, or as Erikson puts it, assimilating and repudiating. Most adolescents accept a great deal of what they have learned from their parents. Some accept it too hastily and uncritically; that is, they do not really assimilate it as their own, perhaps because the risk of repudiating any of it is too great. Others, as we have said, experience uncertainty. For them, the identity crisis is a more conscious one. Even when the crisis is conscious and the conflicts are painfully real, it is seldom a tumultuous period. The process of choosing one's way is usually a very gradual one. For example, an adolescent rarely makes his vocational choice in the same weeks that he determines his stance on political values or reaches a new level of acceptance of his adult body.

The chapters to follow will examine specific areas and issues involved in identity formation: the body, sex and intimacy, vocation, values, and authority (Chapters 8 through 12). I will then consider some different styles of handling the identity crisis, including the older style of forging ahead on the most traveled road (early identity formation) and the newer style, a conscious and deliberate search for the path which is right for each individual (prolonged adolescence).

Obviously the order of presentation is somewhat arbitrary, and the issues, though seldom settled all at once, are intertwined. Involved throughout the process of identity formation are the various persons and groups that influence the adolescent most: parents and family, identification figures outside the family, nonparental authorities and the impersonal institutions of society, the peer group, and his closest friends. Generally speaking, these groups are not in direct conflict. The peer group, for the most part, affirms the values of the adult society, yet there are times when the youth must choose between them. The process of assimilation and repudiation occurs in relation to each of these influences upon his life.

This chapter will continue the discussion of the interaction between parents and adolescents. The peer group is discussed in more detail in Chapter 9; identification figures outside the home in Chapter 10; and nonparental authority in Chapter 12.

No doubt a single adolescent will handle repudiation differently in different circumstances, depending upon the agent attempting to influence him. When boys in a locker room seek to interest the high school boy in more heterosexual experience than he feels ready for, he may repudiate their influence by pretending he has already had such experiences. The deception is only partial, and it may be humorous. A few years later the same boy may feel ready for more sexual experience, when he is self-assured about his ability to handle it. If an impersonal authority such as a college dormitory rule is in conflict with his decision to seek sexual expression, he may simply ignore the rule, or possibly rebel against it.

Repudiation of impersonal authority seems more likely to be expressed in rebellion than does repudiation of parents. When a college student returns home, it is likely that, in subtle ways, the parents will get the cues that some areas of his college experience are not open for discussion. A case study from the longitudinal clinical study of normal boys in their second and third years after high school by Daniel Offer et al. illustrates this. After his move to college, Andy experienced a communication barrier between his parents and himself. "He had told his parents he was a radical student to 'keep them on their toes' but did not tell them he had smoked marihuana. 'I think they know, but neither of us says anything, so why rock the boat?'."[4] The repudiation of the parents' point of view is frequently handled, not by overt rebellion, but through a subtle conspiracy of silence.

## Getting away from parents

The psychoanalytic theory describes the rejection of the parents as an unconscious maneuver on the part of the adolescent in order to separate himself from the oedipal temptation. The move toward independence is understood in terms of this withdrawal of sexual interest from parents and reinvestment of desires in peers. The research reviewed in the preceding chapter gives little evidence for this type of oedipal rebellion.[5]

This is not to say that sexual experience plays no part in the adolescent's developing independence. However, it has to do with experiences outside the home, rather than with intrafamilial conflict. Though the American family is close, sexual topics are still generally taboo, and the area of sexual experience is frequently one of the first in which young people make decisions without informing their parents. No doubt experiences of rewarding sexual encounters, precisely because they did not entail parental involvement and advice, increase the adolescents' confidence in their own ability to handle problems and make decisions—a confidence which may then generalize beyond the area of sexuality.

The sort of repudiation which occurs as part of the process of establishing identity is not a primative and deeply unconscious phenomenon. Rather, the repudiation is selective. The usual pattern is that the adolescent avoids making an issue of it—unless, of course, the parents push it. Another case study from the Offer, Marcus, and Offer study is illustrative:

> Richard regarded himself as partially breaking away from his home and parents. When he was at [college], he was on his own. When he came home, his parents told him what time to be in, which friends he should see, and where he should or should not go. "I am tired of it so I just go out without specifying time or place. My parents pressure me, and I keep quiet. When I tell them that I was able to take care of myself for nine months, they say that while I live with them, things are different. So, then, I tell them any place that pops into my mind just to keep them quiet and happy."[6]

Though I know of no statistical data, I suspect that Andy's situation is more typical than Richard's; usually parents cooperate in the conspiracy of silence. Perhaps they recognize that the adolescent is not intending to reject them, but only wants to reach his own decisions. Even where the break from home is more difficult and where, as in Richard's case, the parents cannot seem to let go, it is striking how frequently the youth seeks to avoid conflict. Richard does not want to rebel, he only wants to be left alone to make his decisions.

It is not an uncommon tactic for adolescents to make some decisions without their parents' knowledge and wait until the decision is in effect before involving their parents, thus reassuring the adolescents that they did not need their parents' advice. A male college undergraduate (who prefers to remain anonymous) reports an instance of this type:

> While many of my friends seemed entirely capable of expressing new ideas and backing up their new-found philosophies with what

seemed at the time infallible arguments, I, on the other hand, found myself still expressing many opinions of my parents. . . . Because I felt this inadequacy around my friends to completely denounce all the views of my family background I made the decision to break away entirely. I began by seeing my "friendly Army recruiter" and telling no one what I was planning lest someone would try to talk me out of it.

Here the fear of being talked out of this line of action could be construed as a recognition on the part of myself that these fears of dependency on the family were not real. Or, on the other hand, if these fears were real then it wouldn't take much to talk me out of enlisting. At any rate, I waited until after enlistment was completed to inform my parents.

Although parents in such situations tend to feel slighted, such a reaction on the part of the adolescent is certainly more honest than asking for unwanted advice. The parents should try to understand that it was not that the youth could not discuss it beforehand, but that he needed to test himself to prove that it was not necessary for him to discuss it. It was a test of his own confidence, not a problem in the breakdown of communications.

The interpretation of adolescence as a search for identity points to an increasing individuation of the person at this stage. The adolescent becomes conscious of himself as a separate individual, and this becomes precious to him. Attempts to separate himself from his parents are not usually signs of a loss of esteem or love for the parents; they are simply manifestations that now he must choose for himself. The move away from dependence upon parents normally begins long before adolescence. If the "declaration of independence" becomes more articulated during the adolescent years, it is because of the increased consciousness the youth now has of his own private self.

## Independence training

It is questionable that adolescence today should be described as a special period of growth in independence. For most children today, the move toward independence is a gradual one and need not entail any sudden break from the parents such as may have been more common in the more authoritarian homes of Freud's time.

Parents of small children gradually shift their rewards from dependent to independent behaviors yet continue to satisfy the child's need for dependency. In the modern American home, children are encouraged, even pushed, toward self-sufficiency from the age of one on. The two-year-old is extremely proud of the areas in which "I can do it myself."

The increasing influence of peers (who reward independent behavior), as well as the direct reinforcement of attaining a goal directly without having to depend upon a somewhat unreliable mediator, generally ensures that the child will give up the advantages of dependency in exchange for greater autonomy.[7] In many aspects of life, American children are trained to be self-sufficient long before adolescence.

The development of independence and self-sufficiency appears to be related to the use of nonauthoritarian child-rearing approaches. The research problems in unraveling such connections are immense; many variables which might confound results are uncontrolled. Thus the results must be considered tentative. Nonetheless, studies have consistently shown that children of warm and permissive parents are more likely to be "active, outgoing, socially assertive, and independent."[8] Middle-class mothers tend to be more affectionate and less punitive than lower-class mothers and to use reasoning and praise more often.[9] Their children show less rigid compliance to authority; that is, they are more able to function independently.[10] Studies relating directly to the adolescent period have been conducted by Glen H. Elder, Jr., to examine the relationship between autocratic, democratic, and permissive parental practices and adolescent autonomy.[11] The parental practices were defined by Elder as follows:

> *Autocratic:* No allowance is provided for the youth to express his views on a subject nor for him to assert leadership or initiative in self government.
> *Democratic:* The adolescent contributes freely to discussion of issues relevant to his behavior, and may even make his own decisions; however, in all instances the final decision is either formulated by parents or meets with their approval.
> *Permissive:* The adolescent assumes a more active and influential position in formulating decisions which concern him than do his parents.[12]

The permissive category was broadened to include "laissez-faire" and "ignoring" parents—those who failed to become involved in adolescents' decisions. In addition to these different parental approaches, another variable was studied. Each of three groups of parents was further subdivided into those who frequently explained their rules of conduct and expectations and those who did not. Adolescent self-ratings were used to measure autonomy, defined as:

1. Confidence in one's own values, goals, and awareness of rules.
2. Independence—a desire to make up one's own mind, with or without listening to others' ideas.[13]

Adolescent ratings were also used to measure the parent variables, a serious limitation of this and many of the studies in the field. The results showed that adolescent autonomy was most likely to develop among the adolescents of those democratic and permissive parents who also frequently provided explanations. It seems fair to summarize the results of studies on the training of independence and autonomy by saying that these traits are encouraged when the parents are warm and involved but allow their children to explore and do things themselves, offering explanations when guidance is given.

Another study by Elder provides evidence that adolescents' involvement in family decisions has increased constantly throughout the present century. A representative sampling of American subjects was asked to recall how much influence they had had in family decisions when they were about 16 years old. Of the oldest (who were 16 before 1916), only 40 percent reported moderate involvement, while in the youngest sample (who were 16 between 1950 and 1957), 77 percent reported such involvement. The data suggest a steady historical trend toward increasing adolescent involvement in family decisions.[14] The study also found that the trend toward democratic child rearing is most pronounced in the working class; that is, more change is occurring there (probably because the working class is becoming more and more middle class in value orientation).

Receptivity toward these trends in family relations is associated with increased use of the mass communications media.[15] The media also may play an important role in keeping parents "up to date," thus diminishing the generation gap.[16] Earlier independence training, greater adolescent participation in decision making, and the effects of mass media may help to explain why the pattern of adolescent rebellion is diminishing.

Though the direction appears to be toward allowing adolescents greater participation in family decisions, it is doubtful that this trend has reached a level of training for responsibility in our culture that it has in some others. The Elder study which reports increasingly democratic parental practices gathered its data from adults reflecting backward on their adolescent years. A more recent study by Denise Kandel and Gerald Lesser questioned high school adolescents in America and compared them to a similar group of Danish adolescents.[17] The authors distinguished between interaction with mother and interaction with father in their report; unfortunately the responses of male and female adolescents were not separately reported. Comparisons of Danish and American adolescents' perceptions of parental authority and parents' explanations of decisions, considering interactions with mothers and fathers separately, are shown in Table 2. When both parents were considered, the predominant parental attitudes reported in Denmark utilized the joint democratic approach, with both parents applying democratic techniques; 41 percent of Danish families compared to 20 percent of American families reported using a joint democratic approach. The predominant American pattern reported was joint authoritarian—32 percent

**TABLE 2**
Perceptions of parental practices reported by Danish and American adolescents

|  | Interaction with mother | | Interaction with father | |
| --- | --- | --- | --- | --- |
|  | U.S.A. | Denmark | U.S.A. | Denmark |
| Parental authority: |  |  |  |  |
| Authoritarian . . . . . . . . . . . . . . | 43% | 15% | 53% | 31% |
| Democratic . . . . . . . . . . . . . . . | 40 | 61 | 29 | 48 |
| Permissive . . . . . . . . . . . . . . . . | 17 | 24 | 18 | 21 |
| Parental communication: |  |  |  |  |
| Parent "always" explains decisions. . . | 30 | 43 | 21 | 33 |

Source: Denise B. Kandel and Gerald S. Lesser, *Youth in Two Worlds: United States and Denmark* (San Francisco: Jossey-Bass Publishers, 1972), Table 11, p. 71.

of American families reported this approach, compared to 16 percent of Danish families. Consistent with their more authoritarian control, American parents were reported to insist on more rules than Danish parents.

Respondents were presented with a list of eight rules and asked to check which ones their parents applied to the teen-age children in their families. Many more rules were checked by American adolescents than by Danish adolescents; 55 percent of the Americans checked three or more rules, as compared to only 29 percent of the Danes.[18] The concreteness of these data increases confidence in their accuracy.

During the teen-age years, the Danish adolescents reported experiencing increasing independence, while this sample of American adolescents perceived their status as remaining stationary.[19] Danish adolescents appeared to have greater participation in decisions and felt freer of control than Americans. Even when American youth stated that they felt "free," half of them did not feel that they were treated as adults. A large percentage of the students in the study complained that their parents failed to give them full respect, trust, and status as persons.[20]

In the face of these data, caution is necessary about inferences regarding the prevalence of democratic child rearing. The differences between these data and those reported by Elder could best be settled by studies which actually observe parent-adolescent interaction, rather than relying solely on verbal reports. In light of the discussion of variables affecting independence training, it is noteworthy that the Danish parents, who reportedly use more democratic methods combined with more explanation, find less need for rules when their children reach adolescence. This suggests that Danish youth have learned enough responsible self-direction so they do not need rules.

Consideration of the experiments relating to growth in autonomy and self-direction will be followed by a look at the subjective side: It is one thing to study the experiments, and another to live through the experience.

## Dual ambivalence

The adolescent is aware that he must prepare to live in a different world from his parents, and he is both excited and apprehensive about this. His ambivalent feelings are compounded by the fact that the parents, too, are ambivalent. The adolescent wishes both to mature into interdependence in the larger world and to regress into the dependence and security of the family home. The parents are proud of his development and delighted that he will no longer be dependent upon them, but they also know that they will miss their child and have qualms about the kind of world he is entering. This state of mixed feelings on the part of both parents and child regarding the child's maturation has been termed "dual ambivalence." Growth ambivalence occurs around each developmental task; the child has an urge to venture forth and yet is tempted to regress to an earlier stage. Whether this task is going to school, managing one's own money, or moving toward heterosexual experience, the parent is also likely to have ambivalent feelings about it. And this is especially true of the move away from home. This dual ambivalence, this complexity of feelings on both sides, is part of what makes communication between generations difficult.[21]

At one moment the adolescent complains, "Why can't I do it; I'm old enough?" At the next he laments that his parents expect too much of him: "You want me to work all the time; I never have *any* fun.'" The parents are at one moment bragging about how mature their child is and at the next protective and fostering dependency. The same vacillation and ambivalence frequently hold in attitudes toward the larger world. The parents push the child to make vocational decisions and stress the freedoms of adulthood: "Someday you'll be big enough to do what you please." But when the adolescent rushes to explore the exciting world, the parents become conscious of its dangers and corruptions. Much of this confusion is because they genuinely care for their children, but frequently the parents themselves have not learned to care for the world. They are not sure the world is worth the risks. Naturally the adolescent picks up this message, and he, too, becomes unsure the adult world is worth it. His own identity is unstable enough; he is not sure he can risk losing it by committing himself to involvement in the world.

It is not necessary to be judgmental about the ambivalence parents feel. Parents of adolescents are generally middle-aged persons, and many of the issues the adolescent is facing as he enters adult life are also reemerging as issues for the parents as they assess their lives. Just as adolescents are self-conscious because of changes in their bodies, the middle-aged parents are aware that their bodies are losing their youthful forms. The parents may indeed envy the children in this regard: "The vigorous, healthy, attractive youngster can be an object of sexual interest to the parent, partly consciously, partly unconsciously."[22] This is particularly true because parents may look enviously at youth's greater sexual freedom and feel regrets at their own sexual demise. Likewise, as the middle-aged parents hear the adolescent accept and reject various vocational alternatives, they are bound to be conscious of the choices that are no longer available to them. If a father is not well on the way toward attaining the professional goals he longed for, he may have to face the fact that he is not going to accomplish what he once dreamed was possible. The parent must reassess his own values as he hears youth question and ridicule the goals of the prior generation. In short, the parents may experience an identity crisis of their own, while trying to cope with the confusion and uncertainties of their adolescent children.

The fact that the ambivalence is experienced by both generations can be a source of strength; it can aid communication and understanding. What frequently happens, however, is that the parents feel a duty to reestablish their earlier role as the "strong ones" who lead and direct the child. Consequently, fearing that they may add to the adolescent's confusion, they repress their own doubts and defend the adult world of their making. Much of the psychological literature tends to counsel parents in that direction, such as this advice: "An attitude that lacks firmness, both in individual adults and in the culture, fails to provide a definitive model for either identification or rebellion."[23] Often the firmness is premature and fails to respond to the ambiguities that the youth so clearly perceives. As one high school student expressed it: "The main thing adults do wrong is that they think things are either black or white, only positive or negative. No compromising. Having this attitude, just makes teens kind of 'burn' inside."[24]

This reaction pushes youth to take the other side: the result is polarization between generations. The communication gap, then, comes partly from the failure to admit the ambivalence within each of us—we project it outside ourselves, polarizing the positions and destroying the common ground upon which communication could be built.

This is not to deny the need for courage in spite of ambiguity, the courage to take a stand in one's life.[25] But in a fast-changing society, the parent provides a more useful model for identification if he can affirm that "this has been right for me" without trying to mold the next generation in his spittin' image. And conversely, when young people really sense the changing times, there should also be a sense of the relativity of history to aid them to recognize that, though the older generation's way is not right for them, this does not mean it was without integrity in its time. A recognition of the dual character of ambivalence might increase generosity on both sides of the generation gap.

## Getting away—physically

Among the things college undergraduates cite as helpful in the development of confidence in their own ability to handle problems and make decisions are their experiences in living away from home. Camp sessions or vacations with relatives prepare for the move away from home, not only by providing practice in dealing with dependency and homesickness but by giving the child a chance to make decisions without checking them out with Mom and Dad. These temporary sortees into the world do not involve the same kind of detachment from the emotional life of home that occurs later, but positive experiences of this sort reduce the crippling bondage to the family that occurs when the adolescent believes that his parents are the only people who can be close to him and satisfy his needs. It has been found, for example, that competent high school students who decide to go to college away from home prepare for this move by engaging in a series of adaptive anticipatory experiences, such as reading harder books, assigning themselves special papers, taking more difficult summer jobs, and (for boys) selecting their own clothes for the first time.[26]

Although the actual move away from home and the emotional separation do not always occur together, frequently there is a readiness for separation that allows students to choose a college far enough away so that they cannot commute, for example.[27] And when students return home following their freshman years, they often are aware that, emotionally, the campus has become their home. Though the late adolescent may not consciously think of his maturation after leaving home as a process of differentiating himself from his parents, he often discovers, once out of the home, that he does not want to do what he earlier felt compelled to do.[28] Thus he begins to experience what *he* really wants to do.

### Rites of passage

The confusion experienced by adolescents and adults about the move into the world is confounded by the fact that our society has little clarity about it. In many cultures, ceremonial rites of passage exist as a way of recognizing a change in relationships, status, or roles. We may look with some envy at societies in which rites of passage clearly proclaim that the boy is now a man, the girl an adult woman. In primitive societies, once the ceremony is over, the adolescent is "honored by new status and responsibilities," the parents or guardians relinquish authority, and all the responsibilities and privileges of adulthood are his.[29] Possibly at an earlier time the marriage ceremony served as a rite of passage in Western society, but it no longer serves that function; many youths (particularly college students) marry while they are still financially dependent upon their parents. Similarly, the move away from home is not a genuine rite of passage, since for a major portion of youth it occurs upon entering college, when the parents still maintain financial responsibility. Some anthropologists argue that our society would function more smoothly if we had a clear, recognized rite which proclaimed at some point in development "you are an adult."

It is wishful thinking to believe that a simple ceremony would rid us of the confusion of becoming an adult in our pluralistic society, however. Rites can function in simpler societies where the youths know exactly what is entailed in the adult roles they will assume. In these societies the adult roles are clearly defined, everybody knows exactly what is expected, and there is no question about what it means to be a man or woman. Usually, the son assumes the same roles he observed in his male elders, and girls become women exactly the same way their mothers did. Ceremonial assumption of roles is possible when the roles are unchanging, but it is no answer for a diversified and fast-changing society.[30]

The search for identity is the price we pay for opening up many possibilities to each child. In a pluralistic society, each youth must struggle to decide which of the many ways of being adult is to be his way. Rather than trying to reestablish some primitive certainty, we must rear our children to be able to tolerate confusion.

### You can't go home again

The courage to move into the world despite uncertainty comes with the realization that "you can't go home again." Both the longing to go home and the recognition that it is not possible in our society have been captured in Thomas Wolfe's novel of that name, in which George Webber, 29 years old, tries to return home. En route on the train, George meets some businessmen from his home town—a judge and some others who have been in New York and are now returning. They tell him of the changes that are occurring at home:

> "You ought to stay around a while, Webber. You wouldn't know the town. Things are booming down our way. That's the way it is all over town. Within a few years, Libya Hill is going to be the largest and most beautiful city in the state. You mark my words. . . ."

George returned to his seat feeling confused and bewildered. He was going back home for the first time in several years, and he wanted to see the town as he remembered it. Evidently he would find it considerably changed. . . . He couldn't make it out. It disturbed him vaguely, as one is always disturbed and shaken by the sudden realization of Time's changes in something that one has known all one's life.[31]

This type of experience is not new to our period of history, however. If we read the Adam and Eve story as a myth of man's development, we are intrigued by the symbol of the Angel. After Adam and Eve have eaten of the tree (that is, have matured sexually, have reached adolescence) they are banished from the garden (they must leave home). And the Angel stands forever at the gate with a flaming sword to make it absolutely clear that there is no going back. For today's young people the recognition that there is no going back means not only that they cannot regress to childhood, but also that their adulthood cannot be the adulthood of their parents.

### Research on the move away from home

Though college-age adolescents repeatedly testify to the import which the move from home has had on their identity quests, surprisingly little research has been done on the subject. This is partly due to the difficulty of following subjects through a geographical move. The move is of real importance in understanding the adolescent's developing view of the larger world and will be discussed in detail in Chapter 12. Two longitudinal studies have assessed the effects of the move on parent-adolescent relations. Both are impressionistic and based on a series of interviews.

The first study, conducted in the early 1960s by Elizabeth Murphy and Earle Silber, consisted of a series of interviews with 20 students, beginning with the senior year of high school and continuing through the freshman year of college. The purpose was to measure the capacity for autonomous behavior of the subjects and discern patterns of interaction between these students and their parents. The results suggest that some students had to decrease their involvements at home in order to become more independent; as they grew in autonomy their feelings of relatedness to their parents decreased. Other students, however, grew more autonomous, while maintaining or even increasing their feelings of closeness to the family.[32]

The second, more recent study is the longitudinal study of normal post-high-school boys by Offer, Marcus, and Offer, to which reference has already been made. Two cases illustrating repudiation were quoted earlier in this chapter, and the general conclusions of the study were summarized in Chapter 6. The majority of the boys studied felt their relationships with their parents were as good as or better than before they left home. A significant minority did express annoyance with their parents, particularly during the first two years after high school.

Not all of these subjects had left home. For those who had done so, the problems often centered around increased autonomy while away which was not respected when the youth returned home, judging from the few cases reported.[33]

Related evidence comes from a pencil-and-paper study comparing personality test responses of ninth-graders to responses on the same test during their freshman year of college. The results indicate that males may experience more family strain as college freshmen than they did four years earlier, though this was not the case for females.[34]

It is difficult to summarize this scant and impressionistic data encompassing the move from home. Clearly there are different styles of handling autonomy. Apparently rebellion is rare, but increased autonomy may be guarded through silence or other maneuvers when the parental view has been repudiated. And apparently sex differences are important (though, unfortunately, few of the studies have systematically observed them).

## Sex differences in the development of autonomy and identity formation

Two of the variables relating to independence training appear to be sex-typed in our culture. Parents tend to give more warmth and affection to girls but allow greater freedom to explore and do things to boys. For girls the result often is overdependency. More adolescent girls than boys exhibit strong dependency; further, dependent adolescent girls tend to remain dependent on their families into adulthood.[35] One study found that dependent women "consulted with their mothers before making major purchases, preferred to live close to the family, and felt strong need to keep a close tie to their family."[36]

Research on the process of identity formation is just beginning. Anne Constantinople developed preliminary scales in an attempt to measure the resolution of the developmental crises formulated by Erik Erikson.[37] Erikson's fourth, fifth, and sixth developmental stages[38] are of most interest here:

| Stage | Crisis | Period of life |
|-------|--------|----------------|
| 4 | Industry v. Inferiority | School years |
| 5 | Identity v. Identity diffusion | Adolescence |
| 6 | Intimacy v. Isolation | Early adulthood |

Each crisis is described by Erikson in terms of successful and unsuccessful resolution. The scales used in Constantinople's studies consisted of five items for each successful and unsuccessful resolution.[39] The subjects were asked to indicate the degree to which each item was characteristic or uncharacteristic of them. Examples of an item from each possible resolution help explain the meaning of Erikson's terms:

1. *Industry:* (I am) serious, have high standards.
   *Inferiority:* (I am) ineffective, don't amount to much.
2. *Identity:* (I) know who I am and what I want out of life.
   *Identity diffusion:* (I) never know how I feel.
3. *Intimacy:* (I am) candid, not afraid to expose myself.
   *Isolation:* (I am) very lonely.

Constantinople conducted a cross-sectional study, administering the scales to almost 1,000 college students and comparing students in different years of college. (The difficulties of inferring developmental change from cohort groups were discussed above, p. 96.) She followed up the study by collecting the same data again each year throughout the period the students remained in college, thus obtaining longitudinal data as well.

A factor analysis of the cross-sectional data indicated that the identity factor was clearer in males than in females. Results from the longitudinal study also indicated sex differences: Although both sexes showed increases in identity formation, females did not show a consistent decrease in the opposite scale which measured identity diffusion. The girls increased on the intimacy scale but also increased on the opposite scale concerning isolation. Boys showed more identity diffusion than girls when they began college. Girls appeared more mature than boys when they first came to college but showed an increase in diffusion during the college years.

The preliminary character of the personality scale makes it difficult to interpret these results. However, these data are supplemented by a large series of studies by James Marcia which use a different approach to operationalizing Erikson's identity theory. Marcia's studies, which focus upon different styles of moving through the identity process, use structured interviews to determine identity statuses. In a work in progress, he reports his conclusions regarding sex differences. Independence and the increasing differentiation of personality appear to be central issues in male identity and are supported in the college environment, but these qualities do not seem to be supported for college females. Instead, females are allowed to remain more dependent, and early identity commitments rather than personality differentiation seem to be encouraged.[40]

Only one American study of identity statuses has drawn males and females from the same population and analyzed the data for sex differences. This study measured variables relating to the way partners are perceived in a laboratory game situation and does not relate to the present discussion.[41] My own study of identity statuses, which was conducted on a population of Danish youth of about 18 years of age,[42] included a personality test measurement of autonomy. When the four identity status groups were placed in an inferred developmental sequence, the male subjects showed a progressive increase in autonomy, moving up the developmental scale. The study was not a longitudinal one, but these results clearly fit the pattern of increased autonomy as males progress toward identity formation. The Danish women in the study showed no significant differences between identity status groups on the measurement of autonomy. This was the most striking sex difference found in the study. Since Danish society emphasizes sex roles far less than our own, it seems likely that the same sex differences would be found in an American sample of youth perhaps even to a greater degree. The study deserves replication in America.

A tentative summary and interpretation of the findings on sex differences in identity formation indicates that the identity process in boys continues to reflect the cultural expectation of greater independence in males. Male college youths are encouraged during the college years to develop increasingly autonomous, highly differentiated personalities. Girls, in contrast, enter college looking more mature, due to their greater acceptance of adult authority and their stronger identification with their sex role.[43] Intimacy is a more important concern to them than to their male peers, but the competitive college environment does not necessarily reward intimacy. Thus we find evidence of both growth in intimacy and increasing isolation in the girls' scores in Constantinople's study. The college woman is caught between the traditional feminine role in which her identity centers around love and intimacy, and the alternative of a career which involves trying to integrate her achievement aspirations into a less traditional feminine role. Consequently her identity, relatively firm and mature when she enters college, shows a mixture of growth and increasing diffusion.

The above summary must be considered a series of propositions in need of further research validation. Research of sex differences in identity formation is scant and leaves much to be desired in the way of methodology. Fortunately, consideration of specific content areas in the chapters to come will make the picture somewhat clearer.

## Summary

In closing this chapter it is important to contrast the theory of adolescence presented here to the traditional view. Traditionally it has been held that adolescence is a period of crisis which reaches its peak in early adolescence, focusing on emerging sexuality and the struggle for independence and taking the form of rebellion against the parents. The viewpoint I am presenting here is that adolescence is a period of choices, a time for making important life decisions. Personal and social conflict reaches its peak in late adolescence, focusing on value issues which result from the adolescent's confrontation with society. The real crisis of adolescence, I believe, is not rebellion but the problem of affirming one's unique identity in relation to society. It is accurate to describe adolescence as a period of personal crisis: At no other time in an individual's life does one's view of one's self change and develop so rapidly. Further, it is accurate to describe adolescence, especially late adolescence, as a period of social crisis: At no other time does the individual make so many decisions affecting the remainder of his life in the world.

Adolescence can best be understood as the period of the move into the world. Normally the physical move into the world outside the home is made during late adolescence. It is late adolescence, then, that is usually the time of greatest crisis. Family identifications have already been well internalized. The process of assimilation and repudiation, necessary to the adolescent's finding his own way, occurs in relation to all influences upon personality, not just the family. Usually the repudiation that occurs in relation to parents is limited to specific issues and does not involve globalized rebellion or a loss of affection. The crisis is not primarily intrafamilial, but personal and social. The basic conflict is between one's view of one's self and the expectations of others in the world outside the home. The adolescent stands at the intersection. Eventually he must move forward into the world. Hopefully he can do it in an integrated way.

## Notes

1. Robert Frost, "The Road Not Taken," from *The Poetry of Robert Frost*, edited by Edward Connery Latham, Copyright 1916, © 1969 by Holt, Rinehart, and Winston, Inc. Copyright 1944 by Robert Frost. Reprinted by permission of Holt, Rinehart and Winston, Inc.

2. Peter Blos, "The Second Individuation Process of Adolescence," *Psychoanalytic Study of the Child*, 22 (1967): 162–87.

3. Erik Erikson, *Identity and the Life Cycle* (New York: International Universities Press, 1959), p. 113.

4. Daniel Offer, David Marcus, and Judith L. Offer, "A Longitudinal Study of Normal Adolescent Boys," *American Journal of Psychiatry*, 126 (1970): 917–24. Copyright 1970, the American Psychiatric Association.

5. A portion of this theory may hold for a small group of adolescents. Our child-rearing patterns tend to emphasize a close nuclear family in which all early needs are met. As family size has decreased, *some* families have become emotionally inbred, with the family "warmth" serving as an overprotectiveness against the outside world. If such a family fails to encourage the movement of the child toward peers, or at least toward others outside the family, then when sexual feelings do develop, they are forced to arise in the home and cause family conflict. One need not consider

it a "reemergence of oedipal conflicts" to understand that this new need will seek gratification from the same sources that have satisfied most prior needs.

6. Offer, Marcus, and Offer, "Longitudinal Study of Normal Adolescent Boys."

7. For a more complete account of the techniques of developing self-sufficiency in children, see Boyd R. McCandless, "The Socialization Process," in *Children: Behavior and Development*, 2d ed. (New York: Holt, Rinehart & Winston, 1967), chap. 10.

8. P. H. Mussen, John J. Conger, and Jerome Kagan, *Child Development and Personality*, 3rd ed. (New York: Harper & Row, Publishers, 1969), pp. 485–96.

9. Ibid.

10. L. Dolger and J. Ginandes, "Children's Attitudes toward Discipline as Related to Socio-Economic Status," *Journal of Experimental Education*, 15 (1946): 161–65. For a critical review, see Wesley C. Becker, "Consequences of Different Kinds of Parental Discipline," in *Review of Child Development Research*, ed. Martin L. Hoffman and Lois W. Hoffman (New York: Russell Sage Foundation, 1964), vol. 1, pp. 169–208.

11. Glen H. Elder, Jr., "Parental Power Legitimation and Its Effect on the Adolescent," *Sociometry*, 26 (1963): 50–65. Reviewed in Mussen, Conger, and Kagan, *Child Development and Personality*.

12. Mussen, Conger, and Kagan, *Child Development and Personality*, p. 627.

13. Ibid., p. 630.

14. Glen H. Elder, Jr., "Democratic Parent-Youth Relations in Cross-National Perspective," *Social Science Quarterly*, 49 (1968): 216–28.

15. Ibid., p. 220.

16. Bengt-Erik Andersson, of Göteborg University, Sweden, made this point in a discussion at a conference sponsored by Project for Youth Research, Copenhagen, October 1973.

17. Denise B. Kandel and Gerald S. Lesser, *Youth in Two Worlds: United States and Denmark* (San Francisco: Jossey-Bass Publishers, 1972). The population used in this study is described in Chapter 6 above.

18. Ibid., p. 70.

19. Ibid. Also see Denise Kandel and Gerald Lesser, "Parent-Adolescent Relationships and Adolescent Independence in the U.S. and Denmark," *Journal of Marriage and the Family*, 31 (1962): 348–58.

20. See Elizabeth Herzog and Cecelia E. Sudia, "The Generation Gap in the Eyes of Youth," *Children*, 17 (1970): 53–58.

21. See Lawrence Stone and Joseph Church, *Childhood and Adolescence*, 2d ed. (New York: Random House, 1968), pp. 204 and 446, for a discussion of "dual ambivalence." See also Group for the Advancement of Psychiatry, eds., *Normal Adolescence* (New York: Charles Scribner & Sons, 1968), section on "Dynamics of Adult Responses to Adolescents."

22. Group for Advancement of Psychiatry, *Normal Adolescence*, pp. 98–99.

23. Ibid., p. 96.

24. Herzog and Sudia, "The Generation Gap."

25. The late theologian Paul Tillich elucidated the relationship of ambiguity and courage as a major theme in his writings. See, for example, *The Courage to Be* (New Haven, Conn.: Yale University Press, 1952), p. 27.

26. Earle Silber et al., "Adaptive Behavior in Competent Adolescents: Coping with the Anticipation of College," *Archives of General Psychiatry*, 5 (1961):354–65.

27. Even before coming to college, students who choose to live on campus differ from those who will remain at home, on personality variables related to attitudes toward authority. See review in Chapter 12 below of David R. Matteson, "Changes in Attitudes toward Authority Figures with the Move to College: Three Experiments," *Developmental Psychology*, 10 (1974): 340–347.

28. See Joseph Katz, *No Time for Youth* (San Francisco: Jossey-Bass Publisher, 1968), p. 154–55.

29. Ernest R. Hilgard and Richard C. Atkinson, *Introduction to Psychology*, 4th ed. (New York: Harcourt, Brace & World, 1967), p. 91.

30. For a discussion of events in our society similar to rites of passage, see Rolf E. Muuss, "Puberty Rites in Primitive and Modern Societies," *Adolescence*, 5 (1970): 109–28.

31. Thomas Wolfe, *You Can't Go Home Again* (New York: Dell Publishing Co., 1963), pp. 66, 68–69. Originally published, 1934, by Harper and Row Publishers.

32. Elizabeth B. Murphey and Earle Silber, "Development of Autonomy in Parent-Child Interaction in Late Adolescence," *American Journal of Orthopsychiatry*, 33 (1963): 643.

33. Offer, Marcus, and Offer, "Longitudinal Study of Normal Adolescent Boys."

34. O. E. Thompson, "Student Values in Transition," *California Journal of Educational Research*, 19 (1968): 77–86.

35. Becker, "Different Kinds of Parental Discipline," p. 201; Urie Bronfenbrenner, "Toward a Theoretical Model for the Analysis of Parent-Child Relationships in a Social Context," in *Parental Attitudes and Child Behavior*, ed. J. C. Glidewell (Springfield, Ill.: Charles C Thomas, 1961); Mussen, Conger, and Kagan, *Child Development and Personality*, p. 634.

36. Mussen, Conger, and Kagan, *Child Development and Personality*, pp. 634–35, citing a study by Jerome Kagan and H. A. Moss, "The Stability of Passive and Dependent Behavior from Childhood through Adulthood," *Child Development*, 31 (1960): 577–91.

37. Anne Constantinople, "An Eriksonian Measure of Personality Development in College Students," *Developmental Psychology*, 1 (1969): 357–72.

38. Erik H. Erikson, *Identity: Youth and Crisis* (New York: W. W. Norton & Company, Inc., 1968).

39. Items were taken from a Q-sort test: A. E. Wessman and D. F. Ricks, *Mood and Personality* (New York: Holt, Rinehart & Winston, 1966).

40. Marcia's studies are reviewed in detail in Chapter 14, which also points out the limitations of these studies.

41. Marvin H. Podd, James Marcia, and Barry M. Rubin, "The Effects of Ego Identity Status and Partner Perception on a Prisoner's Dilemma Game," *Journal of Social Psychology*, 82 (1970): 117–26.

42. David R. Matteson, "Alienation vs. Exploration and Commitment: Personality and Family Correlaries of Adolescent Identity Statuses," Report from the Project for Youth Research (Copenhagen: Ungdomsforskning, 1974).

43. See Chapters 4, 6, and 12.

# 8

•

# CRISIS ONE
## *The body: I got life!*

Physiological changes
Effects of physical changes
    Awkwardness
    Peer standards and stereotypes
    Self-consciousness about appearance
Early and late maturation
Facing finitude
Affirmation of physical identity
Summary

## *Physiological changes*

ADOLESCENCE, as it is usually described, begins when the genital organs attain maturity and the person is capable of procreation. Other bodily changes also occur about this time, probably due to the same endocrine changes that precipitate sexual maturation. The growth spurt, the changes in body build, and the development of secondary sex characteristics are the most noticeable of these changes and have the greatest social implications for the adolescent.

The common observation that girls mature earlier than boys is based on their more visible changes in height and weight. For girls, the peak rate of growth occurs at about 10.9 years of age, with the growth spurt lasting from about age 10 through 12.5. The peak rate for the average boy does not occur until he is more than two years older than the girl, about age 13.2; the average boy's growth spurt begins when he is about 12 and lasts until 14.5.[1] There is a wide range of ages in which these changes can occur; an individual may undergo the physical changes much earlier or later than is statistically normal, without being abnormal medically. However, being out of step with one's age-mates does frequently have psychological consequences in our society, as will be noted later.

For girls, the growth spurt is well underway before menarche occurs to clearly signal the girl's entrance into physical adulthood. The average American girl has her first period at about 12.6 years of age;[2] 97 percent have first menstruation between 10.5 and 14.5. Yet girls may reach menarche as early as their ninth or as late as their 16th year of life without there being any physiological abnormalities.[3]

If there is a physical occurrence that has equivalent psychological import for the boy, it is probably first ejaculation, which usually occurs when the boy is 12 or 13 (though studies vary considerably in the mean ages reported).[4] Since it is difficult to trust memories and verbal reports of first ejaculation, a more objective research criterion is needed to establish early or late maturation. Most commonly, observations of the developmental stage of pubic hair are made in the context of a physical examination. Sparse, slightly pigmented hair usually begins to appear in the genital area at about age 12, becoming dark and coarse a year or so later.[5] A large variation occurs among healthy boys; first ejaculation occurring as early as 9 years or as late as 15 years is still within the normal age range.[6] It is likely that most boys have experienced first ejaculation before the growth spurt has reached its peak. Thus boys may begin to deal with new sexual feelings prior to experiencing changes in their body as a whole, while girls must deal first with a new body image.

During the growth spurt, adolescents, both boys and girls, must cope with the fastest changes that their bodies have undergone since the first year of life. Not only is the body growing faster, it is changing in its general proportions. For girls there is a broadening of the hip area, an enlargement of the breasts, and the addition of fatty tissue which results in a more rounded figure. For boys, an increase in musculature occurs, with a proportionate reduction of fatty tissue and a broadening of the shoulders and chest. The result is a more angular physique. An increase in pubic and axillary hair occurs in both sexes, of course. For boys, the appearance of a beard is of special import as visible evidence of male maturation.

In addition to the increase in growth and emergence of secondary sex characteristics, adolescence brings the maturation of the reproductive organs and the new experience of sexual excitement. The psychological aspects of sexual maturation are discussed in the next chapter. This chapter deals with the effects of the pubescent changes on the adolescent's image of his or her own body. The material presented focuses upon adolescent identity and little attention is given to physical fitness, but its importance should not be minimized. It is well established that psychological well-being is generally enhanced by physical fitness.[7]

## Effects of physical changes

### Awkwardness

It is widely believed that the growth spurt results in adolescent awkwardness, at least for many adolescent boys. However, tests of motor coordination and basic athletic performance do not support this view. Most longitudinal studies show that boys improve on all measures of motor performance throughout adolescence. Girls improve on some measures and decrease or show little change on others. One study of boys reported the usual overall increase in performance during adolescence but showed a leveling-off period beginning immediately after pubescence and lasting one or two years. During that period skills continued to improve, but at a slower pace. Later in adolescence the improvement in performance was accelerated.[8]

Unfortunately, the data in these studies were presented in terms of chronological age, so the effects of pubescence are blurred by differences in age at the onset of these phases. It would be valuable if future studies would use physiological age in the grouping of data. If changes in motor skills are found, they could be directly associated with stages of biological maturation, and a clearer picture of the effects of physical development on motor skills might emerge.

The impression of adolescent awkwardness has been explained in several ways. Perhaps a minority of adolescents are conspicuously awkward. Group data would not show these individual, but dramatic, exceptions, but informal observers would notice them and possibly overgeneralize from them. Another explanation is that adolescents, after their growth spurt, may look awkward because others confuse their adult size with older age, termed size-age confusion. That is, the adolescent may look like a man but may not yet have developed adult coordination.[9] This explanation seems unlikely, both because most adult men are actually less coordinated than adolescents, at least in terms of athletic skills, and because adolescent roles and dress in our society make such age confusion unlikely.

A more likely explanation is that the motor skill tests fail to show the kinds of awkwardness that occur in strained social situations. Indecision and lack of confidence, rather than neuromuscular inability, may result in jerky or clumsy movements. These would not be as likely to occur in the performance of specific motor skills in the all-male (or all-female) setting of a motor coordination test. Both the setting and tasks of these tests may be inappropriate to answer the question of adolescent awkwardness. The fact that different parts of the body grow at different rates ("asynchrony of growth")[10] might affect coordination in tense social settings. Boys' feet tend to grow long before full height is reached, which conceivably could be the reason adolescent boys trip over their feet more often than younger boys or adult men do.[11] The fact that some parts of the body may grow faster than others can result in conspicuous disproportions for some adolescents in phases of their growth. Common instances are short-waistedness due to the legs growing faster than the trunk, a bottom-heavy look when the hips develop faster than the shoulders, and odd facial features when the nose increases in size before the jawbone catches up.[12] These disproportions may be painfully embarrassing, but they seldom last.

Certainly the area of adolescent awkwardness deserves further empirical study. Whether or not psychologists succeed in measuring awkwardness, adolescents feel awkward and self-conscious about their bodies. Rapid bodily change (during periods of rapid growth or in illness) leads to self-consciousness about the body. One's sense of self, is closely associated with one's body.[13] In a real sense, when one's body changes, one is not one's self anymore. Further, the body provides a reference point from which one learns one's sense of external space.[14] An adolescent remarked after experiencing several inches of growth in one summer, "Even the ground has changed—it's moved so far away from me!"

## Peer standards and stereotypes

The self-consciousness produced by the adolescent's own changing body is accentuated by comparison with peers. Though the individual variations may be perfectly normal from a medical or psychological viewpoint, parents and teachers may unwittingly make comparisons or allow statistics to produce a "tyranny of the norm" that increases the adolescent's self-consciousness. And in the age-graded, competitive school system, the adolescents can scarcely avoid making comparisons themselves. For example, girls in the seventh grade are likely to be taller and heavier than their male peers of the same age; since the boys and girls of the same age are in the classroom together much of the day, they are sure to notice the differences.

Often the peer group amplifies the physical concerns of its members to the point that physical attractiveness appears to be the "chief criterion of social acceptability in adolescence."[15] In a study of the personality characteristics of socially accepted, neglected, and rejected students in junior high schools, the trait of accepted girls most frequently mentioned by peers was "good-looking." "Tidy" was the next most frequently mentioned. For popular boys the trait of "active in games" was the most frequently mentioned, with "good-looking" sharing second place with "tidy" and "likable."[16]

At the high school level, another study revealed that boys possessing superior strength, physique, and physical fitness tended to have social prestige, popularity, and satisfactory personal adjustment, while boys with low physical strength, while not disliked by classmates, tended to be ignored. They were more shy and retiring and had poor scores on personal adjustment inventories, both during and after adolescence.[17]

Another study compared students in 5th and 11th grades on factors influencing popularity.[18] Academic performance was not an important contributor to popularity at either grade level, while physical attractiveness and perceived similarity of attitudes were positively correlated with popularity at both grade levels. A statistical technique for determining the relative influence of each variable, called the percentage of variance, was calculated. For fifth-graders, physical attractiveness proved far more important than perceived similarity of attitudes for boys' attraction to girls and to other boys. For girls, physical attractiveness was important in their attraction to the opposite sex, but not in their relationship to other girls. The picture was different for the older sample, the 11th-graders. At that stage the belief that the other person held similar attitudes was far more important in girls' selections of friends than physical attractiveness. The same was true for boys' selections of other boys. Physical attractiveness was more important than perceived attitude similarity only in the case of boys' choices of girls.[19] This would seem to suggest a decline in the importance of physical attractiveness during the adolescent years, except in the boy-choosing-girl situation. However, a study using college students shows no indication of such a decline.

The importance of physical attractiveness at the college level was demonstrated by an ingenious study of college freshmen who participated in a "computer matched" blind-date dance during orientation week.[20] While they were filling out applications for dates, the students were rated on physical attractiveness by two male and two female observers. During the dance intermission the freshmen were briefly interviewed regarding their desire to date their partners again and on related variables. Four to six months later a follow-up was done to determine how frequently the couples had actually dated or one had asked the other for a date. Test data, also obtained during orientation week, included the Minnesota Multiphasic Personality Inventory, the Minnesota Counseling Inventory, Berger's Scale of Self-Acceptance, and a number of measures of intellectual and academic achievement. The experimenters had hypothesized that freshmen would seek partners near their own level of attractiveness and with similar personality traits. Instead, it was found that the subject's own attractiveness played no role in how he viewed his partner. The only significant determinant of how much the partner was liked, was desired as a future date, and was actually asked out was his or her physical attractiveness. The authors warn against generalizing from this large-group "display" situation. Yet it is striking that physical attractiveness, rated on a few seconds of observation, was more valuable in predicting adolescent behavior in this circumstance than any of the tests used.

Rather than emphasing the value of individual differences, adolescent peer groups (and much of the larger society) tend to encourage stereotyping; there is a fairly consistent view of the "ideal" body image for each sex. The communications media contribute to the adolescent's stress by "overemphasizing unrealistic standards, glorifying the ideal body, and degrading the deviant."[21]

William H. Sheldon delineated three body types,[22] which have been described as:

> mesomorph, in which strong muscles and bones predominate, with large head, broad shoulders and chest, and minimal fat; endomorph, who has a round head, large abdomen, weakly muscled arms and legs with much fat, but slender wrists and ankles, much subcutaneous fat; ectomorph, possessing a thin, narrow face and body, spindly arms and legs. . . .[23]

In an experimental test of body stereotyping, three groups of male subjects, preadolescent, adolescent and late adolescent were asked to view a series of pictures of men fitting Sheldon's body types. The subjects scored each picture on 15 personality traits. The mesomorphic body type was associated with socially positive personality traits by all three age groups. In fact, the only negative trait more frequently associated with mesomorphs was "puts his own interests before others." Endomorph and ectomorph pictures were frequently associated with negative personality items, with many of the negative traits being associated with both of these body types.[24]

This result is consistent with findings of earlier studies which used college students as subjects. In the next two studies to be reported, the three major body types described above were further subdivided into "balanced" and "extreme" categories. For example, "the balanced mesomorph was characterized as well built with well-distributed muscles, while the extreme mesomorph was the muscle-bound type. The balanced endomorph was stout, and the extreme endomorph was unusually so."[25] The earliest study of this type compared male students in a Negro university and in a mostly white university. The two samples did not differ significantly in their responses. Both groups more often attributed negative traits to the extreme ectomorphs and endomorphs, including phrases like "unpopular" and "doesn't have many friends." The two mesomorph types fared best, frequently being described as "popular."[26]

Another study used the balanced and extreme subdivisions of the male body types and compared the responses of males and females. Females rated the balanced mesomorphic type as the most attractive. Males were more inclined to prefer the extreme mesomorph, the muscleman, than the females were.[27] As other studies have shown, the extremely tough aspects of masculinity are more valued by males themselves than by females.[28]

Fewer data are available concerning stereotypes of the ideal female body. A common ideal for femininity appears to be a small, dainty body. A study similar to the ones cited for male body types asked several hundred high school students to rate silhouette pictures of different body types for both sexes. The mesomorphic body type was regarded as ideal for boys, but the more ectomorphic silhouettes were overwhelmingly considered to be ideal for girls.[29]

### Self-consciousness about appearance

The adolescent's self-consciousness about his body and his looks is perhaps most easily observable in his concern about his clothing. One study showed that "if he does not feel properly dressed . . . the adolescent feels inadequate."[30] There is no reason to assume that the present popularity of denims and casual clothes indicates any decrease in the importance of the clothes to the adolescent. The fact established in Chapter 6 that peer conformity first surpasses conformity to parents in the area of clothes and grooming supports the view that the body is the first focus of the adolescent identity struggle.

As the adolescent compares his own body to his image of the ideal body, he is likely to be highly self-critical and to wish for something different from what he sees when he looks into a mirror. Physical appearance was shown to be a major factor in a study of the concern of 580 adolescents with physique by Alexander Frazier and Lorenzo Lisonbee. Complexion problems were the most frequent cause of worry; acne and other facial blemishes were reported as present by 57 percent of tenth-graders of each sex. Other concerns regarding facial appearance included oily skin, irregular teeth, and glasses. Girls were apt to be concerned that their noses were too big, their skin was too dry, or they were just too homely. Facial characteristics of some type concerned over 50 percent of the boys and 82 percent of the girls.[31]

Evidence of the degree of concern adolescents experience regarding their bodies comes from the following observation made during a longitudinal study: "One-third of all boys and one-half of all girls became sufficiently concerned about at least one aspect of their growth at some point that they *spontaneously* express[ed] their concern to the physician investigator."[32] The fact that girls express greater concern about their bodies than boys may reflect a greater focus upon the body in our culture's definition of female identity. Or it may simply be that girls can more openly admit their difficulties and concerns than boys can.[33] Some evidence for the first interpretation comes from studies in which it was found that the correlations between body concept and general self-concept are higher for women than for men, though the correlations in the studies were high for both sexes.[34]

While girls expressed the greatest concern about complexion problems and hair, in the Frazier and Lisonbee study, boys emphasized stature and strength as the areas of greatest dissatisfaction. In view of the ideal male body type's description as the large, strong mesomorph, it is not surprising that boys dissatisfied with their own bodies wish they were larger and stronger.[35] For a boy, to be taller may not only satisfy his image of masculinity, it may have social advantages. It has been found that if a group of adolescents who do not know one another is asked to select a leader, it tends to choose a large boy.[36] Thus, Frazier and Lisonbee found that short boys may be concerned about their height, but tall boys are unlikely to be dissatisfied. Along the same line, boys frequently wish to put on weight, which they associate with heavier muscles and bones.[37] Boys show seven times as much concern about being too thin as about being heavy. One third of tenth-grade boys in the Frazier and Lisonbee study considered their upper arms "thin"; 30 percent stated they had thin forearms, and 27 percent, thin chests. Boys also were found to be more likely to think of themselves as slow in development (which is true, of course, if they compare themselves to girls).

It seems probable that self-esteem for males is affected not only by physique but by the rate of maturation of the genitals and the secondary sex characteristics. Comparisons in the boys' locker room are common, but scientific data are scarce and clinical and anecdotal accounts must be relied on. The visibility of the male genitalia invites comparisons between boys as to size and development. As is usual in our culture, high value is placed on largeness and speed of development. It is common to believe that the size of the genitals is directly related to virility and potency. Clinical evidence reveals that many men, even of college age, continue to be disturbed that their genitals are "too small."[38] Women sometimes express a parallel anxiety about the size of their breasts.

Girls' concerns with stature and body proportions, like boys', reflects the stereotypic ideal for their sex. Since the ideal is different for girls, their concerns are different. Among boys it is the shortest who express the highest level of concern. But since girls usually wish to be petite, it is the tall girls who express concern.[39] In the same line, girls are more concerned about being overweight than underweight. They often confuse being above the average in weight-for-height with being obese; thus girls who are actually below average in body fatness but have large frames and builds often go on diets which are uncalled for and potentially dangerous.[40] Girls who actually are obese may believe the stereotype that fat girls lack willpower. One study, which compared obese girls to nonobese girls, found that the obese girls said that they ate more than the average-weight girls, when in actual fact they were characterized by an extremely low level of physical activity but not

an abnormally high food intake.[41] It is indicative of girls' self-consciousness about weight that they frequently underreport their weights, while
boys do not.[42]

The degree of concern which adolescent girls experience in regard
to their own bodies is evidenced by an analysis of retrospective essays
written by 20-year-old women.[43] Asked which aspects of development
caused them the most anxiety, they most frequently mentioned being
too tall or too heavy. One reviewer of this study concluded:

> The rapid physical changes of adolescence produce a rapid change
> in body image, and typically lead to a rejection of the physical self
> as well. It is rare that an adolescent is accepting of his physical self.
> Something is always wrong; height, weight, degree of physical maturity,
> pimples, hair, or a multitude of other possible subjective defects become
> central concerns and lead frequently to self-rejection.[44]

Physical development is so important to the adolescent's view of himself
that one can predict more about an adolescent's self-concept from objective ratings of physical development than from chronological age.[45]

Certainly there can be no doubt that concerns of body image weigh
heavy on the adolescent's mind. Not all the concerns are realistic ones,
but peer pressure and the desire to be "normal" are very strong. In
spite of this, not all adolescents with actual defects in maturation suffer
from body image disturbances.[46] The child raised to appreciate his own
body and to respect human differences is not doomed to self-rejection
if he does not fit the cultural ideal. The fact that two thirds of the
adolescents interviewed in one study expressed a desire for some change
in their physiques[47] may indicate an ability to look at oneself with some
degree of objectiveness and to criticize oneself, but concern does not
necessarily mean self-rejection.

## Early and late maturation

Further, though I would not wish to gloss over the pain of peer
rejection, it should be noted that some personality benefits come from
the experiences of conflict and uncertainty. Sometimes investigators at
one stage of development suggest negative effects of conflict; later fol-
lowup studies may reveal that the conflict has had positive effects in
the long run. An example of this is found in a long series of investigations on the personality differences between early- and late-maturing
boys.[48] The differences in the rates of maturation of the boys studied
are well within the normal range, yet the social factors already mentioned
are apparently sufficient to amplify the differences and produce significant personality effects.

When tested during adolescence, the late-maturing boys seem to have been hurt psychologically. In one study they showed more feelings of inadequacy and rejection, stronger motivations to escape from or defy authority, and stronger needs for heterosexual affection (on Thematic Apperception Test projections). Trained observers rated the late maturers lower in physical attractiveness, grooming, and matter-of-factness, but higher in sociability and eagerness. The same boys were seen by peers as less good-looking and grown-up, more attention getting, restless, and bossy.[49] Another study included average maturers as well as the two extremes; few differences were found between early and average maturers, but the late maturers scored lower on dominance and higher on succorance (seeking help) on the Edwards Personal Preference Schedule.[50]

Since the early maturers are taller, heavier, and stronger than their peers during adolescence (late maturers do catch up, at least in height), they are likely to be better athletes and consequently may be better accepted by peers. They also may be more secure about their own physical development and masculinity and thus more confident socially. Further, acceptance by peers may result in their being given more positions of leadership, which result in greater development of the dominant or assertive behaviors. Some studies of high school leadership roles have found physical characteristics to be correlated with leadership in athletic activities but not with elective and appointive positions; for these, biological maturity did not seem significant.[51] A more recent study comparing early and late maturers during their adolescent years has somewhat contradicted the negative image of the late maturer presented in the earlier studies just cited.[52] Care must be taken in the interpretation of these studies not to infer too much on the basis of test scores alone.

Both personality tests and behavioral data were used in follow-up studies of early and late maturers conducted when they had reached middle adulthood.[53] These studies by Mary C. Jones provide the most solid base for challenging the view that early maturers make the best psychological adjustment. Tests showed the early maturers to be more dominant, more responsible, and more concerned with making a good impression. They were more often in executive positions, and their life histories showed greater employment stability. The late maturers, by contrast, continued to score higher in rebelliousness, impulsivity, and succorance.

These findings have been interpreted to mean that early maturers are better adjusted, both during adolescence and later. It might be more accurate to infer that the early maturers fit the image of the strong, dominant male and are admired by their peers, though not necessarily better liked. Early maturers move more quickly and assuredly into the masculine culture—and this has lasting effects upon their personalities. It should be noted, however, that the late maturers were found to be more flexible and "more sensitive to their feelings and more ready to admit and face them openly."[54] In Jones's follow-up interviews the late maturers showed an "ability to cope, humor, tolerance of ambiguity and of individual idiosyncrasies, perceptiveness, and playfulness in the service of the ego."[55] They exhibited fearfulness and vulnerability more frequently than the early maturers, but this may simply have been an indication of their more open acceptance of negative feelings.[56] Jones found the early maturers, by contrast, to be rather rigid in cognitive processes and attitudes and more moralistic—reflecting the responsible, socialized, conventional syndrome. Another researcher found that early maturers pride themselves on being "objective and rational"[57] and Jones concluded that early maturers "escape prematurely into adulthood, while late maturers take more time to integrate their impulses and capacities."[58]

The earlier development of the adult masculine body, combined with peer group interaction, may lead to an early acceptance of the male image and an early closure of the identity struggle. The late maturer moves with more hesitation and conflict, but as a result achieves a better integration of masculine and feminine roles. His expressive learning is not lost through conforming to society at an early age.[59] Tangential evidence for this interpretation comes from another study which showed that men who had more masculine interests during adolescence (as appears to be the case for the early maturers) were less happy and less well adjusted in middle adulthood than those who had more feminine interests during adolescence.[60]

Certainly those traits that I consider most desirable in today's adolescents—integration, continued expression of emotions, originality, and greater individuation—could occur regardless of the time of the individual's physical maturation. The fact that they occur less commonly in early-developing males is not due to any biological cause. There is clearly nothing wrong with having an athletic, mesomorphic body type. But our society encourages a boy with this ideal body build to view himself as superior. Rather than accepting his body as his, he is pleased that it fits the socially approved stereotype. Thus his identity becomes stereotypic.

The situation for girls is somewhat different. Similar studies have compared early- and late-maturing girls,[61] but the findings have not been consistent.[62] It is possible that physical acceleration does not have the consistent peer advantages for girls that it has for boys during the adolescent years. In an interesting study, students in grades six through nine were asked to "guess who" to a series of positive and negative descriptions, filling in names of girls in the class. The responses were analyzed in relation to the menarchial age of the girls mentioned. In the sixth grade the majority of girls were prepubertal; it was the prepubertal girls who received the highest rate of mentions on items significantly related to prestige, such as "popular," "friendly," "assured adult," and so on. In the seventh grade (which was the modal grade for menarche) students positively evaluated postpubertal girls, those slightly ahead of the average in physical maturity. In eighth and ninth grades, girls four to six years past menarche received the most positive mentions.[63] It appears that at first it is a disadvantage to be an early-maturing girl, but it becomes increasingly advantageous as far as peer prestige is concerned. It would be interesting to differentiate between boys' and girls' ratings of girls, to see if boys award prestige to girls at the same level of physical maturation that girls chose.

A number of variables must be considered in comparing the consistent effects of early maturation in boys to the inconsistency of findings for girls. First, the early-maturing boys are the most likely to develop the ideal body type, the mesomorphic build. Early-developing girls are also prone to develop a more solid build, but this is not as esteemed in girls. On the other hand, late development frequently results in an ecto-morphic build; the slimness is valued in women, but the extreme tallness is not. It is possible (though not clear from direct research evidence) that the rate of maturation is more closely related to the desired body type for boys than for girls.

Second, the early-developing male has a better chance of perfecting leadership qualities. But if the same were true for the female, it would be a mixed blessing; our culture positively evaluates leadership traits in men but is ambivalent about the same traits in women. Popularity in girls is perhaps not so closely correlated with leadership as it is in boys. This, too, needs empirical exploration.

Third, the relationship of body concept to the total self-concept may be different for the two sexes. On the one hand, women in our culture are generally more focused on body interests than are men. The studies reviewed report a higher incidence of concern about the body in adolescent girls and a higher correlation between body concept and self-concept for women than for men.

Body image stereotypes, however, appear to be closely tied to male views of sexual potency. Since sex-role identifications are generally less secure in men than in women, late maturation and the failure to develop the ideal body type might be more traumatic for men. Two studies provide indirect evidence for this. A careful test of the relation between body types, rated for degree of masculinity and other physical and personal characteristics, found that boys who are less masculine in physique tended to be the most masculine in terms of interests, which the author interpreted as "overcompensation." The same result was not found for female subjects.[64]

Similarly, overcompensation appears to play a role in choice of sports for men. R. G. Harlow predicted that men who had inadequate masculine self-concepts would be more likely than strongly sex-typed men to take up sports designed to develop the more obvious secondary sex characteristics. For example, men who preferred weight lifting predictably would be less masculine in personality and more insecure about their masculinity than other men in a carefully matched group who were interested in sports like basketball or volleyball. Consistent ratings from responses to two projective tests (T.A.T. and sentence completions) provided considerable support for the predictions. The differences were significant for nearly all variables tested.[65]

Differences in the nature of male and female peer groups may account for the fact that males consistently show more psychological effects related to age of physical maturation. Adolescent boys frequently interact with their male peers in groups which place strong positive emphasis on physical prowess. Girls more often associate with a few close friends in smaller, more intimate groups which are less likely to place high importance on physical traits. My impression is that girls are more tolerant of differences in other girls' appearance, at least until heterosexual concerns begin to predominate. Possibly boys, more than girls, judge themselves and others of their own sex in relation to that sex's cultural ideal rather than affirming their particular body characteristics and those of others. When they move from same-sex to heterosexual groupings, boys' concern for the ideal body may be displaced onto girls, and they seek good-looking girl friends to bolster their own self-esteem. Since boys can more overtly take the initiative in determining who is dated and accepted, to a large extent they determine the values for the heterosexual peer group. (These are, of course, hypotheses which need to be tested by empirical studies that trace the development of body consciousness and stereotyping in adolescence.)

One thing is clear: the effects of maturation rates on personality are culturally determined. A study of Italian boys raised in Italy, in contrast to American-Italian boys, showed no noticeable effects on personality variables due to time of maturation—perhaps, the researchers suggested, "because physical size and strength and hence the characteristics of 'maturity' and 'independence' are not as highly prized in Italian culture as they are in American."[66]

It is interesting to speculate about changes in American culture that might decrease the effect that maturation rates have on male personality development. Increased contact with male figures might allow boys to make more personal identifications and thus reduce the insecurity about masculinity which leads to anxious acceptance of a stereotypic role.[67] This might lead, in turn, to a decrease in peer emphasis on athletic prowess and a reduction of the negative evaluation of the slow maturers. A change in dating patterns might also reduce the psychological consequences of late maturation. If girls are given more freedom to take the initiative, their lesser concern for a particular body type might result in more dating experience and greater self-acceptance than is presently the case among late-maturing boys.

There are some suggestions in the popular literature that American culture is already changing in these directions, but the empirical evidence is scanty.[68] For a time college adolescents did seem to be decreasing in their support for athletic teams and their attendance at athletic functions. Although this might have been interpreted as evidence for a decline of the male stereotype, it is equally possible to view it as part of the general decline in interest in organized activities on the college campus, perhaps in reaction to the overorganization of activities that youth experience in high school, junior high, and even elementary school.[69] Recent studies have confirmed the continued importance of athletic ability for friendship choices among boys in early adolescence (ages 10 to 14 years).[70] Perhaps the most that can be said is that there is no clear evidence, as yet, for a decline in male stereotyping.

## Facing finitude

We have examined the importance of the body in the adolescent's struggle for self-acceptance and peer recognition. The adolescent's consciousness of his own body has another important consequence: He becomes personally aware of his own finitude. In adolescence, as in times of illness or other bodily changes, a person becomes not only more self-conscious about his body but also more personally aware of the end in store for all mortals: death. Further, as the adolescent prepares for adulthood he gives much more realistic attention to the future than he had previously. The future becomes less a land of fantasy escape. In middle adolescence, young people begin to understand the future realities available to them and then invest themselves emotionally in planning for the future.[71] Death is an inevitable part of that future. The adolescent begins to realize that he has one life to live, that he must live it with his particular body, and that life in that body will end.

It is depressing to many adults that a young person should be concerned with thoughts of death. Clinicians have noted, however, that many of the characteristics of adolescence are similar to the clinical syndrome labeled "depression." [72] Freudian analysts attribute this to the "mourning" over broken libidinal ties with the parents.[73] It seems to me more appropriate to view the concern with death as having two aspects. The first is a mourning for elements of childhood that the adolescent feels forced to leave behind—both those elements of dependency that he realistically must give up and those positive childlike traits that our depersonalized society demands he surrender. But secondly, the concern with death is part of an honest confrontation with what it means to be human. No longer is the magic thinking of childhood an option for the adolescent. Some children in the stage of thinking Jean Piaget termed "preoperational," when asked "How do you make dead things come back to life?" responded with answers such as "Keep them warm" or "Give them hot food."[74] The answers of a small but significant percentage of children imply that death need not be permanent. The adolescent is more realistic. To recognize that his identity is very much tied up with his body, that when his body ceases to function, he dies, is not pathological but realistic. The concern with death is simply the other side of taking seriously one's life, one's identity. It cannot be separated from the decisions concerning what to do with one's life and the struggle to find one's own values and philosophy of life. The increase in religious interest which once was considered typical of adolescence reflects both the search for life's values and the recognition of life's finitude.[75]

## Affirmation of physical identity

The end of adolescence has no biological marker; it usually is considered to have ended when the crises of identity have been resolved and the individual has assumed adult roles in society. Though the crisis of body image is usually the first of the identity issues to be experienced, it is not necessarily the first to be resolved. In fact many adults—perhaps most adults in our culture—have not really accepted their own bodies. The last vestiges of Victorian attitudes, including not simply a rejection of sexuality but a general distaste for the sensual, still can be found throughout society.

There are signs, however, particularly in adolescent culture, that we are moving beyond Victorian fears and their Freudian antitheses to a joyous acceptance of the body. Nowhere is this better expressed in the popular culture than in the musical *Hair*, when Claude affirms his own body: "I got life, Mother!" he declares. The song opens with the defensiveness and conflict of early adolescence but increasingly becomes a simple, joyful affirmation of the body:

> I got my hair; I got my head;
> got my brains; got my ears;
> got my eyes; got my nose;
> got my mouth.
> I got my teeth.
> I got my tongue; I got my chin;

> got my neck; got my teets;
> got my heart; got my soul;
> got my back.
> I got my ass.
> I got my arms; I got my hands;
> I got my fingers; got my legs;
> got my feet; got my toes.
> Got my liver.
> Got my blood.
> Got my guts.
> I got my muscles.
> I got LIFE, LIFE, LIFE![76]

Claude's acceptance of life in the flesh is profound in its concreteness. In affirming this body as life, it affirms mortality; it recognizes the limits of humanness while celebrating its sensual delight. Further, the phrase "I got life" shows an implicit awareness that to accept the body is to accept process. Adolescence brings change in the body. The resolution of adolescence is not simply a resignation to the new adult body but a realization that the body is always changing. The end of adolescence is not defined by an acceptance of the status quo but an affirmation of change itself. The neo-Freudian discussion of a "resolution to the adolescent identity crisis"[77] seems too final, as if identity could be finally and permanently established. Perhaps one of the most significant discoveries of adolescence is that "I change," that identity is not static. It would be malfunctional for the adolescent simply to affirm the present state of the body, for it will continue to change. Claude affirms life in his body—not an abstract principle, but incarnate experience.

Claude's affirmation comes, in part, with the positive acceptance of himself which he experiences within the "hippie" subculture. The affirmation is interpersonal, not simply individual, as it is in all the issues of identity. We learn to accept, appreciate, and rejoice in our bodies as we are accepted by others. For most Americans, especially those in the older generation, it is probable that this mutual acceptance of the body itself (not just of sexuality) first occurs in the intimacy of marriage. But for some of today's youth, at least, the affirmation of the body is being worked out within the peer group. Today's adolescent may experience an openness about the body and an acceptance from members of both sexes. As in Claude's affirmation, their acceptance of the body is not based upon sexuality and does not wait for permanent heterosexual commitments.

The early adolescent questions of "Who am I?" are invariably bound up with "my body." Adolescence is not over until the individual can feel, with real affirmation: "This is me; this is my body—I accept it, I enjoy it. I got life!"

## Summary

The adolescent's growth spurt, changes in body build, and the development of secondary sex characteristics have social and personal implications for the adolescent. Girls generally experience bodily changes, the growth spurt, and the development of a mature female figure before they become sexually awakened. For boys the reverse is true; sexual awakening precedes the other bodily changes.

Adolescents frequently feel awkward and self-conscious about their bodies; our age-graded schools encourage comparisons between and within sexes, frequently increasing the self-consciousness of those who develop out of step with the others or fail to fit the stereotypes of physical attractiveness for their sex. Data on late-maturing boys suggest that some positive personality benefits occur as a result of the experiences of conflict and uncertainty. Early acceptance of the male image appears to have social benefits during adolescence itself, but does not correlate with psychological health later in life.

Healthy identity formation includes an affirmation of one's unique body. This entails overcoming stereotyped images. It also involves a realistic recognition of one's finitude. There are some signs that youth culture is increasingly supporting a joyous affirmation of the body.

## Notes

1. All of the figures given in the text are adjusted for the "secular trend," the fact that since 1840 puberty has been occurring about four months earlier for each decade—Rolf E. Muuss "Adolescent Development and the Secular Trend," *Adolescence*, 5 (1970): 267–84. Regardless of the dates of the reference, the figures are approximately what would have been average in 1970. Means for peak growth-spurt ages are based on A. Nicholson and C. Hanley, "Indices of Physiological Maturity: Deviations and Interrelationships," *Child Development*, 24 (1953): 3–38. The span of time for the growth spurt is based on J. M. Tanner, "The Adolescent Growth-Spurt and Developmental Age," in *Human Biology: An Introduction to Human Evolution, Variation, and Growth*, ed. G. T. Harrison et al. (Oxford: Clarendon Press, 1964), pp. 321–39.

2. A. H. Byron, "Methods for Analyzing and Interpreting Physical Measurements of Groups of Children," *American Journal of Public Health*, 44 (1954): 766–71.

3. F. K. Shuttleworth, "The Physical and Mental Growth of Girls and Boys Age Six to Nineteen in Relation to Age at Maximum Growth," *Monographs of the Society for Research in Child Development*, Series 22, 4 (1939), no. 3.

4. J. E. Horrocks, *The Psychology of Adolescence: Behavior and Development*, 3rd ed. (Boston: Houghton Mifflin Co., 1969), pp. 388–89.

5. J. M. Tanner, *Growth at Adolescence*, 2d ed. (Oxford: Blackwell Scientific Publications, Ltd., 1962).

6.  G. R. Medinnus and R. C. Johnson, *Child and Adolescent Psychology: Behavior and Development* (New York: John Wiley & Sons, 1969), p. 665.

7.  A. Espenschade, "Motor Performance in Adolescence," *Monographs of the Society for Research in Child Development*, 5 (1940), no. 1; Howard H. Hopwood and Starr S. Van Iden, "Scholastic Underachievement as related to Sub-par Physical Growth," *Journal of School Health*, 35 (1965): 337–49. Also see Mollie S. Smart and Russell C. Smart, *Adolescents: Development and Relationships* (New York: Macmillan Publishing Co., 1973), pp. 15–23, for a review of the literature regarding adolescent physical care and health.

8.  H. S. Dimock, *Rediscovering the Adolescent* (New York: Association Press, 1937), p. 245.

9.  E. R. Hilgard and Richard C. Atkinson, *Introduction to Psychology*, 3rd ed. (New York: Harcourt, Brace & World, 1962), p. 96; Harold W. Bernard, *Adolescent Development* (Scranton, Pa.: Intext Educational Publishers, 1971), p. 120.

10.  Dorothy Rogers, *Adolescence: A Psychological Perspective* (Monterey, Calif.: Brooks/Cole Publishing Co., 1972), p. 35; Johanna Dwyer and Jean Mayer, "Psychological Effects of Variations in Physical Appearance during Adolescence," *Adolescence*, 3 (1968–69): 353–80, especially p. 354.

11.  Smart and Smart, *Adolescents*, p. 27.

12.  Dwyer and Mayer, "Effects of Variation in Appearance," p. 355; Rogers, *Adolescence*, pp. 35–36.

13.  Kurt Lewin was among the first to emphasize this. See R. E. Muuss, *Theories of Adolescence*, 2nd ed. (New York: Random House, 1968), p. 93.

14.  Newell C. Kephart, *The Slow Learner in the Classroom* (Columbus, Ohio: Charles E. Merrill Publishing Co., 1960). See especially the discussion of "laterality."

15.  E. Walster et al., "The Importance of Physical Attractiveness in Dating Behavior," *Journal of Personality and Social Psychology*, 4 (1966): 508–16.

16.  Norman E. Gronlund and Loren Anderson, "Personality Characteristics of Socially Accepted, Socially Neglected, and Socially Rejected Junior High School Pupils," *Educational Administration and Supervision*, 43 (1957): 329–38.

17.  H. E. Jones, "Adolescence in Our Society," in *The Family in a Democratic Society*, Anniversary Papers of The Community Service Society of New York (New York: Columbia University Press, 1949), pp. 70–82.

18.  Norman Cavior and Paul R. Dokecki, "Physical Attractiveness, Perceived Attitude Similarity, and Academic Achievement as Contributors to Interpersonal Attraction among Adolescents," *Developmental Psychology*, 9 (1973): 44–54.

19.  Ibid., p. 50, Table 4. It should be noted that the authors fail to differentiate the two age groups in their discussion of results and thus reach different conclusions from those stated.

20.  Walster et al., "Physical Attractiveness in Dating Behavior."

21.  William A. Schonfeld, "The Body and the Body-Image in Adolescents," in *Adolescence: Psychosocial Perspectives*, ed. Gerald Caplan and Serge Lebovici (New York: Basic Books, 1969), pp. 27–53, especially p. 46.

22.  W. H. Sheldon, S. S. Stevens, and W. B. Tucker, *The Varieties of Human Physique* (New York: Harper & Row Publishers, 1940).

23.  Smart and Smart, *Adolescents*, p. 31.

24.  Richard M. Lerner, "The Development of Stereotyped Expectancies of Body Build-Behavior Relations," *Child Development*, 40 (1969): 137–41.

25. Rogers, *Adolescence*, p. 37.

26. C. M. Brodsky, *A Study of Norms for Body Form Behavior Relationships* (Washington: Catholic University of America Press, 1954).

27. G. Calden, R. M. Lundy, and R. J. Schlafer, "Sex Differences in Body Concepts," *Journal of Consultng Psychology*, 23 (1959): 378.

28. See "Garden Variety Sexism: Rampant among Psychologists," *Psychology Today*, February 1973, p. 9.

29. See Dwyer and Mayer, "Effects of Variation in Appearance," for a report of a study by J. T. Dwyer et al. entitled "Body Image in Adolescents: Attitudes toward Weight and Perception of Appearance in Adolescents."

30. Richard Schmuck, "Concerns of Contemporary Adolescents," *Bulletin of the National Association of Secondary School Principals*, 49 (1965): 19–28.

31. Alexander Frazier and Lorenzo K. Lisonbee, "Adolescent Concerns with Physique," in *Adolescent Behavior and Society: A Book of Readings*, ed. Rolf E. Muuss (New York: Random House, 1971), pp. 88–98; see especially pp. 90–91.

32. H. R. Stolz and L. M. Stolz, "Adolescent Problems Related to Somatic Variations," in *Adolescence: 43rd Yearbook of the National Society for the Study of Education*, ed. N. B. Henry (Chicago: University of Chicago Press, 1944), pp. 80–99; as reported in Dwyer and Mayer, "Effects of Variation in Appearance," p. 356. Underscoring mine.

33. Support for *either* interpretation can be found in a comparison of mental illness statistics for males and females.

34. L. C. Johnson, "Body Cathexis as a Factor in Somatic Complaints," *Journal of Consulting Psychology*, 20 (1956): 145–49; P. F. Secord and S. M. Jourard, "The Appraisal of Body-Cathexis: Body-Cathexis and the Self," *Journal of Consulting Psychology*, 17 (1953): 343–47.

35. H. V. Cobb, "Role-Wishes and General Wishes of Children and Adolescents," *Child Development*, 25 (1954): 161–71; S. M. Jourard and P. F. Secord, "Body Size and Body-Cathexis," *Journal of Consulting Psychology*, 18 (1954): 184, M. G. Magnussen, "Body Size and Body-Cathexis Replicated," *Psychological Newsletter* (NYU), 10 (1958): 33–34. Calden, Lundy, and Schlafer, "Sex Differences in Body Concepts.

36. Dwyer and Mayer, "Effects of Variation in Appearance," p. 365.

37. R. L. Huenemann et al., "A Longitudinal Study of Gross Body Composition and Body Confirmation and Association with Food and Activity in a Teen-Age Population: Views of Teen-age Subjects on Body Conformation, Food, and Activity," *American Journal of Clinical Nutrition*, 18 (1966): 323–38.

38. Rogers, *Adolescence*, p. 52.

39. Frazier and Lisonbee, "Adolescent Concerns with Physique," pp. 90–91; S. M. Jourard and P. F. Secord, "Body-Cathexis and the Ideal Female Figure," *Journal of Abnormal and Social Psychology*, 46 (1955): 130–38; Abe Arkoff and Herbert B. Weaver, "Body Image and Body Dissatisfaction in Japanese-Americans," *Journal of Social Psychology*, 68 (1966): 323–30, which compared Japanese-Americans to Caucasian-Americans. Calden, Lundy, and Schlafer, "Sex Differences in Body Concepts," found that females generally desired to be smaller and lighter in all dimensions except bust.

40. J. T. Dwyer, J. J. Feldman, and Jean Mayer, "Adolescent Dieters: Who Are They? Physical Characteristics, Attitudes, and Dieting Practices of Adolescent Girls," *American Journal of Clinical Nutrition*, 20 (1967): 1045–56.

41. B. A. Bullen et al., "Attitudes toward Physical Activity, Food, and Family in Obese and Nonobese Adolescent Girls," *American Journal of Clinical Nutrition,* 12 (1963): 1–11.

42. Dwyer et al., "Body Image in Adolescents."

43. H. Angelino and E. V. Mech, "Fears and Worries concerning Physical Changes: A Preliminary Survey of 32 Females," *Journal of Psychology,* 39 (1955): 195–98.

44. Medinnus and Johnson, *Child and Adolescent Psychology,* p. 670.

45. W. D. Smith and D. Lebo, "Some Changing Aspects of the Self-Concept of Pubescent Males," *Journal of Genetic Psychology,* 88 (1956): 61–75.

46. H. Caplan, "Some Considerations of the Body-Image Concept in Child Development," *Quarterly Journal of Child Behavior,* 4 (1952): 382.

47. M. C. Jones and Nancy Bayley, "Physical Maturing among Boys as Related to Behavior," *Journal of Educational Psychology,* 41 (1950): 129.

48. Ibid.; M. C. Jones, "The Later Careers of Boys Who Were Early- or Late-Maturing," *Child Development,* 28 (1957): 113–28; Paul Henry Mussen and Mary Cover Jones, "Self-Conceptions, Motivations, and Interpersonal Attitudes of Late- and Early-Maturing Boys," *Child Development,* 28 (1957): 243–56; Mary Cover Jones and Paul Henry Mussen, "Self-Conceptions, Motivations and Interpersonal Attitudes of Early- and Late-Maturing Girls," *Child Development,* 29 (1958): 491–501; D. Weatherley, "Self-Perceived Rate of Physical Maturation and Personality in Late Adolescence," *Child Development,* 35 (1964): 1197–210; Mary Cover Jones, "Psychological Correlates of Somatic Development," *Child Development,* 36 (1965): 899–916.

49. Mussen and Jones, "Early and Late Maturing Boys."

50. Weatherley, "Self-Perceived Rate of Physical Maturation."

51. A. J. Latham, "The Relationship between Pubertal Status and Leadership in Junior High School Boys," *Journal of Genetic Psychology,* 78 (1951): 185–94.

52. H. Peskin, "Pubertal Onset and Ego Functioning," *Journal of Abnormal Psychology,* 72 (1967): 1–15.

53. Jones, "Later Careers of Boys"; Jones, "Psychological Correlates of Somatic Development."

54. Mussen and Jones, "Early- and Late-Maturing Boys."

55. Jones, "Psychological Correlates of Somatic Development."

56. Weatherley's finding that late maturers scored lower on intraception (on the EPPS) cannot be taken as evidence against their greater sensitivity, both because the finding was not at an .05 level and because this scale of the EPPS is very poorly validated (see L. J. Stricker's review in Oscar K. Buros, *The Sixth Mental Measurements Yearbook* (Highland Park, N.J.: Gryphon Press, 1965), p. 388.

57. J. Block, *The Q Sort Method in Personality Assessment and Psychiatric Research* (Springfield, Ill.: Charles C. Thomas, 1961).

58. Jones, "Psychological Correlates of Somatic Development."

59. There are striking parallels between the data just presented and the studies of the foreclosure identity status reported in Chapter 14.

60. P. H. Mussen, "Long-Term Consequences of Masculinity of Interests in Adolescence," *Journal of Consulting Psychology,* 26 (1962): 435–40; Medinnus and Johnson come to similar conclusions in *Child and Adolescent Psychology,* pp. 666–67.

61. Jones, "Adolescence in Our Society," pp. 70–82; Jones and Mussen, "Early- and Late-Maturing Girls"; Weatherley, "Self-Perceived Rate of Physical Maturation."

62. Medinnus and Johnson, *Child and Adolescent Psychology*, pp. 666–67.

63. Margaret Siler Faust, "Developmental Maturity as a Determinant in Prestige of Adolescent Girls," *Child Development*, 31 (1960): 173–84.

64. Nancy Bayley, "Some Psychological Correlates of Somatic Androgyny," *Child Development*, 22 (1959): 47–60.

65. R. G. Harlow, "Masculine Inadequacy and Compensatory Development of Physique," *Journal of Personality*, 19 (1951): 312–33.

66. P. H. Mussen and H. Boutourline-Young, "Relationships between Rate of Physical Maturing and Personality among Boys of Italian Descent," *Vita Humana*, 7 (1964): 186–200.

67. See Chapter 4 for background data supporting this conclusion.

68. Charles Reich, *The Greening of America: The Coming of a New Consciousness and the Rebirth of a Future* (New York: Random House, 1970); Jesse Bernard, "Teenage-Culture: An Overview," in *Teen-age Culture*, ed. Bernard (Philadelphia: American Academy of Political and Social Science, 1961), p. 338; Talcott Parsons, "Youth in the Context of American Society," *Daedalus*, 91 (1962): 97–123.

69. Dr. Margaret Ross, Marietta College, personal communication.

70. Leslie H. Krieger and William D. Wells, "The Criteria for Friendship," *Journal of Social Psychology*, 78 (1969): 109–12.

71. Elise E. Lessing, "Extension of Personal Future, Time Perspective, Age, and Life Satisfaction of Children and Adolescents," *Developmental Psychology*, 6 (1972): 457–68.

72. Peter Blos, *On Adolescence: A Psychoanalytic Interpretation* (New York: Free Press, 1962), pp. 12 and 40.

73. Anna Freud, *The Ego and the Mechanisms of Defense* (New York: International Universities Press, 1946), p. 188; Anna Freud, "Adolescence," *Psychoanalytic Study of the Child*, 13 (1958): 264; J. Lample-de-Groot, "On Adolescence," *Psychoanalytic Study of the Child* 15 (1960): 98.

74. Gernald P. Koocher, "Childhood, Death, and Cognitive Development," *Developmental Psychology*, 9 (1973): 369–75, especially p. 373.

75. See Chapter 11 for a discussion of the role of religion in adolescence. Also note Medinnus and Johnson, *Child and Adolescent Psychology*, p. 485.

76. G. Ragni and J. Rado (lyricists), "I Got Life," *Hair: The American Tribal Love-Rock Musical*. Copyright © 1966, 1967, 1968, James Rado, Gerome Ragni, Galt MacDermot, Nat Shapiro, United Artists Music Co., Inc. All rights administered by United Artists Music Co., Inc., New York.

77. Blos, *On Adolescence*.

# 9

## CRISIS TWO
## Sex: The beauty of difference

SEXUALITY is not the central issue of adolescence; it is one aspect of the issue of identity and makes sense only in the context of the acceptance of the body. The adolescent boy may associate his newly experienced genitality with the male image but fail to affirm his particular and unique way of being a man. Similarly, the adolescent girl may accept fairly traditional female roles, revising them slightly to fit with her peers' view of sex, without really integrating the two or discerning her own way of being a woman. The task of adolescence is not simply the discovery of the male or female role but the creation and affirmation of the individual's particular style of being a man or woman.

145

## Socialization for adult sexuality

There are differences between the sexes in the biological characteristics of the sexual emergence. In our culture, these differences are accentuated by differences in the socialization process. Not only are males
and females taught different sexual roles in this process, they are taught
different attitudes toward sexuality, and, to some extent, they are trained
by different persons. It is useful to look at the general pattern of socialization for each sex before attempting comparisons and discussing the
import of sexual experience in identity formation.

### Social-sexual development in girls

*Puberty and the family.* Although many girls have already experienced the initial enlargement of breasts and the appearance of pigmented pubic hair before menarche, it is the first menstruation which
is usually the symbol of a girl's awakening to mature sexuality. It will
be a year or so before the girl is sexually fertile, but in all other physical
respects, once she experiences menarche she is sexually mature.[1] A study
by Gordon Shipman found that the majority of girls are prepared for
first menstruation by their mothers, most of whom do reasonably well
in their explanations of menstruation. Only 10 percent of girls develop
negative feelings in anticipation of the occasion, and at the time of
menarche about 10 percent are shocked and frightened. At the opposite
extreme, Shipman cites the following case:

> After describing how well her mother had explained the approaching
> menarche the girl went on to say, "When I discovered it, I called
> my mother and she showed me what to do. Then she did something
> I'll never forget. She told me to come with her and we went into
> the living room to tell my father. She just looked at me and then
> at him and said, "Well, your little girl is a young lady now!" My
> Dad gave me hug and congratulated me and I felt grown-up and
> proud that I was a lady at last. That was one of the most exciting
> days of my life. . . . I was so excited and happy."[2]

This case is clearly exceptional, though Shipman believes there is a
growing tendency to ritualize the menarche in middle-class families.
If so, this is the one bright spot in the general picture of family sex
education. Since mother usually is at home more, it could be expected
that she would have fairly good communication with her children when
sex-related issues arise. In fact, there is more exchange of sexual
information between mothers and daughters than between the other
parent-child dyads (mother and son, father and son, father and
daughter). Nonetheless, most girls do not get much sex information

from their mothers, except in preparation for menstruation. While 64 percent of the girls in the study reported at least adequate education from mother regarding this event, the figure dropped to around 25 percent on other matters of sex education. Although the majority of girls first learn about menstruation from mothers and sisters, they usually learn about intercourse first from their peers.[3]

*Peer group influences.* When it comes to providing sexual information, parents in our culture play a minimal role. Though many adolescents

Sex education should be handled by the people closest to it. Those with firsthand experience. Not the school, not the parents, but the kids in the street!

Reproduced by special permission of *Playboy* Magazine; copyright © 1971 by *Playboy*.

report good communication with parents in other areas, they generally state that they do not discuss sexual issues with them. Even studies that show continued positive parent-child communication throughout adolescence note that sexual issues are not discussed.[4] For example, one study showed that "The parents are interested in all the activities of their children, and the adolescents, except for the area of sex, frankly discuss their own behavior and problems with them."[5] Though our culture permits more open discussion of sex than in the past, it appears that sex is still a taboo topic between parent and child. The child must move to the peer group to learn about sex and to gain experience in this area.

The peer group for the girl usually consists of a few close, intimate girl friends, at least during early adolescence.[6] Previous training in sex roles and affiliation in same-sex play groups ensures that, by the time sexual differences between boys and girls emerge in puberty, they have already developed different interests and attitudes. While activity in the boys' peer group centers around athletics and cars, girls value clothes and other things related to attractiveness and social success.[7] Girls' close friends are obviously a help in understanding self and others and in making the move away from dependence upon parents. When the physical changes of puberty occur, girls' peer reference groups respond in a different way than boys' groups do. In the female, the body as a whole undergoes changes first, before menarche. The changing body proportions which result in the appearance of a more womanly adult figure are the focus of attention, since they occur first. Thus the peer group's concern with attractiveness is amplified by the type of body change which is most noticable in women. Even when mature genitality is attained, the female reproductive organs are more hidden and thus are less likely to be the focus of comparisons and discussions.

Partly because the female genitals are more hidden, the girl is less likely to experience sexual arousal through accidental stimulation. These biological factors, as well as cultural expectations, make the sequence of sexual learning different for boys and girls. While sexuality for adolescent boys is focused upon the genitals, as will be noted in the next section, adolescent sexuality in females tends to be more diffuse. Probably the majority of girls never experience full sexual arousal or orgasm until they have reached the stage of heavy petting in a relationship with a boy; they are first "turned on" sexually through heterosexual experience. Until then, their sexuality is not particularly genital in nature. Not surprisingly, then, genital fantasies and sexual dreams, both of which are common in adolescent boys, are relatively rare in girls.

*Biological and cultural factors.* Comparisons with other cultures suggest that biological factors are not the major reasons for the genitalless diffuseness of adolescent female sexuality. Social learning for girls has stressed the acceptance of emotions and their interpersonal expression. When the new sexual feelings emerge, it is easy for them to be experienced as an increase in emotionality and a desire for romance. The cultural double standard discourages the acceptance of clearly genital sexuality in women. Generally the peer group, as long as it remains a same-sex group, supports this romantic view of sexuality in women.

For most American children the move to increased involvement with the peer group precedes adolescence, and its effects are not limited to the area of sexual learning. Around the age of puberty, both biological and social changes are occurring, and it is difficult to untangle the two. There is evidence for both sexes that biological changes correlate with changes in interests and desires, even when age and grade level are controlled. Subjects who have reached puberty differ from their peers of the same age and in the same social setting. An early study of the interests and desires of pubescent girls showed that those who had reached menarche were more interested in boys, and in their own physical appearance, than girls of the same status and age who were premenarchal. The postmenarchal girls demonstrated less desire for vigorous physical exercise, stronger tendencies to daydream, and greater concern about conflicts in family life.[8] Such studies suggest that some of the increase in activity rates and impulsive behavior during early adolescence is directly attributable to the growth spurt, the new sexual feelings, and the endocrinal changes which underlie them.

However, it is very possible that social and cognitive factors are central to even these changes. The roles for each of the sexes have been learned long before adolescence. Social expectations of how an adolescent should act are strong; television, movies, and popular magazines portray a clear script of "typical" adolescent behavior. When the distinctively sexual feelings begin to emerge in adolescence, they are expressed in the forms the culture has taught. Even before the girl is sexually awakened, once menarche has taken place she is likely to label herself an adolescent. Thus the occurrence of menarche may serve as a cue that she can now assume the roles she has been carefully observing and learning for some time. It is as if the culture, and particularly the peer group, had prepared a script, much of which has been read and learned before adolescence. Once the girl has labeled herself an adolescent, she feels permitted to act it out.[9]

## Social-sexual development in boys

*Puberty and the family.* The level of communication between parents and sons in regard to sexual matters is even lower than with daughters. The boy usually experiences his entrance into mature sexuality in a psychological and cultural void. Shipman notes:

> . . . the ritualization of the menarche in American family life . . . gives the girl so much satisfaction. Imagine an American boy coming to the breakfast table exclaiming, "Mom, guess what! I had my first wet dream last night. Now I'm a man." It is not without significance that such an imaginary episode is greeted in American culture with laughter.[10]

Possibly the family can be more comfortable about menstruation than about boys' first ejaculation because they can desexualize the former and treat it simply as a biological event. As Shipman says, "The boy and his parents know full well that the first ejaculation is sexual."[11] Thus the tendency is to abide by the taboo against sexual discussion between parents and children. Despite the failure in our culture to prepare boys for first ejaculation, my clinical impression is that this event is a profound experience for many boys, an impression which is supported by autobiographical materials . The incidence of fright at puberty appears to be greater for boys, and wholesome anticipation of puberty is very much less common. Shipman found that:

> Whereas about half the girls reacted to the menarche with feelings of gratification or elation, only 6 percent of the boys estimated that they had feelings of satisfaction at the time of their first ejaculation which they associated with the beginning of manhood. Also, only 6 percent of our male respondents felt that they had been adequately prepared for this event by parents.[12]

For a large percentage of boys, ejaculation first occurs in a nocturnal dream; 15 percent of these boys experience fright. The other major source of first ejaculation is from masturbation; 20 percent of boys who first ejaculate as a result of masturbation are frightened, reporting "It scared the hell out of me," "It was frustrating and shocking to me." Fears that they are ill or have hurt themselves or, in the case of nocturnal emission, that they have regressed and wet the bed are common. Many of the boys attempt to hide stains on the sheets and pajamas, and though they are very curious they are afraid to ask their parents about it.[13]

For the boy, as has been noted, genital maturity is often reached before the growth spurt and the attainment of an adult male body. Usually the testes show the first signs of growth at about age 11.[14] Soon after, pigmented hair begins to appear at the base of the penis. A year or so later the beginning enlargement of the penis occurs, and the boy generally experiences his first ejaculation.[15] In the next two years the boy generally experiences his fastest growth, develops axillary hair and a beard, undergoes changes in the sweat glands, and lives through the social embarrassment of marked voice changes.[16]

*Sex as a private experience.* Since first ejaculation frequently occurs before the growth spurt and the development of the male secondary sex characteristics, and since it is clearly a sexual experience and subject to family taboos, the sexual emergence of the adolescent boy in our culture is usually a private experience. Further, since the male sexual organs are easily visible and manipulable, arousal through accidental stimulation or through the curious exploration of his own body is nearly inevitable. Nearly all boys have heard about masturbation before they attempt it themselves, and many have observed companions masturbating.[17]

Boys tend to be frank with each other about their new sexual feelings. Though it cannot be said that middle-class culture condones masturbation (and lower-class culture clearly does not), locker room talk and joking about "jerking-off" make it evident to the adolescent boy that he is not alone in this practice. The joking and banter are not direct enough to assure most adolescent boys that masturbation is a natural and appropriate beginning to mature sexual experience. Though adolescent boys tend to value and openly brag to one another about the new sexual arousal they are experiencing, they may be unsure and less than candid about their own masturbation. Sexual worries are reported slightly less often by boys than girls, but they are still frequent; 21 percent of prepubertal boys, 44 percent of those in puberty, and up to 71 percent of adolescent boys report worries about sexual matters.[18] The greatest worries for adolescent boys focus on masturbation. Apparently most adolescent boys still consider masturbation somehow wrong or abnormal; they would probably be surprised to learn that 90 percent of their peers admit privately to the act.[19] Despite whatever guilt the adolescent male experiences, sexuality normally begins as a private, personal experience, and men quickly recognize the very pleasant character of genital sexuality and increase the frequency of their sexual experiences throughout their adolescent years.[20]

Since male sexuality normally begins with masturbation, some comments on the adult culture's lack of candidness on this matter are in order. It would seem healthier if men could frankly admit to masturbation as an acceptable private pleasure. The study by Alfred Kinsey, *Sexual Behavior in the Human Male*, noted that a major percentage of married adult males continue to engage in masturbation.[21] Not only is it incorrect to view masturbation as deviant, it should not even be considered immature or adolescent. For most males of the college level, masturbation provides the chief source of sexual gratification up to the time of marriage. The guilt and aloneness that many adolescent boys (and girls) feel would be somewhat alleviated if adults could be more open about the naturalness of the act. It is well established that there are no harmful effects from masturbation, and it seems plausible that masturbation and the fantasies that accompany it play a positive role in the boy's preparation for heterosexual relations.[22] However, some adverse consequences may result from the inhibited and passive manner in which many boys masturbate. Frederick Perls has suggested that passive masturbation, or, to use his phrase, "the rape of the genitals by the hand" trains the boy to experience orgasm without the pelvic thrusting and the full organic responses normally involved. This results in incorrect preparation for heterosexual intercourse.[23] It might be said that sex education should not only condone masturbation but should teach adolescents enough about sexual intercourse so that these responses become integrated into masturbation fantasy and technique.

If the cultural orientation toward masturbation were a more positive one, boys might be aided in their attempts to accept their own bodies. The mental health concerns surrounding masturbation are conjectures from clinical data; the lack of empirical data is itself a measure of our culture's avoidance of this subject. It may be that, whether adult culture initiates it or not, a change in attitudes is occurring within segments of the youth culture. A song from the musical *Hair* marks a move toward the joyful acceptance of the body when it proclaims simply and directly: "Masturbation can be fun."

*Social factors: The peer group.* Social factors, such as the view of adolescence presented on television and in movies and popular magazines, greatly affect adolescent behavior and probably account for the behavior of youths who are enticed to dance, date, and otherwise act like adolescents before they reach puberty.

Just as the affirmation of the body is a social process, experimentation with sexual roles and the creation of individual sexual identity also depend upon interpersonal interactions. For boys as well as girls, sexual maturation may function as a cue to the adoption of adolescent roles. Thus it is difficult to distinguish changes due to physical causes from those due to cultural expectations. In any case, boys who have reached puberty differ on psychological dimensions from their peers in the same social setting who have not reached puberty.

Projective instruments were used to measure three variables in pubescent boys: defense against impulses, intensity and frequency of anxiety and emotional reactions, and amount of fantasy and abstraction. Increases in all three variables were found not only as age increased but with the onset of puberty, when age was held constant.[24]

The importance of social factors is attested to by the fact that boys begin dating at the same age as girls do, in spite of the fact that they are at least a year behind the girl in physical materation. In this instance, the pressure to date may come from the girls. In early adolescence, for boys as well as girls, the main peer reference group consists of friends of one's own sex. Nonetheless, there is considerable awareness of the opposite sex, even before puberty.

Since the home provides even less sex information to sons than to daughters, adolescent boys are more dependent upon peers for their information—or misinformation. The influence of the peer group appears inversely related to the availability of the same-sex parent as a model, so far as sex education is concerned.[25] That is, parental influence is strongest in the case of girls, since mother is usually in the home and provides a direct model. Because a male model is generally less available, the peer group is more influential in boys' sex-role learning. Among lower-class boys, where father absence is particularly common, the all-male peer group has an even stronger influence than is the case for boys from middle and upper classes.[26] Modeling after a parent tends to make sex-role learning more personal, whereas peer group learning generally increases stereotypic views of the sexual roles.[27]

For the most part, the adolescent peer group reinforces the cultural norms that have been transmitted by the parents.[28] Adult and peer reference groups generally agree regarding the conventional male and female statuses and role relationships, and on the desirable characteristics sought in a date.[29] As a rule, the peer group does not represent a separate youth culture; its norms generally reflect those of the adult society around it. The one important area of difference is that youth is more often explicitly concerned with having a good time, whereas parents, feeling responsible for their offsprings' futures, place more stress on long-range goals. This difference between adolescents and adults can be easily exaggerated. On the one side, parents often gave high priority to having fun when they themselves were adolescents; to some extent they want this for their children. On the other side, youth generally are not wildly irresponsible in their sexual activities and attitudes. Thus, "The evidence shows more conservatism and responsibility than one might expect."[30]

*The all-male peer group.* Boys and girls develop different interests during the years of late childhood, because of their different identifications and the different sex roles encouraged by the culture. These differences are amplified in the all-boy and all-girl peer groups in preadolescence and early adolescence. My impression is that the initiative for same-sex peer groups comes from the boys; it is related to their rejection of the feminine and their defensive sex-role formation. Boys attempt to find a masculine identity by asserting their autonomy and independence. In preadolescence, this is primarily an assertion of autonomy from the constraints of female domination in home and school. By adolescence, it has more to do with the struggle to be a man, in terms of both genital sexuality and adulthood.

In contrast to the affiliation girls develop with a few close peers, boys tend to seek support from a larger peer group.[31] The importance of the same-sex group in male pubescence has been alluded to: the locker room comparisons and jokes, the emphasis on athletic prowess, the bragging about conquests. Perhaps it is because he is less secure in his sexual identity that the boy relies not on a few close friends but the whole gang. Within the gang, however, he is also likely to develop pals. Thus intimacy, at least so far as same-sex relationships are concerned, may develop prior to mature genitality, even for boys.[32]

It is pertinent at this point to note the role of homosexual experience in the development of sexual identity. Since in our society the child, up through pubescence, attaches himself most closely to peers of the same sex and learns about sexual matters from these peers, it should not be surprising that some of the adolescent's earliest erotic feelings may be directed toward intimates of the same sex. Erotic feelings for early adolescent girls tend to be diffuse and do not usually result in any genital contact. Boys' sexuality, by contrast, is clearly goal directed toward genital contact. While homosexual experiences in adolescence appear to occur more frequently among boys than girls,[33] it is difficult to be sure of their incidence. Our society is one of the world's most phobic in regard to homosexuality, and self-report measures may involve response bias and social desirability factors.[34] In 1948, over 40 percent of Kinsey's male subjects reported having some homosexual experiences after puberty. A far less careful survey in 1970 conducted for *Psychology Today* found approximately the same percentage reporting homosexual experiences.[35]

Some clinicians have argued that a homosexual period may aid masculine identification, and homosexual experience in early adolescence may actually be healthier than no such experience. There are even societies that have institutionalized homosexual experience for adolescent boys, the rationale being that only an adult male can teach a boy how to be a man.[36] Other cultures, for example in France, maintain that a boy should be initiated into adult sexuality by an experienced woman. The point is that there are many ways in which the movement toward mature sexuality can occur, and adolescent homosexual experiences should certainly not be considered cause for alarm.[37]

Erik Erikson has called attention to the confirming effect a label has on a juvenile struggling to find his identity. For example, a confused adolescent who breaks a law and gets labeled "delinquent" may accept that label, which at least provides him with a clearer identity. A similar dynamic is possible in adolescent homosexuality. High school counselors occasionally become so alarmed over a report of a boy's homosexual activities that they involve the parents, school authorities, and psychiatrists. If the boy is unsure of his masculine identity to begin with, such overconcern about his homosexual behavior may serve to confirm homosexuality as a self-definition.

Many boys (even that majority who never experience homosexual contact) go through a period of activity in all-boy groups before moving into heterosexual activities. In our culture it is the peer group which provides the most incentive for the individual to move on to heterosexual experience.

The importance of the male peer group in setting the goals for the adolescent boy's sexual behavior has been demonstrated in an experiment which examined the relationship between sexual aggression and sexual frustration. Information gathered from a random sample of 400 male students in a co-ed Midwestern university showed that 20 percent could be labeled as sexually aggressive; they reported being involved in sexual interactions in which the girl cried, fought, screamed, or pleaded when they pressed for sexual intimacy. Compared to the remaining 80 percent, these men had more sexual experience and were eagerly seeking further experience. They persistently sought sexual activity and used more exploitive techniques (seduction, false promises, professions of love) to gain it. In spite of their higher rate of "successful" sexual activity, their degree of satisfaction was low; 50.6 percent of the aggressive males described themselves as frustrated and dissatisfied, whereas only 30.7 percent of the nonaggressive males reported feelings of sexual frustration. A basic source of the differences in the two groups appeared to be peer group affiliation. When asked to what degree their friends pressured one another to seek premarital sex experience, 42 percent of the nonaggressive males reported feeling no pressure. Among aggressive males, only 13.8 percent felt no pressure. The results suggest that "sexual satisfaction is largely a function of the nature of peer group associations [and expectations], rather than of a given quantity of sexual outlets."[38]

### The double standard

Some of the differences in male and female sexual development have to do with the double standard in our culture. Generally, the teen-age code restricts the girl to petting when the relationship involves affection, but this restriction is not expected to apply to boys.[39] A cross-cultural study revealed that the double standard is much more acceptable to American and Canadian adolescents than to those in England and Norway.[40] When males move from private sexual experience to heterosexual experience, their first sexual relationships with girls are commonly self-centered and exploitive. The suggestion that sex is everywhere available which is communicated by movies and popular music makes "the boy who chooses to abstain or has trouble finding a partner [feel] more freakish than ever," and males may feel "under more pressure than ever before to prove themselves through the sex act."[41] Obviously, social scripts concerning the male image (reinforced by *Playboy* and James Bond movies, among others) influence the goal-oriented manipulative character of this stage of male sexuality.

This goal-oriented character of male sexuality is illustrated by William Masters and Virginia Johnson's experience with couples having sexual problems.[42] The first aspect of their treatment program is to teach the couple to enjoy touching and pleasing each other without any plans or goals in mind. They find that couples have to be taught to enjoy foreplay in and of itself, tending to be obsessed with the assumption that bodily contact must end in coitus. Clinical experience suggests that it is most frequently the man who is driven toward (and fearful of) the goal and has trouble enjoying physical contact for its own sake. The woman has the opposite problem; she can accept other physical expressions of love but may be hesitant when it comes to genital contact.[43]

By attempting to live out an image, the male deprives the sexual experience of his unique personal qualities. Because he feels he must be superior and goal directed, the male looses spontaneity, flexibility, and sensitivity—each of which is essential to a fully erotic experience. Our culture denies to men their full sexuality by depriving them of their sensitivity, their *care*fulness. Conversely, it deprives women of full selfhood by training the girl to be genitalless and selfless and by treating her virginity as something to be preserved, as if she would be contaminated if she experienced her own sexuality. The beauty of the heterosexual experience is that one comes to accept one's self and to enjoy another who is different. Unfortunately, the double standard and the sex-typing in our culture make it difficult for the meeting of the sexes to occur in a way which enhances the identity of both persons.

## When girl meets boy: Socialization continued

### Toward the heterosexual peer group

The move toward heterosexuality can be described in terms of changes in the social groupings of adolescents. On a basis of a field investigation of adolescent peer groups conducted in Australia, Dexter C. Dunphy has identified five stages in the sociological process of such groups. Thirteen-year-olds were found to cluster mainly in "unisexual cliques" (Stage 1). The cliques' chief activity is informal conversations; they function to provide information about and preparation for the members' entrance into larger groups—the crowd. In Stage 2 the young adolescents interact with the opposite sex, but only within the cliques; that is, group-to-group interaction of a boys' and a girls' clique paves the way for a single heterosexual clique. In Stage 3, individual-to-individual heterosexual interaction is initated by the upper status members of the unisexual cliques, and the first dating occurs. These members of the new heterosexual groups still retain leadership in the unisexual cliques and set the pattern which the other members follow, until a number of heterosexual cliques develop in close association (Stage 4: the fully developed crowd), and the unisexual cliques dissolve. Finally, as couples begin to go steady or get engaged, the crowd disintegrates and couples meet together in cliques.[44]

Care must be taken in generalizing from Dunphy's observations. Some subsocieties within American culture clearly do not move into the latter stages in the manner described. In lower-class society, for example, though the male moves into heterosexual relations, he retains the all-male group as his social base.[45] Instead of recreation shifting largely to couples' groups, as it does in middle-class culture, the male returns to the bar and poolroom to be with the guys. These males never become as accepting of feminine ways as middle-class husbands do. Instead, they generally become more stereotyped in their views and more hostile toward women.

Now that dormitories have become sexually mixed on many university campuses, it would be valuable to know whether these socialization patterns have changed. The traditional men's dorm seems surprisingly like the lower-class society just described. The male moves into heterosexual relations but maintains the all-male group as a social base. If this pattern is retained, it is likely that exploitation and the double standard will continue to receive social support.

It may be that the most important changes are occuring long before the adolescent faces the issue of mixed dorms, however. Dunphy described the first stage as one of unisexual cliques. Recently available data raise questions about that description. There is some evidence that preadolescent boys do not shun girls to the extent that once was the case. Studies in the twenties and thirties reported that friendship choices across sexes dropped to near zero from about third to eighth grade. A 1961 study in which preadolescents were asked to list "whom they liked best" found that 40 to 50 percent of students in grades five through seven made at least one cross-sex choice. The great majority of boys claimed to have a "sweetheart," declining from 86 percent in fifth and sixth grades to 74 percent in the seventh grade. (The percentages were higher for girls but followed the same pattern.) In fifth grade, 45 percent of the boys and 36 percent of the girls claimed to have dated, rising to 70 percent and 53 percent, respectively, in the seventh grade.[46]

A study conducted in 1963 verified the change in levels of preadolescent and adolescent heterosexual interest by using the identical questionnaire which had been used in a 1942 study, in the same schools as the original study. Of course, the population of the communities involved had changed in the 21 years between studies, but this is as close to a historical follow-up as is likely to be accomplished. Each subject was asked to indicate his first and second choice of companions for nine activities. The procedure of analyzing the data was to calculate the proportion of children of each sex and grade level (6th, 9th, and 12th) who made at least one choice involving a member of the opposite sex. For all six groups (boys and girls at each of three levels), heterosexual choices increased, as compared to the same groups in the earlier study. The changes were greater for girls but significant in all cases but one, the sixth-grade boys. Another finding was that boys chose girls more often than girls chose boys in the older grades, but in the sixth grade, girls made slightly more cross-sex choices than boys. In percentages chosen by a member of the opposite sex, the only reliable change was that more boys were chosen by girls in the sixth grade in 1963 than was the case in 1942. Thus the greater interest in heterosexuality is evident in choosing, but not in being chosen. Approximately the same proportion of boys and girls attracted choices from the opposite sex in 1963 as earlier.[47] Apparently a larger proportion of students than previously are wishing for friendships with members of a popular clique.

It is not clear from these two studies whether greater heterosexual interaction is really occurring or is merely being wished for. The data of the second study suggest that if any change in heterosexual interests has occurred at the sixth-grade level, only the girls have changed. The apparent conflict between results on these two studies for boys in the late elementary school grades could best be resolved by observational studies. Probably all-boy groups are still common in the socialization of boys, but it is questionable that preadolescence and early adolescence can still be thought of as a unisexual period.

Dunphy's Stage 3, the individual-to-individual heterosexual interaction, also appears to be changing. Some youths claim formal dating is a thing of the past; dates are less often planned in advance and are increasingly casual. There is a need for an up-to-date study similar to Dunphy's to determine the nature of the adolescent peer group process in our society today.

## The difficulty of getting together

Whatever the exact social process by which boy meets girl, when they get together they realize they have important differences in attitudes. In view of the differences in sex-role learning and sexual expectations, and the differences between male and female peer groups, this should not be surprising. To the boy and girl in the situation, however, it often comes as a surprise to discover the differences in their desires and goals.

The difference between the attitudes of young men and women regarding love and sex was first demonstrated in Winston Ehrmann's study of the dating behavior of 1,000 college students. Males stressed eroticism first and romanticism second; females reversed the priority.[48]

As stated, boys begin sexuality as a private personal experience and later move to sociosexuality. Girls, though less active sexually, are trained to view themselves self-consciously and to consider boys as desirable mates. They define attractiveness in sexual terms and include far more than genital pleasure in their interpretation of sexuality. A study of psychosocial development found that:

> Girls appear to be well-trained precisely in that area in which boys are poorly trained—that is, a belief in and a capacity for intense, emotionally-charged relationships and the language of romantic love. When girls during this period describe having been sexually aroused, they more often report it as a response to romantic, rather than erotic, words and actions.
>
> In later adolescence, as dates, parties and other sociosexual activities increase, boys—committed to sexuality and relatively untrained in the language and actions of romantic love—interact with girls, committed to romantic love and relatively untrained in sexuality. Dating and courtship may well be considered processes in which each sex trains the other in what each wants and expects. What data is available suggests that this exchange system does not always work very smoothly. Thus, ironically, it is not uncommon to find that the boy becomes emotionally involved with his partner and therefore lets up on trying to seduce her, at the same time that the girl comes to feel that the boy's affection is genuine and therefore that sexual intimacy is more permissible. . . .
>
> The male experience does conform to the general Freudian expectation that there is a developmental movement from a predominantly genital sexual commitment to a loving relationship with another person. But this movement is, in effect, reversed for females, with love or affection often a necessary precondition for intercourse.[49]

Erikson's theory of psychosocial stages[50] states that identity must precede intimacy. Before one can really meet another person with respect, one must be reasonably firm in his own identity. Thus early loves (both homosexual heroes and heterosexual crushes) have more to do with finding one's self than with discovering the other. This progression fits male experience rather well.

For boys the new sexuality is generally first experienced through masturbation and then through heterosexual experiences, which are likely to be viewed as conquests or proof of masculinity rather than as signs of intimacy. Later, when male sexual identity has been confirmed, the young man becomes secure enough to lose himself in another person and thus to accept the personhood of the woman as part of his experience.

For adolescent girls, the progression is different. Girls generally learn to accept the broader social and emotional aspects of love first; the act of love, the sexual act, is accepted only later, in the context of an intimate relationship. Since only a minority of females masturbate before they have experienced sexual relations with a partner,[51] and since for the majority of females first intercourse becomes possible only in stable relationships or those with strong bonds,[52] it would appear likely that girls do not really learn to accept their bodies, specifically their genital sexuality, until they have attained intimacy. In the area of sexuality, for girls, intimacy precedes identity and self-affirmation. In other areas of adolescent concern, issues of identity probably precede intimacy for the girl as well as for the boy; personal relationships in early adolescence have to do with self-discovery, and only later does the adolescent girl overcome her preoccupation with herself and learn to focus on the other, to meet him as a person without primary regard for fulfillment of her own needs. The girl, like the boy, must accept herself before she can accept others.

### From groups to pairs

Scientific knowledge of how individuals select the partners they will marry is lacking, but the process by which casual acquaintances develop into serious pairs is beginning to be understood. Couples at first perceive similarities; this leads to the development of rapport between the two. A mutual trust develops, which allows self-disclosure. As each learns the other' needs and desires, they begin to assume roles in relation to each other. These steps in the developing relationship of couples have been carefully enough defined to allow one psychologist, Robert A. Lewis, to predict with some success which dating couples would still be together after two years.[53] Theoretically, the role taking is followed by a testing of role fit, which, if successful, leads to confirmation of the couple's relationship (such as engagement). This last part of the theory has not been tested successfully. The social and interactional aspects of mate selection merit much further study.

Earlier theories focused upon individual dynamics in mate selection. Psychoanalytic theory, for example, claimed that children grow up to seek a mate similar to their parent of the opposite sex. Research has now shown this is not necessarily the case; the ideal mate more often resembles the most loved parent, regardless of sex.[54]

Perhaps in the future interactional theories (such as that used by Lewis to predict dating) will provide a link between sociological processes (such as in Dunphy's field study) and individual variables. Data are too scattered and scanty to attempt such an integration now. Lewis' model includes the discovery of the partner's needs and the establishment of mutually compatible roles. One wonders what effects changes in sex roles may have on this process of mate selection.

### *Sexual intimacy and identity*

The problems of communication which occur when boy meets girl clearly reflect the splitting of their roles into expressive and goal-directed orientations. The male brings to the interaction a positive affirmation of sexuality; however, his goal directedness may lead to exploitative and manipulative interactions which are destructive to the girl's identity and, indirectly, to his own. The girl brings a desire for warm, personal interaction which may be tinged with dependency; her interactions may restrict and inhibit them both. For the interaction to progress positively, each must learn something from the other. The boy must help the girl discover the sexual aspects of her identity. The girl must teach the boy about caring and intimacy.

Erikson has noted that early adolescent boy-girl relations include a type of interchange in which intimacy serves identity. The boy and girl interact, he suggests, not so much to understand the other as to get feedback on their own identity. This puppy love is very much an event in the identity quest, rather than an act of mature intimacy.[55] Certainly the young adult who has learned to accept himself is more able than the adolescent to give to another and to focus the relationship upon the other's needs. In that sense, mature intimacy is less concerned with finding oneself. But even in the later form of intimacy, when a person seeks to understand the other, he is affected by the other and changes and grows. In every real sharing experience, both persons grow; identities are rediscovered and altered. There is no clear pattern to suggest that identity must precede intimacy; intimacy also alters identity. Identity and intimacy appear much more closely intertwined than Erikson's system suggests.

In the area of sexuality, identity and intimacy seem very closely linked indeed. Following the usual pattern, males have a somewhat autonomous identity (in this case, a private sexual experience) before moving to intimacy. For girls, the discovery and acceptance of mature genital sexuality most frequently occurs during an intimate relationship with another person. The area of sexual identity provides an important illustration of the necessity of interpersonal interaction in the affirmation of identity. Unfortunately, our culture's sex-role training frequently results in negative interactions, to the detriment of identity and intimacy.

## Problems with sexual training in our culture

The degree of sensationalism in popular press accounts of adolescent sexuality makes it difficult to assess the real difficulties. The adolescent peer culture is neither so sensational nor so deviant from the adult cultural norms as it is usually portrayed. There are real problems, but they are not directly attributable to youth culture; they are the problems of American culture as a whole.

One way to assess the adequacy of our culture's system of sex education is to ask if youth is correctly informed regarding sex. The answer is that there is considerable misinformation about sex among young people. Reliable data are scarce, but it appears that even college students are poorly informed, despite their appearance of sophistication. Data from a study of Canadian university students, mostly freshmen, showed that self-ratings on adequacy of sex knowledge had no relationship to actual scores on a sex knowledge test. Males greatly overestimated their understanding of the structure and function of sex organs and their knowledge about venereal disease. Females also were much more poorly informed on VD than they claimed and overestimated their knowledge of conception and masturbation.[56]

Ignorance about masturbation is surprisingly widespread. The false belief that mental illness can be caused by masturbation was held by 50 percent of the graduating class of one school. Though the study is dated (1961), the statistic is still surprising because the subjects were medical students. Supporting my contention that the problem is not limited to youth, the study discovered that 20 percent of the faculty of the medical school also held this misconception![57]

An unfortunate aspect of adult silence on sex is that the individual adolescent experiences strong desires for sex and faces tremendous pressure for conformity from the peer group, but gets little help in placing sex in total life perspective. Since the adolescent is denied opportunities for adult roles in other aspects of society,[58] sex may become the one area in which he proves his adult status. Thus the act of intimacy becomes burdened with the excess baggage of other issues, confusing further the attainment of identity and genuine intimacy. The use of sex to prove male prowess was noted in the discussion of the double standard. Girls also use sex to serve other needs; they may allow sexual intimacy to counteract insecurity about their own worthiness of love. Clinicians generally agree that such ulterior motives are frequently involved in out-of-wedlock pregnancies; thus it is difficult to know to what degree these pregnancies are due to inaccurate sex information. What is clear is that unprepared-for pregnancies are common among youth. A large percentage, if not the majority, of marriages involving a partner 18 years old or under are precipitated at least in part because of pregnancy.[59]

The most serious problems with sex training in our society concern such deeper issues as the stereotyping of sex roles and the manipulative view of sex. One contributer to these problems is the lack of available identification figures for the late adolescent. Adults in the past have played an important role as identification figures and objects of early adolescent love before the youth was ready to involve himself in intimacy with a peer of the opposite sex. Some sources consider crushes on an older person part of the normal progression toward mature love.[60] Since the adolescent's search for sexual identity occurs concurrent with his increased separation from his nuclear family, it is appropriate for the adolescent boy, for example, to observe adult males other than his father before crystalizing his own style of masculinity.

One way in which youths do find adult identification figures is through involvement with the families of their dates, particularly when a couple go steady. Many an adolescent has expressed, in retrospect, the importance of the steady's family in providing him with a close look at another pattern of family interaction and sex roles. Students in counseling have reported after breaking up with a steady, "I missed her family almost as much as I missed her." This opportunity to observe adult models outside one's own family, but to see them in a personal setting, is crucial to avoiding a premature or stereotyped sex identification. Adults who are willing to enter into personal interaction with adolescents, going beyond their roles as parents of the girl friend, or teacher, or group leaders, serve an important function in adolescents' quests for their own style of being a man or woman.

During late adolescence, adult models could be most valuable. It is then that the reassessment of values usually occurs and sharply different attitudes toward sex emerge between adolescents and their parents.[61] Since the college student has normally left the home, he may be most open at this point to other styles of home life and adult roles. Unfortunately, the increasing depersonalization of the college campus and the professionalization of the teaching role deprive many late adolescents of a chance to know adults personally. Instead, they become engulfed in a culture made up almost entirely of people in their own age group, and their interaction with adults is usually limited to the contractual relations of teacher-student, administrator-student, and so on. Research on a large number of campuses has documented that most faculties are ineffectual as models and teachers in areas of values; when change occurs in the student's values, it is usually the result of the peer group.[62] The solution to the vacuum on college campuses lies not in a reassertion of institutional authority but in providing the structures and incentives which encourage the faculty to dare to be more personal.

A lack of accurate sex information, a lack of personal models for sexual identity and for support in the struggle to affirm personal values, and the confusion of differing goals when boy meets girl combine to make the area of sexuality a tense and alienating one. The youth is caught between feminine aspects of the culture, which treat sex as a guilt-producing aspect of self, and masculine orientations, which encourage a manipulative grabbing "for what he can get." The first alienates the youth from himself; the second alienates him from the other. Thus aspects of the cultural training in sexuality handicap both his attainment of identity and his development of intimacy.

Perhaps we can find hope in the possibility that cultural attitudes are changing.

### Parent-youth differences: Have sexual attitudes changed?

Studies show sharp differences between parents and adolescents on sexual values, particularly between mothers and daughters with reference to premarital chastity.[63] The fact that parents are more conservative in the sexual standards they hold for their children does not indicate that sexual behavior has changed. Ira Reiss has gathered considerable evidence that one's views about premarital sex become more conservative when one becomes a parent.[64] Many individuals who advocated a more permissive sexual ethic in their youth become concerned for protecting the institution of the family when they assume parental roles. It seems that the difference in roles, rather than age difference or change in sexual attitudes, is the main factor in the gap between adolescent and parental attitudes toward sexual behavior.

The real revolution in sexual behavior appears to have occurred in the twenties. Youth in that decade reported a higher incidence of premarital intercourse than previously. Though the popular media proclaimed that sexual behavior was changing in the fifties and sixties, scientific studies failed to show much change.[65] Little change was documented from the twenties up to the early sixties. Perhaps what was occurring then was a change in attitudes to match the change in behavior which had already occurred. What appeared to popular writers to be a sexual revolution was primarily an acceptance of behavior that the older generation had already practiced, but (and this is an important change) youth was openly affirming the behavior and positively valuing it, while the older generation practiced it privately and with conflict.

While the dominant adult values continue to affirm love and marriage as the prerequisites for coitus, peer group standards often accept some premarital sexual relations, provided the girl is in love.[66] A shift can be discerned at least in an important minority of youth, away from the double standard and toward an acceptance of premarital intercourse in the context of an affectionate relationship, as will be discussed more fully below. Ehrmann found that "In the past, emphasis was placed on the girl's virginity at the time of marriage; but today, many young people may only emphasize her being a virgin until she is in love, which may mean at the stage of going steady or engagement."[67]

The difference in parents' and adolescents' sexual attitudes may be a source of conflict. By the time the children have reached adolescence they have sensed that it is not wise to discuss sex openly with their parents. Thus the difference between the older and younger generations' values in regard to sex are generally handled by a "conspiracy of silence."[68] Robert Bells' study of college coeds found that while 83 percent of the girls' mothers felt their daughters should freely answer the mother's questions regarding the daughter's attitudes toward sexual intimacy, only

37 percent of the daughters felt they should be expected to answer such questions. The sharp differences between mothers' and daughters' attitudes toward premarital sexual behavior do not generally emerge until the girl is around age 20.[69] But even in early adolescence it is likely that duplicity on the part of the parents and lack of effective adult definitions for adolescent behavior contribute to the adolescent's increasing reliance on his peer culture for both his information and his values regarding sexuality.

The declining influence of parents on the sexual behavior of youth[70] can be seen in the context of the increasing autonomy of the individual in the selection of a spouse. Courtship used to be a social institution through which the parents helped in mate selection. As the extended family diminished in importance, choice of mate increasingly became a decision between the boy and girl; gradually unchaperoned dating replaced older forms of courtship. Increasing affluence, which allows youth more privacy (in cars, dormitories, and so on), and diminished fears of prolonged relationships resulted in the form of dating called "going steady." Earlier it had been important to keep dating from leading too early to preparation for marriage; dating served as a transitional social institution which encouraged "play relations" to avoid "getting serious."[71] Now young people who long for deeper personal relationships are painfully aware of dating as a game, and many of them are attempting to reformulate their own sexual values.

The separation of the generations in regard to sexual attitudes and behavior may be necessary at this stage in history in order for youth to develop more consistent and humane values than those sanctioned by the larger culture. The negative aspects of the lack of adult involvement in youth's sexual decisions have been alluded to: the overevaluation of the importance of sexual experience, regardless of its personal meaning; the youthful stress on fun, without adequate concern for future consequences; the acceptance of stereotypic standards of physical beauty, to name a few. It remains to be seen whether future changes in sexual behavior will reflect a more humane value orientation or simply a breakdown in older standards.

### The new morality: A trend?

The student in college, even though he may be isolated from personal interaction with mature adults, is at least likely to be confronted within his peer group with value orientations different from his own. No apologies should be needed for incorporating a discussion of morality in a psychology book; value orientations are crucial in analyses of the identity quest. A campus psychiatrist, Dana Farnsworth, has clarified three attitudes toward sexual morality that are common on the campuses today:

traditional morality, amorality, and the new morality.[72] He associates the traditional morality with Freudian psychology and the belief that repressive authoritarian control is necessary to the survival of civilization. Restraint allows sublimation of sexual energy into more socially productive tasks.

The amoral viewpoint is in some ways the polar opposite. Social concern is not stressed but is presumed to occur automatically, as in laissez-faire economics. "The central belief," Farnsworth stated, "is that no restrictions are needed. If sexual impulses are allowed free rein, tension, anxiety, and frustration will be lowered, and happiness, satisfaction in living, and effectiveness increased."[73]

The new morality stresses personal fidelity and interpersonal concern, caring, and love of the sexual partner and opposes exploitation.

Another campus psychiatrist, Robert Nixon, has spoken out in defense of the new morality as follows:

> [The older generation] is afraid that the new mode of control is totally relativistic, entirely shorn of the comfort and security of moral absolutes; but in my view [they] are wrong. When I was young the absolutes were spelled out, but they were not defined. A sign high on the wall of the university gym read "Don't smoke; smoking leads to drinking. Don't drink; drinking leads to petting. Don't pet; petting leads to something else." Today the absolutes have not yet been spelled out, but they are in the process of being defined. The first one has to do with pregnancy; the youthful generation is aware of the responsibility of pregnancy and they intend their sexual gropings to stop short of that result until and unless they themselves are ready to assume the responsibility. And the second absolute has to do with man's relation to his fellow man. The youthful generation does not condone sex for the sake of controling, manipulating, or exploiting others, or as a defense against others, or as a means of aggrandizing oneself or as a dehumanized source of "kicks." In short, the young are trying to discover the appropriate place of sex in the mature life, and in their efforts they have pared down the moral absolutes to concrete issues.[74]

Is there a shift toward the new morality, or has the popular press simply reported a surface phenomenon, as was the case in the fifties and sixties? Hard data suggesting that such a change is occurring are scarce and limited to studies of college students. Nonetheless, it appears that there has been some behavioral change in the past two decades.

In the midsixties the Institute for Sex Research surveyed a sample of college students in order to make comparisons with the Kinsey data which had been collected some 20 years earlier. The comparisons on one aspect of sexual behavior, first intercourse before marriage, showed that the differences between how males and females view love and sex are still present. The study found that females still "surrender their virginity to males they love, whereas males are much less emotionally involved."[75] Love was involved in 70 to 90 percent of the cases for the girl, but in only 11 to 14 percent for the boy. It is noteworthy, however, that the percentages of boys having first intercourse with someone they loved had tripled, compared to the 1 to 5 percent of the earlier Kinsey report. Prostitution, on the other hand, had become quite insignificant as a source of the male's first intercourse, dropping from 20 to 25 percent in the earlier study to between 2 and 7 percent in the later one. The former pattern of first intercourse being between an older male and a younger female seems to be breaking down; first intercourse was reported most often between those of the same age.

All these changes suggest that the double standard in which the male exploits the female, though still dominant, is breaking down. The consequences of such a breakdown appear positive.[76] The study showed no great change in the age at which first intercourse occurred for men; it still was taking place in the later years of high school and the early years of college, when youth is being freed from parental restraints. There was a great increase in the percentage of college girls who reported experiencing intercourse, jumping from 20 percent in 1953 to between 35 and 40 percent in 1965.[77] In the earlier studies, a much larger percentage of college males than females reported they were experienced in intercourse, reflecting the fact that males were not having their experiences with women with whom they had the closest contact. Apparently the view that there are two kinds of girls, those males can have fun with and those they respect and would consider marrying, is less predominant today. The Institute's survey also revealed a marked trend toward greater enjoyment of first intercourse, especially among girls, finding that "the figure for coed freshmen who reported enjoying initial intercourse is 73 percent as compared to only 46 percent in the older study. There [was] also an increase in the number of girls reporting orgasm in initial intercourse."[78] Dr. Paul Gebhard, who heads the Institute for Sex Research at Indiana University, interpreted the data as follows: "All of this sounds like a continuation of the trend toward sexual equality with the female being regarded both by males and by herself as less a sexual object to be exploited and more as a person with her own needs, expectations, and rights."[79]

Two extensive longitudinal studies have been conducted which resulted in findings similar to those reported above. Three classes of Vassar College students (women) were tested in their freshman and senior years,[80] and both men and women students at the Stanford and Berkeley campuses in California were followed through their college years from 1961 to 1965.[81] These studies showed that the students' attitudes grew increasingly permissive as they became more experienced sexually during their college years. The California study showed little change in the frequency of coitus for college males, as compared to previous studies, but the interpersonal character of those experiences had changed. Formerly, college males usually had their early experiences with girls with whom they had little personal relationship: party girls or prostitutes. Today's males far more frequently have their experiences within the context of a serious dating relationship. Consequently, the rate of premarital intercourse for college women appears to be rising.[82] There is little reason to fear that this rise will lead to a permissive promiscuity. Though college students hold increasingly liberal attitudes toward sexual relations, they reject the idea of a promiscuous society.[83] Rather, we seem to be moving toward the Scandinavian model of sexual behavior, which condones premarital sexual relations between people in love.[84] The move reflects a changing norm, not a normlessness.

An integration of personal and sexual intimacy, though still limited to a minority of youth, appears to be becoming the norm. An analysis of sociological factors involved in this change suggests that the trend will continue.[85] The present attempt to integrate personal and sexual intimacy also involves exploration with new forms.

The noted anthropologist Margaret Mead suggested decades ago that our culture needed to experiment with some less repressive way of institutionalizing sexuality during the period from pubescence to marriage, since we have extended that period to nearly a decade in our society. She suggested the possibility of an early marriage concerned primarily with the development of intimacy rather than the establishment of a family, with a later marriage for the purpose of child rearing. Perhaps such a pattern is beginning to develop. Increasingly in campus areas serious young couples are living together in trial marriages, and such arrangements have become more and more acceptable, at least among the peer group. It is far too early to evaluate such arrangements; sociological studies on them have just been begun.[86] Judging from those students who have come for counseling, it appears to me that many such arrangements provide a healthy growing experience. The experimentation with new forms has started. Certainly there will be errors and mistakes, but at least individual styles may be developed, and stereotypes may be left behind. Nixon concluded that youths "are making mistakes, some of them pretty drastic, but mistake making is in the nature of learning by experience."[87]

## Mature sexuality: Caring for self and others

This chapter has explored the physical and psychological differences between men and women and the struggle of their meeting in a way that enriches both. The physical, social, and moral issues are complex and cannot be summarized neatly, but a symbol drawn from the youth culture may be helpful.

A friend was walking with me near a college campus when a number of students passed us on the street. The friend, very much a part of the older generation, remarked with scorn, "I can't even tell if those were boys or girls." The changes in male hair styles and the increase in unisex clothing seem to me symbolic of adolescence today, standing as a symbol that the central issue is not sex but being an individual in contemporary society. My friend was conscious of similarities between male and female hair and dress, but he failed to take note of the remarkable diversity in individual clothes and grooming. Instead of every boy wearing his hair in essentially the same style, there were myriads of styles, a different cut for each unique face. Unisex is not, then, the destruction of differences but the search for the individual's unique way of being a person.

What these youths are recognizing and affirming is that every genuine meeting is the coming together of two unique individuals. Sexuality, then, is not an issue in itself. It is simply a part of the larger issue of identity and intimacy. The question is not so much finding one's masculinity or feminity, but discovering one's humanness.

Since the beginning of adolescence is marked by the emergence of adult sexuality, traditionally the closure of adolescence has been described as the establishment of heterosexual commitment. It would seem more appropriate today to describe adolescence as being completed when the individual is able to affirm his individuality and yet lose himself in intimacy. Both the image of closure and the focus on male and female roles and heterosexuality seem inappropriate and dated. It is not the declaration "I am a man" and the ability, consequently, to love a woman which is central. Sexuality is merely an aspect of carnateness—and the affirmation "This body is me" and "I can love and care for other bodies" marks maturity. Harry Stack Sullivan has described intimacy as occurring when a person can be as concerned for the needs of another as he is for his own.[88] What today's youth seem to be sensing, in their experimentation with new styles, is that genuine caring is not an absorption in the other and does not deny one's separateness and individuality. Mature love is not a bond. As expressed in a contemporary folk song, it's not "the inkstains on some page that bind us":

> And it's knowing I'm not shackled by
> forgotten words and bonds
> and the inkstains that have dried
> upon some line . . .
> That keeps you ever gentle on my mind.[89]

The following extract from *The Prophet*, by Kahlil Gibran, though given in the context of a discussion of marriage, expresses well the mature love of a secure identity:

Then Almitra spoke again and said, And what of Marriage, master? And he answered saying: You were born together, and together you shall be forevermore. You shall be together when the white wings of death scatter your days. Aye, you shall be together even in the silent memory of God. But let there be spaces in your togetherness, and let the winds of the heavens dance between you.

Love one another, but make not a bond of love: Let it rather be a moving sea between the shores of your souls. Fill each other's cup but drink not from one cup. Give one another of your bread but eat not from the same loaf.

Sing and dance together and be joyous, but let each one of you be alone, even as the strings of a lute are alone though they quiver with the same music.

Give your hearts, but not into each other's keeping. For only the hand of Life can contain your hearts. And stand together yet not too near together: For the pillars of the temple stand apart, and the oak tree and the cypress grow not in each other's shadow.[90]

## Summary

The development of sexual identity provides a prototype for male/female differences in the total identity crisis. Girls receive more sex instruction from mother and are more dependent upon the norms of the family than boys are. For girls, sexual interests are kept diffuse and romanticized, with the support of a small group of intimate friends. When the girl moves into a heterosexual relationship, her primary goal is to find love.

Adolescent males receive little sexual information from the family and are less tied to family prescriptions of sexual behavior. Usually early sexual experience is private; the all-male peer group supports the transition to genital, goal-directed heterosexual behavior. Typically, when boy meets girl, he is looking for sex, she is searching for love.

The split in sex roles and the double standard frequently make it hard for the sexes to develop mutually satisfying and enriching relationships. There is some evidence that college youth, at least, are moving away from the double standard. The limited data suggest that they are moving not toward permissiveness but toward a more principled sexual morality.

## Notes

1. The timing and order of development may vary. See Howard V. Meredith, "A Synopsis of Pubertal Changes in Youth," *Journal of School Health*, 37 (1967): 171–76.

2. Gordon Shipman, "The Psychodynamics of Sex Education," in *Adolescent Behavior and Society: A Book of Readings*, ed. Rolf E. Muuss (New York: Random House, 1971), p. 331. The nature of Shipman's sample is not clearly described.

3. Gene R. Medinus and Ronald C. Johnson: *Child and Adolescent Psychology: Behavior and Development* (New York: John Wiley & Sons, 1969), p. 662.

4. Clay V. Brittain, "Adolescent Choices and Parent-Peer Cross-Pressures," *American Sociological Review*, 28 (1963): 385–91; M. C. Dubbe, "What Teen-Agers Can't Tell Parents and Why," *Family Coordinator*, 4 (1956): 3–7.

5. Frederick Elkin and William A. Westley, "The Myth of Adolescent Culture," *American Sociological Review*, 20 (1955): 680–84.

6. Elizabeth Douvan and Joseph Adelson, *The Adolescent Experience* (New York: John Wiley and Sons, 1966).

7. John E. Horrocks, *The Psychology of Adolescence: Behavior and Development*, 3rd ed. (Boston: Houghton Mifflin Co., 1969).

8. C. P. Stone and R. G. Barker, "The Attitudes and Interests of Pre-menarchial and Post-menarchial Girls," *Journal of Genetic Psychology*, 54 (1939): 27–71.

9. William Simon and John Gagnon, "Psychosexual Development," *Transaction* (March 1969): 15–16.

10. Shipman, "Psychodynamics of Sex Education," pp. 333–34.

11. Ibid., p. 334.

12. Ibid., p. 333.

13. Ibid.

14. E. L. Reynolds and J. V. Wines, "Physical Changes Associated with Adolescence in Boys," *American Journal of Diseases of Children*, 82 (1951): 529–47. The correction for secular trend has been made as described in Chapter 8, note 1.

15. Alfred C. Kinsey, Wardell B. Pomeroy, and Clyde E. Martin, *Sexual Behavior in the Human Male* (Philadelphia: W. B. Saunders Co., 1948).

16. Group for the Advancement of Psychiatry, eds., *Normal Adolescence* (New York: Charles Scribner and Sons, 1968), pp. 21, 105.

17. Kinsey, Pomeroy, and Martin, *Sexual Behavior in the Human Male*, p. 501.

18. Shipman, "Psychodynamics of Sex Education," p. 334.

19. A. C. Kinsey, et al., *Sexual Behavior in the Human Female* (Philadelphia: W. B. Saunders Co., 1953), p. 717, Figure 1, "Comparisons of Female and Male Experience and Orgasm."

20. Kinsey, Pomeroy, and Martin, *Sexual Behavior in the Human Male*, p. 302, Table 69.

21. Ibid., pp. 277 and 512.

22. Peter Blos, *On Adolescence: A Psychoanalytic Interpretation* (New York: Free Press, 1962), pp. 160–61 and 169.

23. Frederick S. Perls, Ralph F. Hefferline, and Paul Goodman, *Gestalt Therapy* (New York: Julian Press, 1951).

24. Mazie G. Gurin, "Differences in Psychological Characteristics of Latency and Adolescence: A Test of the Relevant Psychoanalytic Propositions Utilizing Projective Material," unpublished doctoral diss., University of Michigan, 1953.

25. The availability of the model does not, of course, ensure that the model will be imitated. Another important factor is the adolescent's prior adjustment in the family. Poor adjustment in the family increases the youth's susceptibility to peer influences. Charles E. Bowerman and John W. Kinch, "Changes in Family and Peer

Orientation of Children between the Fourth and Tenth Grades," *Social Forces,* 37 (1959): 206–11.

26. Walter B. Miller, "Lower Class Culture as a Generating Milieu of Gang Delinquency," *The Journal of Social Issues,* 14 (1958).

27. See Chapters 4 and 5.

28. Most of the recent research supports this view: Denise Kandel and Gerald S. Lesser, *Youth in Two Worlds: United States and Denmark* (San Francisco: Jossey-Bass, Publishers, 1972); Ira L. Reiss, "Sexual Codes in Teen-Age Culture," *Annals of the American Academy of Political and Social Sciences,* 338 (1961): 53–62. The view that peer groups are an antiadult culture finds most of its empirical support in James S. Coleman, *The Adolescent Society: The Social Life of the Teenager and Its Impact on Education* (New York: Free Press, 1961). Unfortunately, Coleman did not gather direct data from parents; the differences found are based on adolescents' perceptions.

29. Lee G. Burchinal, "Adolescent Dating Attitudes and Behavior." In H. T. Christensen, ed., *Handbook of Marriage and the Family* (Chicago: Rand McNally, 1964).

30. Reiss, "Sexual Codes in Teen-Age Culture," p. 62.

31. Douvan and Adelson, *Adolescent Experience.*

32. Henry Stack Sullivan, *The Interpersonal Theory of Psychiatry* (New York: W. W. Norton & Co., 1953), pp. 245–46.

33. Wardell B. Pomeroy, *Boys and Sex* (New York: Delacorte Press, 1968), chap. 5, pp. 59–76.

34. "Response bias" means that those subjects who answer questionnaires or surveys are not a random sample; for example, those with more sexual freedom might be more willing to answer, thus inflating the percentages responding in a "deviant" manner. "Social desirability" refers to answering questions falsely in the direction approved by our society; for example, respondents may agree to answer surveys but then present their sexual histories in such a way as to sound more "normal" than they are. In this case, the two effects might cancel each other out.

35. See Merle Miller, "What It Means to Be a Homosexual," *New York Times Magazine,* January 17, 1971, pp. 9–11, 48–49, 57, 60.

36. Clellan S. Ford and Frank A. Beach, *Patterns of Sexual Behavior* (New York: Harper & Row, Publishers, 1951).

37. It is questionable whether adult homosexuality, when it is not a symptom of fear of intimacy with the opposite sex, should be labeled pathological. A cross-cultural perspective might lower our tendency to overreact.

38. Eugene J. Kanin, "An Examination of Sexual Aggression as a Response to Sexual Frustration," *Journal of Marriage and the Family,* 29 (1967): 428–33.

39. P. H. Landis, "Research on Teen-Age Marriage," *Marriage and Family Living,* 22 (1960): 266–67. Also see I. L. Reiss, *The Social Context of Premarital Permissiveness* (New York: Holt, Rinehart & Winston, 1967).

40. E. B. Luckey and G. D. Nass, "A Comparison of Sexual Attitudes and Behavior in an International Sample," *Journal of Marriage and the Family,* 31 (1969): 364–79.

41. Seymour L. Halleck, "Sex and Mental Health on the Campus," *Journal of the American Medical Association,* 200 (1967): 684–90.

42. William H. Masters and Virginia E. Johnson, *Human Sexual Inadequacy* (Boston: Little, Brown & Co., 1970).

43. Inflexibility and domination are most dramatically evident among lower-class

males, where it is sometimes considered perverse for a man to assume any position in intercourse other than the "superior" one—the man on top.

44. Dexter C. Dunphy, "The Social Structure of Urban Adolescent Peer Groups," *Sociometry*, 26 (1963): 230–46.

45. Walter B. Miller, "Lower Class Culture as a Generating Milieu of Gang Delinquency," *Journal of Social Issues*, 143 (1958).

46. Carlfred B. Broderick and Stanley E. Flower, "New Patterns of Relationships between the Sexes among Preadolescents," *Marriage and Family Living*, 23 (1961): 27–30.

47. Raymond G. Kuhlen and Nancy B. Houlihan, "Adolescent Heterosexual Interest in 1942 and 1963," *Child Development*, 36 (1965:) 1049–52.

48. Winston W. Ehrmann, *Premarital Dating Behavior* (New York: Holt, Rinehart & Winston, 1959).

49. Simon and Gagnon, "Psychosexual Development," p. 15. Published by permission of Transaction, Inc. Copyright © 1969 by Transaction, Inc. Similar descriptions of differences in attitudes between the sexes are presented in Carlfred B. Broderick, "Going Steady: The Beginning of the End," in *Teen-Age Marriage and Divorce*, ed. Seymour Farber and R. H. L. Wilson (San Francisco: Diablo Press, 1967), and in W. B. Pomeroy, *Boys and Sex*, pp. 90–91.

50. Reprinted from *Identity: Youth and Crisis* by Erik H. Erikson. By permission of W. W. Norton & Company, Inc. Copyright © 1968 by W. W. Norton & Company, Inc. Austen Riggs Monograph No. 7.

51. Wardell B. Pomeroy, *Girls and Sex* (New York: Delecorte, 1969), p. 128.

52. Simon and Gagnon, "Psychosexual Development," p. 128.

53. Robert A. Lewis, "A Longitudinal Test of a Developmental Framework for Premarital Dyad Formation," *Journal of Marriage and the Family*, 35 (1973): 16–25.

54. Willard Waller and Reuben Hill, *The Family* (New York: Dryden Press, 1951).

55. Erikson, *Identity: Youth and Crisis*, p. 132.

56. A. McCreary-Juhasz, "How Accurate Are Student Evaluations of the Extent of Their Knowledge of Human Sexuality?" *The Journal of School Health*, 37 (1967): 409–12.

57. R. K. Greenbank, "Are Medical Students Learning Psychiatry?" *Pennsylvania Medical Journal*, 64 (1961): 989–92.

58. Paul Goodman, *Growing up Absurd* (New York: Random House, 1956).

59. Lee G. Burchinal, "Trends and Prospects for Young Marriages in the United States," *Journal of Marriage and the Family*, 27 (1965): 243–54.

60. Harold W. Bernard, *Adolescent Development* (Scranton, Pa.: Intext Educational Publishers, 1971), pp. 204–5.

61. Robert R. Bell, "Parent-Child Conflict in Sexual Values," *Journal of Social Issues*, 22 (1966): 34–44.

62. P. E. Jacob, *Changing Values in College* (New York: Harper Bros., 1957); Theodore M. Newcomb, "Student Peer-Group Influence," in *The American College: A Psychological and Social Interpretation of the Higher Learning*, ed. Nevitt Sanford (New York: John Wiley & Sons, 1962), pp. 469–88.

63. Bell, "Parent-Child Conflict in Sexual Values."

64. Ira L. Reiss, *The Family System in America* (New York: Holt, Rinehart & Winston, 1971).

65. Ira L. Reiss, *Premarital Sexual Standards in America: A Sociological Investi-*

*gation of the Relative Social and Cultural Integration of American Sexual Standards* (New York: Free Press, 1960).

66. Bell, "Parent-Child Conflict in Sexual Values."

67. Ehrmann, *Premarital Dating Behavior.*

68. Ernest A. Smith, "The Date," in *American Youth Culture* (Glencoe, Ill.: Free Press, 1956).

69. Bell, "Parent-Child Conflict in Sexual Values."

70. Reiss, *Premarital Sexual Standards in America,* pp. 246–47.

71. Smith, "The Date"; Burchinal, "Adolescent Dating Attitudes and Behavior."

72. Dana L. Farnsworth, "Sexual Morality and the Dilemma of the Colleges," *American Journal of Orthopsychiatry,* 35 (1965).

73. Ibid.

74. Robert E. Nixon, *The Art of Growing* (New York: Random House, 1962), p. 99.

75. Isadore Rubin, "Changing College Sex: New Kinsey Report." Reprinted from *Sexology Magazine* © 1968 by Sexology Corporation.

76. Reiss predicted this breakdown in *Premarital Sexual Standards in America,* arguing that the standard of "permissiveness with affection" would have the best cultural integration and most positive value consequences. See Reiss's chap. 8, p. 178 ff.

77. Paul Gebhard, quoted by Lucia Nouat, "Not All Students Want to Srap the Rules," in *Christian Science Monitor,* April 22, 1967.

78. Rubin, "Changing College Sex."

79. Ibid., p. 781.

80. Mervin B. Freedman, "The Sexual Behavior of American College Woman: An Empirical Study and an Historical Survey," *Merrill-Palmer Quarterly of Behavior and Development,* 11 (1965): 33–39.

81. Joseph Katz, ed., *No Time for Youth* (San Francisco: Jossey-Bass, Publishers, 1968).

82. R. R. Bell and J. B. Chaskes, "Premarital Sexual Experience among Coeds, 1958 and 1968," *Journal of Marriage and the Family,* 32 (1970): 81–84.

83. Halleck, "Sex and Mental Health on the Campus."

84. H. T. Christensen, "Scandinavian and American Sex Norms: Some Comparisons with Sociological Implications," *Journal of Social Issues,* 22 (1966): 60–75.

85. Reiss, *Family System in America,* p. 172, and *Premarital Sexual Standards in America,* p. 247.

86. See, for example, Jason Montgomery, "Toward an Understanding of Cohabitation" (Ph.D. diss., University of Massachusetts, 1972).

87. Nixon, *The Art of Growing,* p. 99.

88. Sullivan, *Interpersonal Theory of Psychiatry,* chaps. 14, 15, and 16.

89. John Hartford, "Gentle on My Mind." Copyright © 1967 and 1971 by Glaser Publications, Inc. Used by permission.

90. Reprinted from *The Prophet,* by Kahlil Gibran, with permission of the publisher, Alfred A. Knopf, Inc. Copyright 1923 by Kahlil Gibran; renewal copyright 1951 by Administrators C.T.A. of Kahlil Gibran Estate, and Mary G. Gibran.

# 10

## CRISIS THREE
### Work: Vocation or drudgery?

IN WESTERN HISTORY, the identification of the boy with his father facilitated his occupational role learning. In the agrarian society the boy worked in the fields beside his father and learned from him, taking over the same piece of land when his elders could no longer manage it. Even centuries later, as specialization increased, it still was assumed that the cobbler's son would become a cobbler. Work was learned through the personal model closest at hand. Even where there were too many sons to be supported by the farm, those who left to become apprentices learned their trade by doing it beside a more skilled craftsman. For the most part, one's vocation was assigned, not chosen, and was learned contiguous with the rest of growth and learning. One's status in life was simply accepted as part of the given order of things. It was not chosen.

At the time of the Protestant Reformation, early rumblings of the Industrial Revolution were being heard. The effects of the printing press in spreading Reformation teachings are well known. Martin Luther's sensitivity to the historical changes of his time was reflected in his concept of a doctrine of vocations as a foundation stone of Reformation theology. Vocation means, literally, one's calling, and Luther argued that not only is the ordained priest called to his task, but that:

> . . . a cobbler, a smith, a peasant, every man has the office and function of his calling. . . . All alike are consecrated priests and bishops, and every man should in his office or function be useful and beneficial to the rest, so that various kinds of work may all be united for furtherance of body and soul, just as the members of the body all serve one another.[1]

The emphasis Luther placed on vocations in his theology can be seen as a recognition of the importance one's work has in the formation of one's identity. In many ways, the Protestant Reformation brought a renewal of the secular in Christian theology. If man is to be saved in the (secular) world, then the work in which he spends much of his time must have been ordained by God.

Perhaps it is because Erik Erikson was raised in a Lutheran country that he was so alert to the importance of vocational choice in adolescent identity formation. He noted:

> If the desire to make something work, and to make it work well, is the gain of the school age, then the choice of an occupation assumes a significance beyond the question of remuneration and status. It is for this reason that some adolescents prefer not to work at all for a while rather than be forced into an otherwise promising career which would offer success without the satisfaction of functioning with unique excellence.[2]

Functioning with unique excellence carries some of the same personal meaning as being "called." One's work is in some sense ordained, specially one's own, expressing one's unique identity. According to Erikson, "the adolescent looks most fervently for men and ideas to have *faith* in, which also means men and ideas in whose service it would seem worth while to prove oneself trustworthy."[3] The most passionate striving of adolescence, Erikson claims, is the quest for fidelity. As youth moves into the adult world, he needs an adult task, but one which is authentically his own. In the seeking of self-expression in a realistic occupation, the struggle to blend the past and present and future in a way that will make a legitimate contribution acceptable by society is especially clear. The area of vocational choice illustrates most sharply that the adolescent struggle is with both self and society, both personal and social.

There is an implicit recognition in our culture that one's job is closely connected with one's identity. When people are introduced, they ask "What do you do?" and classify one another by their occupations. In recent years, vocational choice has had an important place in the theory of adolescent identity formation. Unfortunately, research relating vocational choice to the identity process is meager. Most of the research regarding adolescents and their vocational choices is focused on the validation of vocational tests.[4]

## Sex roles and vocational identity formation

The research which is relevant here approaches vocational choice from a developmental perspective or relates vocational decisions to sex-role orientations. As a rule, occupational choice plays a central role in boys' identity, so central that the degree to which a boy is handling this aspect of his future is one of the best indicators of his overall identity achievement. For girls, however, vocational identity is usually secondary. This difference is part of a more general difference in male and female identity formation noted in the representative study of adolescents by Elizabeth Douvan and Joseph Adelson. They observed that boys focus the identity struggle on autonomy and independence, while girls "attempt to establish identity by affiliating themselves with others."[5]

Very similar findings occurred in another study, in which it was concluded that:

> To attain masculine sex identity, boys need identification with a vocational goal, preferably one that is characterized by a meaningful or prestige-conferring activity. Girls, on the other hand, tend to attain their feminine sex identity primarily through intimacy in interpersonal relations—i.e., success in marriage—whereas identification with a vocational goal appears to play a secondary role in their quest for identity.[6]

This is also reflected in the differences in occupational values between the sexes. Boys, more frequently than girls, rate as important the opportunity to be leader, to be boss, to receive high pay, and to gain fame. Girls more frequently value jobs which allow them to express their abilities and to help other people.[7] Girls also set lower sights for themselves vocationally; they are much more likely than boys to choose minor professional goals. This sex difference, is, of course, culturally learned. A study of vocational goals in adolescents from 16 to 19 years old was conducted in the United States, East and West Germany, Chile, Poland, and Turkey. The sex difference in vocational aspirations was more pronounced in the United States than in any of the other nations studied.[8] The place of vocational choice in identity formation is clearly part of the traditional roles for the two sexes in our culture.

Thus it again becomes apparent how much Erikson's developmental theory has focused upon male development and failed to note sex differences. Erikson considers the preadolescent period to be the key time for the development of "industry,"[9] or a "sense of competence."[10] According to psychoanalytic theorists, the focus on skill building and the manipulation of objects is possible in these years before adolescence because the basic interpersonal conflicts of the oedipal period have been resolved. This theory fails to note the differences between boys and girls in this latency period. Research indicates that by age seven or eight both have made sex-typed identifications and have begun to discriminate sex-typed roles. Males, more than females, tend to move away from strong family dependencies and toward independence in the all-boy peer group during preadolescence. It seems likely that it is this move away from dependency, encouraged in boys, which allows them to focus more upon skill development and other objective achievements in the preadolescent years. Boys precede girls in the development of skills and objective achievements.[11] They generally develop a stronger motivation to achieve and move toward earlier vocational maturity.

## Developmental studies

It has been stated that vocations are no longer assigned from father to son. Of course this does not mean that parents are unimportant in youth's vocational decisions. Probably less than 10 percent of boys choose the same occupation as their fathers,[12] and even those who do are more likely to do so because of identification rather than "forced inheritance."[13] Yet youth of both sexes name parents most frequently as persons who had great influence on their vocational plans. (Teachers are usually named second, and friends third in importance as influences.)[14]

The usual assumption is that parents influence youth's vocational development through the types of child-rearing methods they employ, the values they instill, the ways in which they encourage mastery, the social aspirations they hold, and so forth. Probably the most extensive attempt to relate occupational choices to child-rearing practices has been undertaken by Anne Roe. After a decade of studies, she concluded that her major hypothesis was not substantiated. All the attempts to predict vocational choice from knowledge of parental attitudes toward the child had failed.[15]

Another approach focuses upon the development of particular traits within the personality. Donald Super has formulated propositions concerning the development of self-concepts and occupational concepts which he believes determine adolescent vocational choice.[16] Unfortunately, his theory has not been adequately tested using the longitudinal method. One of his propositions, that self-concepts begin to form prior to adolescence and become clearer in adolescence, has been supported by cohort data from a study of the four classes in a Catholic boys' school. The self-concepts of these boys in the areas of interests, aptitudes, work values, and general values were clarified and became more realistic during the adolescent years. The investigators compared subjects' estimates of their present status with regard to aptitudes, interests, social class, and values to their standing in each of these categories, as revealed by tests or statements of preference. They found that as the boys moved through high school they made more and more accurate estimates of their own test results, (that is, the correlations between self-estimates and test data became increasingly positive) in all areas except social class. This suggests that the adolescents became increasingly clear in their attitudes, interests, and values, though their preceptions of their social class status remained inaccurate. The highest correlations between self-concepts and objective ratings were in the areas of work values and interests ($r = .67$ to $.84$), which suggests that these concepts are formulated prior to developing clarity about aptitudes; self-estimates of aptitudes were considerably lower ($r = .44$ to $.69$).[17]

A proposition similar to Super's has been developed by David Hershenson: "The individual must have a view of himself before he can determine what his strengths and limitations are, and he must determine these before he can select vocational goals for himself."[18] This proposition was tested on a handicapped population. The priority of worker self-concept over development of competence held up well, although caution in interpreting this is necessary, since the longitudinal method was not used.

From these experiments one might infer that the preferred developmental sequence is to clarify values and interests before attempting to test aptitudes and develop skills. However, there is no assurance that the clarification of values will occur in the high school years. One study of less advantaged high school students showed no change in the accuracy of work-value and interest self-estimates from 10th to 12th grade.[19]

Though males and females do not necessarily have the same occupational values and interests, girls, like boys, generally move toward a clarification of their values and interests, which become increasingly realistic.[20] A longitudinal study of career development in boys and girls from eighth grade through high school showed that, though general goals of satisfaction and interest remained most important at all ages tested, other priorities shifted from "idealism" (giving priority to social service, personal goals, travel) to "realism" (marriage and family, preparation and ability, advancement).[21] Though girls were more people oriented and boys more career oriented throughout, the change toward realism held for both boys and girls.

There is some evidence that girls advance more rapidly than boys through this early stage of vocational development, the clarification of work values and interests.[22] After this phase, a gradual move through consideration of abilities and outside realities to tentative occupational choices is posited.[23] Boys apparently complete this later part of the process of vocational choice earlier than girls do. The boys generally have a "clearer concept of their future occupational roles, and are more realistic in their vocational planning."[24] Girls tend to keep their vocational plans more tentative and flexible,[25] which has its own kind of realism: girls stress more people-oriented needs and prepare to meet them by focusing on marriage, with career plans remaining flexible until the marriage partner is known.[26]

Personality factors which develop long before the actual vocational choices are made appear to influence the individual's later vocational development. Leona Tyler conducted an extensive 12-year longitudinal study of boys and girls, testing them in grades 1, 4, 8, and 12. As early as the fourth grade, boys who later became interested in scientific vocations differed from the other boys. It was not that scientific interest itself had clearly emerged; rather, the scientist group made more masculine choices on personality scales than did the nonscientist boys. The most predictable aspect of female vocational development concerned the traditionally feminine noncareer orientation of the majority of the girls, and the strong career orientation developed by a significant minority of the girls. These two groups could be differentiated as early as the eighth grade. The career group scored higher on scales of responsibility, self-control and achievement, though their parents' social and educational backgrounds were similar.[27]

Tyler proposed, on the basis of this study, that an important variable in understanding vocational choice is the decisions individuals make about the use of time. She suggested that interests and traits are not themselves continuous; rather, they affect the ways children program their use of time. Later skills and interests are developed out of the experiences in which the individual engages as a consequence of these choices of activities. This suggestion may prove more fruitful in future research than the hypothesis of direct correspondence between parental approaches and children's interests.

It is clear from Tyler's results that early developmental factors are important to later vocational choice, in spite of the inability of experiments, as yet, to isolate those factors. It can be assumed, that family, peers, social class, and other factors affect the total personality in ways which influence vocational decision making, but only social class effects have been well documented experimentally.[28]

Tyler's hypothesis regarding the use of time provokes some speculations on the development of nontraditional roles in girls. Girls who later assume nontraditional roles may not, in their early development, have any clear concept that their activities do not fit traditional sex patterns. Some girls may simply not have been indoctrinated to traditional sex roles in the childhood years. They may not have been restricted to distinctively feminine activities and may have spent more time in activities which others see as masculine. Thus they may have developed values and interests which are similar to those typical of males. It is not that they have thought of themselves as masculine, but the culturally approved sex-typing has not been part of their training. In adolescence, when they are confronted with the fact that the roles they desire are sex-typed by the culture, they are forced to formulate a nontraditional view of sex roles. Their formulation of sex roles does not lead to their nontraditional behavior. Rather, the formulation develops out of a conflict between the behavior which has long been part of their identity and the teachings of the normative culture. Their formulation is an attempt to develop self-constructs congruent with already existing behavior.

Once the conflict has been experienced and a position on sex roles has been formulated, it is possible that this self-construct will affect future behavior. At first, however, these girls are forced to formulate a nontraditional sex-role concept to resolve the dissonance between what they have experienced as part of themselves and what the culture labels masculine.

## Nontraditional female roles

Though the traditional sex roles are important to understanding vocational identity formation in the great majority of youth, it is also important to note the exceptions. A significant minority of girls do not define themselves in the traditional way. Feminine role concept appears to be a noteworthy factor in vocational development, as the experiments discussed below demonstrate.

Girls in their junior year of high school were tested on three scales: A feminine-role rating inventory distinguished between fulfilling oneself through affiliation (traditional role for women) or achievement (nontraditional). Other scales measured positive and negative self-concept and maturation in vocational development. The results agreed with Super's proposition regarding development of self-concept in adolescense, in that positive self-concept development scores were predictive of vocational maturity. Girls holding nontraditional feminine concepts showed greater maturity in their vocational development than those with traditional views.[29] This may be interpreted to mean that girls who hold less traditional sex roles consider vocational choice more important to their identity formation and thus have developmental patterns more similar to boys.

Two studies have approached this issue by comparing students in traditionally female and traditionally male areas of study. High school girls whose current vocational goals were medicine, mathematics, or a natural science were found to have interests and patterns of vocational development similar to those typical for boys, including early career decisions. This was in contrast to the patterns of girls planning on nursing or teaching careers.[30] This finding strengthens the interpretation given to the previous study. It is interesting to note that college women in "male" fields, compared to those preparing to teach, reported that the significant men in their lives did not hold traditional views of sex roles. These women were more concerned with male support in their own career goals than women entering more traditionally female occupations.[31]

It is not surprising that female career choice is influenced by "what women think men think,"[32] as illustrated in an interesting experiment with working women over 40 years old.[33] The Strong Vocational Interest Blank was administered to each subject twice, under normal conditions, and again in a group situation in which they were instructed to:

> Pretend with me that men have come of age[34] and that:
> 1. Men like intelligent women.
> 2. Men and women are promoted equally in business and the professions.
> 3. Raising a family well is very possible for a career woman.[35]

Under these conditions, both married and single women showed significant increases in scores on the career-oriented scales and decreases on the home-oriented vocation scales.

### Implications of this research

Vocational choice is one aspect of the identity search. It appears wise to delay vocational commitment until self-concepts are well explored, particularly concepts of sex roles, work values, and interests. Donald E. Super has demonstrated, in a complex, masterful study, that the vocational preferences of ninth-grade students are not realistic, consistent, or wise. This does not mean that these early vocational preferences are unimportant. They should be used as leads for self-exploration, but it is foolish to take them as a basis for decisions about curriculum and vocational preparation. To quote Super:

> The best way to let this information help the pupil is to aid him in assimilating it into his concept of himself. This is best done by beginning, not with the data, but with the self-concept. The statement of a vocational preference is one way of expressing a self-concept.[36]

## *The achievement motive and sex roles*

Another productive approach to understanding vocational development has been to study a particular character trait. One trait that has proved extremely important in modern society is the achievement motive. The extensive developmental and cross-cultural studies on this subject by David McClelland and team have been reviewed elsewhere;[37] the focus here is upon the implications for vocational identity of sex differences in the achievement motive.

Because the achievement motive has been studied in the context of success and social mobility, issues such as status seeking and competitiveness have obscured the central meaning of achievement, which is "the concern with performance evaluated against a standard of excellence."[38] Central to the concept is the confidence that goals can be achieved, that one is able to make effective contact with the physical and social environment. Though in our culture this is often associated with rivalry, competition, and the desire to be ahead of others, concern with competence need not involve competition, and the two should not be confused. The achievement motive itself is simply "the internal impetus to excel."[39]

Certain characteristics of parent-child interaction in early childhood, specifically the "withdrawal of love" approach to child rearing, probably contribute to the achievement motive long before the specific competencies related to adult achievement appear.[40] A longitudinal study by H. A. Moss and Jerome Kagan suggested that striving to achieve a self-imposed goal (mastery behavior) exhibited by young elementary school children may be a reasonably good indicator of achievement behavior in adolescence and adulthood.[41] That is, achievement motivation appears to be a stable personality characteristic.[42] Mastery behavior appears earlier and with greater intensity in boys,[43] and achievement orientation is generally thought of as masculine. As is the case with many aspects of masculinity, mothers appear to play a more important role than fathers in the training of achievement orientation.[44] This is due, of course, to the reduced role of father in American child rearing.

Young boys generally have a higher level of aspiration than girls; they set higher standards of performance for themselves, and are more persistent in task performance.[45] It could be said that boys have a higher need to achieve. However, in actual performance, especially in academic achievement, girls are superior to boys by the time they enter school. This may reflect, in part, the passive teaching techniques of our schools, which are more congruent with the girls' sex-role learning. Differences in areas of achievement reflect the sex-typing of passive versus active roles even in adulthood; girls continue to do better on the verbal scales of intelligence and achievement, while boys excel on spatial and motor tasks.

But by adolescence, boys, at least those from middle-class homes, have learned that achievement is more important for them than it is for girls. Boys are under more pressure to prepare for their future, whether it be for college or a vocation. Thus, in the high school years, boys catch up to and surpass girls in academic achievement.[46] Cultural expectations that males will be more active and more goal oriented encourage achievement among males. It appears that girls soon realize that the world of vocations is essentially a man's world. It has been noted that female occupational choice occurs later. Even when women have entered the work world, they do not place the same importance on a career as men do.[47] Among nurses queried, 60 percent stated that having a career was important to them, yet only 25 percent said they would be very displeased if they married and never worked at nursing again.[48] Even those vocational commitments that women do make have a lower priority for them. As the high school or college girl looks ahead to the adult female role in our society, she may be inhibited from investing too much in her vocational aspirations. The word "inhibited" is carefully chosen, for the limited data available suggest that the need for achievement is strong for girls but does not become operative (in the area of vocational goals, for example) because of sex-role expectations. Much of what superficially appears as less competitive or less aggressive behavior on the part of girls[49] may actually be an indication of fearfulness of appearing masculine. Three experiments have supported this interpretation.

Achieving and underachieving girls in a highly competitive school were asked to view pictures designed to elicit stories about academic achievement. Girls who were high achievers produced more achievement-oriented stories to the pictures showing women achieving. The underachievers, by contrast, increased in achievement-oriented responses when shown pictures of men achieving.[50] These results suggest that high-achievement girls see academic goals as a relevant part of their own female roles. The underachievers apparently see academic achievement as more relevant to the male role. Thus the girls who hold less traditional sex-role definitions are more likely to succeed under strong academic competition than are those holding more traditional views.

A second study directly tested the importance of girls' perception of woman's role as it relates to academic achievement efforts. High school girls who accepted the traditional sex role did not appear to compete against boys in their classroom. There was no relationship between their attitudes toward achievement and their actual grades, when verbal ability was controlled for. However, for girls who endorsed the role definition that "women do many things including being leaders in politics, the professions, and business (the same as men do)," the interaction was significant.[51] That is, of the more liberated girls, those who had high achievement needs apparently implemented their needs in the classroom, with the result that they obtained higher grades than those with low achievement motivation, even though they were no more gifted than their peers.

A third study is noteworthy for its use of a direct observational measurement of competing against men or women. This study of college women tested the hypotheses that women's fear of success is related to their fear of competing against men. It was found that women who showed fear of success imagery in completing a projective test performed more poorly when competing against men than when working alone or when competing against women. Women in this group also performed more poorly when a task was labled masculine than when it was labeled feminine. The reverse was true of women who did not show fear of success imagery; they performed best when competing against men and when performing tasks labeled masculine. The women who exhibited fear of success held more traditionally feminine orientations: they considered home and family more important and a personal professional career less important than did the women not exhibiting this imagery. "There were no differences between groups on the importance they placed on being 'feminine' " (though they apparently defined "feminine" rather differently), nor on their view of competition per se.[52]

These three studies illustrate how an interpretation derived from unexpected results (in the first study) can be progressively tested by pencil-and-paper means and finally by direct laboratory observation. While early research on the achievement motive and vocational orientations in women tended to generalize about all women compared to men,[53] more recent studies such as the three just reviewed illustrate the importance of discriminating between women with traditional and those with more liberated sex-role orientations.

These studies have important implications. In the previous section, experimental results were discussed which showed the importance of sex-role definition in women's vocational maturation and decision making. The studies just reviewed suggest that sex-role definitions not only influence women's decisions but affect their actual achievement in circumstances in which they compete with males (as they do in the adult work world).

## Social causes of women's inhibition of achievement

The inhibition of achievement in women is part of the constrictive female sex role which has been discussed throughout this book. It has been noted that girls excede boys in academic achievement throughout grade school but are surpassed by boys in high school. Though early school experiences whet girls' appetites for achievement, by high school girls begin to be discriminated against as they plan for future education or jobs. A girl who may be recognized at the junior high level as gifted still is likely to be "shuttled into nursing instead of medicine, elementary school teaching instead of college teaching, etc." by counselors and teachers who encourage acceptance of traditional sex roles rather than assisting the girl in her own self-concept formation.[54] Without adequate support, the gifted adolescent girl may also be subject to heterosexual pressures to be feminine. Results from a study of high school girls suggested that, in order for girls to pursue less traditional academic and vocational roles, support must be forthcoming from significant males in their lives.[55] Such support is not the rule, for studies consistently show that men feel threatened by professional women. When the American man seeks a wife, he usually rejects women of equal intelligence, earning power, or accomplishment. It is also a common pattern that truly gifted and creative women frequently must look outside their own peer group for supportive male companions. Such women frequently seek men from other countries as husbands, a phenomenon many sociologists call "marrying down" but which is better described as "marrying out."[56]

Full discussion of discrimination in the work world is reserved for Chapter 16. Very real cultural pressures do exist which encourage the majority of girls to inhibit their desire to achieve, though a significant minority are no longer accepting traditional sex-role orientations.

### Sex-typing of values implicit in the achievement motive

The more recent research on the achievement motive has brought to the fore the effects of sex-typing on achievement. The encouragement of the achievement motive in males and its inhibition in females is not an isolated phenomenon but is part of a larger pattern of sex-typed values.

It is easy to review these studies without ever clarifying the possible assumption that achievement motivation is a trait which should be encouraged in all children. Clyde Kluckhohn and Florence Kluckhohn have abstracted from cross-cultural studies five value dimensions which are imminent in the human situation, regardless of culture. Three of these dimensions are directly related to achievement motivation and provide a beginning framework for an examination of the positive and negative aspects of achievement motivation:

1.  Activistic-passivistic orientation: The degree to which a society fosters belief in the possibility of manipulating the physical and social environment to his advantage, in contrast to the notion that individual efforts at change are futile.
2.  Present-future orientation: The laying of stress on the merit of living

in the present, emphasizing immediate gratifications, or on the importance of planning and sacrificing in the present to ensure future gains.

3. Familistic-individualistic orientation: One aspect is the importance of maintaining physical proximity to kin, as opposed to mobility and independence from family ties.[57]

The achievement motivation in our culture stresses the activistic, future, and individualistic poles of these orientations. The traits of activism and future orientation have been noted in the previous discussion of the instrumental orientation, that constellation of traits that are considered masculine in our culture. The third of the Kluckhohns' dimensions, the familistic-individualistic value orientation, also appears to be sex-typed. Boys in our society are encouraged toward earlier and more complete independence than girls, and they reach vocational maturity earlier. Probably because boys are freed earlier from family dependency, they are more able to focus upon skill development and other objective achievements than girls are.

This earlier focus upon achievement in boys may be accomplished at the cost of some interpersonal learning. While the traditional sex roles allow males greater activity in shaping things, boys learn to "do" but not to "be." The focus on future orientation (goal directedness) may be to some extent contrary to the need to "stay in the present" if one is to develop intense interpersonal relationships. And the individualistic orientation may encourage an isolation from deep personal contacts. In short, an examination of the values implicit in the achievement orientation, and a comparison of these polarities to the traditional sex roles, will raise the question of social goals. How desirable is it that women become more like men in their value orientation? Or is it crucial to the survival of humanity that men move toward more interpersonal value orientations?

The fallacy in this discussion is that one becomes locked into thinking in polarities. The value dimensions of the Kluckhohns were conceptualized to define one culture's orientation relative to another's. Perhaps they are suitable indicators in homogeneous societies. There is a need, then, for research that recognizes the value dimensions implicit in such psychological constructs as the achievement motive. It is not sufficient, however, to approach this problem in a gross way, using demographic data. It is important to find out whether the learning of objective skills does, in fact, deter the learning of interpersonal skills, for example. But the generalization that most boys excel over girls in objective skills but are inferior in interpersonal skills does not tell us whether these two types of learning are necessarily opposed. Carefully controlled learning experiments are necessary to determine whether or not there is negative transference between the two areas of learning. If negative transference is discovered, further experiments are needed to determine whether discriminations can be taught to reduce or eliminate the effects of such transference. To do this, measurements must be developed which do not assume that an increase on one trait results in a decrease on others.

To summarize, the research to date seems to indicate that the traditional sex roles inhibit women from implementing their wish to achieve. This raises questions about the desirability of increasing achievement motivation in our society, which is already highly achievement oriented. These questions suggest the need for research to determine whether expressive and instrumental skills are actually opposed to one another. Is it possible not only to break down the identification of expressive roles with women and instrumental roles with men but, further, to develop both roles within a person without producing conflict and negative transference?

## *Job satisfaction and the expressive-instrumental role split*

Almost two decades have passed since Paul Goodman argued in a popular book, *Growing Up Absurd,* that to become a man the adolescent needs the confirmation society gives when it expects of him a man's job. "A man's work" means to create or produce something of worth.[58] The situation today is essentially the same as Goodman described it in the 1950s, except that I would extend the argument to include women. The unfortunate fact is that few jobs are available to youth, and many of the jobs available are not worthwhile. They are not creative, and the small part the worker has is in the production of something for which a demand is synthesized through advertising. Thus the jobs, even if they were available to adolescents, neither allow the individual to express a part of his identity nor give him the satisfaction of doing something of value. As a youth begins to experience the types of jobs that are available to him, he may easily become cynical in his attitude toward life's work. He begins to question whether it is realistic to consider who he is in his vocational decision, and he is tempted to give up seeking self-expression and resign himself to asking "What is available?"

Once again the tragic separation of instrumental versus expressive roles provides the key for an analysis of adolescents' perception of the world. Seeking to find his place in society and to make his contribution to it, he longs for meaningful work, but often he is forced to make life decisions with little or no experience of such work. The view of work as a calling, a vocation, yields to a purely instrumental view, as noted by Kenneth Keniston:

> Work . . . in technological society . . . requires a dissociation of feeling, a subordination of passion, impulse, fantasy, and idealism before cognitive problems and tasks. As breadwinners, most Americans neither find nor even seek "fulfillment" in their jobs. Work, split away from "living" by convention and tradition, becomes instrumental, a dissociated part of life that makes possible, yet often vitiates, the rest of a "living."[59]

Instead of work being a fulfilling expression of life, it becomes a drudgery to be endured so the rest of life can be lived.

Worker dissatisfaction in American society seems to be on the increase. In 1969, 13 percent of workers of all ages stated that they were displeased with their jobs. Three years later, in 1972, the percentage of displeased workers had risen to 19 percent.[60] The alienation caused by the instrumental view of occupations has been poignantly expressed by C. Wright Mills: "Each day men sell little pieces of themselves in order to try to buy them back each night and weekend with the coin of 'fun.'"[61] One researcher in youth employment concluded that "Fun, not work, becomes the core around which one builds his personality."[62]

The dissatisfaction with work and the focus upon fun for life's meaning is reflected in statistics on absenteeism, especially in routine jobs. In auto plants, absenteeism has doubled since the early 1960s, with 5 percent of the work force being absent each day. On Mondays and Fridays the average percent absent is 15, and union leaders report that their members now value leisure time more than time-and-a-half pay.[63]

The adolescent may give up searching for his vocation and merely accept work as society defines it. In doing so, he appears to have grown up, but in fact he has not been able to integrate his earlier playful self with his adult tasks. He lives "schizophrenically",[64] existing through the adult role in order to be free at another time to be a child again—that is, to play games having no life-changing consequences.

The adolescent who refuses to plunge into the society as given but waits on the threshold in search of more integration astutely perceives the split in the adult work world. This split is characteristic of what Reich calls Consciousness II, the modern technocratic experience:

> Thus a crucial aspect of Consciousness II is a profound schizophrenia, a split between his working and his private self. It is this split that sometimes infuriates his children when they become of college age, for they see it as hypocrisy or selling out. But it is schizophrenia, not hypocrisy. The individual has two roles, two lives, two masks, two sets of values. It cannot be said, as is true of the hypocrite, that one self is real and the other false. These two values simply coexist; they are part of the basic definition of "reality"; the "reality" of Consciousness

II is that there is a "public" and a "private" man. Neither the man
at work nor the man at home is the whole man; it is impossible to
know, talk to, or confront the whole man, for that wholeness is precisely
what does not exist. The only thing that is real is two separate men.[65]

Classical views of adolescence, focusing upon sexuality, have noted
the vacillation between ascetic self-denial and hedonistic flings. This
description is of questionable accuracy but suggests a parallel in the
work world. The ascetic denial of sex has its counterpart in a stoic
resignation to the drudgery of work, but this is only livable if it is
counterbalanced by periods (weekends, vacations) of self-indulgence
and pointless fun. A mature integration, it would seem, should occur
when the playfulness can be channeled creatively into socially fruitful
products. When the product of work is a creation—the fruit of one's
self skillfully produced for others—an integration occurs of expressive
and instrumental, play and skill, self and society.

Today's adolescent is faced with two philosophies of labor. Is work
a necessary evil to be endured, or can it be a self-fulfilling achievement,
a meaningful contribution to society? It is legitimate to ask if the second
alternative is realistic (and we will return to that question below), but
we must not avoid the question of whether technological, objective reality is worth living for. Certainly Keniston was correct when he stated:

> Americans mention 'working for a living' a hundred times more often
> than they mention 'living for their work'.
>
> Yet to spend one's days at tasks whose only rationale is income and
> whose chief requirements are cognitive is another demand in our lives
> which makes our technological society less than likely to inspire
> enthusiasm.[66]

## Work, values, and personality variables

A number of the issues that have been discussed—the coordination
of inner exploration with the developing awareness of the objective
world, the assessment of cultural expectations in regard to achievement,
and the search for vocational identity that is congruent with personal
identity—suggest that vocational decision cannot be made apart from
the articulation of one's own value system. To be more explicit, since
one's vocational decision is so important to one's lifestyle, it must develop
out of one's total value stance. The relationship between value orientations and vocational choice has received limited attention. The general
area of the development of value orientations is just beginning to be
charted, so it may be too early to search for interactions between these
two aspects of identity formation.

Some early work in this field attempts to relate interpersonal styles to vocational choices. In a study by Morris Rosenberg, responses to indirect questions were used to classify individuals into one of Karen Horney's three styles of relating to others: moving toward, moving away, and moving against. The personality classifications were termed (respectively) the compliant type, the detached type, and the aggressive type. As might be expected, the occupational values of those who moved toward people emphasized working with people and being helpful. Those more concerned with being independent or detached valued freedom from supervision and sought creative and original jobs. The aggressive type, concerned with mastery, control, domination, and conquest, valued jobs which brought money, social status, and prestige.[67] Members of this last group seem to have accepted unquestionably the values we have associated with the male image. The results were interpreted as indicating "that the way a person characteristically relates to others will influence the type of career he selects."[68] Though the study is suggestive, it is limited because it simply relates two types of verbal (pencil-and-paper test) responses. Follow-up studies are needed using observational measures of interpersonal styles. Further, the study shares with all correlational studies the problem of discerning cause and effect. When two variables are measured simultaneously (as are vocational choice and interpersonal orientations in this study), we can only conclude that there is an interaction. Perhaps, as the author infers, the personality styles influenced the vocational decision. But it is also possible that vocational choices and commitments crystalize values.[69] Developmental studies, preferably using the longitudinal design, are needed to determine the direction of the interaction.

A more recent approach to research relating personality variables to occupational choice involves the use of factor analysis to determine the important variables related to particular career choices.[70] Such studies also involve several pencil-and-paper measures taken simultaneously and share the flaws of the study reviewed above. They have the advantage, however, of avoiding predetermined categories by using complex statistical methods to determine what clusters of related data emerge. A separate factor analysis for 250 male and 250 female college seniors was performed on their responses to a group of life-goal and self-rating items. Life goals such as comfort, prestige, and altruism proved to discriminate significantly the 36 categories of vocations chosen.[71]

The preliminary character of this type of research must again be emphasized. Nonetheless, results to date suggest that the work values are integrally related to vocational decision making, which seems to imply that satisfaction in one's work depends upon choosing a vocation in harmony with one's self-concept. This has been set forth as a hypothesis: "The degree of satisfaction the individual attains from his work is related to the degree to which he has been able to implement his self-concept in his work."[72] Unfortunately, I have been unable to locate any empirical research directly testing this proposition.

## Preparation for vocational decisions

As young people attempt to clarify their own vocational self-concepts, they need to assess their particular value stance. Among the questions they may ask themselves are the following:

1.  What is the relationship between my own needs and the needs of others? How much do I owe to each?
2.  How much security do I demand in life? How much creative insecurity can I tolerate or do I desire?
3.  What level of material goods provides a base from which I can function well?
4.  What kinds of rewards do I need? Am I rewarded by prestige through things, prestige through status, aesthetic experience, intimate personal experience, the possession of power, or others?

Three interrelated processes that aid in vocational decision making may be noted:

1.  The clarification of one's self-concept, particularly the articulation of one's value stance.
2.  The use of fantasy to test out tentative value orientations and possible vocational choices.
3.  The expansion of self-concept and the development of skills through active involvement in work.

It has been stated that the first priority in vocational counseling should be the clarification of the individual's self-concept. Yet the self-concept is clarified not in a vacuum but in relationship to the real world. It can be argued that when guidance counselors use objective measures (vocational tests) to clarify reality, they are in fact dealing with fantasy. By treating the results objectively, the counselor clarifies neither the objective situation nor the youth's self-concept. Certainly there is something ludicrous about spending hours asking a seventh grader to:

> Decide which of the three activities you like most:
> Be an expert on cutting jewels
> Conduct research on developing a substitute for rubber
> Be a radio music commentator[73]

Because he is unlikely to have experienced any of these, his response can only be a projection of his fantasies. The point is not that fantasies should be ignored; rather they should be explored as facets of adolescent personality.

When the protagonists in J. D. Salinger's *Catcher in the Rye* was asked what he would like to be, Holden Caulfield answered with a salient example of a fantasy rich in personal meaning.[74] He is not ready to be pinned down to a realistic vocation and resists his sister's attempts to be realistic. When Phoebe asks what he'd like to be, he daydreams about kids playing freely in a field of rye. He pictures himself near a cliff at the edge of the field; his job is to catch the kids if they start to go over the cliff. What Holden wants to be is "the catcher in the rye."

Before he can decide what to do with his life, Holden needs to know himself. Unfortunately, all "old Prexy" could teach Holden was objective facts and skills essential to his role as an adult. Holden had to reject this, but in doing so he was himself rejected, and he internalized much of that rejection. That is, though he fought the "phoney" world and its depersonalization, he rejected himself for being unable to succeed in it. Suppose (let us fantasize) that a guidance counselor was able to hear Holden's fantasy as a personal statement, to recognize that, despite his rejection of relationships with others ("they're all phonies"), Holden has a sensitivity and caring that could be developed as a skill. Suppose (many interviews later) that Holden was able to admit that he created not only the fantasy of the "catcher" but of the children in need of being caught—that both are his own projections; that his own sensitivity comes in part from the depth of his need. And suppose the counselor, not being too hung up on his authority as the interpreter of tests, is able to confess to Holden that in being a counselor (a catcher) he too satisfies some of his needs to be cared for (a child). Suppose, in short, that instead of meeting "grown men" living out roles, Holden is able to meet a man who knows and accepts the child within himself. Is it not possible this expressive child can be nurtured to accept himself and others as of worth?

This is not, of course, enough. There are still essential skills to be learned. And if (to continue the fantasy) Holden identifies himself with his counselor and decides to become a helping person himself, he must begin to differentiate himself from the counselor. He may need other close relationships—let us say with a teacher of literature this time— before he can decide which vocation expresses him most. Further, he must (whatever helping role he chooses) learn to fulfill his needs in ways that do not harm those he is charged with helping. These are skills learned best through interpersonal relations, not through books, but they must be learned before Holden can accept the impersonal discipline of more objective learning. The failure to develop these personal characteristics in Holden made the "educational" experiences he had merely experiences in rejection. He was too sensitive to reject his inner experience; instead of repressing it and becoming a man, he, like Biff in Arthur Miller's *Death of a Salesman,* could not "take hold of some kind of life."

The role of fantasy in vocational development has not received much attention in research. Eli Ginzberg theorized that occupational choice progresses through three periods: fantasy choice, tentative choice, and realistic choice.[75] The theory has the merit of recognizing the importance of subjective components in appropriate vocational decisions. So far, however, research stemming from this theory has limited itself to exploring and further differentiating the period of tentative choice.[76]

Some conjectures can be drawn from research on the role of play in the development of children. Girls are more likely to use play for the development of social and interpersonal skills, whereas boys use play as preparation for realistic roles in later life.[77] This is, of course, a generalization which reflects the traditional sex roles. The fact that a positive relationship between play preferences and future occupational goals has been confirmed for boys[78] suggests that play activities may be a means of experimenting with adult roles in a safe way. It can be speculated that fantasy explorations would serve the same function.

Not only are fantasized activities worthy of attention, fantasized relationships appear to be important to the development of the "ego ideal," one's concept of the self one strives to be. The role of imaginary relationships in identification is instructive:

> The child from the age of six to about eight generally chooses a parent or some other family member [as an identification figure]. Most children then move on to a choice either of a glamorous person or an attractive, visible young adult. The age for choosing a glamorous person is about eight to sixteen. The choice of an attractive, visible young adult may start at eight or ten and continue all through adolescence, or it may give way to a more abstract ego-ideal in the form of a composite imaginary person. The final and mature stage of the ego-ideal is the composite of desirable characteristics, drawn from all of the persons with whom the individual has identified himself during his childhood and adolescence.[79]

This suggests that the mature ego ideal develops out of both real and fantasized relationships and depends upon the ability to abstract and project a composite imagery. Healthy growth does not entail the repression of fantasy; rather it means learning to forge dreams into realities.

### The need for involvement

In addition to exploration of self-concept, youth needs experience with real people in the real work world. There are many reasons why direct involvement in the work world is valuable for adolescents: It provides them with some vocational experience, the earnings reduce their sense of financial dependence, and it allows the adolescent to be recognized as an adult with a real contribution to make.[80] It is a shame to waste youth's most creative years in thinking about work but not really doing any.[81]

All of these are important reasons, but my concern goes beyond these. Education without involvement is always second-hand education, at least once removed from reality. This seems especially dangerous in adolescence, when intellectualism is already overused as a defense mechanism.[82] Symbolic processes develop to their peak in adolescence. It is easy, in the academic world, to become so involved in symbols and words that one learns words about words and thoughts about thoughts and loses contact with direct experience. Adolescents need the opportunity to conceptualize experience; they also need some direct experience to conceptualize. Learning only from books and lectures can result in living in the realm of symbols, but with nothing to symbolize.

This dearth of experience simply increases the adolescent's self-consciousness. As psychological experiments have shown, any person deprived of external stimuli begins to create his own stimuli by hallucinating.[83] Similarly, youth deprived of contact with the work world of adult society is forced to focus upon itself. Self-consciousness is normal during adolescence, but introspection can become morbid. The self in a vacuum is not a growing self—growth comes from self-experiencing, not from introspection alone.[84]

Many youths who are intellectually alive and anxious to explore feel stymied and out of touch in the college setting. A large percentage of college dropouts or "stopouts" are youths who feel they must leave in order to educate themselves by real involvement.[85] To quote from a letter to parents one student shared with me:

> The goal or purpose for staying in college has vanished. School has been reduced to taking courses to fulfill requirements for a degree. The incentive is gone, and the goal-less future is too hazy to bear. I am weary of the seemingly endless preparatory years and the dependence which they necessitate. I want desperately to enter the world beyond the ivory-covered walls and stake out my claim. Drifting along accepting society's conventions and goals which others set and expect of me, I believe, is worse than stepping adventurously forth with joy to embrace life and to accept the inevitable mistakes which are a part of living.

Genuine vocational preparation must be personal and integrative. Such preparation involves exploration of both the inner and outer worlds, and exploration of reality comes not just from reading about it, but becoming involved in it. In this way the experience of reality can be a personal one which affects and is affected by one's own fantasies.

Reality testing of job fantasies stimulates educational motivation; school experiences become more real, and dropouts diminish.[86] As Douvan and Adelson discovered, concrete work experience is a very important factor in the enhancement of adolescents' self-esteem.[87] One study of the occupational plans of high school and college women found that students regarded relevant work experience as the most important source of influence in their vocational decisions, citing it even more frequently than parental influence.[88]

While it is important that the job experiences of adolescence be carefully chosen, it might be wise to involve the youth directly in the process of job hunting through such programs as work-study. When economic threat is low, the interview process can be a useful experience in self-concept clarification. So often interviews amount to a game in which the prospective employee tries to present himself in the manner he assumes the interviewer desires, while the interviewer describes the position to fit his view of what the prospective employee will find attractive. No real dialog occurs, since each participant is assuming postures and painting images. Occasionally a youth has the self-assurance to present honestly what he feels he has to offer and to state how he would define a particular job. Then the interviewer is encouraged to reciprocate with a more honest description of what his need is. A job description begins to emerge from an honest confrontation of the needs of the individual and the needs of the institution; or perhaps a clear recognition that the two do not mesh occurs. In either case, the possibility is enhanced that the job will really be his own or that a decision will be made against it. The youth uses the interview to demonstrate an identity, to show that he has something to offer. Frequently the employer respects such self-direction, though of course his firm has its own needs. The future employee is then more likely to see clearly the needs of the firm and can decide whether or not he can respect and fit into them. Whatever the actual decision, a clearer sense of one's self in relation to real possibilities is likely to emerge.

### Let's be realistic

Having argued that vocational preparation and vocational decision making should occur in the context of broad personal learning, utilizing both inner and outer experiencing, it is appropriate to ask how realistic this is in a technological society. A complete examination of this issue would be a book in itself. A few observations are in order.

First of all, despite the common observation that highly specialized education is needed for jobs in today's society, the fact is that very few persons now spend their lives in one specialized job. H. L. Wilensky found that a very low proportion of the subjects he studied had orderly work careers in which each job was preparation for the next one. A high proportion of his population exhibited a great many job changes.[89] It may be wise, instead of preparing the individual for a specific job, to think in terms of a set of basic skills or an orientation which will serve the individual in the course of his life.[90] It is interesting that a number of industries seeking college graduates for employees now stress that they want them to have a broad liberal arts education.[91]

Not only are vocational patterns no longer linear, but the nature of our industrial society is changing. We are moving from a mechanistic period to one of automation. While mechanization of a process is "achieved by fragmentation", according to Marshall McLuhan, automation involves a return from specialization to generalization.[92] The fact that, paradoxically, automation makes liberal education mandatory indicates the need for an integrative education as training, even for technological vocations. In addition, there is the acute human need for personal insight to live with the mobility expected in these vocations. Finally, an increasing majority of jobs in our society are service oriented rather than production oriented.[93]

It becomes apparent that vocational training cannot be separated from the process of identity formation. The quest for self-understanding must be concurrent with the attempt to understand the world in order for the individual to choose an area of work that is truly a vocation and be able to function creatively in that field. To develop technique and methodology without deep understanding may provide the individual with an occupation which occupies his time, but not with a calling. The result of such a life is captured in an Indian proverb:

> I have spent my time stringing and unstringing my instrument
> And the song that I came to sing remains unsung.

## Mature vocational identity

Though I have been critical of contemporary society for its depersonalization and division of roles, this viewpoint must be placed in context. If it were not for the Industrial Revolution, it is unlikely that the adolescent would face an identity crisis over vocations at all; he simply would have no alternatives among which to choose.

The opportunity to choose an area of work that fits one's identity is a rare one in the perspective of history and cultural anthropology, and one which should not be taken for granted. Some anthropologists have lamented the failure of our culture to provide a smooth transition from home to world and have noted the grace with which some cultures make the transition through a single ceremony, a rite of passage. Where adulthood possibilities are restricted to a few clearly defined roles, a quick and direct transition into adulthood is possible. While the multitude of possibilities in a pluralistic society makes adolescence more difficult, it also makes the period richer. Nowhere is this clearer than in the area of vocational choice.

When a person can confidently enter into interaction with the environment, with both care and competence, his vocational identity can be considered established. The resolution of the crisis of identity in the area of work is poorly defined in terms of some final choice of a particular job; our society is too fluid for that. Rather, vocational identity involves a realistic awareness of one's values and one's areas of competence, with an openness to be changed as well as to change. A mutual respect for self and environment and a commitment to interaction rather than coercive domination form the achievement motive appropriate to a humane society. Thus, in the area of vocations, as in the previous areas surveyed, adult maturity is reached, not when some absolute and final choice is made, but when the individual knows himself well enough and has enough confidence to enter genuinely mutual interactions.

## Summary

The adolescent has a wide choice of vocations to consider as he searches for one which satisfies his needs, expresses his unique contribution, and yet is realistically attainable. Occupational choice plays a central role in male identity. In our society, women's vocational aspirations are generally lower than men's, with the clear exception of women who affirm nontraditional sex-role orientations. It appears that achievement motivation is suppressed in most women by the fear of appearing masculine.

Men get into a different bind; they split work and pleasure and find themselves working to stay alive but not enjoying their work. To make authentic vocational decisions, the adolescent must determine what he values in a job and in life. His search may necessitate exploring his own world of fantasy, as well as the objective world of reality.

## Notes

1. Martin Luther, "Address to the Christian Nobility of the German Nation," in Harry Emerson Fosdick, *Great Voices of the Reformation* (New York: Random House, 1952), pp. 99–100.

2. Erik Erikson, *Identity and the Life Cycle* (New York: International Universities Press, 1959), p. 113.

3. Ibid., pp. 128–29.

4. For a critique of the test approach to vocational research, see Henry Borow, "Development of Occupational Motives and Roles," in *Review of Child Development Research* ed. Lois W. Hoffman and Martin L. Hoffman (New York: Russell Sage Foundation, © 1966), vol. 2, pp. 395–96.

5. Elizabeth Douvan and Joseph Adelson, *The Adolescent Experience* (New York: John Wiley & Sons, 1966).

6. Josef E. Garai and Amram Scheinfeld, "Sex Differences in Mental and Behavioral Traits," *Genetic Psychology Monographs*, 77 (1968): 260–61.

7. O. E. Thompson, "Student Values in Transition," *California Journal of Educational Research*, 19 (1968): 77–86.

8. G. H. Seward and R. C. Williamson, "A Cross-National Study of Adolescent Professional Goals," *Human Development*, 12 (1969): 248–54.

9. Reprinted from *Identity: Youth and Crisis* by Erik H. Erikson. By permission of W. W. Norton, Inc. Copyright © 1968 by W. W. Norton & Company, Inc. Austen Riggs Monograph No. 7.

10. Robert W. White, "Motivation Reconsidered: The Concept of Competence," *Psychological Review*, 66 (1959): 297–333.

11. Garai and Scheinfeld, "Sex Differences."

12. O. D. Duncan and R. W. Hodge, "Education and Occupational Mobility: A Regression Analysis," *American Journal of Sociology*, 68 (1963): 629–44.

13. Edward Gross, "The Worker and Society," in *Man in a World at Work*, ed. Henry Borow (Boston: Houghton Mifflin Co., 1964), pp. 67–95.

14. L. G. Burchinal, A. O. Haller, and M. Taves, *Career Choices of Rural Youth in a Changing Society*, Bulletin no. 458, Agricultural Experimentation Station, University of Minnesota (Rosemount, 1962); W. L. Slocum and L. T. Empey, *Occupational Planning by Young Women*, Bulletin no. 568, Agricultural Experimental Station, State College of Washington, (Pullman, 1956).

15. For a review of research on Roe's theory, see Borow, "Occupational Motives and Roles," pp. 401–7. For other broad developmental theories see Borow, ed., *Man in a World at Work*.

16. Donald E. Super, et al. "Some Generalizations Regarding Vocational Development," in *Selected Readings in Adolescent Psychology*, ed. Joseph Duffy and George Giulani (Berkeley, Calif.: McCutchan Publishing Corp., 1970).

17. Robert P. O'Hara and David V. Tiedeman, "Vocational Self-Concept in Adolescence," *Journal of Counseling Psychology*, 6 (1959): 292–301. One must be cautious about such interpretations; the differences in the tests used in each area may have contributed to the differences in the correlations.

18. David B. Hershenson and William R. Langbauer, "Sequencing of Intrapsychic Stages of Vocational Development," *Journal of Counseling Psychology*, 20 (1973): 519–21; see also D. B. Hershenson, "Life-Stage Vocational Development System," *Journal of Counseling Psychology*, 15 (1968): 23–30.

19. Roger J. Tierney and Al Herman, "Self-Estimate Ability in Adolescence," *Journal of Counseling Psychology*, 20 (1973): 298–302. See also David V. Tiedeman, "Comment on Self-Estimate Ability in Adolescence," pp. 303–5.

20. Ibid., p. 301, and Barbara A. Putnam and James C. Hansen, "Relationship

of Self-Concept and Feminine Role Concept to Vocational Maturity in Young Women," *Journal of Counseling Psychology,* 19 (1972): 436–40.

21. Warren D. Gribbons and Paul R. Lohnes, "Shifts in Adolescents' Vocational Values," *Personnel and Guidance Journal,* 44 (1965): 248–52.

22. R. P. O'Hara, "The Roots of Careers," *Elementary School Journal,* 62 (1962): 277–80.

23. The complex sequence of vocational development conceptualized by Eli Ginzberg is reviewed in Borow, "Occupational Motives and Roles," pp. 398–401. Only those portions of the developmental theory which have been subjected to empirical test are reviewed here.

24. Douvan and Adelson, *Adolescent Experience.*

25. Shirley S. Angrist, "Role Constellation as a Variable in Women's Leisure Activities," *Social Forces,* 45 (1967): 423–31; Eli Ginzberg et al., *Occupational Choice* (New York: Columbia University Press, 1951); Lenore W. Harmon, "Anatomy of Career Commitment in Women," *Journal of Counseling Psychology,* 17 (1970): 77–80; Arnold Rose, "The Adequacy of Women's Expectations for Adult Roles," *Social Forces,* 30 (1951): 69–77.

26. Shirley S. Angrist, "The Study of Sex Roles," *Journal of Social Issues,* 25 (1969): 215–32.

27. Leona E. Tyler, "The Antecedents of Two Varieties of Vocational Interests," *Genetic Psychology Monographs,* 70 (1964): 177–27.

28. Research regarding the influence of social class on vocational choice is reviewed in Borow, "Occupational Motives and Roles," pp. 382–95.

29. Putnam and Hansen, "Vocational Maturity in Young Women."

30. Agnes G. Rezler, "Characteristics of High School Girls Choosing Traditional or Pioneer Vocations," *Personnel and Guidance Journal,* 45 (1967): 659–65.

31. Peggy Hawley, "Perceptions of Male Models of Femininity Related to Career Choice," *Journal of Counseling Psychology,* 19 (1972): 308–13.

32. Peggy Hawley, "What Women Think Men Think: Does It Affect Their Career Choices?" *Journal of Counseling Psychology,* 18 (1971): 193–99.

33. Helen S. Farmer and Martin J. Bohn, Jr., "Home-Career Conflict Reduction and the Level of Career Interest in Women," *Journal of Counseling Psychology,* 17 (1970): 228–232.

34. "Come of age" is used here in its popular literary sense, that men have "grown up" to be modern, 20th-century men. See also Chapter 11, p. 226 below.

35. Farmer and Bohn, "Home-Career Conflict Reduction," p. 229.

36. Donald E. Super, "Consistency and Wisdom of Vocational Preference as Indices of Vocational Maturity in the Ninth Grade," *Journal of Educational Psychology,* 52 (1961): 35–43.

37. See Roger Brown, *Social Psychology* (New York: Free Press, 1965), chap. 9, pp. 423–76. See also David McClelland, *The Achievement Motive* (New York: Appleton-Century-Crofts, 1953).

38. Bernard C. Rosen, "The Achievement Syndrome: A Psychocultural Dimension of Social Stratification," *American Sociological Review,* 21 (1956): 203–11.

39. Ibid. See also Paul H. Mussen, John J. Conger and Jerome Kagan, *Child Development and Personality,* 3d ed. (New York: Harper & Row, Publishers, 1969), pp. 346–49.

40. Rosen, "Achievement Syndrome."

41. H. A. Moss and Jerome Kagan, "Stability of Achievement and Recognition

Seeking Behavior from Early Childhood through Adulthood," *Journal of Abnormal and Social Psychology*, 63 (1961): 504–13.

42. Ibid., and R. D. Tuddenham, "The Constancy of Personality Ratings over Two Decades," *Genetic Psychology Monographs*, 60 (1959): 3–29.

43. Garai and Scheinfeld, "Sex Differences," p. 228.

44. Alice S. Rossi, "Naming Children in Middle-Class Families," *American Sociological Review*, 30 (1965): 499–513.

45. Garai and Scheinfeld, "Sex Differences," pp. 228–29.

46. William Simon and John Gagnon, "Psychosexual Development," *Transaction*, 6 (1969): 15–16.

47. Garai and Scheinfeld, "Sex Differences."

48. Goldsen and White. A study of teachers had similar results, Mason et al. 1959.

49. For example of this interpretation, see Jerome Kagan, *Understanding Children: Behavior, Motives, and Thought* (New York: Harcourt Brace Jovanovich, 1971), p. 20.

50. Gerald S. Lesser, Rhoda N. Krawitz, and Rita Packard, "Experimental Arousal of Achievement Motivation in Adolescent Girls," *Journal of Abnormal and Social Psychology*, 66 (1963): 59–66.

51. P. S. Houts and D. R. Entwisle, "Academic Achievement Effort among Females: Achievement Attitudes and Sex Role Orientation," *Journal of Counseling Psychology*, 15 (1968): 284–86.

52. Vivian P. Makowsky, "Fear of Success, Sex-Role Orientation of the Task, and Competitive Condition as Variables Affecting Women's Performance in Achievement-Oriented Situations" (Paper presented to the 44th Annual Meeting, Midwestern Psychological Association, Cleveland, May 1972).

53. For an excellent review of the general sex differences, see Garai and Scheinfeld, "Sex Differences," pp. 217–24.

54. Joan Joesting and Robert Joesting, "Future Problems of Gifted Girls" (Paper presented at the 17th Annual Meeting of the National Association for Gifted Girls, New Orleans, November 1969).

55. Rezler, "Traditional or Pioneer Vocations."

56. Alice Rossi, "Changing Sex Roles and Family Development" (Paper presented at the meeting of the American Psychological Association, Washington, D.C., September 1971).

57. Clyde Kluckhohn and Florence Kluckhohn, "American Culture: Generalized Orientation and Class Patterns," in L. Bryson et al., *Conflict of Power in Modern Culture* (New York: Harper Bros., 1947).

58. Paul Goodman, *Growing up Absurd* (New York: Random House, 1956).

59. Kenneth Keniston, *The Uncommitted: Alienated Youth in American Society* (New York: Harcourt, Brace & World, 1965), p. 267. Copyright © 1962, 1965 by Kenneth Keniston. Reprinted by permission of Harcourt Brace Jovanovich, Inc.

60. *Life*, September 1, 1972, pp. 30–41.

61. C. Wright Mills, *White Collar: The American Middle Classes* (New York: Oxford University Press, 1951), p. 237.

62. H. Kirk Dansereau, "Work and the Teenager," in *Annals of the American Academy of Political and Social Science*, vol. 338, November 1961.

63. Donald M. Morrison, in *Time*, October 30, 1972, pp. 96–97.

64. Schizophrenia is used here in its popular sense of split personality, which is correctly termed dissociated personality.

65. Charles Reich, *The Greening of America* (New York: Random House, 1970), p. 78.

66. Keniston, *Uncommitted*, pp. 226 and 267–68.

67. Morris Rosenberg, "Occupational Orientation," in *Society and the Adolescent Self-Image* (Princeton, N.J.: Princeton University Press, 1955), pp. 224–39.

68. Morris Rosenberg, "Personality and Career Choice," in *Occupations and Values* (Glencoe, Ill.: Free Press, 1957).

69. Borow, "Occupational Motives and Roles," p. 406.

70. For a brief explanation of factor analysis, see Chapter 7.

71. Alexander W. Astin and Robert C. Nichols, "Life Goals and Vocational Choice," *Journal of Applied Psychology*, 48 (1964): 50–58.

72. Rosenberg, "Personality and Career Choice."

73. Kuder Preference Record, Vocational Form CH, 2d revision (Chicago: Science Research Associates, January 1950).

74. J. D. Salinger, *The Catcher in the Rye* (New York: Signet Books, 1945), pp. 155–56.

75. Ginzberg et al., *Occupational Choice.*

76. O'Hara and Tiedeman, "Vocational Self-Concept in Adolescence."

77. Garai and Scheinfeld, "Sex Differences," pp. 212–13; Brian Sutton-Smith, B. G. Rosenberg, and E. F. Morgan, "Development of Sex Differences in Play Choices during Preadolescence," *Child Development*, 34 (1963): 119–26.

78. S. Krippner, "Sex, Ability and Interest: A Test of Tyler's Hypothesis," *Gifted Child Quarterly*, 6 (1962): 105–10.

79. Carol Quigley, "Youth's Heros Have No Halos," *Today's Education*, February 1971, pp. 28–29.

80. Mollie S. Smart and Russell C. Smart, *Adolescents: Development and Relationships* (New York: Macmillan Publishing Co., 1973), p. 181.

81. The difficulty of the transition from school to work has prompted an extensive study in Britain by J. M. M. Hill and D. E. Scharff, *Between Two Worlds*, in process.

82. Anna Freud, *The Ego and the Mechanisms of Defense* (New York: International Universities Press, 1946), pp. 172, 191.

83. D. D. Schultz, *Sensory Restriction: Effects on Behavior* (New York: Academic Press, 1965); J. P. Zubek, *Sensory Deprivation: 15 Years of Research* (New York: Appleton-Century-Crofts, 1969).

84. Frederick Perls, Ralph E. Hefferline, and Paul Goodman, *Gestalt Therapy: Excitement and Growth in Personality* (New York: Julian Press, 1969).

85. Alan S. Waterman, Patricia S. Geary, and Caroline K. Waterman, "Longitudinal Study of Changes in Ego Identity Status from the Freshman to the Senior Year at College," *Developmental Psychology*, 10 (1974): 387–92.

86. Irwin M. Marcus, "From School to Work: Certain Aspects of Psychosocial Interaction," in *Adolescence: Psychosocial Perspectives*, ed. Gerald Caplan and Serge Lebovici (New York: Basic Books, 1969), pp. 157–64.

87. Douvan and Adelson, *Adolescent Experience;* H. D. Carter, "The Development of Vocational Attitudes," *Journal of Counseling Psychology*, 4 (1940): 185–91; D. E. Super, et al., *Career Development: Self-Concept Theory* (New York: College Entrance Examination Board, 1963).

88. Slocum and Empey, "Occupational Planning by Young Women."

89. H. L. Wilensky, "Orderly Careers and Social Participation: The Impact of Work History on Social Integration in the Middle Class," *American Sociological Review*, 26 (1961): 521–39.

90. Edward Gross, "A Sociological Approach to the Analysis of Preparation for Work Life," *Personnel and Guidance Journal*, 45 (1967): 416–23.

91. Personal communications with interviewers for engineering, business, and sales positions.

92. Marhall McLuhan, "Automation: Learning a Living," *Understanding Media: The Extensions of Man* (New York: McGraw-Hill Book Co., 1964).

93. Alan Gartner and Frank Riessman, *The Service Society* (New York: Harper & Row, Publishers, in press).

# 11

## CRISIS FOUR
## Values: The fall of the gods

A THEME OF this book has been that the adolescent identity crisis is aggravated by the discontinuity in American child rearing by which children are reared in a female-dominated home and then expected to take adult roles in a society dominated by masculine values. Within the American home there are two gods: the imminent mother god of sensitivity and warmth, and the transcendent father god of power and effectiveness. The mother god is loved; the father god is respected and revered.[1]

To a child, parents are somewhat like gods, for they tower above; they appear to have incredible knowledge and power. It is they who decide the way things are and declare what is right and what is wrong. In day-to-day living, the preschooler begins to learn that his parents have limitations, but they still remain the highest gods he knows. When the child enters school, he meets some minor gods (teachers) and gradually recognizes that there may be other ways to do things, that the primary gods are limited in the domain they rule. It appears at times that they are not omniscient, but still the child looks up to them.

As relationships with playmates and school friends develop, the child's world of interactions becomes less hierarchical. Not all personal interactions are defined in terms of who is above and who is below. The child feels less alone in his status as one of the lesser ones. But that does not diminish the status of the parents; it is only when the child begins to sense that there are differences in what is considered right and wrong that the parents' status comes into question. In early adolescence, the peer group increases in importance and comparatively more of the individual's time and enthusiasm are expended with peers. Differences in values begin to emerge. Yet, even then, when it comes to decisions that matter, the parents' views are generally trusted.

It is only in late adolescence, when the youth experiences the world on his own, that it dawns on him that the world of his parents is only one view of the real world. The experience of an anonymous college student, written retrospectively, is indicative of this discovery:

> I knew that there were other opinions and other beliefs before. In fact, I didn't always agree with my parents, even in junior high school. But still it seemed clear that there was one thing which was right. There was a Right and Wrong, even if we didn't agree completely. When teachers in the classroom raised questions, I could intellectually toy with the issues—but I could always return safely to the oasis of home, where the ground was solid and secure. But now the questions of the classroom are only the beginning. When I return to the dorm, there is no agreement there, either. The worst of it is, it's the Jewish kids from the city who intrigue me most. But at times I can hardly take it. The doubts keep rising: Maybe there is NO truth. Maybe neither Mom nor my professors, neither the Christians nor the Jews are right. They can't all be right. So maybe no one is right. It feels like there's just nothing you can count on anymore.

For this student, the gods have fallen. This is the "shaking of the foundations" of which the theologians speak.[2] In secular terms, this young man has felt the "nausea" of "nothingness."[3]

It is not simply that the college youth is homesick and misses Mom. Clearly the grief over the loss of home is part of it. But there is that other god who falls as well, the father god, that distant, powerful image. The whole masculine image begins to be questioned. Not only does the youth miss the warmth of home, he questions the value of moving into the masculine world. Perhaps all values are called into question, and he may ask himself, "What is the sense of continuing in college if nothing matters anyway?"

At the core of the identity quest is the struggle to affirm some values by which the individual can live out his life in society. The process of value formation has its roots, of course, in early childhood. But early value judgments are not issues of identity, as they are in adolescence. At first the child simply accepts the values of his parents. Psychoanalytic theory describes this as the introjection of the superego, which I referred to metaphorically as the swallowing whole of the apple (Chapter 1). And now, in adolescence, this somewhat dissociated portion of the personality, this apple, has to be coughed up and chewed; some of it must be spit out, and some digested, that is, reassimilated into the total identity.

## The development of values

### The cognitive approach

Out of the work of Jean Piaget and others has emerged a cognitive-developmental approach to understanding the socialization process. The viewpoint recognizes the importance of learning in the socialization of the child but emphasizes the structural components of learning. That is, learning is not understood as merely the development of new associations or the shaping of new behaviors (as in classical and operant conditioning). According to Lawrence Kohlberg, "Basic development involves basic transformations of cognitive *structure* which . . . must be explained by parameters of organizational wholes or systems of internal relations."[4] Kohlberg goes on to define his terms as follows:

> Cognitive structure refers to rules for processing information or for connecting experienced events. Cognition (as most clearly reflected in thinking) means putting things together or relating events, and this relating is an active connecting process, not a passive connecting of events through external association and repetition. In part this means that connections are formed by selective and active processes of attention, information-gathering strategies, motivated thinking, etc. More basically, it means that the process of relating particular events depends upon prior general modes of relating developed by the organism.[5]

The cognitive viewpoint emphasizes the active role of the person in making sense of his environment. The attempt to understand involves not only receiving experience but acting on it to order and arrange it. The interaction of the individual with the social environment is seen as an active attempt of the child (or adolescent) to work things out for himself.

Obviously, there are close parallels between this view and the themes of active identity struggle which are central to this book. The cognitive theory suggests that the individual continually seeks a more consistent structure or framework through which to interpret experience. When new experiences do not fit his conceptions, he must seek some way to resolve the conflict. Sometimes he can do so by forming a new gestalt, a new, more inclusive "structured whole" which integrates the new experience. The developmental sequence of stages implies that each stage constitutes a structured whole. Research to date suggests the fruitfulness, for research in socialization, of "defining social behavior in terms of developmental sequence instead of in terms of traits."[6]

## The developmental sequence

The uncritical acceptance of parental values has been termed "moral realism" by Piaget, a pioneer in the attempt to understand the development of values as an aspect of cognitive growth.[7] Piaget noted three aspects in the hierarchial stages of moral development:

1. Goodness is defined as obedience to adult commands; acts that do not conform are bad.
2. Rules are perceived as given from above; they are externally imposed and consequently demand external compliance to the letter of the law rather than the spirit.
3. An act is evaluated in terms of its consequences rather than its intentions. Punishment is incurred for behavior, regardless of the person's intentions.[8]

As the child is more and more influenced by peers, Piaget states that the child gradually ceases to view morality in terms of "unilateral authority" and shifts to a focus on rules as necessary for cooperation among peers.[9] In other words, the child moves from a hierarchial stage to a cooperative stage of moral reasoning. Piaget's stages of moral development have been extended and elaborated by Kohlberg in a manner which has allowed considerable productive research.[10] Qualitative changes in the criteria for moral judgment may occur into late adolescence; after that, generally, the changes which occur reflect increased integration and consistency rather than the development of a new, higher stage of judgment. Thus Kohlberg views the six stages in his theory as complete and universal. These stages have been clearly summarized by Mollie S. Smart and Russell C. Smart as follows:

> I. *Preconventional level, on which impulse gratification is modified by rewards and punishments.*
>     Stage 1. Punishment and obedience orientation. The reason for doing anything or for not doing something is to avoid punishment. "Being right" means obeying an authority. There is no concept of *a* right.
>     Stage 2. Instrumental relativist orientation. The reason for behavior is to get pleasure for oneself, often in the form of rewards from another person. Everyone has a right to do what he wants with himself and his possessions, even though his behavior conflicts with the rights of others. Reciprocity is pragmatic and has nothing to do with loyalty or gratitude or justice.

II. *Conventional level, where conduct is controlled by the anticipation of social praise and blame. Meeting the expectations of family or nation and maintaining such groups is valuable regardless of consequences.*

Stage 3. Good-boy, nice-girl morality, or maintaining good relationships and the approval of other people. Conformity to stereotyped notions of majority or "natural" behavior. Intention becomes important in judging behavior. The concept of everyone's rights is the same as in Stage 2, with the addition that nobody has the right to do evil.

Stage 4. "Law and order" orientation. Right behavior consists of following fixed rules, respecting authority, maintaining the established social order for its own sake. When legitimate authorities disapprove or punish, the youngster feels guilty. A right is a claim on the actions of others, usually an earned claim, such as payment for work.

III. *Postconventional, autonomous, principled level. Morality of self-accepted moral principles, in which the person regulates his behavior by an ideal which he holds, regardless of immediate social praise and blame.*

Stage 5. Social-contract legalistic orientation. Morality of contract and of democratically accepted law. Community respect and disrespect are powerful motivators. The concept of human rights emerges here. There are rights linked to role and status and also unearned, universal, individual rights as a human being.

Stage 6. Morality of individual principles of conscience. Motivation is feeling right with oneself. The idea of rights includes all that expressed in Type 5 plus the notion that the life and personality of every individual is to be respected. Acceptable principles, such as the Golden Rule, have logical comprehensiveness, universality, and consistency.[11]

Not all people reach the highest level of moral development; in fact, for the majority of males, Stage 4, the "law and order" orientation, gradually becomes the predominant level of judgment. Females, on the average, are more likely to consolidate their moral development at Stage 3, the "good girl" morality.[12] There is variation within individuals, with different judgments being made at different levels, and of course there is a wide span of variation between individuals of the same sex. Though research has been done on class and cultural differences, the interest here is in the general scheme of individual development. Before considering research on the topic, some comments are in order on the influences of various agents of socialization in the progression of moral stages.

Piaget emphasized the importance of peers in late childhood development. During late childhood and early adolescence, social conformity defines the moral code; the child becomes increasingly "socialized" in the sense of obedience to the norms of society. Peers are clearly important in this process, though there is little reason to believe they are the primary agent of socialization. Parents continue to function as important references for moral judgments, and other adult figures are increasingly influential.

Though conventional morality is less egocentric than the preconventional level, it still involves an uncritical attitude toward authority. In this stage, obedience is given to the larger society and its legitimate authorities, rather than to the parents. It is as if the sources of moral rules have shifted, but rules continue to be given from outside.

As the agents of outside influence increase, many adolescents begin to experience some conflict. Often this conflict reflects discrepancies between the values of the home and those of the peer group.[13] These tensions are expressed in comments such as: "I don't always agree with [my friends] and it bothers me," "Sometimes you can't convince kids that they're wrong," and "I don't agree with what some of the girls do on dates."[14] Conflicts may also arise as the adolescent is brought into closer contact with nonparental authorities. He begins to note that what is okay in one home is not accepted in another. There are different ways of doing things; the values of home are not the universal values. This broadening social experience is the first of two factors which contribute to the changes in moral orientation that occur next.

The second factor producing change in moral attitudes is the development of new cognitive skills. The adolescent develops the ability to think about himself as an object and to symbolize self-attributes. He learns to think logically, to formulate hypotheses, and to deduce consequences. He is now able to use symbols about symbols, and this allows him to construct ideals and to postulate contrary-to-fact situations.[15] This ability will affect the adolescent's decision making processes, as has been noted by David Elkind:

> The capacity to deal with combinatorial logic and to consider all possible factors in a given problem solving situation lays the groundwork for some characteristic adolescent reactions. One consequence of the capacity for combinatorial logic is that, particularly in social situations, the adolescent now sees a host of alternatives and decision-making becomes a problem. He now sees, to illustrate, many alternatives to parental directives and is loath to accept the parental alternatives without question.[16]

The adolescent's increased ability to use symbols and logic allows the value struggle to emerge, in middle and late adolescence, as a conscious process. More than ever before, the adolescent is able to see inconsistencies and conflict. Conflicts between his different reference groups and conflicting messages from the same agent of socialization become clear to him. For example, adult authorities may urge him to "Do unto others as you would have them do unto you," and at another time they will advise him to "Take care of no. 1 first." The youth's new cognitive tools encourage him in a quest for a consistent ethic, a philosophy of life.[17] Those who attain the third, postconventional, level of morality are cognizant that rules and laws are inventions of man for his own benefit. The appeal to external authority declines. It is those adolescents who reach this principled level who may experience the fall of the gods.

Although Kohlberg, following Piaget, believes that the order of these cognitive changes is universal, in our own culture they occur in interaction with the social and psychological changes we have noted.[18] The recognition that laws are human inventions which can be changed is aided by the adolescent's awareness of the changes between generations. The adolescent's increased interaction with the outside world leads him to position himself within society's framework, not just within his own family's.[19] The conscious struggle for identity and the need for inner consistency encourage the emergence of the final stage, an orientation toward the decisions of conscience and toward self-chosen ethical principles appealing to logical comprehensiveness, universality, and consistency.[20] Principled thought (Stage 5) begins in adolescence, but this final stage (Stage 6) does not usually crystalize until the early twenties, if it develops at all. As noted, conventional morality is the highest level reached by most people in our society. Adult development is primarily a matter of a diminishing use of childish modes of judgment rather than continued movement to higher modes.[21]

### Family and peer influences on the child's values

So far the discussion of moral development has been restricted to changes in the level of moral judgments, using Piaget's and Kohlberg's formulations of levels and stages. Another approach to the study of value development focuses upon the content of the values. Both the content and the level of values are important—the reader must be alert to note which of the two is the focus of whatever research he is studying.

There is considerable evidence that values held by family members are similar even after the children have reached college age. One well-designed study tested similarity in values and other personality traits in college students and their parents to determine which family pairs showed the greatest similarity: mother-father, mother-son, mother-daughter, father-son, or father-daughter. The conclusion was that members of a family resemble one another in values and, to a lesser extent, in other personality traits. The values measured which showed significant correlations for nearly all the family pairs were: dedication to causes, conventional moralism, intellectualism, humanitarianism, and achievement need. For these values, correlations between the parents were higher than those between parent-child pairs. Correlations between the parents were also significant for self-realization, aestheticism, practicality, and materialism.[22]

It cannot be determined from this study whether the greater parent-to-parent similarity on values and interests reflects a similarity present before the parents chose each other, is due to their years of living together, or is a function of differences between age groups, generations, and social roles. No patterns of difference were found when the four parent-child pairs were compared. For all of these pairs (father-son, father-daughter, mother-son and mother-daughter), the associations of values were similar in strength.

A number of studies have sought to clarify the process by which parents facilitate their children's moral development. These studies have measured the degree of self-control or level of moral judgment in the children, rather than focusing on specific value content. A series of studies by Martin Hoffman and Herbert Saltzstein demonstrated relationships between the form of discipline used by mother and the moral development of seventh-graders. Four measures were obtained of the child's reactions to being caught doing something wrong: the child's judgments of stories, the child's story completions, the teacher's evaluations, and the mother's evaluations. The withdrawal of love as discipline did not seem related to moral development. Assertion of power, including physical punishment and deprivation of objects or privileges, seemed negatively related to internalization of moral standards. The most effective parents were those who responded to wrongdoing by appealing to the child's guilt potential, stating the consequences his action had for other people involved. No clear effects of fathers' responses were obtained.[23]

In another study, Constance Holstein measured moral development in eighth-grade students and their parents, using Kohlberg's stages. The level of moral reasoning employed by the mother proved to be a very good predictor of the child's level of moral development. As in the Hoffman study, no clear effects were found related to the fathers. However, when Holstein pursued the analysis of the data further, she found that for a subgroup of fathers who were high on expression of warmth and affection, significant relationships between father and child levels of moral judgment did occur.[24] This suggests that fathers can be important in children's moral development if they develop a closer relationship with the child than is typical of most American fathers.

Holstein's data indicate that high levels of moral development in children are not directly due to warmth and affection from parents. Rather, these factors act as mediating variables in homes where the parents encourage children's participation in decision making. This is reminiscent of the data indicating the importance of explanation in the development of autonomy.[25] Holstein's study included direct observation and measurement of family interaction, in an attempt to validate the importance of parental encouragement of the child's participation in decision making. A sample of family discussions on moral issues was scored on measures of parental encouragement (rated by independent observers). Results showed that the parents of children more advanced in moral reasoning provided much more encouragement for the child to participate in the discussion. These children did, in fact, participate more than other children, as measured by the percentage of the total time the family spent in discussion.[26] This study provides actual observation of family interaction, rather than verbal report, and is to be commended as a model for future research.

These studies are sufficient to indicate the role of mothers in moral development (and the potential role of fathers who are willing to involve themselves in child rearing). The socializing effects of peers have not been as adequately researched. Morton Birnbaum conducted an interesting study of relevance to both parent and peer socialization, using seventh-grade students to test the role anxiety plays in making moral judgments.[27] Students were asked to write down their moral judgments regarding situations in which a child violated or adhered to a moral rule which conflicted with the circumstances. For example:

> When Fred was seven, he cut himself with his father's saw. His father told him to use the saw only when he was around. Now Fred is 13 and experienced with saws. To finish a school project Fred used his father's saw even though no one else was at home.

After the students had completed four such stories, the experimenter made some comments intended to introduce anxiety about parents, peers, or physical harm. In the group subjected to anxiety about parental rejection, the experimenter stated that "A lot of kids really don't know what their parents think of them." Then students were asked how they thought their parents would rate them—as good or bad, smart or dumb, and so on. Following this, responses to four more moral stories were solicited. Twice while they were working on these, the experimenter again aroused their anxiety by making statements like "It looks to me like some of you are still worrying about what your parents may think of you, but it's important now that you get down to work on these stories."

The procedure was the same for the two other experimental groups. Peer anxiety was elicted by the statement "We have found many kids who don't have many friends," after which students were instructed to list three classmates they liked "So we can find out who is hardly ever picked." The third experimental condition, anxiety over bodily harm, was included to test Freud's theory of castration anxiety. Students were led to believe dentists would come to school for checkups and were asked to provide information on "how good your teeth are and how much drilling and cleaning the dentist may have to do." (It was assumed any threat of bodily harm would be more likely to elicit castration anxiety than would threats of parent or peer judgments.) A fourth group simply took a "food preference inventory" between the two sets of moral stories; this group functioned as a control with no induced anxiety.

Birnbaum's experiment was designed to see what shifts toward flexibility or rigidity in moral judgment would occur under the different anxiety conditions. It might be more accurate to describe the variable measured as the degree of adherence to rules given by authorities versus the ability to make independent judgments. The effects were the same for boys and girls. In the control condition, no anxiety, there was a tendency for subjects to become slightly more flexible on their second set of four moral judgments. The same pattern held for the dentist anxiety condition, suggesting no effect; this fails to substantiate the Freudian view of castration anxiety as an important factor in moral development of adolescents. Significant shifts in moral judgments occurred under the other two conditions. Students subjected to anxiety about parent rejection became more rigid in their moral judgments (adhering to rules given by authorities); those encouraged to worry about peer rejection became more flexible (making more independent judgments).

These results may be interpreted as indicating that anxiety increases conformity to the salient reference group. That is, when students are encouraged to worry about what their parents think, they produce moral judgments which more rigidly adhere to adult rules. When the experimenter's comments brought the peer group to mind, that became the salient reference group, and responses were closer to those the peer group would approve. The shift in responses is consistently in the direction of greater conformity; the content of value responses changes, depending on the reference group to which the student is conforming.[28]

### The search for a philosophy of life: Trends in late adolescence

As a youth seeks to make decisions about vocations, sex and intimacy, and the other content areas, and as he seeks to reconcile his past identifications with the influences of new reference groups, he is confronted throughout with the issue of value. Though the struggle to make autonomous decisions begins much earlier, it is usually not until late adolescence that the youth can cut to the heart of the struggle and see clearly the value issues involved. Only in late adolescence do the conflicts between parent and child center around differences in beliefs and attitudes.[29]

At one time the adolescent crisis in values was probably experienced as a religious crisis, sometimes culminating in a conversion experience. Among the earliest social psychology studies, research by E. D. Starbuck

(1899) and E. T. Clark (1929) suggested that "a sudden highly emotional commitment to believing . . . was almost exclusively an adolescent phenomenon."[30] Gradual "religious awakenings" also appeared to be most common in adolescence. It has been noted, however, that since the turn of the century:

> . . . the role of the believer seems to have lost its power as a unifying alternative for adolescent identity. Clark's data from the 1920's suggest that this decline had begun by then. More of his subjects seem to have become committed as a matter of conformity rather than through a choice made in crises.[31]

Even where there is an increase in church attendance during adolescence, it does not signify an increase in willingness to believe. While in some areas the frequency of churchgoing is higher among adolescents than adults, the incidence of belief is lower.[32] The general observation is that church attendance declines markedly during adolescence in today's society, probably because the church's approach to value questions has tended to be inflexible and doctrinaire.[33] This decline in interest in organized religion is especially noticeable among the best educated youth. In one study, freshmen at two Eastern universities, Harvard and Clark, were compared on religious attitudes to freshmen at the same universities 37 years earlier. It was clear that attitudes toward the institutional church have become less favorable. For example, in the early 1930s 78 percent of the freshmen believed that "the church is a divine institution and it commands my highest loyalty and respect." In the latest poll, only 17 percent of the freshmen believed this.[34] This does not necessarily indicate a decline in the importance of religious issues for the adolescent, to whom religion seems to be of interest more as a way of raising value issues than as a belief system. Religious beliefs tend to become more abstract and less literal during the high school years and after.[35]

There is little indication of either increased religious fervor or widespread rebellion against religion during the high school years.[36] For the most part, the attitudes and values of high school adolescents continue to mirror those of their parents. There is even some evidence that the first reaction to the emergence of a value crisis may be a defensive retreat to the parental values and an increase in stereotyped thinking with regard to religious matters.[37] This evidence is not uniform; earlier studies found that religious views became more tolerant and less dogmatic during the high school years.[38] There is a need for longitudinal studies of changes in values and religious attitudes during the high school years.

Perhaps an interest in developing a philosophy of life is the more common expression of the value quest among today's adolescents. When high school students are asked to rank the issues they consider "problems," concern with a philosophy of life has low priority during the early years of high school. During the senior year, however, it generally becomes one of the three most important problems.[39] It is likely that the move away from home, and the concomitant broadening of experiences, intensifies this value struggle[40] and that the value crisis reaches its greatest intensity in the years immediately following the move away from home. When tests have been administered throughout the four years of undergraduate education, the scores show that the greatest personality changes occur during the earlier part of the college career, when the student is experiencing the greatest environmental changes, especially those connected with the move away from home.[41]

Beliefs (in the sense of particularist doctrine) do not hold up well as youth move farther away from home and meet more diverse viewpoints. The adolescent becomes increasingly aware that his way is not the only way. He continues to search for what is right for him, regarding both values and religious attitudes, but he is less inclined to be dogmatic about it.

While the great majority of college students continue to affirm their belief in God, in many cases this belief becomes increasingly tenuous or is interpreted in a more abstract manner during the college years. For some youths, the first reaction to new experiences may be to retreat. Although the overall direction of attitude change in late adolescence, at least for college students, is toward increased tolerance, there may be a period of confrontation during which the late adolescent attempts to cling to his earlier views. In a national study, 53 percent of the freshmen stated that college had not changed their religious beliefs, and 23 percent said it had increased their faith. Only 23 percent reported that it had raised doubts for them. Among college seniors, however, only 34 percent reported no change, while 45 percent said college had raised doubts about their beliefs, and only 20 percent reported an increase in faith.[42] Again it should be clarified that such increased doubts and loss of trust in institutionalized religion do not indicate a lack of concern during the college years for the central value issues of religious teaching. In fact, 50 percent of the national sampling of seniors in the study cited above continued to characterize themselves as "fairly religious," and an additional 20 percent claimed they were "very religious." Youth may be putting more emphasis upon personal rather than institutionalized religion.[43]

The youth, in particular the college student, encounters many possibilities—not just in terms of vocation, but in terms of lifestyle as well. These are not just academic possibilities; as they meet and develop friendships with persons from many different ways of life, they consider changes in their own lifestyles. This widening world is both exciting and anxiety producing. No one way is the only way anymore. No right seems absolutely right; no wrong is wrong for everyone. There are no absolutes. The gods have fallen.

## The humanizing of values

Where youth is able to move into involvements with the world and intimacy with peers and adults, the direction of attitude change is usually toward increased tolerance. Longitudinal investigations of changes in student values and attitudes in the late 1920s and early 1930s generally showed changes "in the direction of a more liberal attitude on social issues and a more tolerant attitude toward persons."[44] Psychological research in the 1940s was considerably more complex, but the results were similar: "In general, students in college changed in the direction of greater liberalism and sophistication in their political, social, and religious outlooks. There was also evidence of broadening interests during the college years."[45]

Despite the well-publicized Jacob report (1957) which highlighted a number of important research problems, most of the more recent studies of values have shown changes resembling those reported in previous years. Students who remain in college become significantly less ethnocentric (that is, show less parochialism and ethnic prejudice) than they were when they entered. In religious and political views, students become more liberal.[46]

The most recent extensive research along these lines was done at the Stanford and Berkeley campuses in California and followed the incoming class of 1961 through their four undergraduate years.[47] A consistent pattern of change emerged:

> The changes [in scores] all reflect a movement toward greater open-mindedness and tolerance, a rejection of a restricted view of life, and a humanization of conscience. The complexity of the world is more and more recognized, and there is less tendency to demand pat answers. Along with this, the stereotyped view of right and wrong gives way to a broader acceptance of human diversity.[48]

The many colleges that have contributed research regarding personality change during the college years show impressive differences in the mean scores on the instruments used, but the direction of change has consistently been in the direction of greater tolerance. The direction of growth in values during the late adolescent period has been summarized by Robert White, out of a 20-year longitudinal study of Harvard and Radcliffe students, as follows: "The growth trend observed in the study of young adults is in a sense a continuation of Piaget's trend toward relativism. We prefer to call it a *humanizing* of values."[49] Change in values during the college years is not continuous and does not hold for all students. A great many students, perhaps even the majority, do not change significantly during the college years. The majority of students choose the middle ground; while they are not particularly harsh in their moral judgments, neither do they become particularly liberal.[50] The great majority of late adolescents, even in the middle class, never move beyond conventional morality.[51]

The social environment plays an important role in whether or not students mature in their moral perspective. Though Kohlberg's stages of moral development are correlated with intelligence ($r = .31$), an even higher correlation occurs ($r = .59$) between age and moral development when mental age is controlled.[52] This suggests the great importance of age-linked experience in making moral judgments and supports a concept of moral development as a product not only of cognitive learning but also of social learning.[53]

The amount of personal interaction between college students and faculty appears to be an important factor in student progress in moral development. More change has been reported in schools where student-faculty interaction is common.[54] Failure to mature in value orientation may be attributable, in part, to the lack of opportunities for new identifications, where informal student-faculty interaction is rare. The fact that most academic programs are so book oriented may be largely accountable for the failure of colleges to facilitate personal maturation. Studies which have tried to ferret out the factors that lead to attitude change have generally concluded that changes in information are not effective (despite instructors' wishes to believe that they are); rather, new experiences and involvements result in changes in attitudes and values. Harold Korn concludes that: "It seems from this research that a logical aim of education would consist in increasing the opportunities for diverse kinds of new experiences."[55]

Though the humanizing of values has been best documented on the college campus, it cannot be assumed that it is limited to college students. Research on late-adolescent development among noncollege youth is extremely limited and has produced conflicting data. Walter Plant reported a longitudinal study comparing students attending a state college with college-age subjects who had applied to, but not attended, the same college. After two years, he concluded that youth who did not pursue college education did not show the decrease in ethnocentric attitudes exhibited by those who continued.[56] That is, only the college students gave evidence of a humanizing of values. After four years, however, the noncollege sample showed changes in the direction of increased tolerance similar to those found in the college sample.[57] One interpretation is that the college environment speeds up changes that would have occurred anyway.[58] Unfortunately, no information was given as to whether the subjects had moved away from home or not, so possible effects of this variable are not clear.

## Sex roles and differences in value development

Changes in value orientation appear to occur earlier in boys. In a clinical study of 14- and 16-year-old boys and girls,[59] Elizabeth Douvan successfully predicted that:

> 1. Adolescent girls will show less concern with values and with developing behavioral controls than will boys; that is, character will show rapid development in boys during adolescence, while girls will be less preoccupied with establishing personal, individual standards and values.
> 2. Personal integration around moral values, though crucial in the adjustment of adolescent boys, will not predict adjustment in girls. Rather, sensitivity and skill in interpersonal relationships will be critical integrative variables in adolescent girls and will predict their personal adjustments.[60]

The reasons for these differences seem directly related to the sex-role expectations. Adolescent girls stay closer to home and remain more dependent upon their parents. This and other studies have shown that adolescent girls are more likely than boys to continue to accept parental regulation. Boys, who have been allowed more freedom and greater aggressivity, move toward greater autonomy than girls, but consequently they must develop more self-control. Douvan's measures of value orientation focus upon the issue of self-control, and her data show that boys more often worry about controls, particularly controls on their aggressive impulses. Douvan uses a neo-Freudian model and interprets this in relation to "the more imperious nature of the [sexual] impulses they must handle."[61] Yet the data suggest that boys experience the control issue more acutely around aggression than sexuality.

Since our culture generally encourages greater independence in boys than in girls, it is not surprising that the internalization of independent moral standards occurs earlier and more completely in boys. It was noted earlier that our culture gives more encouragement to boys than girls to undergo the process of personality differentiation and integration. Thus confirmation of Douvan's second hypothesis is not surprising; while for boys, well-internalized controls are highly related to other measures of integration, this is not the case for girls. Boys move from their previous identification with parental values toward the construction of their own more conscious and rational control system. Girls, by contrast, tend to remain dependent upon external controls, and girls who do this, Douvan says, "do not show the disintegration and demoralization that mark the noninternalized boy."[62] Douvan concludes that "In our culture there is not nearly as much pressure on girls as on boys to meet the identity challenge during the adolescent years."[63]

Studies using Kohlberg's stages of moral development indicate that, for the general population, women continue to lag behind men in this factor. One study found that during the high school years the same percentage of boys as girls were in the third stage of moral development, the "good boy, good girl" conventional morality.[64] Stage 3 appears to be a stable adult stage for women, but not for men. In one college population, only half as many boys as girls remained in Stage 3.[65] In a population of middle-aged parents, about four times as many women as men were still in Stage 3.[66] Most adult men, in both middle- and lower-class samples, move on to "law and order" conventional morality, Stage 4.[67] Thus, as Kohlberg summarizes it, "The breed of conventional morality which stabilizes in adulthood depends upon one's adult social sex role."[68] As a general rule, boys progress further in establishing internal controls and in moving beyond conformity to parents and toward a sort of conformity to the larger society.

The fact that most youths stabilize their moral development at a conventional level, with some type of conformity, suggests that they really do not develop an autonomous base for making value judgments in the midst of ambiguous circumstances. It could be argued that the person has not begun to integrate value decisions as part of his identity until "there is a clear effort to define moral values . . . apart from the authority of the groups of persons holding these principles and apart from the individual's own identification with these groups."[69] That is, the value crisis is not a conscious aspect of the identity struggle except for those who reach the postconventional, autonomous, or principled level of moral development. Among college students probably only 25 percent of the men and under 12 percent of the women reach the principled stage during the college years.[70]

Though the data regarding the level of moral judgments consistently favors males, this is not the case for the content of moral judgments. Though women may be more conforming, they also have more humane values. The series of longitudinal studies showing a pattern of change during the college years toward more tolerant, more humane values has been described. In one of these studies, which compared college and noncollege groups, the results suggested that the college experience speeded up the changes in values which would have occurred anyway.[71] This facilitative effect was most noticeable for college women.[72] The more recent research at Stanford and Berkeley indicated strong trends away from rigid, punitive moralizing and toward more flexible and more tolerant views. These trends were strong for both sexes. No analysis of sex differences was reported, but calculations from the data presented indicate that women have more humane values their freshman year and undergo slightly greater change in that direction during the four years of college.[73] Both of the studies just surveyed drew their subjects from California campuses; I know of no other available data. Whether the superiority of these women in value content can be generalized to others is a question for further research.

## Regressions in moral development

The chapter to this point has described a normal sequence of upward movement in levels of moral judgment throughout childhood and adolescence, with consolidation occurring in early adulthood. A surprising exception to this rule was found in about 20 percent of the boys in a longitudinal study by R. Kramer which followed the boys from age 10 to 24, taking measurements of their moral development at eight points during that span of years.[74] Though the general progression was toward consolidation at higher stages of moral judgments,

> . . . the most dramatic finding . . . [seemed] to fit neither [the] generalization that adult change is functional stabilization nor [the] generalization that developmental change is forward and sequential. These generalizations hold true for our longitudinal subjects at every age and social class with one exception, the college sophomore. . . . Between late high school and the second or third year of college, 20% of our middle class sample dropped or retrogressed in moral maturity scores. . . . This drop had a definite pattern. In high school [these 20%] . . . were among the most advanced [in moral development], all having a mixture of conventional (Stage 4) and principled (Stage 5) thought. In their college sophomore phase, they kicked both their conventional and their Stage 5 morality and replaced it with good old Stage 2 hedonistic relativism, jazzed up with some philosophic and sociopolitical jargon.[75]

To what can this regression be attributed? Kohlberg and Kramer suggest that, since these students were more concerned with moral issues than their high school peers, they are more upset by the disappearance of the moral world in which they had believed in childhood. They are more acutely aware of what I have termed the fall of the gods. When those students left high school, Kohlberg and Kramer note, "they thought that people lived by conventional morality and that their rewards in life depended on living that way too." One of the students explains: "College accounts for the change. You see what a dog-eat-dog world it is. Everyone seems to be out for himself."[76]

As Kohlberg and Kramer point out, the aspect of protest is clear, but the protest is not so much against the authority of their parents as it is against the immorality of the world. In short, the move from the moral supporting environment of the home to the wider world confronts young people with both the relativity of values and the gap between even conventional moral expectations and actual life. No doubt this regression to a selfish life (whether it was given Yippie or Ayn Rand type rationalizations) serves some integrative needs, allowing youth to free itself of some guilt. Yet the regressors do not really give up higher levels of morality—they justify their stance by criticizing the culture from the perspective of higher morality. And, after college, they return to "the suburbs of contractual and conventional rules."[77] When they leave college, the "moratorium" from adult responsibilities is brought to an end. Erik Erikson has formulated the concept that extended education allows youth to experiment with possibilities for identity, with hedonism or idealism, without really having to suffer the consequences.[78] In this light, the regression can be seen as a temporary experiment in nonconformity, staged in a setting safe from adult responsibilities. The college environment provided a context in which they "didn't care about having an ideology that 'worked', that formed a foundation for life-long responsibility or commitment."[79]

As noted in the preceding chapter, the search for vocational values can lead to an empty idealism when it is conducted apart from realistic experience. The search for values, conducted in a moratorium, can also lead in the opposite direction—to an empty hedonism. Chapters 14 and 15 will discuss the moratorium in more detail. Once again, it is clear that youth must be involved in order to successfully carry on its identity quest.

## The need for involvement

The loss of the absolutes and the identifications that they once trusted may cause young people to feel impoverished. The need for personal involvements and identifications is intense. As noted in the preceding chapter, there is a need for youth to work beside adults who will encourage them to share in responsibilities and decision making. When the adolescent gets to know styles of adulthood different from those of his parents and home community, his individuation from the family is encouraged and his expanding philosophy of life is nourished. But the close, personal involvement with adults is terribly limited on our college campuses, which tend to structure living experiences into a rigid age stratification.[80] College students eat, socialize, and sleep only with persons within four years of their own age. Adults enter their lives only in highly structured and formalized roles, behind the lecture podium or behind the administrator's desk—roles which offer little opportunity for personal involvement and identification. Formal education, even prior to the college years, tends to shirk responsibility for helping the student develop his own values, or even his own ideas. As Arthur Combs has put it, "We teach children not to look at the personal meanings. We say to the child, 'Jeannie, I'm not interested in what you think about this . . . What does the book say?'"[81] Education focuses upon the learning of facts, and consequently the student frequently perceives formal education as irrelevant to his personal growth. The protest against impersonal authority is not limited to those 20 percent who undergo a moral regression. Changing attitudes toward nonparental authority will be examined in the next chapter.

In some ways the college environment is an exceptionally tolerant one which provides a good place for growth, in spite of the educational system. The greater diversity and tolerance of academia are testified to by the fact that dropouts generally form their enclaves of counterculture in areas adjacent to colleges and universities. But academia also encourages ivory tower attitudes. The faculty of institutions of higher education is often markedly isolated; members avoid getting involved with or committed to the "dirty work" of the world outside.

Although our culture glamorizes youth and portrays it as the period of greatest enjoyment, it keeps young people isolated from real achievement and decision making. This is particularly dangerous to the development of values, for youth is taught ideals while being deprived of experience. Value learning tends to be largely verbalization, a mere matter of words. The adult in the work world tends to accept the practical and stops noticing the ambiguities. When the protected idealism of youth confronts this adult realism, the consequence is frequently a disillusionment that leads to cynicism.[82]

Since the world of academia tends to be isolated from the problems of the everyday world, the learning of values tends to be a practice in fantasy, dissociated from reality. Students are encouraged to develop their ideas out of the ideas of the experts, to feed back on tests the answers they have gained secondhand. Education becomes an experience in rearranging words, largely separated from personal experience. To be socially meaningful, however, values must develop out of social experience. The search for ideals is best conducted in direct contact with the social realities. The consequence of our isolation of youths is that they "acquire ideals not fully operative in the social organization."[83]

## Values and identity

The formation of one's own value orientation in isolation from society is simply a reflection of our society's misconception of the identity process as an intrapsychic issue focused primarily on internal integration. The establishment of ego identity has frequently been perceived as the gradual integration of past identifications. If the ingredients of the mature ego were already present at the point of the adolescent's departure from home, a moratorium for their integration would be appropriate; the late adolescent's search for self would be simply an attempt to discover something that is already there, present within himself. His task, however, is not that simple. The identity struggle is more than an attempt to find himself; he must "*create* a personality."[84] Even the concept of self is misleading if it suggests something that exists in isolation from the world. It may be preferable to describe the developmental task of adolescence as defining one's stance in the world. The youth must deal with the identifications he has with parents and other adults, but he does this more through a process of contact with the world than through introspection. For he must compare the impressions of the past generation to his own phenomenological experience of the world and reject those conceptions that do not fit.

The cognitive changes of adolescence make speculation and introspection all too easy defenses against contacting the world, and the isolation of academia encourages this pathology. Self-analysis or introspection as a way of growth is much like the proverbial snake which chews on its own tail; it is subject to the law of diminishing returns.[85] The self is experienced not in isolation, but in contact. Youth must find its stance by experiencing the wider world.

## Achieving a mature value stance

Among the most difficult of the identity issues is the task of establishing one's own value system, for it involves the integration of the two worlds that America's society and its child-rearing practices have split apart. The humanizing of values, when it is actually achieved, involves a union of the feminine and masculine identifications: "Firm identity would imply acceptance of both expressive and goal-directed orientations; both are necessary for a true comprehension of what is valuable."[86] The move toward humane values involves a decentering of one's world, with emphasis on greater objectivity and seeing the world for what it is. At the same time, it involves a deeper subjectivity and identification with the feelings of others. Rationality and feeling are combined. To take one's stance in the world implies the strength usually associated with masculinity. To affirm it as an ethical stance implies an open expressiveness that we tend to call feminine.

Paradoxically, the loss of authorities, the fall of the gods, leads to the recovering of that earlier childhood loss, the repression of the feminine. The recognition that there no longer is an absolute truth opens the way to the reacceptance of subjective experience. This need not imply a return to the womb (or the garden), for it is a new integration, not a romantic regression. The strength of masculinity learned in late childhood and early adolescence is now directed by the deep human values learned in closeness to mother. The courage to move into the world is expressed beautifully in Bob Dylan's song:

> Oh, where have you been, my blue-eyed son?
> Oh, where have you been, my darling young one?
> I've stumbled on the side of twelve misty mountains,
> I've walked and I've crawled on six crooked highways,
> I've stepped in the middle of seven sad forests,
> I've been out in front of a dozen dead oceans,
> I've been ten thousand miles in the mouth of a graveyard,
> And it's a hard, and it's a hard, it's a hard, and it's a hard,
> And it's a hard rain's a-gonna fall.
>
> Oh, what did you see, my blue-eyed son?
> Oh, what did you see, my darling young one?
> I saw a newborn baby with wild wolves all around it,
> I saw a highway of diamonds with nobody on it,
> I saw a black branch with blood that kept drippin',
> I saw a room full of men with their hammers a-bleedin',
> I saw a white ladder all covered with water,
> I saw ten thousand talkers whose tongues were all broken,
> I saw guns and sharp swords in the hands of young children,
> And it's a hard, and it's a hard, it's a hard, it's a hard,
> And it's a hard rain's a-gonna fall.
>
> And what did you hear, my blue-eyed son?
> And what did you hear, my darling young one?
> I heard the sound of a thunder, it roared out a warnin',
> Heard the roar of a wave that could drown the whole world,
> Heard one hundred drummers whose hands were a-blazin',
> Heard ten thousand whisperin' and nobody listenin',
> Heard one person starve, I heard many people laughin',
> Heard the song of a poet who died in the gutter,
> Heard the sound of a clown who cried in the alley,
> And it's a hard, and it's a hard, it's a hard, it's a hard,
> And it's a hard rain's a-gonna fall.
>
> Oh, who did you meet, my blue-eyed son?
> Who did you meet, my darling young one?
> I met a young child beside a dead pony,
> I met a white man who walked a black dog,
> I met a young woman whose body was burning,
> I met a young girl, she gave me a rainbow,
> I met one man who was wounded in love,
> I met another man who was wounded with hatred,
> And it's a hard, it's a hard, it's a hard, it's a hard,
> It's a hard rain's a-gonna fall.

Oh, what'll you do now, my blue-eyed son?
Oh, what'll you do now, my darling young one?
I'm a-goin' back out 'fore the rain starts a-fallin',
I'll walk to the depths of the deepest black forest,
Where the people are many and their hands are all empty,
Where the pellets of poison are flooding their waters,
Where the home in the valley meets the damp dirty prison,
Where the executioner's face is always well hidden,
Where hunger is ugly, where souls are forgotten,
Where black is the color, where none is the number,
And I'll tell it and think it and speak it and breathe it,
And reflect it from the mountain so all souls can see it,
Then I'll stand on the ocean until I start sinkin',
But I'll know my song well before I start singin',
And it's a hard, it's a hard, it's a hard, it's a hard,
It's a hard rain's a-gonna fall.[87]

## A personal word

I have tried to make clear that the crisis experienced by the more sensitive youth is not just the identity diffusion of individuals with too many options open. It is not simply an individual problem or pathology. It is a social crisis. And the youth is terribly aware that it is wrong to treat him as if he were just suffering from a personal problem (though it is that). He fears talking to a psychologist or counselor, or any adult, because he is afraid they may reduce his struggle to an intrapsychic problem. The adult may treat his struggles as "just a stage" he's going through. The youth is acutely aware of the transcendent character of his crisis. It is not just that he is confused; the very values upon which our society is based have been called into question. His perception of reality shakes the foundations of the real world into which he is supposed to move.

If the adult were to tell him that the problem is his, that only he thinks the gods have fallen, the student might succumb and, in his shaken security, accept the label and call himself sick. But at some level the student may also know that this is, after all, only the evaluation of another generation. It is his value judgment against theirs. The adult world may very well be as delusional as his.

And so I take my stand with youth. The late-adolescent critique is a healthy attempt to integrate what outdated family structure and child rearing have split, and, even beyond this, what the last centuries of Western civilization have split: the subjective and the objective worlds, the expressive and the instrumental.

I have compared the move away from home to the rites of passage

of primitive societies. For today's youth, the move into the world provides a revelation as profound as that experienced by the Indian boy
in the Zuni puberty rites:

> After being whipped by the "scare kachina"—the punitive masked god
> unto whom he has ascribed supernatural powers up to this point—[he]
> becomes terrified when the kachina mask is lifted from the "god" and
> placed on the initiate's head, and when he is also given the yucca whip
> and ordered to strike the kachina himself.[88]

To come of age is to realize that the creation of values lies in our
hands. We now wear the masks of the gods.[89]

## Summary

As children develop, they are increasingly socialized by persons outside the immediate family. Through the influence of adults other than
parents and interaction with peers, children become aware of values
which are alternatives to those espoused at home. Cognitive theory suggests an active attempt on the part of the adolescent to work out his
own integration of values. In late adolescence, this cognitive process
allows some youths to progress into the principled level of moral development. Encouragement of the child's participation in decision making
seems to be a major factor facilitating his progression to higher levels
of moral development.

Concern with developing a philosophy of life often becomes a focal
area of the identity quest in late adolescence. During the college years
the trend is toward a humanizing of values. Males are more likely than
females to move beyond conformity to parents. Nonetheless, only 25
percent of college males move into the principled level of moral development. A moratorium from adult responsibilities during late adolescence
results in a regression in moral values for about 20 percent of college
students, highlighting a need for more involvement with adult society
during this period.

## Notes

1. The intent of this section is to convey a subjective experience common to
adolescents involved in the identity quest. Experimental data regarding value development appear in the section that follows.

2. Paul Tillich, "The Shaking of the Foundations," sermon in a book by the
same title (New York: Charles Scribner's Sons, 1948), pp. 1–11.

3. These terms come from existentialism. See Jean Paul Sartre, *Being and
Nothingness* (Secaucus, N.J.: Citadel Press, 1965), and *Nausea*, a play, trans. Alexander Lloyd (New York: New Directions Press, 1960).

4. Lawrence Kohlberg, "Stage and Sequence: The Cognitive-Developmental Approach to Socialization," in *Handbook of Socialization Theory and Research,* ed. David A. Goslin (Chicago: Rand McNally & Co., 1969), p. 348. For related experiments see Elliot Turiel and Golda R. Rothman, "The Influence of Reasoning on Behavioral Choices at Different Stages of Moral Development," *Child Development,* 43 (1972): 741–56, and Elliot Turiel, "Conflict and Transition in Adolescent Moral Development," *Child Development,* 45 (1974): 14–29.

5. Kohlberg, "Stage and Sequence," pp. 349–50.

6. Ibid., p. 370.

7. The term "realism" has a special meaning in Piaget's writings, referring to the belief that the rules are concrete and inalterable, a reification of morals. Readable summaries of Piaget include Herbert Ginsburg and Sylvia Opper, *Piaget's Theory of Intellectual Development: An Introduction* (Englewood Cliffs, N.J.: Prentice-Hall, 1969), and John L. Phillips, Jr., *The Origins of Intellect: Piaget's Theory* (San Francisco: W. H. Freeman & Co., Publishers, 1969).

8. Jean Piaget, *The Moral Judgement of the Child,* trans. M. Gabain (New York: Harcourt, Brace & World, 1932).

9. Gene R. Medinnus, "Moral Development in Childhood," in *Selected Readings in Child Psychology,* ed. Joseph Duffy and George Giuliani (Berkeley, Calif.: McCutchan Publishing Corp., 1970), pp. 166, 277.

10. Lawrence Kohlberg, "The Child as Moral Philosopher," *Psychology Today,* September 1968, pp. 25–30, see especially p. 26 (a popular treatment), and "Development of Moral Character and Moral Ideology," in *Review of Child Development Research,* ed. Martin L. Hoffman and Lois W. Hoffman (© 1964, Russell Sage Foundation), vol. 1, pp. 383–432.

11. Mollie S. Smart and Russell C. Smart, *Adolescents: Development and Relationships* (New York: Macmillan Publishing Co., 1973), pp. 196–97.

12. R. Kramer, "Moral Development in Young Adulthood" (Ph.d. diss., University of Chicago, 1968); Lawrence Kohlberg and R. Kramer, "Continuities and Discontinuities in Childhood and Adult Moral Development," *Human Development,* 12 (1969): 93–120.

13. Clay V. Brittain, "Adolescent Choices and Parent-Peer Cross-Pressures," *American Sociological Review,* 28 (1963): 385–391.

14. Richard Schmuck, "Some Relationships of Peer Liking Patterns in the Classroom to Pupil Attitudes and Achievement," *The School Review,* 71 (1963): 337–59.

15. These cognitive changes are summarized in readable form in David Elkind, *Children and Adolescents* (New York: Oxford University Press, 1970), especially Chapters 4 and 5.

16. Ibid., p. 77.

17. Henry Kaczkowski, "Sex and Age Differences in the Life Problems of Adolescents," *Journal of Psychological Studies,* 13 (1962): 165–69.

18. The attempt to prove "universals" is fraught with difficulties. See, e.g., Jacqueline J. Goodnow, "Problems in Research on Culture and Thought," in *Studies in Cognitive Development: Essays in Honor of Jean Piaget,* ed. David Elkind and John H. Flavell (New York: Oxford University Press, 1969), pp. 439–62.

19. See, e.g., "The Shattering of Community," in Kenneth Keniston, *The Uncommitted* (New York: Harcourt Brace Jovanovich, 1965), p. 248 ff.

20. Kohlberg, "Development of Moral Character and Moral Ideology."

21. Kohlberg and Kramer, "Continuities and Discontinuities in Moral Development," p. 106.

22. Lillian E. Troll, Bernice L. Neugarten, and Ruth J. Kraines, "Similarities in Values and Other Personality Characteristics in College Students and Their Parents," *Merrill-Palmer Quarterly*, 15 (1969): 323–36.

23. Martin L. Hoffman and Herbert D. Saltzstein, "Parent Discipline and the Child's Moral Development," *Journal of Personality and Social Psychology*, 5 (1967): 45–57.

24. Constance E. Holstein, "The Relation of Children's Moral Judgment Level to That of Their Parents and to Communication Patterns in the Family," in *Adolescents: Development and Relationships*, ed. Smart and Smart, pp. 238–48.

25. G. H. Elder, Jr., "Parental Power Legitimation and Its Effect on the Adolescent," *Sociometry*, 26 (1963): 50–65. See also Chapter 7, on the development of independence.

26. Holstein, "Children's Moral Judgment Level," pp. 244–45.

27. Morton P. Birnbaum, "Anxiety and Moral Judgment in Early Adolescence," *Journal of Genetic Psychology*, 120 (1972): 13–26.

28. The interpretation given by Birnbaum is couched in Piaget's theory but is not at variance with my interpretation, just stated. See Ibid., p. 22.

29. Elizabeth Douvan and Joseph Adelson, *The Adolescent Experience* (New York: John Wiley & Sons, 1966). See also Chapter 6 of this text.

30. Martin Gold and Elizabeth Douvan, eds., *Adolescent Development: Readings in Research and Theory* (Boston: Allyn & Bacon, 1969), p. 319, citing E. D. Starbuck, *The Psychology of Religion* (London: Walter Scott, Ltd., 1899), and E. T. Clark, *The Psychology of Religious Awakening* (New York: Macmillan Publishing Co., 1929).

31. Ibid., p. 320.

32. Derek Wright and Edwin Cox, "Religious Belief and Co-education in a Sample of Sixth-Form Boys and Girls," *British Journal of Social and Clinical Psychology*, 6 (1967): 23–31.

33. Gene R. Medinnus and Ronald C. Johnson, *Child and Adolescent Pscyhology: Behavior and Development* (New York: John Wiley & Sons, 1969), p. 679.

34. Vernon Jones, "Attitudes of College Students and Their Changes: A 37-Year Study," *Genetic Psychology Monographs*, 81 (1970): 3–80.

35. R. G. Kuhlen and M. Arnold, "Age Differences in Religious Beliefs and Problems during Adolescence," *Journal of Genetic Psychology*, 65 (1944): 291–300.

36. P. H. Mussen, John J. Conger and Jerome Kagan, *Child Development and Personality*, 3rd ed. (New York: Harper & Row, Publishers, 1969), p. 699.

37. J. McNeil, "Changes in Ethnic Reaction Tendencies during High School," *Journal of Educational Research Archives*, 53 (1960): 199–200, and "Rebellion, Conformity and Parental Religious Ideologies," *Sociometry*, 24 (1961): 125–35.

38. Kuhlen and Arnold, "Age Differences in Religious Beliefs."

39. Kaczkowski, "Sex and Age Differences in Life Problems." This study is a revision and replication of D. B. Harris, "Sex Differences in the Life Problems and Interests of Adolescents," *Child Development*, 30 (1959): 453–59. The Kaczkowski study used subjects from rural Wisconsin, with results similar to those of the Harris study, which used urban subjects.

40. Medinnus and Johnson, *Child and Adolescent Psychology*, p. 678.

41. Reports of the importance of the move away from home are found in Joseph Katz and associates, *No Time for Youth* (San Francisco: Jossey-Bass, Publishers, 1968), pp. 63–64. Similar data are reported in Harold Webster, Mervin Freedman,

and Paul Heist, "Personality Changes in College Students," in *The American College: A Psychological and Social Interpretation of the Higher Learning,* ed. Nevitt Sanford (New York: John Wiley and Sons, 1967), p. 823.

42. "Campus '65," *Newsweek,* March 22, 1965, pp. 43–54.

43. J. Shepherd, "The *Look* Youth Survey," *Look,* September 20, 1966, p. 44–49.

44. Webster, Freedman, and Heist, "Personality Changes in College Students," p. 823.

45. Ibid., p. 824.

46. Ibid., pp. 825–28.

47. Harold A. Korn, "Personality Scale Changes from the Freshman Year to the Senior Year," pp. 162–84, in *No Time for Youth,* ed. Katz.

48. Ibid., p. 166.

49. Robert W. White, *Lives in Progress: A Study of the Natural Growth of Personality,* 2d ed. (New York: Holt, Rinehart & Winston, 1966), p. 397.

50. Russell Eisenman, "Values and Attitudes in Adolescence," in *Understanding Adolescence,* ed. James F. Adams (Boston: Allyn & Bacon, 1968), p. 190.

51. Kohlberg and Kramer, "Continuities and Discontinuities in Moral Development."

52. Lawrence Kohlberg, "Moral Development and Identification," in *Child Psychology: Sixty-second Yearbook of the National Society for the Study of Education,* ed. H. W. Stevenson (Chicago: University of Chicago Press, 1963), pp. 277–332.

53. See R. F. Peck and R. J. Havighurst, *The Psychology of Character Development* (New York: John Wiley & Sons, 1960).

54. Harold Taylor, "Freedom and Authority on the Campus," in *The American College,* ed. Sanford, chap. 23.

55. Korn, "Personality Scale Changes."

56. Walter T. Plant, "Changes in Ethnocentrism Associated with a Two-Year College Experience," *Journal of Genetic Psychology,* 92 (1958): 189–97.

57. W. T. Plant, *Personality Changes Associated with a College Education,* USOE Cooperative Research Project 348, San Jose State College, 1962.

58. See Thomas T. Frantz, "Student and Nonstudent Change," *Journal of College Student Personnel,* January 1971, pp. 49–53.

59. Elizabeth Douvan, "Sex Differences in Adolescent Character Processes," *Merrill-Palmer Quarterly,* 6 (1960): 203–11.

60. Ibid., p. 203.

61. Ibid., p. 205. Note the differences in attitudes toward parents described in Chapter 9. Girls are consistently more accepting toward nonparental authority as well, as will be noted in Chapter 12. What appear to be negative responses toward authority on the part of boys may indicate instead their greater independence in thinking and behavior.

62. Ibid., p. 206.

63. Ibid., p. 210.

64. Elliot Turiel, "Developmental Processes in the Child's Moral Thinking," in *New Directions in Developmental Psychology,* ed. P. H. Mussen, Jonas Langer, and M. Covington (New York: Holt, Rinehart & Winston, 1969).

65. Norma Haan, M. Brewster Smith, and Jeanne H. Block, "Moral Reasoning of Young Adults: Political-Social Behavior, Family Background and Personality Correlates," *Journal of Personality and Social Psychology,* 10 (1968): 183–201.

66. Holstein, "Children's Moral Judgment Level."

67. Kramer, "Moral Development in Young Adulthood."

68. Kohlberg and Kramer, "Continuities and Discontinuities in Moral Development," p. 109.

69. Ibid., p. 109.

70. Ibid., Table 1, p. 101. Kramer's data show about 23 percent of college males at Stage 5, plus 3 percent at Stage 6. The college sample of Haan, Smith, and Block, which included both sexes, found 12 percent at postconventional levels. It seems safe, in the light of the sex differences just discussed, to assume that the female percentage is below 12 percent.

71. Plant, "Changes in Ethnocentrism."

72. Frantz, "Student and Non-student Change."

73. Joseph Katz in "Four Years of Growth, Conflict, and Compliance," pp. 3–73, in Katz, *No Time for Youth.*

74. Kohlberg and Kramer, "Continuities and Discontinuities in Moral Development."

75. Ibid., p. 114.

76. Ibid., pp. 114 and 115.

77. Ibid., p. 117.

78. Reprinted from *Identity: Youth and Crisis* by Erik H. Erikson. By permission of W. W. Norton & Company, Inc. Copyright © 1968 by W. W. Norton & Company, Inc. Austen Riggs Monograph No. 7.

79. Kohlberg and Kramer, "Continuities and Discontinuities in Moral Development," p. 117.

80. Social interaction in our society is generally structured in terms of age; age segregation is not limited to the college setting.

81. Arthur W. Combs, recorded interview, Western Reserve High School Vocational Workshop, 1968.

82. For a discussion of idealism, realism, and cynicism, see Eisenman, "Values and Attitudes in Adolescence," pp. 184–88.

83. Kingsley Davis, "The Sociology of Parent-Youth Conflict," *American Sociological Review*, 5 (1940): 523–35.

84. The metaphor is taken from a sermon by Dr. George Buttrick, Lawrence, Kansas, 1957.

85. L. J. Stone and Joseph Church, *Childhood and Adolescence*, 2d ed. (New York: Random House, 1968), p. 306. Italics added.

86. Brian Caterino, Marietta College, Marietta, Ohio, unpublished paper, 1972.

87. Bob Dylan, "A Hard Rain's A'gonna Fall," © 1963, M. Witmark & Sons.

88. Rolf Muuss, "Puberty Rites in Primitive and Modern Societies," *Adolescence*, 5 (1970): 109–28.

89. The phrase "coming of age" refers not only to individual development but to our particular time in history, where man has "come of age" in that he no longer needs gods for stopgaps. See Deitrich Bonhoeffer, *Letters and Papers from Prison* (New York: Macmillan Publishing Co., 1967), pp. 140–44, 164, and 187–88.

# 12

## CRISIS FIVE
### The confrontation with impersonal authority

Validation of a concept
Research on late adolescent development
Formulation of research results
Implications: Critical attitudes and alienation
Coping with the move into the world
Summary

THE MOVE AWAY from home demands that the adolescent cope simultaneously with two adjustments: the loss of the parents as personal identification figures, and the confrontation with impersonal authority. The adolescent's increasing independence from parents has been discussed in previous chapters. The confrontation with impersonal authority is the subject of the present chapter.

The relevant research data focus upon attitudes toward nonparental authority and come largely from studies using college students. There appears to be enough consistency in the results of the available studies to permit generalizing about college students, but the samples used in the studies cannot be taken as representative of late adolescence as a whole.

The importance of distinguishing between attitudes toward parents and attitudes toward nonparental authority was stressed in Chapter 6. The concept of nonparental authorities needs to be examined before the evidence regarding changes in attitudes toward authority during late adolescence is reviewed.

## Validation of a concept

The belief that there are generalized attitudes toward authority figures has usually been associated with the concept that childhood interactions with the family determine the basic patterns of relationships that continue throughout life.[1] The roots of attitudes toward authority figures, it is asserted, lie in childhood attitudes toward parents. A generalized attitude toward authority, from this perspective, is simply a transference of attitudes originally held toward parents, particularly attitudes toward the father.[2]

The research on attitudes toward authority provides a good illustration of some of the difficulties involved in building scientific concepts. It is not enough for the social scientist simply to choose a construct such as "attitudes toward authority" and proceed to measure them. It must be determined whether or not the category is a valid one. It is necessary to decide, empirically if possible, whether this is an appropriate way to cut the cake or just an arbitrary division.

Exploratory data suggest that attitudes toward parents tend to be more positive than attitudes toward nonparental authority.[3] Attitudes toward parents do not generally become more negative during late adolescence,[4] whereas attitudes toward nonparental authority become increasingly negative.[5] The inference from these data is that attitudes toward parents do not vary together with attitudes toward other authorities, but the experiments involved were not a direct test of this issue.

As far as I know there is only one study (by LeRoy Burwen and Donald T. Campbell) which has attempted to test this issue directly.[6] Before looking at that study, the issue of degrees of covariance needs explanation. If the construct of generalized attitudes toward authority is a valid one, then attitudes toward particular authorities should vary together. That is, if a person feels positively toward a high school principal, the probability should be that he will also feel positively toward other authority figures, such as a senator. It is known that responses to these and similar items do covary; there is a positive interitem correlation on instruments measuring attitudes toward authority.[7] What must be determined, in addition, is whether these responses are more highly correlated than other attitudes. It might be that the similarity found between attitudes toward different authorities simply reflects a broader generalized response. The similar responses may not be due to generalized attitudes toward authority in particular; instead, they may reflect a general response toward people as a whole or (to give another example) a general tendency to respond positively to questions.[8]

In the study by Burwen and Campbell, the method used to determine whether there are generalized attitudes toward authority was to compare attitudes toward father with attitudes toward nonparental authorities and with attitudes toward peers.[9] The experimenters sought to determine whether attitudes toward nonparental authorities were more like attitudes toward parents than they were like attitudes toward peers. (Remember that it is not enough to know that these attitudes are similar. Unless the similarity is greater than other similarities, we cannot attribute it to the issue of authority; it may simply represent a broader, generalized response.)

A series of objective instruments was used to test these similarities. It could be argued that objective instruments do not tap a deep enough emotional response to provide a fair test. Frequently projective tests are assumed to measure deeper levels of personality. However, it is impossible to use projective instruments to test this hypothesis, for these instruments by their very nature do not distinguish between parental and nonparental authorities.[10] Burwen and Campbell argued, in a very sophisticated treatment of the problem, that many of the correlations that had previously been found between attitudes toward parents and attitudes toward authority were simply a result of "apparatus factors" in the instruments used; the positive correlations occurred not because attitudes toward authorities and parents were alike, but because items on the instruments being correlated were similar. To test their hypothesis, they used a large variety of measurements of attitudes toward father and attitudes toward other authorities, but they eliminated all similar items that might inflate positive correlations. Their results showed that attitudes toward father and toward nonparental authority were no more highly correlated with each other than with attitudes toward peers.

This experiment effectively demonstrates, at least for this population and this setting, that no clear generalization occurs from father to nonparental authorities. This is an important finding, for it refutes the traditional view that attitudes toward authority are transferences from attitudes toward father. The study deserves replication and extension; since mother is the more important authority in child rearing, it would be valuable to compare attitudes toward nonparental authority with attitudes toward mother, with a comparison of degree of similarity to attitudes toward peers.

An earlier study by Ross Stagner compared responses of college men on a ten-item test of acceptance of nonparental authority to expressed liking for mother and father. Though he reported a tendency for students who were accepting of authority to express liking for both parents, the results were not statistically significant.[11] The failure to find significant differences appears to support Burwen and Campbell's findings.

The rejection of the hypothesis that attitudes toward nonparental authority are transferred from attitudes toward the parents does not invalidate the concept that generalized attitudes toward nonparental authority may exist. What evidence is there that attitudes toward authority (hereafter used to refer to nonparental authority) exist as a cluster of covarying responses? Stagner, in the study just cited, claimed that "a generalized attitude of accepting or rejecting authority . . . can be identified in college men."[12] His study does not appear to be subject to the apparatus effects criticized by Burwen and Campbell, though there is no assurance that the covariance is higher than for peers or other persons not included in the study.

A much-publicized study of prejudice by T. W. Adorno et al., *The Authoritarian Personality*, claimed results showing a congruent pattern of personality variables which included acceptance of authority.[13] This study was appropriately criticized for its reliance on clinical impressions, with insufficient rigor in methodology.[14]

What is sought in the attempt to validate categories or constructs is a group of responses that "hang together" and form a cluster somewhat consistent internally but different from responses outside the cluster. Factor analysis, a highly complex statistical technique, has been developed to reveal the clusters into which responses fall. The results of studies using this technique provide the most important support for the validity of "attitudes toward authority" as a construct. Items from many personality tests, responded to by large samples, are analyzed by computers to determine the main orthogonal factors (a complex mathematical construct which can roughly be translated as "clusters"). Repeatedly such studies have found that one of the important clusters which emerges has to do with "acceptance or rejection of authority."[15] It appears, then, that though attitudes toward authority are not simply transferred from attitudes toward parents, there is a generalized response to nonparental authorities.

## Research on late adolescent development

Since attitudes toward nonparental authority appear to be somewhat generalized, their measurement provides an interesting means of assessing changes that occur during late adolescence. The transition period between high school and college (or the move away from home) provides an important period for experimentation. Such experimentation provides valuable practical knowledge about this difficult period of adjustment and helps to clarify some theoretical issues concerning the nature of the adolescent conflict, as will be evident in what follows.

The traditional assumption has been that the adolescent's conflict centers around difficulties between him and his parents; negative attitudes toward authority are assumed to reflect this parental conflict.[16] If these assumptions are correct, the move away from home should reduce the conflict the adolescent experiences with his parents and thus should result in a decrease in negative attitudes toward authority. Whether the adolescent physically moves away from home, or merely shifts his emotional investments, *the traditional theory leads to a prediction that negative attitudes will decrease.*[17]

In opposition to the traditional view, evidence presented in Chapters

6 and 7 suggests that the struggle with parental authority is not the central crisis of adolescence. Family ties continue to be strong in early and middle adolescence. In the context of the contrast between the personal home atmosphere and the instrumental orientation of American society, I hypothesize that the break with family and the move into the outside world will increase conflict. *This theory leads to a prediction that negative attitudes will increase after the move away from home.*

Despite the obvious importance of studies covering the transition period between high school and college, such studies are very rare, probably because of the difficulty of gathering data in several locations. To my knowledge only one study previous to my own has directly tested the traditional prediction that negative attitudes toward authority will decrease in late adolescence. The author, Marcello Lostia, must be credited with recognizing the need for research spanning this transition period.[18] Unfortunately, the study was methodologically unsound. An objective questionnaire of attitudes toward authority was used with four cohort groups: students in their first, third, and fifth years of a scientific high school, and students in their first year of a college of chemistry and physics. The problems of infering developmental change from cohort groups were discussed in Chapter 6. The Lostia study compared high school students to subjects from a college, and the two groups may well have differed in intellectual ability, economic status, and other uncontrollable variables which would affect their attitudes toward authority.[19]

Using as a starting point a hypothesis derived from psychoanalytic theory, I conducted two longitudinal studies which directly assessed the changes in adolescents' attitudes toward nonparental authority occurring during the transition from high school to college, and the effects of the move away from home on these changes.[20] The hypothesis was that negative attitudes toward authority reflected conflict with the parents and would therefore decline with the move away from them. In both the original study and the replication, instruments testing attitudes toward authority figures were administered to incoming freshmen the summer prior to their admission to college and again after they had been in college for a number of months. Both studies found that negative attitudes increased during the transition period, rather than decreasing, as would be predicted by the traditional theory.

Figures 2 and 3 present data from the second study regarding the changes in attitudes which occurred on the sentence completion test for those students who moved away from home. In that study the students were also tested a day or two after they had arrived on campus. At that point their attitudes toward nonparental authority were more positive than they had been when tested at home three months earlier. But after they had lived away from home for a year and a half, their

**FIGURE 2**
Changes in male and female proauthority responses

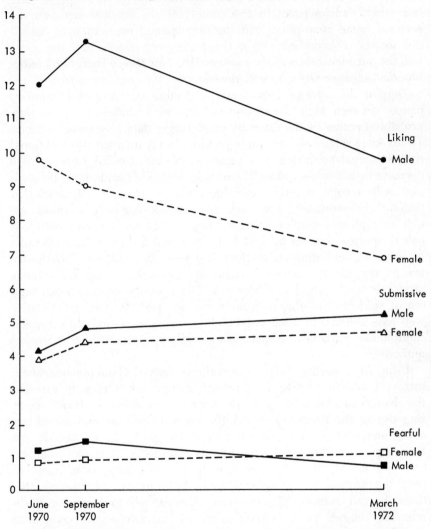

From David Matteson, "Changes in Attitudes toward Authority Figures with the Move to College: Three Experiments," *Developmental Psychology*, 10 (1974): 345, Figure 1. Copyright 1974 by the American Psychological Association. Reprinted by permission.

attitudes were considerably more negative toward authority. Since the data show that negative attitudes do not subside with the move away from home, the object of the negative attitudes can hardly be the family, as traditionally assumed. Instead, the crisis of late adolescence appears to involve a conflict with the impersonal authority in the outside world.

Another result in both studies was the indication on the earliest testing that students who planned to leave home were different from those

**FIGURE 3**
Changes in males and females antiauthority responses

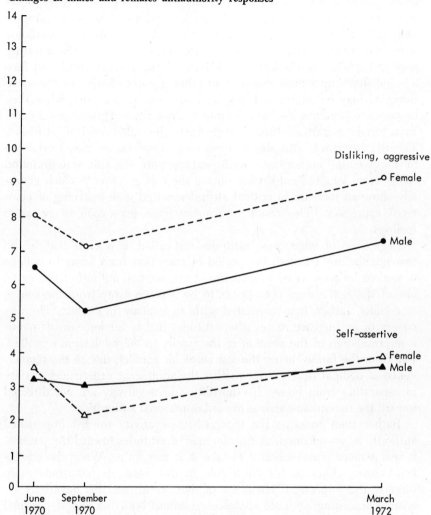

From David Matteson, "Changes in Attitudes toward Authority Figures with the Move to College: Three Experiments," *Developmental Psychology*, 10 (1974): 346, Figure 2. Copyright 1974 by the American Psychological Association. Reprinted by permission.

who planned to continue living at home and commute to college.[21] Perhaps those students who were going to leave home had already begun to face the outside world; they scored significantly more negative in their attitudes toward nonparental authority than the other students did. Students who remained at home may have reacted to the first testing more in terms of the personal authorities they had known, and thus they responded more positively. Once they entered the college world, however, their attitudes changed even though they had not ceased to live at home, and they increased in critical attitudes until their responses were nearly identical to those of the students who had moved to campus. One interpretation is that the students who were ready to leave home were a more mature group; their greater negativity on the first testing may indicate a critical attitude as they prepared, realistically, to face a somewhat impersonal world. The other group's change in the same direction may be interpreted as a later maturation, occurring when they began to experience the world more realistically.[22] Perhaps what have been termed negative attitudes might better be called "critical" attitudes. The rise in critical attitudes is apparently based on increased exposure to nonparental authorities. Additional support for this interpretation comes from longitudinal studies during the college years,[23] which generally show an increase in critical attitudes paired with a freeing of emotional expression. The result is a more open expression of negative feelings.

Regardless of what these attitudes are called, it is clear that in the two populations I tested, the period of transition from home to college is marked by an increase in criticism of nonparental authority. The move out of the home does not appear to be a move away from the source of conflict; rather, it is associated with an increase in conflict. The discovery of an increase in negative attitudes in late adolescence demands a reformulation of the relation of the family to the adolescent's conflict. Far from the family being the source of his conflict, due to the reemergence of oedipal issues, it seems that the adolescent experiences anxiety in separating from home. His hostility and negativity are not directed toward the parents so much as toward impersonal authority.

Rather than construe the increase in negativity toward impersonal authority as an unconscious transference of attitudes toward the parents, it seems more parsimonious[24] to take it at face value. When the adolescent moves closer to his adult role in the world, he confronts more directly the impersonal character of that world, and his negativity increases accordingly.[25] Late adolescence entails both the loss of personal authorities and the confrontation with impersonal ones. It should not be surprising, therefore, that negative attitudes toward authority increase during this period.

## Formulation of research results

The increase in critical attitudes, the crisis in values—in fact, the experience of an identity struggle in late adolescence—must not be taken as normative for adolescents in general. These aspects of contemporary adolescence are the results of particular historical and cultural events.

Even today, it is likely that only the more alert and sensitive youths are consciously aware of the crises and can articulate them.

The data presented in this book, and particularly the data in this chapter, are drawn largely from the college-directed portion of the adolescent population. With this limitation in mind, three findings concerning the late adolescent period can be summarized, as follows:

1. The period of late adolescence is marked by an increase in negative attitudes toward authority.
2. The negativity appears to be directed not toward parental authority but toward impersonal authority.
3. The conflict that produces this negativity appears to be the loss of the home and the confrontation with the world.

It was my interpretation of these data that led me to the reformulation of the adolescent identity crisis presented in the preface of this book. The central point in my formulation is that the major identity conflict is between self and society, precipitated by the move out of the home into the world.

In the remainder of this chapter, some of the implications of the late adolescent's critical attitudes toward authority are explored. In addition, some methods for coping with the issue of impersonal authority are discussed.

## Implications: Critical attitudes and alienation

The increase in critical attitudes during the college years appears to be a reaction to the impersonal character of the world outside the home. Though the break from home is a gradual one, the physical move away involves real loss and is a grief situation. It is appropriate to mourn the breaking of the close ties with the family, and camp counselors, military personnel, and dormitory staffs are well aware that many youths experience the process as grief. As in any appropriate mourning, the result should be a freeing of emotional investments, which can then be reinvested in new relationships.[26]

For a previous generation of parents, the task was to teach independence gradually enough so that sudden rebellion was unnecessary. The more difficult task today is to prevent alienation. It is not so much that youth cannot break its ties with home as that it is not sure it wants to move into the adult world. Young people are unsure that the effort is worth it, and they linger in the limbo of uncommitment. The failure to become reinvolved results in alienation, a withdrawal from society and a continuance of self-absorption.[27]

The confrontation with impersonal authority may lead, negatively, to alienation when the adolescent is unable to transfer involvement from the family to the world beyond the family. This is not always the case; critical attitudes do not inevitably lead to alienation.[28] Nevertheless, alienation does occur, all too commonly, in late adolescence. The factors that push a youth to reject or withdraw from society are extremely complex, and confrontation with impersonal authority is one of them. Impersonal authority seems to pose a direct threat to the identity of many adolescents. It is not difficult to understand why, in light of the importance of autonomy and intimacy to identity formation, and the effects of impersonal authority upon autonomy and intimacy. It has been noted that male identity generally focuses around issues of autonomy, and female identity around issues of intimacy. Authority which appears arbitrary threatens the adolescent's autonomy, and the impersonal quality of the authority threatens the need for intimacy. This threat is compounded by some misconceptions which are prevalent in our culture, as illustrated by American mythology regarding pioneering.

The image of the pioneer, and the move westward in settling America, invariably focuses upon the men involved. Failure to recall the crucial role played by women in the westward move reveals our distorted view of the forces which lead to progress. We perceive the move into the world as requiring masculine instrumentality and reject the vital role of the more personal (feminine) traits. The cultural myth suggests that the way to move into the world is through coercive, manipulative, and controlling techniques: The pioneer conquers the woods, the wild animals, the savage Indians, and so on. Strength is falsely associated with disregard, and self-assertion is confused with manipulation solely for selfish gain. The image is one of fighting nature; caring for the natural is associated with weakness.

This view of the move into the world leads to a mistaken view of independence which feeds into the alienation of youth. The very word "independence" suggests that the direction of adulthood is toward being self-sufficient and dependent upon no one. Perhaps we should discard the term and speak of mutual dependency, or interdependence. Adult humanness involves moving away from passive receiving to an active give and take. Though maturing entails learning to give, it does not mean no longer receiving from others. Rather, there is a mutuality of giving and receiving. One continues to need others.

To be alive as a man is to be emotionally involved, and the goal of self-sufficiency which fails to recognize the need for contact with others is delusionary; it makes man into less than a machine. Even a machine interacts with, depends upon, its environment. To be self-made is to be a rock, inanimate. As the Paul Simon song suggests, "I am a rock; I am an island" is a form of death. Alienation is the natural consequence of this form of independence.

The late adolescent frequently is unable to integrate his styles of contact and to affirm the world through a strong but caring interaction. The only caring he knows is passive dependency; he learns neither to passionately care nor to actively reach out when he needs to be cared for. Unable to integrate strength and care, youth may reject both. The feminine world of home tempts a retreat to weakness and dependency; the masculine world of adulthood demands too much strength and seems to have no room for caring.

Thus the confrontation with impersonal authority may deal a crushing blow to the quest for identity. Healthy criticism may lead to futile cynicism. The myth of going it alone results in alienation.

It is important to repeat that negative or critical attitudes toward authority do not, in themselves, indicate alienation.[29] Youths who are involved in a passionate struggle for integrity are very sensitive to the inconsistencies in our society. Their self-criticism is sometimes reflected outward; they become critical of the areas in which our culture fails to live up to the values it espouses. For some of these youths the criticism leads to a commitment to try to alter society rather than a withdrawal from it. Critical attitudes are common among committed youths, as a more thorough review of the studies of these youths will indicate in Chapter 14.

## Coping with the move into the world

For each of the areas of the identity crisis discussed in the preceding four chapters, I have sought to describe the direction of a healthy resolution. In this final area, the confrontation with impersonal authority, the term "resolution" seems both too optimistic and too centered upon individual development. In my judgment, the issue regarding impersonal authority will not be truly resolved until our society is changed. The most mature state of identity I can envision in our present society is not one which becomes resigned to impersonal authority, but one which learns to cope with it.

Rather than a resolution for this crisis, I would offer a strategy for coping with the impersonal world. The strategy, in a nutshell, involves learning to actively develop a community of persons who provide support and confrontation. What is needed is a way of regaining the level of intimacy previously provided by the family, without restructuring the hierarchical and dependency-prolonging characteristics of parent-child relationships.

It does not seem to me that the family of origin can continue to meet the need for intimacy in our mobile and pluralistic society. Solutions to alienation that prolong the period that adolescents reside with their families[30] fail on two counts. First, they do not provide the youth with new identity figures to help him overcome the inevitable parochialisms of his particular family. A variety of identifications is essential to functioning in a pluralistic society. Second, staying with the family does not force the youth to take the initiative in forming a community of his own.

Youths, after they first move from home, frequently experience the world as cold and unloving. In part at least, this is due to the fact that they have not learned to reach out for intimacy, to seek out and develop new intimate relationships. So many people in our society are lonely for years after each move to a new geographical area; they sit and wait passively for ties to develop. They have not learned to take responsibility for putting down roots, for reinvesting themselves. It is only in a world of intimate humans that one is able to reinvest the whole self, including the childhood self that was uprooted from home. Coping with the move into the world demands, first of all, surrendering the illusion that warmth and closeness should just happen. Dependently waiting for them to happen keeps one from reaching out and actively initiating an experience of community.

Each of us was born into the first community we needed for our development—the family. We were given this, but when we reach adulthood, we have to create our own communities if we are to stay emotionally alive and if growth is to continue. The family of origin provides the social structure for dependency. Marriage, when it existed primarily for childbearing and child rearing, simply changed one's role; the same structure was repeated for another generation. An individual moved from a family in which he was dependent to a family in which he was depended upon. Increasingly, however, the marriage relationship has been seen as a unit of importance apart from the children, a relationship of mutual intimacy. It is a new structure, not hierarchial but mutual. But marriage, even as redefined, is not sufficient to sustain adult growth; the two partners become stagnant unless stimulation is feeding into each of their lives from other sources. We must actively develop intimate, mutually dependent relationships in order for personal needs to be met in adulthood. The adolescent can no longer depend, he must initiate intimacy. To avoid becoming depersonalized, the youth must develop interpersonal skills that allow him to seek out a group of fellow humans who will nurture him and be nurtured by him, confront him and be receptive to his confrontations.

Once one learns to admit his need for others and to actively reach out for community, the immobilizing association of personal need with passive dependency begins to break down. To need others does not mean to be passively at the mercy of others. The need for love is not infantile; all that is infantile is the expectation that one must wait for it to come.

As adolescents begin to take responsibility for their lives with others, the distinction between authorities and peers begins to break down. As adolescents have more opportunities for mutual, interdependent relationships with adults, their fantasies of adult power diminish. They begin to see adults as fellow humans.

The concrete forms in which community may be structured are varied. The development of communes by youth, however short lived and ill conceived particular communes may be, is an exceptionally courageous and healthy example of youth's learning to take initiative in structuring intimacy. The danger with communes is the same as with marriages: they may become escapes from the world,[31] isolated islands in which relationships become closed and stagnant. A healthy community is not an island, but an oasis where one is refreshed to return to involvement outside. But commune living is too radical a step for most youths to take. They need other less demanding opportunities to gain experience in initiating community outside the home. Educational institutions, for example, should allow students to share responsibility with adults for developing their programs and experiences. Adults who do not merely repeat the authority-dependency roles of the nuclear family can provide youths with models for developing their intellectual and interpersonal skills. Many experimental colleges are innovating along these lines.

Another encouraging sign is the increasing interest in group work, particularly groups focusing on personal growth and human potential.[32] There are risks in such groups, especially when unskilled leaders are involved or when individuals are pushed toward opening up without the appropriate support structures being built into the group process. Granted the needed precautions, such groups offer an opportunity for learning how to give and elicit care which is unmatched in most other settings.

The strategy of building one's own community is not an easy solution. For some youths, it is asking too much—they have not developed the resources for doing this. For others, it stops short of what is possible and desirable. With the support and confrontation of a group, they are able not only to keep themselves human but to set out to humanize the world. If they succeed, it may yet be possible to speak of resolution.

The goal is to encourage youth to move into the world and effect change without alienation. To do so demands an integration of strength (which has been called masculine) and caring (which has been termed feminine). This courageous and embracing move into the world is demanded of male and female alike. I suspect that the resolution of the crisis with impersonal authority demands not just the personal integration of sex roles but a new cultural integration. For the crisis of authority is not simply an intrapersonal struggle but a social one.

## Summary

Youths do not have the same pattern of responses to outside authority that they have to their own parents. During late adolescence, there is an increase in critical attitudes toward authority, especially after the youth moves out of the family home. As he moves closer to his adult role in the world, he confronts more directly the impersonal character of that world, and his negativity increases accordingly. Impersonal authority threatens both autonomy and intimacy and thus may deal a crushing blow to the quest for identity. A strategy for coping entails learning how to actively develop a community of persons who provide personal support and confrontation, a replacement for the extended family of earlier times.

## Notes

1. Ross Stagner, "Attitudes toward Authority: An Exploratory Study," *Journal of Social Psychology*, 11 (1954): 197–210.

2. The view that attitudes toward authority generalize from attitudes toward parents is commonly held by Freudian theorists but is also accepted by those with other theoretical perspectives, including many behaviorists.

3. David R. Matteson, "Changes in Attitudes toward Authority Figures in Selected College Freshmen" (Ph.d. diss., Boston University, 1968), and "Changes in Attitudes toward Authority Figures with the Move to College: Three Experiments," *Developmental Psychology*, 10 (1974): 340–47. See Table 1 above, in Chapter 6. Also see J. H. Borup and W. F. Elliot, "College Students' Attitudes toward Laws, Courts and Enforcers," *College Student Survey*, 4 (1970): 24–27.

4. See Chapter 6.

5. Matteson, "Attitudes toward Authority in College Freshmen," and "Changes in Attitude with the Move to College," reported in more detail below.

6. LeRoy S. Burwen and Donald T. Campbell, "The Generality of Attitudes toward Authority and Non-authority Figures," *Journal of Abnormal and Social Psychology*, 54 (1957): 24–31.

7. For a detailed analysis of interitem statistics on three measures of attitudes toward nonparental authority, see Matteson, "Attitudes toward Authority in College Freshmen."

8. Arthur Couch and Kenneth Keniston, "Yeasayers and Naysayers: Agreeing Response Set as a Personality Variable," *Journal of Abnormal and Social Psychology*, 60 (1960): 151–74.

9. Subjects of the study, 155 men assigned to bomber crews at Randolph Air Force Base during the Korean War, were assigned to take a battery of tests. One

must question the validity of tests dealing with attitudes toward authority when they are taken under the command of a superior officer! Further, in these conditions items dealing with nationalistic symbols might elicit spuriously high positive responses.

10. See the discussion of adolescent girls and the *Sturm and Drang* view of adolescence in Chapter 6.

11. Stagner, "Attitudes toward Authority."

12. Ibid., p. 197.

13. T. W. Adorno et al., *The Authoritarian Personality* (New York: Harper & Row, Publishers, 1950).

14. Richard Christie and Marie Jahoda, eds., *Studies in the Scope and Method of "The Authoritarian Personality"* (New York: Free Press, 1954). For a clear, balanced review of the Adorno study and the ensuing debate, see "The Authoritarian Personality and the Organization of Attitudes," in Roger Brown, *Social Psychology*, (New York: Free Press, 1965), chap. 10.

15. See Arthur S. Couch, "Psychological Determinants of Interpersonal Behavior" (Ph.d. diss., Harvard University, 1960), and Robert F. Bales, *Personality and Interpersonal Behavior* (New York: Holt, Rinehart & Winston, 1970), pp. 391–97.

16. Russell Middleton and Snell Putney, "Political Expression of Adolescent Rebellion," *American Journal of Sociology,* 67 (1963): 527–37; Ross Stagner, "The Role of Parents in the Development of Emotional Instability," *Psychological Bulletin,* 30 (1933): 696–97.

17. For a detailed explanation of the rationale for this prediction, see Matteson, "Attitudes toward Authority in College Freshmen," p. 104. Supporting material comes from Peter Blos, *On Adolescence: A Psychoanalytic Interpretation* (New York: Free Press, 1962), pp. 107, 155, 211, and 212, and Robert W. White, *Lives in Progress: A Study of the Natural Growth of Personality* (New York: Holt, Rinehart, & Winston, 1952), pp. 346–47.

18. Marcello Lostia, *"Atteggiamento dei Geovani nei Confronti della Autorita"* ["Attitudes of Adolescents when Confronted with Authority"], *Rivista di Psicologia Sociale, e Archivio Italiano di Psicologia Generale, e Del Lavoro,* April–September 1966, pp. 217–64.

19. The results confirmed the hypothesis: negative attitudes toward authority figures increased with comparison of the mean scores of the first-, third-, and fifth-year high school students but decreased for subjects in the first year of college. The study was conducted in Italy, so it would be wrong to generalize from these results to our own culture, even if the methodology were sound.

20. Matteson, "Attitudes toward Authority Figures in College Freshmen," and "Changes in Attitudes with the Move to College." The populations and methods used in these studies are described in Chapter 6.

21. The same results occurred whether subjects were grouped by preferred residence or by actual residence at the beginning of the freshman year.

22. An alternate interpretation, that these subjects changed through contact with the students who already held critical attitudes, was rejected when the second study demonstrated that the change had already taken place by the first or second day after the subjects' arrival on campus.

23. Relevant studies are reviewed in Chapter 11.

24. In research, the "law of parsimony" refers to the rule of scientific interpretation which states that the "stingiest" interpretation, or the inference which makes the smallest jump from the data, is the best one.

25. Supporting evidence comes from a study of college males which suggested that the college years are experienced as the most stressful of the adolescent period—George C. Thompson and Eric F. Gardner, "Adolescents' Perceptions of Happy-Successful Living," *Journal of Genetic Psychology*, 115 (1969): 107–20.

26. See Erich Lindeman's classic study of grief following the Coconut Grove fire, "Symptomotology and Management of Acute Grief" (Paper presented to the American Psychiatric Association, Philadelphia, May 1944).

27. See Chapter 14 for a review of studies of diffusion.

28. See Kenneth Keniston, *The Uncommitted: Alienated Youth in American Society* (New York: Harcourt, Brace & World, 1965).

29. This confusion is reinforced by the experimental literature, which treats "anomie" as synonomous with "alienation." The most common measurement of anomie, Sroles scale, can more accurately be described as a test of critical attitudes toward middle-class values. See David R. Matteson, *Alienation vs. Exploration and Commitment: Personality and Family Correlaries of Adolescent Identity Statuses*, Report from the Project for Youth Research (Copenhagen, 1974).

30. George Henry Moulds, "The Generation Gap: Causes and Cures," in *Faculty Forum: A Continuing Conversation among Faculty Regarding the Christian Faith*, January 1971.

31. Kenneth Keniston, *The Uncommitted*, p. 218.

32. See, e.g., Carl R. Rogers, *Carl Rogers on Encounter Groups* (New York: Harper & Row, 1970).

# Conclusions to part two

*The critical period of identity formation for today's adolescents occurs after the move away from home in late adolescence. The move out of the feminine environment of home and school and into the masculine society is a difficult transition. The struggle to integrate inner and outer realities, to face objective reality without rejecting the subjective and sensuous, is complicated by the traditional sex-role orientations. This struggle has been elaborated in the discussion of five areas of identity confrontation: the body, sex, work, values, and impersonal authority.*

*Mature identity formation entails a search among alternatives to find a way which is uniquely one's own. The adolescent must learn to develop relationships which will support that identity and encourage continued growth.*

*part three*

# Victories and losses

INDIVIDUALS DIFFER in the ways in which they react to the adolescent crises they experience in the various areas discussed in Part two, and in the personality styles they develop as they enter young adulthood. Several patterns of progression through adolescence and the personality styles that emerge from these patterns will be described in the next three chapters. These types are only suggestive of the variety of individual differences which in fact exist.

The home from which the adolescent moves has been identified with the feminine qualities of warmth and expressiveness, and the outside world to which he or she moves has been described as predominately masculine in value orientation. These characterizations are admittedly oversimplified, but they do provide a structure for analysis. Ideally, an analysis of the patterns of progression through adolescence should clearly distinguish the nature of that progression for each sex. This will be attempted, insofar as the data permit. Unfortunately, much of the research presented in the following chapters has not included an analysis of sex differences.

As I engaged in the attempt to formulate the directions of adolescent development and the possible outcomes, I became aware that this task is not only a fascinating one, it is of profound significance to the future of our society. It is nearly impossible to describe directions of development without raising the issues of which directions are desirable and which are malfunctioning. Frequently the literature does not sufficiently separate the description of outcomes from their evaluation. In what follows, I shall try not to confuse evaluations with facts. I can do this best, I believe, by openly stating my own evaluative judgments.

# 13

## Today's adolescents: Normals, hippies, radicals and such

A BACKGROUND FOR understanding the research on the identity process discussed in Chapter 14 is provided by the survey of literature on various types of contemporary youth which comprises much of this chapter. More importantly, the recent history of psychological study in this area can be viewed as a search for the relevant variables. I shall use this survey of literature to clarify the dimensions of identity development that are crucial to understanding the personality styles which emerge.

## The length of adolescence

One important variable in the development of adolescent identity is the length and intensity of the crisis during the period of identity search. If the socialization of the child in the home were totally congruent with the society into which he must move, the step out of the home into the world would be simple and direct; no period of personal crisis and decision making would be necessary. In previous periods of history, this was indeed the case; for example, adolescence as we know it did not exist during the Middle Ages. After age seven children were seen as small adults who were expected to take on their share of the work in the adult world. Adolescence only developed as a distinct stage during the 19th and 20th centuries, with the Industrial Revolution.[1] As life has become more complex and alternatives have become more numerous, the process of preparation for adulthood has become longer and more difficult. Clinicians working with adolescents have drawn attention, in the last two decades, to the increasingly common option of prolonging adolescence. Their impressions provide a valuable background for the research to be presented later.

## Clinical observations of prolonged adolescence

As early as 1954, Peter Blos formulated a clinical syndrome frequently seen in college men between the ages of 18 and 22 which he termed "prolonged adolescence."[2] His formulation, which grew out of counseling experience, emphasized the pathological aspects of the syndrome. Blos defined prolonged adolescence as the "static preservation of the normally transient adolescent crisis," a "clinging to the unsettledness of all life's issues," and a view of adulthood as not worth the price. He noted that these youths were unlike adolescents who regress; they were, in fact, remarkably resistant to regressive pulls. Yet they differed from most youth in their "persistent avoidance of any consolidation of adolescent processes." In short, they stood on the threshold and kept the adolescent crisis open. They refused to firm up an adult identity.

This "pathology" is not related to insufficient parental love and the resultant lack of self-esteem. Blos observed that these youths feel well regarded by both parents, more empathetically by the mother, who harbors the belief that her son is destined to do great things. The adolescent continues to believe this, but, according to Blos, "substitutes narcissistic aggrandizement for reality mastery." He does not differentiate clearly the inner world of fantasy from the outer world of reality. He dreams about his superior place in the real world but fails to move into the world to make contact. This lack of contact leaves him impoverished, all the more thrown back on his narcissistic fantasies. Group involvements may help rescue him from his daydreams and autoeroticism, but, though such a young man is fairly at ease with women, he tends to be "ill at ease, fearful, and inhibited in dealing with men," a trait Blos relates to homosexual threat. The role of earlier identification with mother is also clear to Blos, who maintains that "passive strivings are always on the verge of breaking through," and the struggle for independence is experienced only in relation to mother, for the boy has never competed with father.

Eight years later, in *On Adolescence*, Blos differentiated prolonged adolescence, which he saw as self-induced (resulting from internal conflict), from "protracted adolescence," which is "culturally determined."[3] The latter construct shows an awareness of social factors which contribute to the lengthening of adolescence. Blos offers a schema of the "specific courses the adolescent process can take":

> The schematic outline which follows is offered as an attempt at classifying observations along typical lines of clinical variances. (1) *Typical Adolescence:* progressive modification of the personality in consonance with pubertal growth and changing social role; (2) *Protracted Adolescence:* a culturally determined prolongation of the adolescent status; (3) *Abbreviated Adolescence:* pursuit of the shortest possible route to adult functioning at the expense of personality differentiation; (4) *Simulated Adolescence:* an intensification of one of the prelatency drive organizations; (5) *Traumatic Adolescence:* aggressive acting out, an example of which is to be found in female delinquency; (6) *Prolonged Adolescence:* preservation of the adolescent process caused by the libidinization of adolescent ego states; (7) *Abortive Adolescence:* psychotic surrender with loss of reality contact and breakdown of differential learning. The first three of these categories are in the range of normal adolescence; the last four represent deviate developments.[4]

This schema is not developed in Blos's book, but the three categories of "normal development," based on the length of time the youth is involved in forming his adult identity, are significant. He indicates an awareness of the need for a long enough identity struggle in order for individuality to develop, citing as a major danger of adolescence proper "the rush into heterosexuality at the expense of personality differentiation."

Blos's awareness of the dangers of too-early consolidation is reflected in his category of "abbreviated adolescents," who fail to achieve full personality differentiation and contact the world in more stereotypic, less individually creative ways.[5] He appears to assume that healthy identity should be consolidated during the late adolescent years. It is not clear whether he sees prolonged adolescence as pathological because it occurs during the college years and is self-induced or because the passiveness and isolation of the condition prevent real growth from occurring.

For Erik Erikson, the central developmental crisis is the adolescent search for identity. A major portion of his writing has attempted to develop the themes of the formation of identity and its opposite, identity diffusion,[6] or, as he later termed it, identity or role confusion.[7] Erikson has stressed throughout that identity is a psychosocial crisis. The individual judges himself "in the light of what he perceives to be the way in which others judge him in comparison to them."[8] Identity formation

involves both an evaluation of self in relation to society and an evaluation of society in relation to self.

Erikson assigns the identity crisis to his fifth age of man, the period
of adolescence, which is precipitated by pubescence:

> The growing and developing young people, faced with this psychological
> revolution within them, are now primarily concerned with attempts at
> consolidating their social roles. They are sometimes morbidly, often
> curiously, preoccupied with what they appear to be in the eyes of
> others as compared with what they feel they are, and with the question
> of how to connect the earlier cultivated roles and skills with ideal proto-
> types of the day.[9]

In Erikson's schema, the resolution of the identity process leads to the
sixth age, the period of intimacy: "It is only after a reasonable sense
of identity has been established that real *intimacy* with the other sex
(or, for that matter, with any other person or even with oneself) is
possible."[10]

Erikson's focus upon the social as well as sexual aspects of adolescence
makes him acutely aware of the historical processes affecting
adolescence:

> As technological advances put more and more time between early school
> life and the young person's final access to specialized work, the stage
> of adolescing becomes an even more marked and conscious period and,
> as it has always been in some cultures in some periods, almost a way
> of life between childhood and adulthood.[11]

All industrialized societies lengthen the span between childhood and
adolescence,[12] and Erikson saw the necessity for this in order for an
integration to occur:

> They need, above all, a moratorium for the integration of the identity
> elements ascribed in the foregoing to the childhood stages: only that
> now a larger unit, vague in its outline and yet immediate in its demands,
> replaces the childhood milieu—society.[13]

There is some ambiguity as to how long Erikson feels this process
should continue. Some interpreters state that he sees the identity crisis
as occurring in late adolescence,[14] though my understanding is that he
intends the term to apply to adolescence proper and generally sees late
adolescence as a period of resolution. Like Blos, he usually associates
prolonged adolescence with pathology. Erikson begins his formulation
of identity diffusion with a line from Arthur Miller's play, *Death of
a Salesman*. Biff, the salesman's son, cries "I just can't take hold, Mom.
I can't take hold of some kind of life."[15] (The statement is rich, for
we find Biff able to communicate this to mother, but the play concerns

a father who is not strong enough in his personal presence to provide an identification figure for Biff.)

The positive aspects of delayed identity formation are perhaps more clearly recognized by Erikson than by Blos. "Where the processes of identity-formulation are prolonged (a factor which can bring creative gain), preoccupation with the 'self-image' prevails,"[16] Erikson states. He suggests that a prolonged adolescence can lead to a more differentiated personality. In the prologue to *Identity: Youth and Crises*, Erikson is keen to observe that youth's negative evaluation of the world increasingly extends the period of identity attainment: "And as for such fancy terms as psychosocial moratorium, [youth] will certainly take their time, and take it with a vengeance, until they are sure whether or not they want any of the identity offered in a conformist world."[17]

It remained for Kenneth Keniston, following in Erikson's footsteps, to formulate "youth" as a separate stage beyond adolescence and to treat prolonged adolescence as historically normal and appropriate. Keniston has extended Erikson's recognition of cultural factors; his writings are an analysis as much of culture as of youth. He puts extended adolescence into historical perspective, stating that youth today must be understood in the context of a postindustrial (technocratic) society. There is now "a separate stage of disengagement from society," a stage of psychological development "which intervenes between adolescence and adulthood" and "provides opportunities for intellectual, emotional and moral development."[18] Keniston sees this cultural development of prolonged adolescence as an advance, for it frees the adolescent:

1)   from swallowing whole the assumptions of the past
2)   from supersititions of childhood
3)   to express feelings more openly
4)   from irrational bondage of authority.

A prolonged development . . . encourages the individual to elaborate a more personal, less purely conventional sense of ethics.[19]

### Personality variables associated with length of adolescence

The impressionistic, clinical formulations reviewed above illustrate how prolonged adolescence has been differently evaluated in different historical situations. I shall defer my own evaluative judgments about the length of adolescence in order to try to clarify the hypothesis implicit in these formulations. This hypothesis can be stated positively or negatively. Stated positively, the suggestion is that length of adolescence correlates with increased differentiation of personality; that a longer period of identity formation results in greater individuality and autonomy. Stated negatively, the hypothesis is that the extension of adolescence results in an inability to make decisions, resulting in diffusion, intellectualization, introspection, and narcissistic passivity.[20]

Once the issue is formulated in more objective terms, it can be realized that it is not an either/or situation. Blos's schema of the courses adolescence can take suggests there may be an optimal length of time during which the identity quest should be continued. This can be stated quantitatively as a curvilinear relationship: Extending adolescence leads to increased personality differentiation up to a point; after that point, the result is diffusion.

Of course, more is involved than length of time. There are other variables in the development of identity which lead to the differences in styles of personality in young adulthood.

## Criticism and commitment as variables: Impressionistic research

Keniston has devoted his efforts to describing the psychological characteristics of the alienated and the radicals[21] and to examining the family and cultural variables that produce these styles of youth. His books, *The Uncommitted*[22] and *Young Radicals*,[23] contain some of the most sensitive and profound analyses of contemporary youth and culture to be found. Many of the differences between these two groups, which Keniston clarified in his interpretations of projective testing and intensive interviews, have been since verified by more controlled studies. Though the popular media, not to mention many social scientists, continued to lump protesters, hippies, longhairs, and drug abusers together, the research consistently showed important differences between those who were actively engaged in efforts to change the system (radicals) and those who had dropped out of the system (alienated). The picture which emerges from research on the alienated will be sketched first, and then the contrasting picture of the young radical will be drawn.

### The alienated

Keniston's data on the alienated come from an intensive, long-term psychological study. The population and design of the study was described as follows:

> From a large group of undergraduate (Harvard) men, twelve were identified by psychological tests as extremely alienated. These were selected for special study, along with another group of twelve who were extremely non-alienated, and a third "control" group of students who were not extreme either way. All were asked to take part in a three year study of their personal development.[24]

These twelve students had in common rejection of American culture and adoption of noncommitment as a way of life. They were above their classmates in IQ and verbal ability but had inconsistent academic records, due to their passionate concentration on topics they considered personally important. They were detached observers in most group situations, focusing their emotional attention upon themselves and ruthlessly examining their own lives. They "made no bones" about their "confusions, angers, anxieties, and problems" and appeared fragmented in their identities:

> To put their plight in a phrase, they suffer from what the psychoanalyst Erik Erikson has called "identity-diffusion"—from an intense feeling of the precariousness and disunity of the self, from doubt about their own continuing capacity to "cope," coupled with a relentless search for some trustworthy foundation for selfhood.[25]

In a more controlled study, alienated "nonstudents" living near the Berkeley, California, campus were compared to a random sampling of the university student population, who served as controls.[26] The alienated youths were found to be "as intellectually disposed, if not more so, than the students." Both groups scored lower than test norms on practicality, the alienated scoring the lowest. The alienated youths seemed not just to tolerate the ambiguous but to seek it out. They scored high on impulse expression and anxiety and low on personal integration compared to the university students. Finally, they did not conform to the traditional sex roles; the alienated males had higher feminine scores and the females higher masculine scores than university students of the same sex.[27] Keniston describes the alienated young men as avoiding masculine values: "The undesirability of adult maleness and adulthood in general, and his own sense of ineffectiveness, lead [the alienated youth] to avoid moving into the world."[28]

### The young radical

The young radical, like the alienated youth, is of superior intelligence,[29] very emotionally sensitive, and lacking in dogmatism and rigidity.[30] Like the alienated, he has struggled with peer acceptance; he has felt a "sense of specialness" and has experienced turmoil in early adolescence which has led him to turn toward self rather than peers.[31] But in his college years, rather than remaining detached from groups, the radical becomes a leader, and he is secure enough to feel less concerned than other students about his social acceptance.[32] Like the alienated, he is highly critical of American culture and politics,[33] in some studies scoring as high as alienated youth on social anomie (normlessness, rejection of the established values).[34] However, he contrasts markedly from the alienated in his commitment to changing the system. While the alienated stresses sensitivity of perception, the radical is not content to stop short of action.[35]

Keniston describes involvement with the radical movement as follows:

> In considering the process of radicalization, "joining" must be distinguished from becoming committed to the Movement, just as being committed must be distinguished from staying committed. The kind of commitment we find in these young men and women almost invariably evolved after they first 'joined' some radical organization. . . .
>
> A gradual but growing sense of nearing the end of the line . . . plagued most of these young radicals in the years before they became involved with the New Left. Out of this sense of stagnation, gradually, slowly, and unreflectedly, they "found themselves" more and more involved with radical activities. Many commented that at the time they were not aware of the direction they were taking.[36]

The process of radicalization is described as involving

> . . . a confrontation with heretofore inexperienced aspects of American life, a growing disenchantment with existing institutions for social change, the development of a new interpretation of American life, [and] a feeling of personal responsibility for social and political change. . . .[37]

Although the radical is self-critical and often doubts that he can get results, his commitment entails a degree of self-confidence and a sense of competence which appear to be missing in the alienated. As one of Keniston's radicals put it: "The job was there to be done. I could do it, and there was no one else at the time."[38] Radicals combine openness with self-confidence,[39] the desire to be deeply involved, and the courage to act according to their convictions.[40] They tend to be both more enthusiastic and more verbally aggressive than their peers.[41]

### Some limitations of these studies

*The possibility of sex differences.* One of the most serious limitations of the studies of radical and alienated youth is the failure to collect data in a manner which allows in analysis of sex differences. The Keniston studies were actually two separate research projects drawn from rather different populations, and only a small proportion were women. This made an analysis of sex differences impossible.

Most of the other studies cited also did not include a report of sex differences. An exception is the series of studies by Watts and Whittaker.[42] An examination of their data shows that when alienated subjects were compared to controls, any differences found were in the same direction for both sexes. That is, if alienated males were higher than male control subjects on a specific measure, alienated females also were higher than female controls on the same measure. This does not mean there were no sex differences. Rather, it demonstrates that the differences occurred within both alienated and control populations and did not affect the pattern of differences between these two populations. The following scores on the measurement for thinking-introversion in one of these studies[43] illustrate this conclusion:

|  | Males | Females |
|---|---|---|
| Alienated | 30. | 32. |
| Control | 28. | 29. |

Though females consistently scored higher than males, the more striking differences are between the control and the alienated groups. Alienated subjects scored higher than controls, regardless of sex. The same type of comparison can be made throughout the Watts and Whittaker data. It appears, therefore, that the patterns of differences already reported between alienated and control subjects hold true regardless of sex.

A comparison of male and female scores for activist youths and the control group leads to similar conclusions.[44] Thus, there is little reason to suspect that sex is a factor in the differences which have been described between activist, alienated, and control groups of youth.

*Sampling problems.* The studies of radical and alienated youth share a methodological difficulty which should be clarified before conclusions are drawn. When different populations are compared, as they are in these studies, many variables are left uncontrolled and may confound the results. For example, some of the differences between Keniston's radicals and his alienated youth may be due to the fact that the radicals are older. Another variable which might account for some of the differences noted in Keniston's studies is the fact that his radicals were in leadership positions. Possibly the ways in which the radicals differed from the alienated in Keniston's studies are due not to the differences in their level of commitment but to the fact that one group has leadership qualities; some of the same differences might occur if the alienated were compared to any group of leaders.

Although these particular variables, age and leadership, do not appear confounded in the more systematic comparisons of alienated, radical, and control groups of youth, it is possible that other, unknown variables have confounded the results. The method of comparing two or more "natural" groups is always subject to this limitation.

### Contributions of these studies to identity theory

Despite the difficulties of sampling and other methodological problems, the studies of the 1960 youth movements clarified some important issues about the late-adolescent identity process. It is regretable that the studies were limited to a group of students with a particular political ideology. Many of the positive traits associated with the young radicals might well have been found in committed youth of rather different ideologies and political orientations.[45] But agreement or disagreement with their viewpoint need not obscure what can be learned from these studies.

**Criticism of established values.** The studies of radicals and alienated youth provide extensive data on two types of extended adolescence. Despite their differences, it is striking to note what the two groups hold in common: a critical attitude toward traditional values and institutions. The move from home to world, where it involves an extended process of searching, has as a central concern a crisis in values. The centrality of the value struggle has been well established for student activists, though no parallel data are available for the alienated.

Intensive interviews with participants in the Columbia "liberation" of 1968 found that the great majority of these students were idealists.[46] Another researcher, also on the basis of interviews with political activists, concluded that these students were turned off on organized religion as an institution but were very interested in moral values.[47] Students in the Berkeley sit-in showed a higher religious orientation (liberal) on the Omnibus Personality Inventory than other Berkeley students did.[48] The studies are consistent in characterizing the activist as possessing a high degree of social idealism and altruism.[49]

Of particular interest is a study using Lawrence Kohlberg's stages of moral development which permits comparison of youths on the same developmental criteria used in the discussion of the crisis in values in Chapter 11. The study compared large numbers of students who participated in protest activities (at San Francisco State and Berkeley) with students who did not participate.[50] As can be seen from the table below,[51] the majority of participants in the protest had reached the principled level of moral development, while the overwhelming majority of nonparticipants were still in the conventional stage:

| | *Preconventional* | *Conventional* | *Postconventional* |
|---|---|---|---|
| Protestors | 10% | 34% | 56% |
| Nonparticipants | 3 | 85 | 12 |

The fact that a slightly higher percentage of protestors than nonparticipants were in the preconventional category suggests that not all those who become critical of established institutions do so because of a higher ethic. Nonetheless, the data impressively support the view that the critical attitudes that emerge from extended adolescence are associated with higher levels of moral development.

Both radical and alienated youth have undergone extended adolescence; they appear to have searched among alternatives and are no longer able to accept the direction of society uncritically. In sum, a value position, which might be described as criticism toward traditional values and institutional authority, appears to be associated with extended adolescence.

*Criticism and commitment.* If the radicals and the alienated are alike in their criticism of established values, they are markedly different in their ability to move with this critical attitude. The radicals put their criticism into action, with sustained involvement. The alienated seem to become apathetic; they avoid sustained contact with mainstream society. The consistent differences found between the radicals and the alienated on many different psychological variables strongly support the view that commitment is an important dimension of the identity process. Later I will attempt to outline the developmental factors which allow one group of youths to undergo extended adolescence, move through a crisis of values, and still sustain involvements, while those in another group become social dropouts.

*Summary of contributions.* The learning derived from the studies of radical, alienated, and average youth can be summarized by stating the two dimensions which emerge as important to the identity process and conceptualizing the styles of adolescence in terms of these dimensions. These dimensions concern the "critical versus conformity" stance on values and the "degree of commitment" the individual has made. If they are viewed as relatively independent dimensions, the picture which emerges from the studies of radical, alienated, and average (control subjects) youth can be summarized as follows:

1. Alienated youth are high on the critical versus conformity dimension but low on degree of commitment.
2. Young radicals are high on both dimensions; they are able to make commitments yet are highly critical.
3. Other activist youths and student leaders are generally able to make commitments but are not necessarily high on the critical versus conformity dimension.

## Factors leading to criticism and commitment

It would be interesting to know what factors allow some youths to face the pluralism of values in today's world and move to a committed stance at the principled level of moral development. There are two aspects of this broad question. First I will attempt to formulate the factors in the identity process itself which are associated with the dimensions of criticism and commitment. Later (Chapter 15) I will look at factors in earlier development, interactions with parents, and other social factors which affect these dimensions.

On the basis of the clinical-impressionistic material presented earlier in this chapter and the studies of radical and alienated youth, some tentative hypotheses can be formulated. It appears that youths who are highly critical have undergone an extended adolescence and have been confronted with a variety of alternatives. Whether they are able to move through the value crisis to commitments appears to be related to their ability or inability to become intensely engaged in the exploration of alternatives. In sum, three factors can be stated as aspects of the adolescent's identity process which have significant bearing on the adult personality that emerges after adolescence:

1.   The confrontation with alternatives. Has the adolescent searched among a number of available alternatives before forming his identity?
2.   The intensity of engagement with alternatives. Has the adolescent involved himself emotionally in the fantasized alternatives? Has he made tentative investments in real-life situations in order to explore the alternatives?
3.   The length of the adolescent process and the timing of commitment in relation to the first two factors. Does the adolescent make decisions early in the process, before exploring among alternatives, and thus close the adolescent process? Does he struggle for long periods over the alternatives? Or does he delay commitments without really engaging himself with the alternatives?

## Formulating the questions

To this point the focus has been upon some rather exceptional styles of adolescence; now it will proceed to the broader picture of college youth. (Unfortunately, research regarding the process and styles of development for noncollege youth is practically nonexistent.) The next chapter will review a series of studies which provide the fullest empirical account of the identity process to date. In these studies, initiated by James Marcia,[52] the three factors formulated above are assessed, at least in a rough way, through structured interviews. On the basis of these interviews, each subject is assigned to one of four categories: two types of committed students, identity achievement and foreclosure, and two types of uncommitted students, diffusion and moratorium. Marcia's categories yield data which provide tentative answers to the following questions derived from consideration of the three factors formulated above:

1.   What personality characteristics result when commitments are made before an intense exploration of alternatives? (The comparative data on Marcia's foreclosure subjects provides a partial answer.)

2. What are the consequences when an adolescent is confronted with the many alternatives of a pluralistic society but is unable to engage himself in serious exploration at a sustained level? (diffusion subjects)

3. What are the outcomes when the youth engages in an intense and sustained search of alternatives during the adolescent years and reaches firm commitments during the college years? (identity achievement subjects)[53]

4. If the process of commitment is delayed even longer, and an intense and sustained search of alternatives continues, what are the consequences? (The moratorium subjects are still involved in the struggle. Follow-up longitudinal studies of the moratorium group provide some information about the outcome.)

Finally, one more question will be asked of the data on identity statuses:

5. Do the factors noted (search of alternatives, level of engagement, and timing of commitment) have the same consequences in female identity formation as they do in the development of male identity?

## Summary

Clinical observations and impressionistic studies suggest that prolonged adolescence leads to a more differentiated personality and to increased criticism of social norms. In some cases this results in cynicism and alienation; in others it results in a commitment to changing the social order.

Research regarding these two types, the alienated and the radical, has been surveyed. Three factors emerging from these studies merit more careful investigation: the confrontation with alternatives, the intensity of engagement with alternatives, and the length of the adolescent process and the timing of commitments. Using these variables, questions have been formulated to provide a focus to the review of identity status research which will be presented in the next chapter.

## Notes

1. Kenneth Keniston, "You Have to Have Grown up in Scarsdale to Know How Bad Things Really Are," *New York Times Magazine*, April 27, 1969, 27 ff.

2. Peter Blos, "Prolonged Adolescence: The Formulation of a Syndrome and Its Therapeutic Implications," *American Journal of Orthopsychiatry*, 24 (1954): 733. Blos credits the term to S. Bernfeld, "*Uder Eine Typische Form De Mennlichen Pubertat*" ["A Typical Form of Male Puberty], *Imago*, 9 (1923).

3. Peter Blos, *On Adolescence: A Psychoanalytic Interpretation* (New York: Free Press, 1962), p. 218.

4. Ibid., pp. 218–19.

5. Ibid., pp. 123, 126 and 219.

6. Erik Erikson, *Identity and the Life Cycle* (New York: International Universities Press, 1959), pp. 88 and 120.

7. Erik Erikson, *Identity: Youth and Crisis* (New York: W. W. Norton, 1968).

8. Reprinted from *Identity: Youth and Crisis* by Erik H. Erikson, p. 22. By permission of W. W. Norton & Company, Inc. Copyright © 1968 by W. W. Norton & Company, Inc. Austen Riggs Monograph No. 7.

9. Erikson, *Identity and the Life Cycle*, p. 89.

10. Ibid., p. 95.

11. Erikson, *Identity: Youth and Crisis*, p. 128.

12. Rolf E. Muuss, "Puberty Rites in Primitive and Modern Societies," *Adolescence*, 5 (1970): 109–28.

13. Erikson, *Identity: Youth and Crisis*, p. 128.

14. Blos, *On Adolescence*, p. 142; James E. Marcia, "Development and Validation of Ego Identity Status," *Journal of Personality and Social Psychology*, 3 (1966): 551–58.

15. Arthur Miller, "Death of a Salesman" in *Masters of Modern Drama*, ed. H. M. Block and R. G. Shedd (New York: Random House, 1962), pp. 1020–54.

16. Erikson, *Identity: Youth and Crisis*, p. 165.

17. Ibid., p. 26.

18. Keniston, "You Have to Have Grown up in Scarsdale," p. 27 ff.

19. Ibid., p. 27.

20. Blos, *On Adolescence*.

21. Different authors have used different labels to refer to these groups of youth. I prefer the labels "radical" and "alienated" and shall use them consistently in what follows.

22. Kenneth Keniston, *The Uncommitted: Alienated Youth in American Society* (New York: Harcourt, Brace & World, 1965).

23. Kenneth Keniston, *Young Radicals* (New York: Harcourt, Brace & World, 1968).

24. Keniston, *Uncommitted*, p. 14.

25. Ibid., p. 102.

26. David Whittaker and William A. Watts, "Personality Characteristics of a Nonconformist Youth Subculture: A Study of the Berkeley Non-student," *Journal of Social Issues*, 25 (1969): 65–90.

27. Ibid., pp. 76–84.

28. Keniston, *Uncommitted*, p. 176.

29. William A. Watts, Steve Lynch, and David Whittaker, "Alienation and Activism in Today's College-Age Youth: Socialization Patterns and Current Family Relationships," *Journal of Counseling Psychology*, 16 (1969): 1–7; Christian Bay, "Political and Apolitical Students: Facts in Search of a Theory," *Journal of Social Issues*, 23 (1967): 77–91. I am indebted to Tom Tintera, Marietta College, 1971, for his help in reviewing research on student activism.

30. Keniston, *Uncommitted*, p. 199.

31. Keniston, *Young Radicals*, pp. 44–78.

32. Larry C. Kerpelman, "Student Political Activism and Ideology: Comparative Characteristics of Activists and Nonactivists," *Journal of Counseling Psychology*, 16 (1969): 8–13; Laurence Gould, "Conformity and Marginality: Two Faces of Alienation," *Journal of Social Issues*, 25 (1969): 39–64.

33. Keniston, *Young Radicals*, p. 127 ff.

34. Watts, Lynch, and Whittaker, "Alienation and Activism."

35. Jeanne H. Block, Norma Haan, and M. Brewster Smith, "Activism and Apathy in Contemporary Adolescents," in *Understanding Adolescence*, ed. James F. Adams (Boston: Allyn & Bacon, 1968), pp. 198–231.

36. Keniston, *Young Radicals*, p. 120.

37. Ibid., p. 124.

38. Ibid., p. 122.

39. Ibid., p. 23. Also see A. L. Greason, "Protest and Reaction: Students and Society in Conflict," *North American Review*, 6 (1961): 48–53, especially p. 51.

40. Richard E. Peterson, "The Student Left in Higher Education," *Daedalus*, 97 (1968): 293–317, especially p. 303.

41. B. B. Winborn and D. G. Jansen, "Personality Characteristics of Campus Social-Political Action Leaders," *Journal of Counseling Psychology*, 14 (1967): 509–13, especially p. 512.

42. Watts, Lynch, and Whittaker, "Alienation and Activism"; Whittaker and Watts, "Noncomformist Youth Subculture."

43. Whittaker and Watts, "Noncomformist Youth Subculture," p. 74.

44. Watts, Lynch, and Whittaker, "Alienation and Activism."

45. Larry C. Kerpelman, *Activists and Nonactivists: A Psychological Study of American College Students* (New York: Behavioral Publications, 1972).

46. See Kenneth Keniston, "Notes on Young Radicals," *Change*, 1 (November–December 1969): 28.

47. Ibid.

48. Paul Heist, "The Dynamics of Student Discontent and Protest" (Paper presented at the meeting of the American Psychological Association, New York, September 1966).

49. William D. Martinson, David G. Jansen, and Bob B. Winborn, "Characteristics Associated with Campus Social-Political Action Leadership," *Journal of Counseling Psychology*, 15 (1968): 552–62.

50. Norma Haan, M. Brewster Smith, and Jeanne Block, "Moral Reasoning of Young Adults: Political-Social Behavior, Family Background, and Personality Correlates," *Journal of Personality and Social Psychology*, 10 (1968): 183–201.

51. Percentages calculated from data presented in Haan, Smith and Block, "Moral Reasoning of Young Adults."

52. Marcia, "Development and Validation of Ego Identity Status."

53. Since most of the studies of Marcia and associates involved students in their middle year of college, those termed identity-achievement subjects have reached commitments during the college years.

# 14

# *Statuses and sex differences*

A SERIES OF 25 or more investigations into the "identity statuses" of college students has been conducted by James Marcia and his followers. Basing his research on Erikson's theory of identity formation, Marcia began his investigations by attempting to operationalize Erikson's alternatives of "ego identity" and "identity diffusion." He used structured interviews to assess each students' degree of commitment, asking questions about the two content areas stressed by Erikson, occupation and ideology (specifically political and religious ideology).

In pilot studies Marcia discovered that commitment was not the only relevant dimension; it also appeared important to assess the *degree of crisis* the subjects had experienced, that is, how much they had struggled with alternatives in their attempts to forge identities. Using these two dimensions, crisis and commitment, Marcia had independent raters assign students to four categories: two types of committed students, identity achievement and foreclosure, and two types of uncommitted students, diffusion and moratorium.[1]

Marcia considers those students who have gone through crisis to commitment to be the most mature. Identity achievement students are those who seem to have gone through some periods of doubt and indecision, times when there were a number of competing possibilities among which they finally made a clear choice. Another type of committed youth, the foreclosure students, appear to have made their commitments without ever having experienced a period of crisis. These students seem to have experienced few doubts and made few conscious choices. They believe what they had always believed and plan to be what they had been expected and expected themselves to be. This category is similar to Peter Blos's abbreviated adolescence. Marcia's choice of the term "foreclosure" indicates his awareness that the degree of crisis may be related to the length of the identity struggle. In Marcia's work, however, the focus is not on the length of the adolescent process but on the variety of alternatives explored and the intensity of the exploration. This seems a significant shift of emphasis from the earlier theories.

The two types of committed youth, then, are those who make their commitment after crisis and those who close off their identity search before experiencing crisis. On the basis of his preliminary studies, Marcia also conceptualized two categories of uncommitted youth. The 2 by 2 (crisis and commitment) paradigm yields a group of students who have experienced no crisis but made no commitments, and a group who have undergone crisis but have been unable to make commitments. The actual descriptions from the early studies do not exactly fit this paradigm.

The group which, theoretically, has experienced no crisis but has made no commitments is not actually described as such. Instead, Marcia described a group he called identity diffusion youth. These youth are diffuse in Erikson's sense of term; they seem unable to firm up an identity. They are clearly uncommitted; they "had neither strong allegiance to an ideology nor specific plans for [the] future." Most striking, they "did not seem particularly concerned about lack of commitment."[2] It is not quite accurate to say that these youth have not experienced crisis. Clearly they are aware of the many alternatives to identity formation, but they seem to float between possibilities, with little concern about coming down to concrete commitments.

The other group of uncommitted youth described by Marcia, moratorium youth, do not actually comprise another outcome category. Rather, they are youths still in the process of crisis. They are moving toward commitments and probably will later achieve identity. The outcome for this group, therefore, will be the same as that for identity achievement youth. Moratorium subjects are keenly aware of alternatives and were anxiously concerned about making commitments.

The categories used in the studies of Marcia and others can be described in terms of the three factors in the identity process which were summarized in the last chapter. These factors can be placed on a developmental continuum. Foreclosure subjects are youths who have made commitments before facing the numerous alternatives available. Diffusion subjects have been confronted with alternatives but do not seem involved in the exploration of alternatives; they have not made commitments and show little inclination for doing so. Both moratorium and identity achievement youth have been involved in the search among alternatives and have moved toward making commitments. It cannot be decided theoretically which are the more mature; all that can be said is that, at the time of a particular study, the achievements have made commitments (perhaps maturely, perhaps prematurely); the moratoriums have not.[3]

## Some limitations of the identity status research

Before looking at the results of these studies, it is wise to note some of their limitations. By assigning the categories on the basis of a single period of data collection, the theoretical distinction between the processes and the outcomes is blurred. As we have noted, the longitudinal research suggests that foreclosure, diffusion, and achievement are usually outcome categories, while moratorium is a process category.

Secondly, the use of a category system precludes measurement of the factors along a continuum. If one were designing research on the effects of the three factors in the identity process (search among alternatives, degree of involvement, and timing of commitments) upon the outcomes of that process, it would be preferable to measure each of these factors separately. Marcia's categories confound the two issues of search among alternatives and degree of involvement in the search. It would also be better to measure the variables in degrees along a quantitative scale, rather than lumping persons into two categories on each variable. As a philosopher of social science noted earlier in this century, the development of a science proceeds from categorization to the isolation of the specific variables and the discernment of their interactions.[4]

Finally, it should be noted that the studies have not been well designed for making an analysis of sex differences. To encourage such an analysis, the results for males and females are reported separately in what follows.

## Identity statuses of college students

All of the studies conducted by Marcia and his followers which are reported here used the structured interview technique to assess degree of commitment and crisis in the content areas of occupation and ideology. Independent raters scored the interviews and categorized the subjects. Subjects were drawn from a variety of campuses, and the four statuses were compared on a number of personality dimensions and in several social laboratory situations. Fairly consistent differences between groups which do not seem to be related to differences in intellectual ability have been reported.[5] Neither do the statuses seem understandable as a continuum of psychopathology, at least as measured by the Welsh Anxiety Scale[6] and the Byrne Repressor-Sensitizer Scale.[7]

## Foreclosure status in male college students

Male students who have moved without crisis to an early commitment differ from other college males in several ways. First, foreclosure students appear to have retained more dependence on their parents than other students.[8] They seem uncritical of their parents and of authority in general. They consistently obtain the highest authoritarian scores on the authoritarian submission and conventionality subscale of the California F scale.[9]

Though foreclosures have made commitments, they seem to rely upon outside cues to guide them. They have a higher need for social approval than the other groups[10] and are less convinced of the importance of immediate personal experience than those in the other statuses,[11] which suggests that they are unwilling to rely on their own experience to make decisions. They have what Julian Rotter calls an "external locus of control";[12] they tend to see things which happen to them as due to outside forces or a matter of chance.[13] Although they see themselves as adults, they continue to see most of the agents of destiny as outside their own control. In a real sense, they fail to take responsibility for themselves in relation to society.

Foreclosures fit Blos's description of abbreviated adolescence; they have pursued "the shortest possible route to adult functioning" at the "expense of personality differentiation."[14] They show the lowest levels of cultural sophistication (interest in art, literature, and so on) of the four groups.[15] Probably because of their continued dependence upon external direction, they uncritically accept traditional cultural values.[16]

A variety of findings suggests that the early commitment of these students is maladaptive and, when placed under stress, leads to a defensive style. Foreclosures perform poorly on a cognitive task when under stress.[17] They become cognitively constricted when they feel uncomfortable[18] and are more impulsive in decision making.[19] C. Mahler's study found them to score in the repressor direction on the Repressor-Sensitizer Scale and to be less able than other students to remember conflict words.[20] Marcia conjectures that foreclosure students cope with the new experience of college by remaining task oriented, not allowing themselves to see the personal relevance of the material they learn, and "forgetting" important information.[21]

The premature move to identity closure, then, generally fails to involve a struggle to reassess society and one's own values.[22] It results in an uncritical acceptance of the stereotyped adult roles. Sex typing is strong: the male affirms the male image and denies emotional dependency. Foreclosure youths depend heavily upon the experience of the past, mistrusting their own experience.[23] The change and ambiguity of the world around them only drive them to cling harder to the values of the past. The premature closure of adolescence results in a provincial (ethnocentric) personality, with a constricted view of the world. Failure to work through the expressive needs of childhood results in immature emotional development.

The lack of personality differentiation which results from too early closure of identity suggests that, though these youths have attained adulthood early, they have attained it incompletely. The resulting personality style may be malfunctional in today's complex and pluralistic society. When put under stress, male foreclosures tend to become rigid.[24] The mere confrontation with alternatives in the college setting appears to make them defensive. These youths have sought swift access to power; they have gained status in the old order, and are now adults in a world of the past.

### Identity diffusion status in male college students

Unlike the foreclosure subjects, those students labeled identity diffusion exhibit little if any commitment to occupation or ideology. The issue of crisis is unclear in this group. Certainly they are aware of alternatives and are floating between possibilities, in a way in which foreclosures are not. Yet they do not seem involved in a serious struggle to identify themselves in relation to alternatives. They give little indication of moving toward commitment.

The impression that diffusion subjects are not firming up an identity was supported in a study using an independent measure of ego identity, an incomplete sentence form designed to reflect Erikson's theory of identity.[25] When independent raters scored the responses to this form, diffusion subjects attained the lowest scores on ego identity, compared to subjects from the other three statuses.

Diffusions are like foreclosures in that they seem to have little autonomy. Both groups have external locus of control;[26] they experience outside agents, or fate, as having control, rather than feeling that they control their own destinies. Diffusions, like foreclosures, are more vulnerable to self-esteem manipulation; that is, their view of themselves changes more when given false feedback regarding their performance on a task.[27] Both foreclosure and diffusions tend to be impulsive rather than reflective in decision making, in contrast to subjects in the other status groups.[28]

Though both foreclosures and diffusions seem vulnerable to outside influences, the limited data suggest that they differ regarding the persons who influence them the most. The foreclosures acquiesce to authority, as shown in authoritarian scores; the diffusions score only slightly higher than the other two statuses on this dimension.[29] Predictably, diffusions would be highly subject to peer influence, but as yet experimental data exist only for female subjects.

Perhaps the most striking difference between these two "low identity statuses" is in their defense patterns. While foreclosures become rigid, constricted, but generally perserverant under threat or stress, diffusions tend to withdraw.[30] It might be said that foreclosures fight for their commitments, whereas diffusions retreat into uncommitment. These two groups had the lowest performance on concept attainment tasks under stress;[31] neither defense pattern is adaptive in this situation.

When James Donovan recorded the interactions of students in an unstructured course in interpersonal interaction, the behavior of the identity diffused in the class reflected withdrawal and noninvolvement. They were particularly resentful of the instructor but were much more likely to leave than to stay and disagree. They spoke little and missed class often.[32] Philip Kinsler, who used a pencil-and-paper measure of intimacy and a behavioral measure (a brief person-to-person encounter), found diffusion subjects consistently less intimate on both measures.[33] Further evidence regarding the withdrawal from personal contact of diffusions comes from a study comparing statuses based on identity issues with those based on intimacy issues, as determined independently from semistructured interviews.[34] Identity diffusion subjects were found to be the most isolated and the least intimate. Three categories of intimacy were used. None of the diffusion subjects were classified in the most intimate category; 67 percent were in the "stereotyped relationships" category and 33 percent in the "isolate" classification. The diffusion group had the highest percentages of any identity status group in each of these least intimate categories.[35]

In short, diffusion subjects appear to avoid sustained contact with others and with the world and to "turn in upon themselves."[36] The controlled studies conducted by Marcia and his followers seem to validate Keniston's early perceptions of the alienated:

> Lacking positive values, the alienated experience themselves as diffused, fragmented, torn in different directions by inner and outer pulls. They find little self-definition or coherence in their intellectual interests or

their social relationships, for these rarely persist beyond the impulses that inspired them. So, too, in their combination of (covert) admiration and (overt) repudiation of those who might become models for them, they reveal both a sense of inner emptiness which leads to excessive admiration and a sense of inner fragility which makes them fear submersion in an admired person. Nor do their pasts provide any clear continuities in behavior and outlook which might unify their conceptions of themselves. Once homebound children, they have now become overt rebels against a kind of world they grew up in; inwardly and unconsciously preoccupied with their lost pasts, outwardly and consciously they live in the present alone.[37]

## Identity achievement status in male college students

Individuals who have passed through a decision-making period (crisis) and who appear committed to an ideology and an occupational direction are said to have achieved an identity. They seem to have achieved the mutual independence discussed in Chapter 12, seeing themselves as separate but related people. They do not seem to need to find their parents, nor are they alienated from peers, as was common for diffusion subjects. They have not retained the dependence on parents and authorities that typifies foreclosure subjects. Functioning at their most optimal level, identity achievers come close to fulfilling Freud's description of the mature person who has an unimpaired capacity to love and to work.[38]

Identity achievers attained the highest scores on a separate measure of ego strength.[39] Along with the moratorium subjects discussed below they showed the least change from self-esteem manipulations and had the lowest scores on the authoritarian scale.[40] Identity achievement subjects and those moving toward identity achievement (the moratorium subjects) seem to have a kind of autonomy not attained by foreclosures and diffusions. As would be expected, they score in the direction of internal locus of control, rather than being convinced that external forces shape their destinies.[41] They are the most realistic in setting goals.[42]

In spite of the fact that the differences in statuses do not appear to be based on differences in intellectual ability, the identity achievers are not only successful in firming up an identity; they achieve in other ways as well. They earn the highest grades,[43] show more perserverance, and make the highest scores under stress on concept attainment tasks.[44] Those who withdraw from college tend to do so in good academic standing.[45] With the moratoriums, identity achievers score toward the reflective end of the impulsivity-reflectivity dimension on measures of cognitive styles.[46] They also score higher on cultural sophistication measures;[47] on these dimensions they appear similar to Paul Heist's sample of student activists, who scored higher than other students on the Thinking Introversion, Theoretical Orientation, Estheticism, Complexity and Autonomy scales of the Omnibus Personality Inventory.[48]

Besides handling objective tasks better, identity achievement subjects appear better able to relate to other persons in depth. Scores from a structured interview regarding intimacy placed 82 percent of the identity achievers in the most intimate category and the remainder in the middle category. None of these subjects was scored as an isolate.[49]

There are insufficient data to sketch the style of defense used by identity achievers; none of the males in the study of defensive styles were classified as in the identity achievement status.[50] Whatever their style, it appears to work well for them in both the instrumental and expressive areas.

## The moratorium period in male college students

The last of Marcia's four classifications, moratorium, concerns those subjects who appear to be still in the midst of identity crisis. "Commitments are vague and general," and there is "a sense of active struggle among alternatives."[51]

In many ways the moratorium subjects are already like those in the identity achievement status; their similarity as regards stability of self-esteem, low authoritarian scores, and internal locus of control have already been noted. Donovan, in his study of interpersonal style and relatedness of the statuses, described moratorium individuals as "competent, autonomous, active . . . [they] possess the interesting capacity to experience and describe their feelings in a clear, immediate way."[52] What distinguishes them from identity achievement subjects is that their search for identity in relation to society is still very much in progress. Marcia notes that the moratorium subjects in Donovan's study "appeared irrepressible in their urge to explore the world and to know others intensely, but above all it seemed that it was an understanding of the self that they sought." Their active exploration is manifested in many ways: "The daily activity of the moratorium individuals was distinct from that of the other subjects. Their lives were less restricted geographically. They traveled more in the city, saw more different kinds of people and left town more often than their peers."[53]

A far larger percentage of moratoriums had changed their majors or dropped out of college during a two and a half year span—80 percent of them, compared to 30 percent in the other statuses. These changes in plans do not appear to be forced on the moratoriums from outside; their academic performance did not necessitate the change.[54] Rather, the changes can be interpreted as reflecting their constant search for identity. They seem to explore and experiment in all phases of life. They reported more sexual activity than students in other statuses[55] and appeared to experiment with "soft" drug use (marijuana and major halluci-nogens) more frequently.[56] Interpersonally, they were the most active in classroom discussion but tended to get engaged and then disengage themselves quickly.[57] A lower percentage of moratoriums (64 percent) were in the most intimate category, as compared to the 82 percent of the identity achievers; 27 percent of moratorium subjects were in the middle classification.[58]

Moratorium students are very sensitive to the experiences they seek out. Donovan described these subjects as "unusually perceptive or re-sponsive people" and noted that each of them mentioned "that he was the 'sensitive' child in the family." Mahler found that they score in the "sensitizer" direction on the Repressor-Sensitizer Scale. They also seem hypersensitive to dissonance and take many issues personally, thus exacerbating their feeling of crisis.[59] Moratoriums have consistently shown higher anxiety on pencil-and-paper measures than subjects in the other statuses; they perform poorly when under stress.[60] It is not clear whether they are actually more anxious, due to their openness, sensitivity, and high goals; perceive themselves as more anxious, due to their greater awareness of themselves; or simply score higher be-cause of their honesty in reporting. Measures of anxiety other than self-report scales have been used in two studies, with conflicting results. Mahler's study cited above, which used physiological indices, found no differences in anxiety between foreclosures and moratoriums when presented with stress words. Other researchers, however, found that in a decision-making situation moratoriums exhibited significantly longer hesitation before responding ("response latency" is generally interpreted as an indication of anxiety).[61]

Moratoriums appear to be in the midst of a struggle with authority. In a group situation, they are "nearly obsessed with leading the group, becoming predominant within it."[62] In contrast to other students, they would not give in to the leader of the group at all; they were the only ones who tried to compete directly with the leader and wrest the group from him. Yet the moratoriums had a strong affinity for the teacher, wanting to be his peer.[63] Further evidence of their struggle with authority comes from their behavior in an experimental game allowing either cooperative or competitive responses. Moratoriums made significantly fewer cooperative responses when playing with an authority figure than when playing with a peer.[64] Still another study found that students who experienced an identity crisis while in college expressed more dissatisfaction with faculty, college administrators, and their fellow students than other students did.[65] The constellation of highly critical responses is similar to that in the studies of attitudes toward authority discussed in Chapter 12.

The moratorium student sees the excitement and freedom of continued exploration yet wants the intensity of deep involvements. Donovan notes that "These individuals, though unsettled about the future, seemed more directly, intensely engaged in self-confrontation and in a quest for a solution to their conflicts than did any of the other students."[66]

There is evidence that moratoriums do succeed in their quest. A four-year longitudinal study showed that 75 to 80 percent of the students who were classified as moratoriums at the end of their freshman year had become identity achievers when interviewed in their senior year of college. The remainder appeared to have become diffusions.[67]

## Identity statuses in female college students

The concern that the identity statuses may simply reflect differences in intellectual ability has been investigated, with similar results for both sexes. As with males, the identity statuses in females do not seem attributable to differences in intellectual ability.[68]

The same structured interview which has been used in the studies of identity status in males was used in an experiment by Podd, Marcia, and Rubin which included both male and female subjects. To this date, it is the only American study of identity statuses which has used subjects of both sexes drawn from the same population and has included an analysis of sex differences. The study provided additional construct validity for the identity statuses by testing some hypotheses regarding moratoriums. As predicted, it was found that moratoriums had contradictory needs both to rebel and to seek guidance.[69] This was evidenced in the moratoriums' more competitive behavior in a laboratory game when they perceived themselves as playing against an authority figure; they were less competitive when they played the same game with peers. Subjects in the other status groups did not show as much contrast in their game strategies and seemed less affected by the authority of their partner than were moratoriums. Because no sex differences were found in this study, it provides initial evidence that moratorium women are similar to moratorium men.

### Problems in comparing results for males and females

For the sake of direct comparisons between the sexes, more studies in which both sexes had undergone the same experimental procedures would be advisable. My own study of Danish youth involved such a comparison, but since our interest here is in American adolescence, I shall refer to this study only where it challenges or clarifies American data on the female identity process.[70] Rather than direct comparisons of the male and female identity processes, Marcia and his followers have chosen another strategy. They have sought to determine whether the same content areas (occupation, politics, and religion) which were used in the male studies are useful in assessing the female identity process. Another validational study, conducted at about the same time as the Podd, Marcia, and Rubin study, sought to compare females' responses to males' responses in the previous studies by using measures similar to those that had been used in the male studies. The design of this study of ego identity status in college women by Marcia and M. L. Friedman[71] was faulty because only female subjects were used. Thus we cannot be sure whether the sex differences found in the comparison were due to general differences between the sexes or to differences between the population from which the female subjects were drawn and the populations used in the previous male studies. This problem of interpretation holds for all of the studies reported in this section except the Podd, Marcia, and Rubin study and my own Danish study; since the sampling methods did not draw males and females from the same population, the data may be confounded with unknown variables.

The comparison of sexes in the identity status research is further complicated by the fact that, except for the Podd, Marcia, and Rubin and the Marcia and Friedman studies, the initial classification of statuses has been made through use of a special, female form of the identity status interview. This structured interview, developed by Susi Schenkel and Marcia, uses the content areas of previous studies, plus a new series of questions on attitudes toward premarital intercourse. This addition to the interview scheme was made on the premise (suggested by previous research) that social relationships, sexual attitudes, and choice of a future mate are important in the establishment of female identity. The predictive validity of the new form was established by the Marcia and Schenkel study, which found that most of the differences among the statuses were attributable to the discriminations made from the religion and sex attitudes sections of the interview. The suggestion was that the occupation and politics sections of the interviews discriminate identity status for men but not for women.[72] Unfortunately, neither the previous studies using women subjects, nor those that followed this one, reported analyses of the predictive power of the different sections of the structured interview. The content areas have been blurred together, and a general identity status has been assigned.

In sum, direct comparisons between the male and female studies are confounded by differences in samples used, differences in interview format, and differences in the measurements of some of the dependent variables. Nonetheless, it is useful to survey the data accumulated to date on female identity statuses and see what generalizations can be made.

## Foreclosure status in female college students

Female foreclosure subjects, like their male counterparts, can be defined in a number of ways. First, they consistently score as more submissive to authority than subjects in the other identity statuses.[73] The same result, an uncritical acceptance of authority, occurred regardless of which interview format was used to determine identity status or which instrument was used to measure attitudes toward authority.

The acceptance of authority does not imply a general susceptibility to outside influence for foreclosures. In the laboratory game used by Podd, Marcia, and Rubin, foreclosures generally fell near the mean in number of cooperative responses.[74] There was no indication of extreme responses, in either the cooperation or competitive directions. In addition to these data for both sexes, data are available on female subjects using other measures of conformity. In a social situation which was designed to encourage peer conformity,[75] female foreclosures fell in the middle range of responses, being neither conformists nor nonconformists.[76] Similarly, Schenkel and Marcia's study, which used perceptual tasks of field dependence, found foreclosure women to be like achievement women in that they were not highly influenced by outside cues.

Still another area in which foreclosures appear alike, regardless of sex, concerns self-confidence. Foreclosure women report high levels of self-esteem and low anxiety.[77] Additional evidence of self-confidence and positive outlook for female foreclosures comes from measurements of negative emotions. Nancy Toder and Marcia used an adjective checklist of hostility; on this self-report measure, foreclosures scored very low.[78] However, self-report measures of negative feelings are highly susceptible to social desirability effects. They do not necessarily reflect observed behavior, as will be noted later in discussion of the research on foreclosure families.

While the foreclosure personality style does not appear to be as functional for males as the moratorium and identity achievement statuses, this does not appear to be the case for females. Unlike foreclosure males, women in this status did not appear inflexible on the cognitive tasks; in fact, they performed as well as women in the other identity statuses. It is interesting that female foreclosures (along with achievements) choose more difficult college majors than subjects in the other categories. Marcia and Friedman suggest that individuals who have achieved an identity should be better able to manage difficult majors.[79] If this were the case, we would predict that foreclosure and identity achievement subjects, regardless of sex, would choose more difficult majors. As yet this issue has not been tested with male subjects in America. In my study of Danish youth, I found the same pattern for females as Marcia and Friedman reported; the foreclosure and achievement women were more likely to enter the more difficult line. Surprisingly, the reverse was the case for male subjects. This may be due to a confounding variable in the study.[80]

It appears that the foreclosure status may be more adaptive for women than for men in our culture. A foreclosure identity does not seem to result in defensiveness in women, though this did seem to occur in male foreclosures. R. Josselson conducted a series of extensive interviews with women in the four identity statuses which provides impressionist portraits to supplement the more objective data.[81] Her descriptions reinforce the view that foreclosures are uncritically positive toward their parents and have not developed much autonomy or individuation. A shallowness and a preference for remaining protected and dependent are suggested. That this type of personality is functional for women has to do, of course, with the continued acceptance of the traditional female role. The failure of our culture to encourage autonomy in women was documented in Chapter 7.

### Identity diffusion status in female college students

Female students suffering identity diffusion are characterized by fear, fantasy, and flight. Josselson's interviews suggested that they prop up their self-esteem by fantasy, finding it difficult to make contact with real people or to make realistic commitments. The evidence regarding the self-esteem and self-confidence of diffusion women is conflicting. Donovan felt that, as a group, these women showed little confidence in themselves. They seldom believed their plans would work out and seemed "always prepared for disappointment." Diffusions scored in the middle range on measures of self-esteem in one study,[82] but another study reported fairly high self-esteem scores for this group.[83] They showed high anxiety[84] and expressed considerably more negative emotions on Toder and Marcia's adjective checklist. In the Marcia and Friedman study of choice of college majors, diffusion women evidenced low self-confidence by choosing the least difficult majors; surprisingly, the diffusion women in the Danish study chose the more difficult line of study more frequently than any other group of women.[85]

Like alienated youth, diffusions seem to conform to peer pressure in a social setting. When subjected to peer influence in a situation in which the subject must decide between trusting his own perception or agreeing with the (false) perception of peers, women diffusions conformed significantly more than those in the other status groups.[86] Diffusion women seem to be even more dependent upon outside cues than is generally the case for women. Moratorium and diffusion women scored higher on Schenkel and Marcia's measures of field dependence than the other two groups.

This susceptibility to outside influence does not imply a conformity to conventions or an acceptance of authority, however. Diffusion women consistently showed less acceptance of authority than female foreclosure subjects, though they were not as critical of authority as were achievement and moratorium women.[87]

Diffusions seemed not to be close to either parents or peers. In the classroom they appeared noninvolved and seemed to withdraw from contact. Avoiding sustained contact with others and with the world, they turned in upon themselves.[88]

### Identity achievement status in female college students

Perhaps the most predominate characteristic of identity achievement women is that they have struggled for independence and have learned to gain support from and contribute to their environment.[89] Their autonomy is demonstrated by the fact that they conform least to peer judgments in the peer-pressure situation.[90] They also score higher in the direction of field independence on perceptual measures, as noted by Schenkel and Marcia. Unlike the foreclosures, however, they do not conform to authority; they consistently score in the middle or upper range of critical attitudes toward authority.[91] In these respects, identity achievement women resemble their male counterparts.

However, Marcia argues that there is evidence that identity achievement in women is not supported by the culture, or even by the college community. When Marcia and Friedman determined the identity achievement status on the basis of interviews regarding occupation and ideology, the women labeled identity achievers scored lowest of all groups on self-esteem. However, when Schenkel and Marcia made the categorization on the basis of interviews which included issues of sex and marriage, the identity achievement group showed the highest level of self-esteem; further, they had the lowest anxiety level of the groups of women. In this study, even when statuses were assigned on the basis of the occupation and ideology sections of the interview, the identity achievement women fell in the middle range on anxiety.

Two comments are in order in regard to the interpretation of these findings. First, care must be used in inferring mental health from low anxiety scores when anxiety is measured with self-report instruments. Donovan commented that his small sample of identity achievement women were able to encounter conflict and depression and acknowledge it, which the foreclosures were not able to do. It may be that the recognition of one's own anxiety indicates self-awareness. Extremely high scores on self-esteem measures may reflect a lack of self-criticism rather than healthy functioning.

Second, Marcia's view that our culture does not support the achievement of identity in women deserves more careful analysis. It may be that if a woman confirms her identity in the traditionally feminine areas first (intimacy and marriage), she can then acceptably pursue the identity quest in other areas. If she attempts to challenge the sex roles and struggles to attain identity in the traditionally masculine areas of politics[92] and vocation without first establishing her credentials as a woman (so to speak), by proving her expertise in the "feminine" areas, she may be deprived of social support.

This conjecture makes sense of the "conflicting" results reported above. When identity achievement is defined solely in terms of sex and marriage, the group consists of those who have established their feminine credentials. These women have high self-esteem and low anxiety. When identity achievement is defined in terms of the other content areas, it is a mixed group, including those who are seeking identity in a "man's world" first; low self-esteem occurs in the group.

Consequently, I believe it is an overgeneralization to state that identity achievement is not supported in women. It appears that women can find support for exercising "their own abilities toward their own goals"[93] *if* they do so in a distinctively feminine way.

## The moratorium period in female college students

Persons in the process of achieving an identity are categorized moratoriums in Marcia's system. The label "moratorium" implies a period of transition rather than a status. In some respects moratorium females already appear like identity achievement subjects. They tend not to accept authority and are critical of it—in fact, more so than women in any of the other statuses.[94] The issue is still conflicted for them, however. They made fewer cooperative responses in Podd, Marcia, and Rubin's laboratory game when playing with an authority figure and showed greater anxiety in that authority situation than when paired with a peer. Perhaps because they are still struggling with authority, they appear more subject to external pressure: in the peer-pressure situation measured by Toder and Marcia they fell in the middle, not conforming as frequently as diffusion women but conforming more than achievement subjects. They showed great dependence on external cues in Schenkel and Marcia's perception experiments, scoring more field dependent than foreclosures or achievements. Unfortunately, none of the experiments on identity status has collected data regarding locus of control from American women.

Like their male counterparts, female moratoriums appear sensitive and vulnerable and in some respects resemble the diffusions. Both moratoriums and diffusions showed high anxiety on the pencil-and-paper measures of Marcia and Friedman and the behavioral measures of Schenkel and Marcia. Even when the status was defined in terms of the sex and marriage responses, the process of searching for identity appeared anxiety producing and self-esteem seemed low.[95] Low self-esteem and negative affect were reported in all relevant studies,[96] and female moratoriums did not appear self-confident when measured by choice of major.[97]

The sensitivity of moratorium students extends to value issues; they have a strong need to know what is right and strive for it.[98] Josselson found that they have internalized the values of their parents, and, at least for female subjects, feelings of guilt are common: guilt for violating the prohibitions of their mothers and for not attaining the ideals of their fathers. Cross-sex identification seems common in moratorium women, consistent with the findings on high-achievement women reported in Chapter 10. They daydream a great deal and seem reluctant to give up their grandiose fantasies.[99]

Marcia's work in process notes that female moratoriums seem to "expect greatness of themselves . . . . They are not happy people in the sense of feeling secure." Their relationships with their parents, particularly their mothers, are characterized by ambivalence and guilt. They are not isolated like the diffusions, however. Instead, Josselyn found, "they have a consuming need for relationships with others, less as a concern for intimacy, perhaps, than as a means of defining themselves." According to Josselyn, "Other people seem to become 'mirrors' for moratoriums . . . a source of identity-establishing feedback."[100] In her doctoral dissertation, Josselyn described female moratorium subjects as follows:

> The moratorium wants everything . . . parents' approval yet [autonomy] to set one's own standards . . . relationships with others yet [the avoidance of being] trapped into any lasting self-definitions which those relationships might impose . . . . to be Free and to be Right at the same time.

> Their ability to see the absurdity in impassioned beliefs or the posturing in just about every life-style is part of what makes them seem so delightful. At the same time, their sensitivity bars a kind of total submission to a set of beliefs or people that they yearn for.[101]

## Conclusions regarding sex differences in the statuses

This survey of identity status research has been presented in an attempt to provide tentative answers to some questions regarding the three variables being considered in the process of identity formation: the search among alternatives, level of engagement, and timing of commitment. The limitations of data and methodology have already been discussed. The questions listed at the end of the preceding chapter can now be reviewed, and some tentative conclusions can be reached.

1. What personality characteristics result when commitments are made before an intense exploration of alternatives? Foreclosure subjects of both sexes appear more dependent upon authority, though the data for females suggest this is not evidence of general susceptibility to outside influence; female foreclosures do not conform more to peers and are not more field dependent. For males, the foreclosure of identity seems to result in a less differentiated personality which is maladaptive in stress. A shallowness and lack of individuation may also result in female foreclosure subjects, but there is no indication of the rigidity which typifies male foreclosures. Perhaps this difference reflects the different cultural expectations for the sexes. Males are expected to move toward independence and autonomy; negative feedback when they fail in this may result in rigidity and defensiveness. Lack of individuation is more acceptable in women; social props support their child-likeness.[102] If sex roles change and women are also expected to develop autonomous, differentiated personalities, the social props which keep female foreclosures from becoming defensive may disappear, and the rigidity typical of male foreclosures may result.

2. What are the results when youths are confronted with alternatives but are unable to engage in serious exploration and sustained involvement? Neither male nor female diffusion subjects seem to be in control of their own destinies. They do not acquiesce to authority, but (at least females) tend to conform to peer pressure. Alienation often leads to conformity (though not to conventionality); diffusions of both sexes appear isolated, somewhat lost in themselves, yet not making much positive progress in their self-definitions.

3. What are the results when intense and sustained searching of alternatives occurs, leading to commitments during the college years? Identity achievement subjects, male and female alike, seem autonomous in respect to both peers and authorities. Yet they are not alienated from either. They see themselves as separate but related people, suggesting the mutual interdependence which is a criterion of healthy development. A study of male subjects showed them to have achieved greater intimacy than subjects in other statuses. There is some evidence that women face more restrictions on the manner in which they may attain identity and suffer greater conflicts in the process.

4. What are the consequences when the process of commitment is delayed and an intense and sustained search of alternatives continues? Those subjects who are still continuing the identity quest are marked by continuing exploration, a resistance to authority, and (at least in women) susceptibility to outside influence, though not at the conformist level. They appear sensitive and vulnerable, but intensely involved. Moratorium subjects who continue the identity process well into the

college years do not become like diffusions; most of them eventually reach identity achievement status.[103]

## Directions for further identity status research

The data presented in this chapter come completely from studies which began with a categorization of subjects. Most of the studies reported above have used the four statuses Marcia described in his first study. Some of the problems with the use of category systems in psychological research have already been noted. As research in identity statuses has progressed, more and more categories have been proposed, to make more refined discriminations. In his work in process, Marcia proposes nine statuses; to the four we have described he adds two new ones: "alienated achievement" and "moratorium character."[104] He also suggests one borderline category, "moratorium-diffusion,"[105] and the subdivision of two of the original categories, discriminating between "schizoid type" and "playboy type" identity diffusions,[106] and between "developmental" and "firm" foreclosures.[107] To continue this proliferation of the statuses seems unwise; the categories are being drawn mainly on an impressionistic level and can multiply infinitely. As suggested earlier, separate measures of the relevant variables would be preferable to categorization.

It is also important to begin to differentiate the different content areas of the identity crisis. Although the interview format has included separate discussions of occupational, political, and religious crisis and commitment, plus (in the female interview form) the area of sexual identity, the categories have generally been assigned on the basis of an overall impression of crisis and commitment. One study of women which included a separate analysis of the content areas used in the interviews led to the discovery that occupation and politics, two of the three content areas used with male subjects, had little predictive power when used with female subjects.[108] Half of the women scored as diffusions in the political area, though only one sixth were considered diffusions as judged from the other content areas in the interview. As other research has indicated, women give lower priority than men to political and occupational commitment.[109]

The separate analysis of content areas needs to be carried further. The issue of which areas are most predictive is an important one. But the underlying assumption that there is *one* single identity crisis needs to be tested. In Chapter 6, I suggested that there may be a series of crises which focus around different content areas at different periods of adolescence. The content areas used in identity status research to date parallel the crises areas of sex and intimacy, work, and values, discussed in Chapters 9, 10, and 11, respectively. Perhaps the dimensions of autonomy and relationship to authority (Chapters 7 and 12) should be treated as content areas, rather than as correlates of the statuses. And perhaps body image (Chapter 8) should be considered a crucial area related to self-esteem. These are only suggestive.

Finally, in order to determine the effects of the different variables on the content areas of the identity crisis, future research must be designed with care to avoid halo effects. For example, it is possible that the impression an interviewer or rater forms of the degree of commitment a subject has on the first section of the interview (occupation) may affect the way he conducts or rates the remainder of the interview. Unless changes are made in the research design, differences between content areas could be obscured by such halo effects.

The identity status research has made a major contributon to our understanding of the identity process. Now changes in design, including the use of the longitudinal method, are necessary in order to test a developmental theory of identity formation. In the next chapter, some beginning developmental longitudinal research and suggestions for such a theory will be presented.

## Summary

The variables formulated in Chapter 13 have been studied using material from experiments in which students were categorized by identity status. Three types of outcomes occur from the interaction of these variables: foreclosed, diffused, and achieved identity. In addition, aspects of the moratorium phase of identity process were studied by examining data from those who are still in the identity crisis.

For males, early identity formation seems to result in a less differentiated personality which is maladaptive when under stress. For females, there is no indication of this rigidity, but a shallowness and lack of individuation does occur. Youths who have been confronted with alternatives but are unable to sustain involvement appear lost in their identity struggles, unable to progress toward definitions of self in relation to society. When a sustained search among alternatives leads to commitments, an autonomy from both parents and peers seems to emerge. This form of autonomy appears to be positively related to intimacy. The achievement of this sort of identity seems to be more difficult for women in our culture.

## Notes

1. James E. Marcia, work in process, Chapter 1. I am heavily indebted to Dr. Marcia for the use of this manuscript reviewing the identity status studies to date.

2. James E. Marcia, "Development and Validation of Ego Identity Status," *Journal of Personality and Social Psychology*, 3 (1966): 551–58.

3. Though moratoriums continue the search among alternatives later than the other groups, we do not know whether they are actually involved in the search longer than the identity achievements, or begin it later in life.

4. Émile Durkheim, *The Rules of Sociological Method*, ed. E. C. George, 8th ed. (New York: Free Press, 1966), p. 46.

5. Marcia, "Development and Validation of Ego Identity Status"; James Marcia and M. L. Friedman, "Ego Identity Status in College Women," *Journal of Personality*, 38 (1970): 249–63; Herbert J. Cross and Jon G. Allen, "Ego Identity Status, Adjustment, and Academic Achievement," *Journal of Consulting and Clinical Psychology*, 34 (1970): 278–81; Dianne Jordan, "Parental Antecedents and Personality Characteristics of Ego Identity Statuses" (Ph.D. diss., State University of New York at Buffalo, 1971); Susi Schenkel and James Marcia, "Attitudes toward Premarital Intercourse in Determining Ego Identity Status in College Women," *Journal of Personality*, 3 (1972): 472–82.

6. Marcia, "Development and Validation of Ego Identity Status."

7. C. Mahler, "The Assessment and Evaluation of the Coping Styles of Two Ego Identity Status Groups: Moratorium and Foreclosure, to Identity Conflict Arousing Stimuli" (Masters thesis, State University of New York and Buffalo, 1969).

8. Alan S. Waterman and Caroline K. Waterman, "A Longitudinal Study of Changes in Ego Identity Status during the Freshman Year at College," *Developmental Psychology*, 5 (1971): 167–73; Alan S. Waterman, Patricia S. Geary, and Caroline K. Waterman, "Longitudinal Study of Changes in Ego Identity Status from the Freshman to the Senior Year at College," *Developmental Psychology*, 10 (1974): 387–92.

9. The California F Scale was developed for a study of prejudice: T. W. Adorno et al., *The Authoritarian Personality* (New York: Harper & Row Publishers, 1950). Its use with foreclosure students is reported in James Marcia, "Ego Identity Status: Relationship to Change in Self-esteem, 'General Maladjustment,' and Authoritarianism," *Journal of Personality*, 1 (1967): 118–34, and "Development and Validation of Ego Identity Status."

10. Jacob L. Orlofsky, James Marcia, and Ira M. Lesser, "Ego Identity Status and the Intimacy versus Isolation Crisis of Young Adulthood," *Journal of Personality and Social Psychology*, 27 (1973): 211–19.

11. J. Dufresne and H. Cross, "Personality Variables in Student Drug Use" (Master's thesis, University of Connecticut, 1972).

12. Julian B. Rotter, "Generalized Expectancies for Internal versus External Control of Reinforcement," *Psychological Monographs: General and Applied*, 80, no. 609 (1966): 1–28.

13. C. K. Waterman, M. E. Buebel, and A. S. Waterman, "Relationship between Resolution of the Identity Crisis and Outcomes of Previous Psychological Crises," in *Proceedings of the 78th Annual Convention of the American Psychological Association*, (1970), vol. 5, pp. 467–68 (summary).

14. Peter Blos, *On Adolescence: A Psychoanalytic Interpretation* (New York: Fress Press, 1962), pp. 218–20.

15. Waterman and Waterman, "Ego Identity Status during Freshman Year"; Waterman, Geary, and Waterman, "Ego Identity Status from Freshman to Senior Year."

16. Dufresne and Cross, "Personality Variables in Student Drug Use."

17. Marcia, "Development and Validation of Ego Identity Status."

18. S. R. Bob and James Marcia, "Ego Identity Status and Two Cognitive Controls" (Report, National Institute of Mental Health, Grant MH13103–01 (Bethesda, Md., 1967); S. R. Bob, "An Investigation of the Relationship between Identity Status, Cognitive Style and Stress" (Ph.D. diss., State University of New York at Buffalo, 1968).

19. Waterman and Waterman, "Ego Identity Status during Freshman Year."

20. Mahler, "Assessment and Evaluation of Coping Styles."

21. Marcia, work in process.

22. Kenneth Keniston, "Student Activism, Moral Development, and Morality," *American Journal of Orthopsychiatry*, 40 (1970): 577–92.

23. Sandford Reichart, "A Greater Space in Which to Breathe: What Art and Drama Tell Us about Alienation," *Journal of Social Issues*, 25 (1969): 138.

24. Bob and Marcia, "Ego Identity Status and Two Cognitive Controls"; Bob, "Identity Status, Cognitive Style and Stress"; Marcia, work in process.

25. Marcia, "Development and Validation of Ego Identity Status."

26. Waterman, Buebel, and Waterman, "Resolution of the Identity Crisis."

27. James Donovan, "A Study of Ego Identity Formation" (Ph.D. diss., University of Michigan, 1970).

28. Alan S. Waterman and Caroline K. Waterman, "The Relationship between Ego Identity Status and Satisfaction with College," *Journal of Educational Research*, 64 (1970): 165–68.

29. Marcia, "Development and Validation of Ego Identity Status."

30. Marcia, work in process.

31. Marcia, "Development and Validation of Ego Identity Status."

32. Donovan, "Study of Ego Identity Formation." I have ignored Donovan's distinction between two types of diffused youth for this analysis. Both types showed the withdrawal pattern. His subjects included both sexes, but no analysis of sex differences was reported in Marcia's review. There were four male and five female subjects in the two diffusion categories.

33. Philip Kinsler, "Ego Identity Status and Intimacy" (Ph.D. diss., State University of New York at Buffalo, 1972).

34. Orlofsky, Marcia, and Lesser, "Intimacy versus Isolation Crisis."

35. The use of a fifth identity status in this study, "alienated achievement," took some less isolated subjects out of the diffusion category. Had only the four statuses been used, the results would not have been as dramatic.

36. Donovan, "Study of Ego Identity Formation."

37. Kenneth Keniston, *The Uncommitted: Alienated Youth in American Society* (New York: Harcourt, Brace & World, 1965), p. 185.

38. Marcia, work in process.

39. Marcia, "Development and Validation of Ego Identity Status."

40. James E. Marcia, "Ego Identity Status: Relationship to Change in Self-esteem, 'General Maladjustment' and Authoritarianism," *Journal of Personality*, 35 (1967): 118–34.

41. Waterman, Buebel, and Waterman, "Resolution of the Identity Crisis."

42. Marcia, "Development and Validation of Ego Identity Crisis."

43. Cross and Allen, "Ego Identity Status, Adjustment, and Academic Achievement."

44. Marcia, "Development and Validation of Ego Identity Crisis."

45. A. S. Waterman and C. K. Waterman, "The Relationship between Freshman Ego Identity Status and Subsequent Academic Behavior: A Test of the Predictive Validity of Marcia's Categorization System for Identity Status," *Developmental Psychology*, 6 (1972): 179.

46. Waterman and Waterman, "Ego Identity Status during Freshman Year."

47. Ibid. Also see Waterman, Geary, and Waterman, "Ego Identity Status from Freshman to Senior Year."

48. Paul Heist, "The Dynamics of Student Discontent and Protest" (Paper presented at annual meeting of the American Psychological Association, New York City, September 1966.

49. Orlofsky, Marcia, and Lesser, "Intimacy versus Isolation Crisis."

50. Marcia, work in process.

51. Rating manual used in Marcia's studies, unpublished (1973).

52. Marcia, work in process. Donovan's moratorium subjects included four males and one female.

53. Ibid.

54. Waterman and Waterman, "Ego Identity Status and Academic Behavior."

55. Donovan, "Study of Ego Identity Formation."

56. Ibid.; Dufresne and Cross, "Personality Variables in Student Drug Use."

57. Donovan, "Study of Ego Identity Formation."

58. Orlofsky, Marcia and Lesser, "Intimacy versus Isolation Crisis."

59. Marcia, work in process.

60. Marcia, "Development and Validation of Ego Identity Status"; Mahler, "Assessment and Evaluation of Coping Styles."

61. Marvin H. Podd, James E. Marcia, and Barry M. Rubin, "The Effects of Ego Identity and Partner Perception on a Prisoner's Dilemma Game," *Journal of Social Psychology*, 82 (1970): 117–26.

62. Donovan, "Study of Ego Identity Formation."

63. Waterman and Waterman, "Ego Identity Status and Satisfaction with College."

64. Podd, Marcia, and Rubin, "Ego Identity and Partner Perception."

65. Waterman and Waterman, "Ego Identity Status and Satisfaction with College."

66. Donovan, "Study of Ego Identity Formation."

67. Waterman, Geary, and Waterman, "Ego Identity Status from Freshman to Senior Year."

68. Marcia and Friedman, "Ego Identity Status in College Women."

69. Podd, Marcia, and Rubin, "Ego Identity and Partner Perception," p. 123.

70. David R. Matteson, *Alienation vs. Exploration and Commitment: Personality and Family Correlaries of Adolescent Identity Statuses*, Report from the Project for Youth Research (Copenhagen, 1974).

71. Marcia, and Friedman, "Ego Identity Status in College Women."

72. Schenkel and Marcia, "Attitudes toward Premarital Intercourse."

73. Marcia and Friedman, "Ego Identity Status in College Women"; Schenkel and Marcia, "Attitudes toward Premarital Intercourse"; Matteson, *Alienation vs. Exploration and Commitment.*

74. Podd, Marcia, and Rubin, "Ego Identity and Partner Perception," Tables 1 and 2.

75. Solomon E. Asch, "Studies of Independence and Conformity: I. A Minority of One Against a Unanimous Majority," *Psychological Monographs*, no. 416, 70 (1956): 9.

76. Nancy L. Toder and James E. Marcia, "Ego Identity Status and Response to Conformity Pressure in College Women," *Journal of Personal and Social Psychology*, 26 (1973): 287–94.

77. Marcia and Friedman, "Ego Identity Status in College Women"; Schenkel and Marcia, "Attitudes toward Premarital Intercourse."

78. Toder and Marcia, "Ego Identity Status and Conformity Pressure."

79. Marcia and Friedman, "Ego Identity Status in College Women," p. 252.

80. Matteson, *Alienation vs. Exploration and Commitment*. The two lines of study in Danish gymnasia are language (or humanities) and mathematics (and science). A higher proportion of young women enter the language line, while the majority of young men enter the math line. Thus the variables of difficulty and of sex-typed area of study are confounded.

81. R. Josselson, "Psychodynamic Aspects of Identity Formation in College Women," *Journal of Youth and Adolescence*, 2 (1973): 3–52.

82. Schenkel and Marcia, "Attitudes toward Premarital Intercourse."

83. Marcia and Friedman, "Ego Identity Status in College Women."

84. Schenkel and Marcia, "Attitudes toward Premarital Intercourse."

85. Matteson, *Alienation vs. Exploration and Commitment*. This is also a choice of the masculine sex-typed line.

86. Toder and Marcia, "Ego Identity Status and Conformity Pressure."

87. Marcia and Friedman, "Ego Identity Status in College Women"; Schenkel and Marcia, "Attitudes toward Premarital Intercourse"; Matteson, *Alienation vs. Exploration and Commitment*.

88. Donovan, "Study of Ego Identity Formation."

89. Josselson, "Psychodynamic Aspects of Identity Formation."

90. Toder and Marcia, "Ego Identity Status and Conformity Pressure."

91. Marcia and Friedman, "Ego Identity Status in College Women"; Schenkel and Marcia, "Attitudes toward Premarital Intercourse"; Matteson, *Alienation vs. Exploration and Commitment*.

92. Stephen I. Abramowitz and Christine V. Abramowitz, "A Tale of Serendipity: Political Ideology, Sex Role Prescriptions, and Students' Psychological Adjustment," *Developmental Psychology*, 1 (1974): 299.

93. Josselson, "Psychodynamic Aspects of Identity Formation."

94. Schenkel and Marcia, "Attitudes toward Premarital Intercourse"; Marcia and Friedman, "Ego Identity Status in College Women." Matteson, *Alienation vs. Exploration and Commitment*, found Danish identity achievement women to be the most critical, with moratoriums second.

95. Schenkel and Marcia, "Attitudes toward "Premarital Intercourse."

96. Toder and Marcia, "Ego Identity Status and Conformity Pressure"; Schenkel and Marcia, "Attitudes toward Premarital Intercourse"; Marcia and Friedman, "Ego Identity Status in College Women."

97. Marcia and Friedman, "Ego Identity Status in College Women"; Matteson, *Alienation vs. Exploration and Commitment*.

98. Marcia, work in process.

99. Josselson, "Psychodynamic Aspects of Identity Formation."

100. Ibid.

101. R. Josselson, "Identity Formation in College Women" (Ph.D. diss., University of Michigan, 1972).

102. Marcia, work in process.

103. Waterman, Geary, and Waterman, "Ego Identity Status from Freshman to Senior Year."

104. For these Marcia draws on data from Orlofsky, Marcia and Lesser, "Intimacy versus Isolation Crisis."

105. Marcia here follows Donovan, "Study of Ego Identity Formation," and Josselson, "Psychodynamic Aspects of Identity Formation."

106. Marcia, work in process.

107. Marcia, draws on Dianne Jordan, "Parental Antecedents of Ego Identity Formation" (Master's thesis, State University of New York at Buffalo, 1970), and "Parental Antecedents and Personality Characteristics."

108. Schenkel and Marcia, "Attitudes toward Premarital Intercourse."

109. Abramowitz and Abramowitz, "Tale of Serendipity"; W. S. Mason, R. J. Dressel and R. K. Bain, "Sex role and the Career Orientations of Beginning Teachers, *Harvard Educational Review*, 29 (1959): 370–83; unpublished paper by R. K. Goldsen and R. F. White cited in Sanford M. Dornbusch, "Afterword," in *The Development of Sex Differences*, ed. Eleanor E. Maccoby (Stanford, Calif.: Stanford University Press, 1966), p. 215.

# 15

## Developmental processes
## and lifestyles

THE IDENTITY STATUSES are intended to describe the present position of an adolescent in the process of his move toward identity. Viewed developmentally, they are not fixed statuses but points or positions in the identity process. Foreclosure might be viewed as the earliest developmental position; the adolescent is still highly dependent upon his parents for identification and has not confronted any alternatives. Many foreclosures become "set" in this position. Those who do progress, because of their external locus of control, would be expected to become diffusions, confused by alternatives yet looking outward for answers. Diffusions appear to be making little progress in the movement toward an integrated identity. The moratoriums, those youths who, for whatever reasons, are able to consider alternatives and yet move toward defining their own stance, can be considered of higher status. And those who progress through moratorium and achieve an identity have reached the highest status, identity achievement.[1]

## Evidence for a developmental progression: Sex differences

There is considerable support for the view that the identity statuses are stages in a developmental progression on which individuals stabilize their identities at particular levels. The studies of psychological development during the college years reported above showed a normal progression which includes increases in such variables as autonomy, complexity, impulse expression, and critical attitudes toward authority.[2] With the exception of attitudes toward authority, these variables have not been tested in American studies on the identity statuses, but my research on identity statuses in Denmark did include measurements of them.[3] Since scores on these variables are known to increase during normal college-age development, the data from these measures provide a test of the hypothesis that the identity statuses represent developmental levels.

The data on male subjects in my study of Danish Youth are presented in Table 3, with the identity statuses listed in the theorized develop-

**TABLE 3**
Developmental progression of identity statuses (Danish males)

|  | Foreclosure | Diffusion | Moratorium | Identity Achievement |
|---|---|---|---|---|
| Autonomy | 2.92 | 3.17 | 3.35 | 3.50 |
| Complexity | 2.70 | 2.86 | 3.01 | 3.34 |
| Impulse expression | 2.51 | 2.52 | 2.96 | 3.08 |
| Acceptance of authority | 2.79 | 2.62 | 2.30 | 2.02 |

Source: David R. Matteson, *Alienation vs. Exploration and Commitment: Personality and Family Correlaries of Adolescent Identity Statuses,* Report from the Project for Youth Research (Copenhagen, 1974), Table 3.

mental sequence, from foreclosure to identity achievement. Note that critical attitudes toward authority were measured by a scale of "acceptance" of authority and thus show a reversed pattern; the scores decline throughout the progression. The developmental progression is the same for all four variables in that foreclosures show the least and identity achievers the most mature pattern of responses. When the high-status groups (identity achievement and moratorium) were compared to the low-status groups (foreclosure and diffusion), the differences in scores were statistically significant for all four variables.

The evidence that the statuses represent a developmental progression is far less clear for female subjects. The same direction of scores was obtained by the women on the measures of complexity and impulse expression. However, the differences were not significant on the complexity variable. On impulse expression, the differences were largely due to the extremely low scores of foreclosure women. The foreclosures were also significantly different on acceptance of authority (they had less critical attitudes), but the other statuses were not significantly different. As previously reported, the status groups did not differ on degree of autonomy; autonomy seems not to typify female development.

Since the identity statuses were determined concurrently in cohort subjects, the Danish study is not a developmental study in the best sense. To determine the developmental sequence of identity formation, it would be preferable to use the longitudinal research method. Anne Constantinople's study using preliminary scales to measure resolution of the developmental crises formulated by Erikson has already been described.[4] Her longitudinal data for male subjects showed a progressive increase in the resolution of identity questions and a progressive decline in identity diffusion. Her data for females were ambiguous; though identity resolutions increased during the college years, identity diffusion also increased markedly in the first year. Though diffusion decreased in the last years of college, the decline was not sufficient to reverse the initial increase in diffusion. Thus the level of diffusion in the last year was as high as in the first year of college.

The preceding chapter noted that women who attempt to achieve identity in the areas of occupation and political ideology do so at greater personal costs than is the case for men. The developmental data presented here lead to a similar conclusion. When the female identity process is assessed using the same criteria that have been used with male subjects, the results suggest that women in our society fail to attain the degree of identity achievement that is typical of men. Perhaps the measurements are culturally biased against women. One must ask whether it is fair to use instruments based on male development to assess female identity. However, the issue of appropriate measurement should not divert recognition of the possibility that the real cause of female inferiority in identity development is cultural discrimination against women. More precisely, the lower level of identity achievement in women may reflect the narrow sex role prescribed for women in our culture.

## Developmental progression in the identity process: Content areas

The one longitudinal study to date which has been based directly upon the identity status categories used male subjects from an engineering college. Alan Waterman, Patricia Geary and Caroline Waterman interviewed the subjects early in their freshman year, late that year, and again during their senior year of college.[5] During the freshman year, many subjects changed in their identity statuses; none of the statuses appeared stable, and the authors discerned little pattern of change. The changes which took place between the end of the freshman year and the senior year, however, tended to confirm the view that the identity statuses are stages in a developmental progression. The most common change was a move from one of the lower identity statuses into the identity achievement status. Students who were already in the identity achievement status at the end of their freshman year tended to remain there; their identity had stabilized. The great majority of moratorium students moved into the identity achievement status. The majority of diffusion subjects were still in the diffusion state three years later, failing to progress toward an identity, as predicted.[6] About one quarter, however, did reach identity achievement by their senior year.[7] A small percentage of diffusions fell back into the foreclosure category. They had reached a commitment but had retained their external locus of control. Like diffusions, many of the foreclosures remained in the same category throughout their college years,[8] though a minority did reach the identity achievement status in their last year.[9]

This study is noteworthy not only because of its longitudinal design but because the authors conducted a separate analysis of the content areas of the identity status interviews. The engineering students moved during their freshman year in the direction of greater maturity when assessed on the occupational area of the interview. But identity statuses as determined from the ideology section of the interview showed regressive changes during the year, a shift toward noncommitment. The authors suggest that this regression may be due to the occupational focus of the engineering school. It seems plausible, however, that this is another indication of a multiple-phase identity crisis. For these students, it is likely that occupational identity is confirmed early, but the crisis of values is just beginning during this first year away from home.

## The crisis in values and the developmental progression

In the opening chapter of Part two, I suggested that the identity struggle may actually entail a series of crises, with issues of independence occurring early and a crisis of values commonly occurring in late adolescence. The Kohlberg and Kramer data on moral development during the college years showed evidence of a regression in some subjects during the first years of college.[10] And Waterman & Waterman's longitudinal study of identity statuses shows, during the freshman year, a move forward in identity in the occupational area but a regression in the area of ideology. Longitudinal studies are rare, and the data are too limited to be conclusive. But the trend of these studies adds support to the hypothesis that the move from home to world precipitates a crisis in the area of values.

For several reasons, the content area of values deserves special attention in the attempt to understand the developmental processes involved in identity formation. Since a clear schema of stages has been formulated for this area, more direct ties between styles of personality and developmental progressions can be made. Further, some longitudinal data have been collected in this area. And finally, data are available which connect adolescent values to parental values. In short, the development of values is better documented than most areas of identity formation, though results must still be considered preliminary.

The developmental schema proposed by Lawrence Kohlberg which charts moral development from preconventional through conventional morals to a principled basis for value decisions was presented in Chapter 11. The Kohlberg and Kramer longitudinal studies have the advantage of using a standardized measurement of moral judgments,[11] by which the scores from one study can be compared to those from others. A disadvantage of standardized tests is that data are not likely to emerge from other areas of life which impinge upon moral development. Open interviews have the opposite advantages and disadvantages. Thus a study by William Perry and associates, using open interviews, nicely supplements the Kohlberg and Kramer studies.

Perry and associates used extensive longitudinal records from open interviews conducted with Harvard students to develop a schema for describing the intellectual and ethical development which occurs during the college years.[12] Their study is provocative, since they successfully validated that schema by using lay judges who scaled records of the interviews with no knowledge of the subjects' year in college. Perry found that most Harvard students undergo two crises in their moral and intellectual development during their four years at college. The first is a crisis in values which involves a move from dualistic thinking (thinking in terms of absolute rights and wrongs) to relativistic assumptions (recognizing that ethical principles are self-chosen from many alternatives). The second crisis is an undertaking of commitments. Perry's schema describes in eight steps the movement from absolutism, through an acceptance of the diversity of human outlooks, followed by a need for personal commitments in a relativistic world, to the development of actual commitments. Perry and associates found that the majority of Harvard youth progressed along this scale. They drew their courage to face the relativity of life and to make commitments from "a sense of community which included not only their peers but their instructors as well." A minority of the Harvard youth studied did not move in this progression; Perry categorized these as three "sidetracks" of development: escape, retreat, and temporizing. Relationships with adults appeared to be a critical factor distinguishing the students who progressed along this developmental path from those who regressed or stabilized their identities at lower levels. The courage to face the relativity and yet make commitments appears to be derived, in part, from seeing members of the faculty as models "and being seen by such models as being in the same boat with them."

The results of this study bear obvious similarities to the findings of Kohlberg and Kramer; the sidetracks that Perry notes are reminiscent of the "regressions" in their data. The Perry study suggests a healthy model for moral development which includes both the recognition of many alternatives and the ability to make specific commitments. It suggests that the ability to reach the principled levels of moral development depends upon adult models and a community of support and confrontation. Apparently most of the students at Harvard were able to experience such a sense of community. The fact that most college students in other studies do not reach the principled level but stabilize their personalities at lower levels suggests that Perry's model (which I have evaluated as healthy) is not normative in the sense of describing the average youth. Rather, it describes what may be possible for college youth, given supporting environmental conditions.

## Social factors in moral development

Perry's study indicates connections between the processes in identity formation and the surrounding environment. The data suggest that early in the college years a crisis occurs, which in the Harvard students resulted in a move away from absolutist moral conceptions. One factor in precipitating this crisis appears to be a confrontation with the diversity of human outlooks. This is one aspect of the move out of the home into a pluralistic world, a factor which would be particularly potent in a heterogeneous student population such as Harvard's. Another precipitant of the crisis of values with the move from home is the discovery of corruption in the world. Though not mentioned in Perry's study, it is noted as a factor in the "regression" in moral development in the Kohlberg and Kramer study[13] and is a common theme in interviews with alienated and radical youth.[14] A third factor is that adult models in the college community provide social support for criticism of conventional values: "Authority itself requires the student to go beyond a defined world . . . [to face] a world of uncertainty."[15]

In sum, it can be concluded tentatively that there are three social factors associated with the move away from home which contribute to a crisis in values:

1. The confrontation with diverse value orientations.
2. The discovery of corruption in the world.
3. An environment which provides support and models for criticizing conventional morality.

The two sets of research that have been reviewed which compare radical and alienated youth and moratorium and diffusion youth suggest the wisdom of distinguishing between the processes of crisis and commitment. Having noted some of the social factors which precipitate the crisis in values, I will raise another question: What are the social factors which aid a movement toward making personal value commitments, once the crisis in values has occurred? Perry's schema is like James Marcia's and Erik Erikson's in that it suggests a developmental process which moves through crisis to commitment. The period during which this process is occurring has been labeled the moratorium phase by Erikson.[16] Kenneth Keniston has added precision to Erikson's description of this phase by defining it as a period of "continuing disengagement from adult institutions."[17] As the research of Marcia and his followers indicates, this is not a period of general disinvolvement. The moratorium youth is not fearful of personal involvement; he appears highly involved in the identity search and becomes intensely engaged with issues and people.

In short, those students who successfully move from crisis to commitment do not appear to do so through a general disengagement from contact with issues and people; the identity search should *not* be described as a turning away from outside involvements toward the self. Rather, a very limited disengagement occurs. Generally, student status involves a disengagement from the adult institutions of marriage and of full-time employment. Thus the student can make commitments to nonconventional value positions and to some nonconventional behavior; he runs less risks of social reprisal than does the person already enmeshed in these adult institutions. This low-risk status is probably one social factor which permits commitments to postconventional (or preconventional) values.

Another social factor which encourages the making of value commitments, as indicated by the data from Perry's study, is support from the college community and, most particularly, from interactions with professors. Thus college professors may provide models for youth in making nonconventional value judgments.

A third factor which may aid youth in the move toward value commitments is the necessity for decisions about jobs or continuing education, especially during the last years of college. Unlike the two factors mentioned above, this factor would not be likely to push the student in the direction of nonconventional commitments. The anticipation of graduation might be a pressure for commitment, but it would not be a pressure for movement to higher levels of moral development. Instead, we would predict that this would be a pressure for consolidation of moral development. Data from Kohlbergs' studies suggest that a consolidation occurs in late adolescence; the individual becomes more consistent in the level of moral judgments he makes and settles into a particular level.

In sum, three social factors appear to be associated with the move toward value commitment:

1. A limited disengagement which reduces the personal risks involved permits commitment to nonconventional values.
2. An environment which provides models and support for commitment to postconventional values encourages youth to take such a value stance.
3. Anticipation of other life decisions encourages a consolidation at a particular level of value judgment.

Though all three factors may encourage the move toward value commitments, they differ in the level of value commitments that they encourage. The second factor, the degree of support and quality of models for commitment to higher levels of value judgments, may prove a deciding factor, since the two other factors are to some extent in opposition to one another.

### Identity status, moral development, and actual behavior

In the preceding discussion of the social factors in moral development, inferences were made concerning the relationship between levels of moral development and the different statuses of identity. There are empirical data which support those inferences.

An interesting study by Marvin Podd attempted to demonstrate a relationship among ego identity statuses, levels of moral development, and moral behavior.[18] The subjects were males in the last two years of college, and the Kohlberg scale was used to measure moral developments. Table 4 shows the distribution (in percentages) of subjects by identity statuses in each level of moral development. Subjects in the achievement and moratorium statuses clustered around postconventional value orientations, while foreclosures and identity diffusions were pre-

**TABLE 4**
Value orientations by identity statuses

|  | Pre-conventional | Conventional | Transitional | Post-conventional |
|---|---|---|---|---|
| Foreclosure | 27% (100) | 54% (74) | 8% (20) | 12% |
| Identity diffusion | 28 (100) | 31 (71) | 31 (40) | 9 |
| Identity achievement | 5 (100) | 44 (95) | 0 (51) | 51 |
| Moratorium | 0 (100) | 36 (100) | 29 (65) | 36 |

Note: All figures are percentages within a particular status. Figures in parentheses are accumulative and indicate percentages of students who have achieved that status or higher.

Source: Marvin Podd, "An Investigation of the Relationship between Ego Identity Status and Level of Moral Development" (Ph.D. diss., State University of New York at Buffalo, 1969).

dominantly conventional and preconventional in their value orientation.

It is fruitful to examine these data in the context of the longitudinal studies of moral development just presented. Those subjects who have experienced an identity crisis, the achievements and moratoriums, seldom respond to moral issues at the preconventional level. They appear to have gone through the value crisis Perry describes as belonging to the early college years. A comparison of the two groups who have experienced this value crisis is instructive. Does commitment during the college years result in a higher level of moral development, as Perry suggests? For these students the answer appears to be negative. The moratoriums, who have not yet made a commitment, appear to be moving toward a higher level of moral development than the identity achievers. None of the moratoriums have consolidated at the preconventional level; and if only half of those in transition consolidate at the postconventional level, the percentage will equal that of the achievers in the highest level. The data suggest, then, that a larger percentage of youth might reach the highest level of development if the moratorium were extended even longer.

The superior moral development of the moratoriums is further suggested by a comparison of subjects' responses. Actual moral behavior was tested in the Podd study, using Stanley Milgram's obedience task in which the subject, on orders from an authority figure, administers what he thinks are increasing levels of electric shock to another person who is a stranger to him.[19] Though the subjects in the different statuses in the Podd study did not differ in the level of shock they administered, there were marked differences in their willingness to continue to give shocks; 57 percent of the foreclosures and 60 percent of the diffusions were willing to repeat their performance, as compared to 43 percent of the identity achievers. Only 17 percent of the moratoriums were willing to do so. One additional finding from this experiment is noteworthy.

Among those who had administered maximum shock, only the foreclosures were willing to do it again; grimly enough, 100 percent of these subjects stated they were willing to repeat their performance!

It should be noted that in the Podd study the subjects were assigned to identity status on the basis of impressions from Marcia's three-part interview (occupation, politics, and religion). Even more striking differences could be expected if subjects were assigned statuses in terms of crisis and commitment on the value dimension alone, rather than on general identity. Kohlberg has shown that the levels of moral development do predict actual moral behavior.[20] Kohlberg's study of the relationship between his moral development measure and Milgram's obedience task revealed that 75 percent of the subjects at the highest stage of moral development refused to continue the task to the level of administering maximum shock. Only 13 percent of subjects at the conventional level discontinued the task.

## Family roots of value orientations

Little careful research exists on what parental influences may lead to higher levels of moral development. The difficulties of researching such a question are immense. Social scientists have begun to discern the types of interaction which lead to the child's feeling guilty and, consequently, to obedient, conventional morality.[21] Even these studies have methodological problems: few longitudinal studies exist. To produce data relating child-rearing practices to moral development in the college years would demand tracing intervening variables through some 15 years of life!

The data presented in this section, then, are largely impressionistic, and the conclusions reached are tentative. The information available comes almost completely from comparisons of the groups discussed in Chapter 13, radical and alienated youths and control groups drawn from student populations.

In Keniston's *Young Radicals* and the ensuing research, it was noted that radical youth confront society not out of rebellion, but out of a continuity with their parents and society based on the values that they have internalized. The home is a warm one which encourages the individual's move into the wider world. Just as the radical youth is able to make political commitments, he is able to commit himself to other people. He moves from childhood dependence to interdependence.

This move is not an easy one for him; his early adolescence, as documented by Keniston, is a tumultuous one.[22] Other studies have shown that young people who reach the principled level of moral functioning regard themselves as intellectually independent of their parents (in contrast to conventionally moral youth).[23] Though independent of parents, the young radical is unable to transfer his dependency to the peer group; he is too much an individual to conform. Like the alienated, he turns into himself rather than to peers. Unlike many alienated, however, he continues to function well in the objective world, achieving academically and frequently moving into positions of social leadership. The strength of these youths results in a "resumption of success" in middle and late adolescence.[24]

Most of the material regarding the development of radical youth comes from the youths themselves. It would be preferable if one were not forced to rely upon youth's perceptions of their parents but could use data gathered from the parents themselves. A study by Charles Derber and Richard Flacks which compared the value systems of radical youth and their parents appears to be the only one to have done this.[25] The sampling of radical students was drawn from lists of students involved in student movement organizations. The control sample was drawn at random from directories of colleges in the Chicago area, matching the two groups for type of college. In 82 of the 98 families included in the study, both parents were interviewed. Though subjects of both sexes were included, no analysis of sex differences was made. A sampling of the interviews was scored on a series of value dimensions, one dimension at a time (to reduce halo effects), by "blind" raters uninformed about the subjects or hypotheses.

The two clusters of values rated were termed "dominant cultural values" and "humanistic values." As would be expected from the previously reported studies, the radical students scored much higher on the humanistic values than did the control group. The real contribution of this study is its verification that these differences in values reflect the value systems of the parents. Parents of radical youth, like the youths themselves, scored higher on romanticism (aesthetic interest and emotive self-expression), intellectualism, authenticity, and humanitarianism. The differences between the two groups of parents were significant on all of these and were especially high for the fathers on humanitarianism. The parents of radicals scored much lower than the control group parents in valuing moralism and self-control, materialism, and status.

On all of these dimensions the values of student radicals appeared to be consistent with their parents'. On two dimensions differences occurred between radical and control students for which no parallel differences were found among the parents. While the career orientations of the parents appeared similar, the male youths were oriented toward two different groups of careers. Males in the control group aspired toward careers in industry and in legal and medical professions. Male radicals were oriented toward academic careers, or they sought vocations outside the established institutions in political action or art. An even more notable difference was the radicals' deep concern for interpersonal intimacy, as compared to control students. No sign of a corresponding difference was found among the parents.

These findings confirm the impressions from other studies by Keniston and his followers. Although the value commitments of radical youth grow out of their home backgrounds, it is apparent that these youths have struggled to arrive at their own integration of values. They do not merely conform to the commonly accepted goals.[26] As Keniston noted, they are not dogmatic or rigid in their values, they have a capacity for deep empathy with the oppressed and an unusual sensitivity to violence, and they avoid direct aggression, at least in personal relationships, preferring verbal argument and compromise.[27] Although radicals consider personal growth an essential element in their political involvement, they reject private goals in favor of humanitarian ones.[28] These young radicals appear to have achieved what was previously referred to as a "humanizing of values."[29] What distinguishes them from the alienated is that they have gained an "appreciation of the relativity of values without losing the capacity to become fully committed to a value position."[30] They have developed the sensitivity of feminine caring, and merged it with "the dominant American value pattern, formulated at the most general level, one of instrumental activism."[31] In short, the young radical, through his prolonged adolescence, appears to have integrated the values and strengths of both feminine and masculine identifications, reassessed them to make them authentically his, and is attempting to implement them by radical efforts for change in the adult world.

Information about the development of values in alienated youth is considerably more limited. In a provocative essay, Melvin Seeman discerned five aspects of alienation: The alienated youth seems to have faced a breakdown in values. He feels the *normlessness* of pluralistic society. His sense of *powerlessness* leads to *isolation* and *self-estrangement,* which persuades him that interacting with the adult world is *meaningless.*[32] It is not that the alienated has set out deliberately to reject adult values; rather, his search for positive values has been unsuccessful, and the "inability to find positive values and goals is closely related to the distrust of commitment."[33] His search for meaning usually centers on a passive experiencing. His resulting style is similar to that of the foreclosure subject in that he does not feel strongly, he does not have passionate emotions. His course of development is very different from the foreclosure's, however; he does not reject emotions as male foreclosures do, but he cannot sustain emotions because of his lack of real contact and commitment. Instead of having passions, he floats from momentary impulse to impulse.[34] His course is not a simple reaction formation resulting in negative identity. His is an authentic struggle;

a real personal battle waged at the cost of internal suffering. But the instrumental world is seen as too strong for him, and he withdraws from engaging in it.

Though the alienated youth approaches life passively, he is a product of the contemporary scene. Thus, the issue of power is a concern for him. Frequently the alienated take part in some of the protests and demonstrations which the young radicals plan and organize. His involvement is casual and ephemeral and is usually viewed by the committed youth as a nuisance.[35] This perception is partly a result of the radical's failure to comprehend the uncommitted's lack of passion and discipline. But it may also reflect the radical's insightful observation: the activity of the passive-aggressive style can easily turn to violence, a protest against the deep-seated experience of powerlessness. The assertion of power is not the skillful tool of the disciplined revolutionary (much as the alienated are fond of speaking of revolution); it is the futile gesture of one who really does not believe anything can work. The cynical, nihilistic attitude even pervades his show of force. Like the Victorian adolescent who vascilated between hedonism and asceticism,[36] this modern adolescent seeks to refute his passivity with sudden bursts of violence. But this is not integrated or sustained strength. In this case, violence becomes a substitute for honest confrontation.[37]

Edgar Friedenberg is correct in seeing that alienated youth are "not struggling to get in; on the contrary, they want out."[38] Friedenberg notes:

> But there are many young people—now usually, if loosely, identified as hippy—whose conflict with us concerns much more profound issues than the question whether they, rather than we, should be in the driver's seat. It would be a better use of metaphor to suggest that they feel as if they were locked in the back of a vehicle that had been built to corrupt specifications, was unsafe at any speed, and was being driven by a middle-aged drunk. They don't want to drive; they don't even want to go where the car is going, and they sometimes distrust the examiners too much even to be willing to apply for a license. What they want is to get out while they are still alive; if they succeed in that, they will try to camp where they happen to be, hoping to make it if they can stay together and leave ambition and the Great Society to us.[39]

One can question whether the alienated youth's perception of himself as "locked in the back" is accurate. The alienated appears beat down in his search for positive values. He fails due to lack of strength, not to lack of sensitivity. Perhaps his perceptions are distorted due to his lack of strength. By contrast, the young radical appears stronger and more ready to risk trying to grab the steering wheel.

I turn now from the issue of values to the issue of strength. A look at the family backgrounds of the different groups of youth that have been studied may reveal the source of the strength that allows some youths to make mature commitments.

## Family backgrounds of radical and alienated youth

Keniston suggests that the family dynamic which produces the alienated son involves parents who sought to break away from the masculine authoritarian home in which they were reared. The mother sought a separate career but gave it up to raise children, and she was disappointed in the collapse of her husband's earlier nonconformity. Thus the mother formed an especially close bond with her son, encouraging in him the sensitivity and nonconformity she had admired in her husband. But the investment in the son was so great, the mother unwittingly tried to prevent him from growing away, discouraging any sign of initiative or independence. The extreme closeness of mother continues to manifest itself in a "fantasy of fusion," a dream of returning to the garden. Alienated youths picture their fathers as "distant, uninvolved with their family." The lack of male identification leaves the alienated with no sense that he can shape the world or be effective in it. He views masculinity as competitive and destructive, though he sees his own father as weak and easily defeated.[40]

Keniston also sought the sources of the radicals' reactions to the social scene in their family backgrounds. The differences between the family backgrounds of the alienated and those of the radical are subtle and open to question, since the interpretation of the interview and projective material was done without blind raters (and therefore prior knowledge of the hypotheses may have biased the results). Although the radical, like the alienated, felt very close to mother, he also felt from mother a push toward independence and achievement. The mother's love, then, did not bind him to the home. In fact, the outside world reached into the home to a remarkable degree; some of the earliest memories of the radicals revolve around social and world events.[41] Both parents were keenly interested in and informed about politics, a difference which has consistently appeared in the follow-up studies.[42] The radical holds a mixed view of his father which contrasts to some degree with the negative view held by the uncommitted:

> Which ever side of the ambivalence is most stressed, there almost always seems to be a quite conscious split in the image of the father, involving the picture of him . . . as idealistic, sympathetic, honest, highly principled, warm, and admirable; but on the other hand, as dominated, humiliated, ineffectual, or unwilling to act on his perceptions of the world.[43]

Radicals frequently speak and write about their fathers, in contrast to the alienated, who seldom mention them. Keniston claims this difference surprised him,[44] and he attaches much importance to it, as I am inclined to do. However, more reliable data on this difference in attitudes toward the father would be welcome. Some data from more objective studies strengthen the evidence that family relationships were different for these two groups of youth. There are data to suggest that the fathers of radicals held higher status positions than those of the alienated, although the families of both were upper-middle to upper class.[45] Conceivably the radical, because of the more prestigious position of his father, learned to take social approval for granted.

An interesting related study contrasted two groups of male college youth, both of whom registered strong antiwar sentiments in regard to Vietnam. One group acted on their beliefs by signing an antiwar petition. The other group did not sign the petition. The nonsigners differed significantly from the signers in their perceptions of their parents. The students whose behavior was inconsistent with their professed attitudes, the nonsigners, reported more unhappiness in their parents' marriage and fewer shared interests and values between their parents and themselves. The nonsigners had less respect than the signers for both parents. They felt less accepted by their fathers, and more of a confidant to their mothers. Youths who acted on their beliefs described their mothers and fathers in similar terms; the nonsigners felt very differently about their mothers than their fathers. In short, the youths who had the strength to act on their beliefs seemed to have a better relationship with their fathers; the inconsistent youths had been close to their mothers, but not their fathers.[46]

A related finding has to do with the communication between youth and parents. A study found the radicals to have excellent communication with their parents on important topics and to be in general agreement with them, in spite of the fact that the parents are less radicalized. The alienated had the least discussion of future goals with their parents; there is clear evidence of family estrangement (although it is not known if this preceded or followed their alienation from society). A control group of normal students fell between these two extremes in regard to family communication.[47] Keniston's belief that the majority of the parents of young radicals accept their child's activity is borne out by another study in which only 35 percent of the parents showed either displeasure or indifference to their children's activity.[48]

Child rearing in the homes of young radicals encouraged freedom of expression but was not permissive, in that there were high expectations, and reasoning and withdrawal of affection ensured the internalization of values.[49] Evidence does not support the view that permissiveness is a factor in the development of young radicals, though this is commonly held to be the case.[50] The homes were not laissez-faire regarding the

children's development; rather, they pushed the child toward independence and achievement and stressed high ethical principles.[51]

The contrast with the homes of alienated youths is clear. The radical
youth, like the alienated, had his closest emotional ties with his mother.
But rather than dominating her son, the mother of the radical youth
was highly individuating force in his life, pushing him toward independence and autonomy. Furthermore, while the alienated son was determined to avoid becoming like his father, the radical youth wished to
live out the values that his father failed to put into practice. The overall
picture, then, is the equalitarian, democratic, individuating environment
of the entire family of the radical in contrast to the overcontrolling,
oversolicitous attitude of the mother in the family of the alienated youth,
where the father was usually excluded from the major emotional life
within the family.

## Family backgrounds of youth in the four identity statuses

Most of the information regarding the parents of young radicals and
alienated youth that has been presented has relied upon the perceptions
of the youths themselves, with the notable exception of Derber and
Flacks's study of parent values. Of the three American studies that have
sought to relate parents' behaviors to the identity statuses of youth,
two were limited to student perceptions of parental behavior.[52] Data based
on children's perceptions of parents are notoriously unreliable. Thus,
in what follows, I will rely heavily upon the third study, the only American study to date which has gathered data directly from the parents.
Dianne Jordan used a written inventory of parental behavior, filled out
by the parents. The inventory consisted of 192 statements, each describing some aspect of the parents' behavior. The youths in this study were
all males.[53]

Even parents' reports of their own behavior are somewhat unreliable,
especially in areas where actual practices were not in line with those
condoned by society.[54] For this reason, my own study of identity statuses
in Denmark included recorded observations of the interaction between
parents and youth.[55] Each family triad (father, mother, and youth)
was asked to reach agreement on possible endings to some incomplete
stories. Each family's recorded interaction was rated by independent
judges on a number of impressionistic scales, and measurements of specific interpersonal acts were counted.[56] This is the only study of the
identity statuses of youth which has directly observed their interaction
with their parents, and a summary of the results for each sex will be
included here. Since the styles of interaction were observed during late

adolescence, it cannot be inferred from this study that the observed parent behaviors caused the youth to form his style of identity. It may be that the youth's style determines the parents' reactions as well. It is also important to keep in mind that the results reported are based on a small sample of families from a somewhat different culture. Replication on an American sample is needed.

In the sections below, Jordan's data on American males will be reported for each of the identity statuses, followed by a comparison with my data on Danish students. Any sex differences which were observed will be noted.

### Foreclosure families

In the Jordan studies, the foreclosures' reports of their family interactions, and the parents' accounts, were extremely positive. Foreclosures described their parents as more child centered than did students in other statuses. They were very positive about their parents' spending time with them as children. Fathers of foreclosures are not seen by the youth as lax, as are moratorium fathers.[57] Instead the foreclosures' fathers appear somewhat intrusive and possessive, and have a close relationship with their sons. The close protectiveness of the parents may make it difficult for foreclosures to risk challenging them, which may also account for the glowing terms in which the youth describe the relationship. In examining these data, it must be kept in mind that foreclosures tend to report things in a socially desirable manner. For this group, especially, verbal reports may be untrustworthy.

The observations of the interactions of Danish foreclosure families both support and refute this positive picture. These families develop an atmosphere which may best be described as task oriented. The fathers are more active than any of the other fathers observed; they can probably be called dominating leaders. When emotions are expressed in the families of male foreclosures, they tend to be negative. This negativity may reflect the difficulty of interaction between fathers and sons in families where fathers dominate. Or it may reflect the instrumental orientation of these families. In any case, it stands in sharp contrast to the positive tones of the pencil-and-paper reports.

The youth in Danish foreclosure families are not passive, however. In fact, they take more leadership in the family interaction than youth of the other statuses. They tend to be idealistic, and the parents frequently encourage them to clarify reality. Parents of female foreclosures frequently encourage their daughters to speak.

The family atmosphere of Danish foreclosures does not appear to be one which encourages the development of individual differences. There is a very low level of expression of emotions of any kind. The families seem to be in close agreement on the story endings used in the study to begin with. Perhaps what differences do appear simply reinforce the conventional sex roles, with the adult male in a position of authority and with more support and encouragement given to daughters.

### Diffusion families

Students in the diffusion status are the most like those considered alienated in other studies, and Jordan's findings parallel Keniston's description of the alienated family. The absent father is clearest in this group:

> The traits of hostile detachment and granting of extreme autonomy, interpreted here as disinterest and lack of involvement, were especially characteristic of diffusion fathers, who, interestingly, appeared somewhat identity diffused themselves, particularly as regards interest in and commitment to their sons. Diffusion mothers were strongly in agreement with the sons' characterizations of diffusion fathers.[58]

Though the alliance against the father fits Keniston's view, the fact that both the fathers and mothers of diffusions in Jordan's study show rejection and detachment does not fit Keniston's picture. Possibly the parents' rejection is a reaction to the youths' unconventional lifestyles and does not reflect the mother's earlier attitudes. Both of Jordan's studies found the father variable most important in differentiating this group.

The picture is close to that portrayed by Keniston. The alienated have learned through mother to revel in their own experience; they value themselves highly. To avoid being dependent, they break the ties with mother,[59] but they fail to invest themselves in other persons. Their rejection of dependence leaves them isolated, and they retreat into their own experience. The tie with mother was warm and expressive, but it did not give them the strength to move out—either to others or to the world. Far from the stereotypic male image of premature identities, these young men accept the richness of their feminine identifications. But their fathers were weak and absent, so what the uncommitted have seen of strength is impersonal and dangerous. They thus reject the masculine; they are feminized and impotent.[60] Keniston noted that the women in the projective stories of uncommitted youth:

> . . . are strong, controlling and dominating; their chief efforts are to make men less sexual, less aggressive, and more socially conforming than they want to be. In none of the stories are there the references to simple, mutual satisfying relationships between men and women which are found in the fantasies of other students.[61]

The Danish sample of diffusion families was extremely small, but the results support the impressions from previous research and add the weight of direct observation to those data. Diffusion youth were very passive in the triad situation, showing almost no signs of initiative. Parents did not encourage the youth, and there were signs of negativity, especially in the families of female diffusions. A striking sex difference occurred. Fathers of diffusion males were the least active of all the fathers, yet the mothers of these boys spoke more (compared to others in the same triad) than any other group of mothers. The pattern for diffusion females was the opposite. Their fathers had the highest ratio of speaking of any group of fathers; their mothers were the least active. Our diffusion triads seemed to consist of a weak, passive youth and a weak, passive parent of the same sex. The most active person was the parent of the opposite sex, but none of the measures suggested much activity or leadership on the part of that parent, either. Whether the youth's diffusion results from an oedipal coalition or simply from a lack of adequate models remains to be determined.[62]

## Moratorium families

The family interactions of the two groups of youth who have not made commitments contrast markedly. Diffusions, defined as passive in the identity search, turn out to be passive and uninvolved in the family interaction as well. Moratoriums, however, appear actively engaged in a struggle with the family, as they are engaged in the identity struggle. The moratorium males in Jordan's study appeared ambivalent in their relationships with their parents, similar to the way moratoricians related to the leader in a group situation.[63] There is more disagreement in relation to parents in moratorium subjects than in youth from the other statuses. Perhaps this disagreement reflects an attempt to break from dependency, as described in the early adolescent years of Keniston's young radicals. Jordan reports that the primary disagreement of moratorium males is with their mothers, which fits the stress in this book on mothers' domination in child rearing. Jordan speculated that some of their negative feelings toward their mothers may be attempts to free themselves from a figure they see as intrusive, possessive, and controlling, in order to identify with a more distant father. In another study, the moratoriums saw their fathers as more lax than did foreclosures and identity diffusions.[64] This finding was based on a small population, and was not replicated in a third study, however.[65]

The fathers of moratorium males were considerably more active than diffusion fathers, in the observations of Danish families. Both male and female moratoriums were assertive in defining themselves. They gave in to parents on story endings less than other youth did and fell between foreclosures and diffusions on measures of leadership.

The atmosphere in the families of Danish moratorium youth was highly active, with a fair amount of emotional expression and little concern for task completion. The families failed to reach agreement more often than the other types. Autonomy and self-expression seemed to be encouraged in moratorium sons. Moratorium daughters were the least submissive of the young women, but there were no signs of continued encouragement of the daughter's autonomy from the parents.[66]

Jordan noted that moratoriums tended more than other youth to see their parents as a unit. In the Danish study, the two parents were much more similar in activity rates than were the parents of other youth, and fewer differences occurred between families with sons and those with daughters. These data suggest that sex typing is diminished and individual differences are encouraged in moratorium families.

## Identity achievement families

The families of identity achievement males appear rather similar to the families of radical youth described earlier. It will be remembered that the young radicals were critical of their parents but maintained good communication. The identity achievers seemed more balanced in their views of their parents than youth in other statuses; they could be critical, like the moratoriums, but were less negative. Like Keniston's radicals, they were ambivalent in their view of their fathers: "fathers were seen as low in acceptance and child-centeredness, high in rejection and hostile detachment, yet moderately positively involved with their sons."[67]

The Danish population was young, and insufficient numbers of achievement families were available for the triad interviews. Therefore no data from direct observations of interaction are available for this group, and no information regarding families of female achievements can be presented.

## Family roots of involvement

Family studies are too scarce and too limited by methological problems to provide conclusions, as yet. The data are suggestive, however. Once a youth enters the college community, he is likely to be confronted with a variety of life alternatives. How he reacts to these appears to be partially a matter of previous family training.

Foreclosure youths appear to come from family environments in which individual differences are not emphasized; the focus is upon getting things accomplished. Perhaps foreclosure youths must defend themselves against alternatives, as Marcia suggests of males. Or perhaps they simply fail to observe differences, except in stereotypic ways which do not affect their images of themselves. Most likely, personality differentiation is not an important goal for them, since it has not been emphasized in their homes.

The other statuses of youth do appear to be sensitive to the variety of alternatives available to them. They are affected by the crisis in values as they move from home to world. They differ in the degree to which they actively involve themselves in the search among alternatives. The strength to become actively involved, even when negative feelings arise, may be directly related to the types of interactions they have experienced in their families. Role models for passive interactions at home reduce the likelihood that a youth can actively engage himself in later struggles. On the other hand, a home atmosphere in which individual differences are valued even when tasks are not always smoothly accomplished no doubt prepares the youth for critical involvement and the struggles which that entails.

## A *summary of styles of adolescence today*

In this section of the book data from a variety of impressionistic categories and typologies have been considered. In order to achieve a summary and integration of these data, it is useful to organize these various category systems in terms of early and prolonged identity formation, as in Table 5.

**TABLE 5**
Summary of youth typologies

|  | Early identity formation | | Prolonged adolescence | |
|---|---|---|---|---|
|  | *Smooth* | *Rebellious* | *Alienated* | *Committed* |
| Erikson. . . . . . . . |  | negative identity | diffusion | identity achievement |
| Marcia . . . . . . . . | foreclosure |  | diffusion | identity achievement (moratorium) |
| Blos. . . . . . . . . | abbreviated |  | prolonged protracted | |
| Keniston . . . . . . . | professionals |  | uncommitted | radicals |

In Table 6, I have attempted to summarize the personality styles which appear to result from these processes of adolescing, in terms of the themes which have been central throughout this book. It should be noted that for some of these the research data are scanty; this table is not intended to obscure the need for more research. Thus it has been labeled "hypothesized consequences," though data for many of these consequences have already been presented.

**TABLE 6**
Hypothesized consequences of three paths toward identity

| Early identity formation | Prolonged: alienated | Prolonged: committed |
| --- | --- | --- |
| Dependency continued, or transferred, or rejected through rebellion, negative identity | Dependency rejected, leading to isolation and narcissism | Dependency shared, mutual, interdependent |
| Mistrusts own experience; undifferentiated self | Retreats into own experience; may have highly differentiated self, but somewhat undifferentiated view of others and world | Uses inner experience to make contact, communicates with others; self and world both well-differentiated |
| Accepts sex-role stereotypes | Rejection of masculine traits | Integration of strength and sensitivity; individuation of self |
| External locus of control | External locus of control | Internal locus of control |
| Attempts to move into or take over the established system | Rejects the system | Critical of the system, but seeks to revise it |
| Assumes adult role in the society same as that of parents' generation | Drops out of society | Involved at the cutting edge of society |

## Early identity formation: Still a majority

*Smooth foreclosure of identity.* For most adolescents, the transition from childhood to adult roles is a smooth one. No doubt most youth do not question the adult social order; they have no grounds for questioning, since they have seen only the immediate adult world in which they are now proving themselves. For the most part, they have not been confronted with alternatives which raise questions.

Probably only a minority of youths in this category go on to college.[68] Unfortunately, our data on late adolescent development is limited almost entirely to studies of the college population. What knowledge we have of early identity formation comes from studies of the college students who have closed the process of identity formation by their first or second year of college. A substantial percentage of college youth does fall in this group. For these young people, college is a practical matter to gain the skills and credentials they need to achieve an already chosen identity. It is not essentially a continuation of the search for identity. Approximately 58 percent of college students view their years of higher education in this practical way.[69] Thus, though college students make up only a minority of those who close the identity process early, the foreclosures are the largest group of adolescents, even in the colleges. These students, like their noncollege counterparts who marry early and enter the work force directly after high school, move directly and unhesitatingly into adulthood.

*The rebellious foreclosure of identity.* No doubt the majority of adolescents move directly from their dependent status while in the public schools to the adult roles of work and marriage. A minority, however, move into adult roles through a process of rebellion. Because the topic is restricted to data from college youth, the rebellious type has not emerged in the data presented in these chapters. The impression is that the rebellious type is less common today than several decades ago. But it must not be assumed that early identity formation always occurs in the smooth manner suggested by Marcia's foreclosure type. There are still some youths who move too quickly into adulthood by rebelling against their parents. These youths fit the classic *Strum and Drang* pattern which has typically been associated with adolescence. Classical rebellion is illustrated by the myth of the young prince who tries to dethrone his father in order to become king. He is not attempting to change the kingdom into a democracy; he simply wishes to be the king. The rebellion is an attempt to break into the adult system. The rebellious adolescent seeks not to change the adult game but to defeat his elders at their own game. Thus he involves himself in the game and ensures that it will continue.[70]

This rebellion is a rejection of childhood status and an attempt to break the ties of dependency.[71] Frequently dependency upon adults is defensively denied, and dependency needs may be transferred from parents to peers.[72] In gang delinquency, for example, youth depends upon the influence and support of its peers to maintain the facade of independence.[73] Every adult demand is opposed. In order to assure himself that he is not still under adult domination, the adolescent styles himself as different from adults as possible. This is not a development of a new value system; it is simply the opposite of the old value system adults have given him. This "negative identity," as Erikson calls it, is a way of overcoming "a pervasive sense of powerlessness."[74] Even in extreme cases of juvenile delinquency and ghetto culture alienation, this is a struggle which seeks a piece of the action.[75] These youths are part of the "perennial generation of restless youth who can't wait to test the power and independence of adulthood, and fight with their parents for that privilege."[76] The rebellion does not change the order of things—these youths become intensely conservative adults, maintaining the same social order.

The result of rebellion is surprisingly similar to the consequences of smooth foreclosure: a conventional personality.

*Conclusions on early identity formation.* The early formation of identity is, undoubtedly, the normative process, speaking statistically. The consequences appear to be a relatively undifferentiated personality, with conventional attitudes and values. The dependency issue is unresolved. For women, a continuation of somewhat childish dependency is considered acceptable. For men, peer group conformity provides a transition from dependency on parents. When the young man marries, the dependency he denies in relation to parents can be expressed in relation to his wife, who frequently mothers him and, often tragically, refers to him as another of her children.

## Prolonged adolescence for a minority

In order for a highly differentiated personality to develop it appears that a prolonged adolescence is necessary. We can predict that increased personality differentiation will become more and more important to functioning in a complex and fast-changing world. As economic conditions have encouraged extending the period of education, with a consequent delay in family and job responsibilities, a period of exploration has become quite possible. Youth can experiment without taking great risks of economic and social disruption.

This freedom to explore alternatives is important to the development of a differentiated personality. Perhaps even more important, it aids the humanizing of values so essential to humane participation in today's world. The ability to look critically at the assumptions of one's own society, to experience the relativity of values, is probably the most significant consequence of the postponing of adult roles.

Two contrasting prototypes which may result from prolonged adolescence have been distinguished: the diffused or alienated youth, who drifts through the alternatives in a disengaged fashion, and the moratorium youth, who recognizes the relativity of values and pursues the value quest, not through disengagement but through involvement which leads to commitment.

*The alienated type.* Frequently, the period of extended adolescence includes not only a delay in family and job responsibilities but a disengagement from society and from personal involvements. Perhaps earlier family experiences have not provided a model for coping with alternatives. For whatever reasons, the youth is unable to actively engage himself with the possibilities and retreats to passive observation. He senses everything and does nothing. Diffusion and isolation result. A family background in which the same-sex models were weak and ineffectual appears to contribute to this diffusion. Another contributor may be the college environment, which is frequently designed to pit students against teachers, youth against adults, in a game for grades and credentials. Living and social arrangements isolate youths in buildings where they are surrounded solely by peers. Few personal contacts are encouraged with persons having more life experience; adult models are available only to those students who are assertive enough to initiate contact with professors. The "work" expected of students is mainly intellectual and encourages an attitude of observing without doing. This type of disengagement is unlikely to lead to creative involvement in the society.

*The committed type.* The committed youth does not retreat into himself at the expense of the real world; his identity is not achieved through a moratorium in that sense. Neither does he accept the world as he finds it. He experiences himself in relation to the world, and the world becomes a medium for self-discovery and expression. These youths have experienced a crisis of values; they have faced pluralism, not only as a fact of the world, but as a personal crisis. Frequently the college environment has provided, for them, adult models who themselves face the ambiguity of life and yet move into life. Perhaps they were fortuitously thrust into the right environment, or perhaps they already had some strength which allowed them to seek out the adult relationships they needed. In part, at least, the courage to get actively involved, to move toward commitments, appears to be a consequence of family experiences. Perhaps the family was already more like the world, in that a multiplicity of viewpoints was represented in the home. Differences were openly expressed, confrontations occurred, and one learned to deal with conflict. Personality differentiation began even before the adolescent years, not through isolated introspection but through communication and direct experience. This is the process which continues in late adolescence.[77] The self grows through contact with others and with the larger society.

*Sex roles and prolonged adolescence.* A prolonged identity struggle and the development of a highly individuated personality do not seem to be encouraged in women to the same extent as in men. The continuation of dependent relationships such as are common in foreclosures appears to be more acceptable in women and does not seem to lead to rigidity. Nonetheless, it is questionable that early identity formation is adaptive, at least in highly pluralistic settings. A longitudinal study at Sarah Lawrence College (for girls) reported that the students who seemed most mature as freshmen did not, in the long run, seem to go as far in their development. It was hypothesized that the emotional cost of too early development may be too great, and that premature resolutions are apt to be limited.[78] The evidence suggests that women who move through crisis to a mature identity place greater importance on the issue of sex and intimacy than identity achievement men do, but they experience crisis in the areas of work, religion, and politics just as men do.[79] It seems likely, since the development of identity in women receives less support from the general culture, that women especially need a strong supportive community in order to accomplish this. Perhaps some separation from direct competition with men is useful.[80] It may be that stable self-definition is more important to female than to male identity development.[81] Certainly once the woman has reached a clear self-definition which rejects the limitations of traditional sex roles, she is in a better position to discover her unique identity.

The sex roles are equally crucial to male identity development, though perhaps men less frequently deal with them in a self-conscious way. The humanizing effect which accompanies an honest recognition of the relativity of values involves getting back in touch with the sensitivity that the young man may have learned from his earlier female identification. When this value stance leads to commitments, sensitivity is utilized by moving into the world with the courage and strength he gained through male identification. Perhaps, some day, sensitivity and strength will no longer carry feminine and masculine overtones. Be that as it may, sensitivity and strength must be integrated if mature, humane involvements are to result.

The young radical provides a useful prototype for this integration of sensitivity and strength. Because he experiences a crisis in values, his protest is not simply the struggle to get in the system but a passion to revise it and steer it in new directions. He wants to participate with his whole self, which means to confront the system with human values he has forged from the best in his childhood and his tradition. He does not stand outside society, he stands in it, but at the growing edge. He is unsure about the power structure, never completely optimistic that he can wrest control of the wheel but committed to giving it a try. Keniston notes that "Some young Americans can do just this: they can live without a guarantee that they have made the best or the only choice: and this capacity to make commitments without guarantees is a prime symptom of strength of character."[82]

They choose a "road less traveled by"—but they do choose.

> . . .
> And sorry I could not travel both
> And be one traveler, long I stood
> And looked down as far as I could
> To where it bent in the undergrowth;
>
> Then took the other, just as fair,
> And having perhaps the better claim,
> Because it was grassy and wanted wear;
>
> . . .
> I took the one less traveled by
> And that has made all the difference.[83]

## Summary

Developmental and longitudinal research has been examined in this chapter to clarify the process of identity formation and the factors in the environment which affect that process. An example is the crisis in values, to which three social factors appear to contribute; the confrontation with diverse value orientations, the discovery of corruption in the world, and the support of models who criticize conventional morality.

Low social risk probably encourages commitment to nonconventional values, while the anticipation of entry into the world of employment and family commitments probably encourages consolidation of values, perhaps at conventional levels. An environment which provides models and support for commitment to postconventional values thus seems crucial to shifting the balance in that direction.

The available data on family backgrounds suggest that sensitivity to a variety of alternatives and the ability to become engaged in the identity struggle are related to a home atmosphere in which individual differences are valued, even when tasks are not always smoothly accomplished.

The outcomes of the different styles of identity process have been summarized, as have the effects of sex-role differences upon the prolonged process of identity formation.

## Notes

1. James E. Marcia, "Development and Validation of Ego Identity Status," *Journal of Personality and Social Psychology*, 3 (1966): 551–58.

2. See Joseph Katz and associates, *No Time for Youth: Growth and Constraint in College Students* (San Francisco: Jossey-Bass Publishers, 1968), pp. 66–68, and Nevitt Sanford, ed., *The American College: A Psychological Interpretation of the Higher Learning* (New York: John Wiley & Sons, 1962).

3. David R. Matteson, *Alienation vs. Exploration and Commitment: Personality and Family Correlaries of Adolescent Identity Statuses,* Report from the Project for Youth Research (Copenhagen, 1974).

4. Anne Constantinople, "An Eriksonian Measure of Personality Development in College Students," *Developmental Psychology*, 1 (1969): 357–72. See Chapter 7.

5. Alan S. Waterman, Patricia S. Geary, and Caroline K. Waterman, "Longitudinal Study of Changes in Ego Identity Status from the Freshman to the Senior Year at College," *Developmental Psychology*, 10 (1974): 387–92. Only about half the original sample of 91 subjects was available for the follow-up study in the senior year of college. A disproportionate number of moratorium subjects had left school. These limitations of the study must be kept in mind in assessing results.

6. Ibid. Separate statistics calculated for statuses based on occupation and on ideology showed that 50 percent based on occupation and 79 percent based on ideology remained diffusions. Where percentages are not reported separately below, the reader may assume they are nearly the same for each content area.

7. 36 percent based on occupation, 14 percent based on ideology.

8. 75 percent on occupation, 29 percent on ideology.

9. 12.5 percent on occupation, 35 percent on ideology.

10. Lawrence Kohlberg and R. Kramer, "Continuities and Discontinuities in Childhood and Adult Moral Development," *Human Development*, 12 (1969): 93–120.

11. On Kohlberg's Moral Judgement Scale, see Lawrence Kohlberg, "The Development of Modes of Moral Thinking and Choice in the Years Ten to Sixteen" (Ph.D. diss., University of Chicago, 1958).

12. William G. Perry, Jr., et al., "Patterns of Development in Thought and Values of Students in a Liberal Arts College: A Validation of a Schema," Bureau of Study Counsel, Harvard University, April 1968, p. 123.

13. Kohlberg and Kramer, "Continuities and Discontinuities in Moral Development."

14. Kenneth Keniston, *The Uncommitted: Alienated Youth in American Society* (New York: Harcourt Brace & World, 1965); *Young Radicals* (New York: Harcourt, Brace & World, 1968); and "Student Activism, Moral Development, and Morality," *American Journal of Orthopsychiatry*, 40 (1970): 577–92.

15. Perry et al., "Patterns of Development in Thought and Values."

16. Reprinted from *Identity: Youth and Crisis* by Erik H. Erikson. By permission of W. W. Norton & Company, Inc. Copyright © 1968 by W. W. Norton & Company, Inc. Austen Riggs Monograph No. 7.

17. Keniston, "Student Activism, Moral Development, and Morality."

18. Marvin Podd, "An Investigation of the Relationship between Ego Identity Status and Level of Moral Development" (Ph.D. diss., State University of New York at Buffalo, 1969).

19. Stanley Milgram, "A Behavioral Study of Obedience," *Journal of Abnormal and Social Psychology*, 67 (1963): 371–78.

20. Lawrence Kohlberg, "Relationship between the Development of Moral Judgement and Moral Conduct" (Paper presented at the Symposium on Behavioral and Cognitive Concepts in Child Development, Minneapolis, March 1965).

21. Lawrence Kohlberg, "Development of Moral Character and Moral Ideology," in *Review of Child Development Research*, ed. M. L. Hoffman & L. W. Hoffman (New York: Russell Sage Foundation, 1964), vol. 1.

22. Keniston, *Young Radicals*, pp. 78–86.

23. Norma Haan, M. Brewster Smith, and Jeanne Block, "Moral Reasoning of Young Adults: Political-Social Behavior, Family Background, and Personality Correlates," *Journal of Personality and Social Psychology*, 10 (1968): 183–201.

24. Keniston, *Young Radicals*, pp. 86–92.

25. Charles Derber and Richard Flacks, "An Exploration of the Value System of Radical Students and Their Parents" (Paper presented at the annual meeting of the American Sociological Association, San Francisco, August 28–31, 1967).

26. James W. Trent and Judith L. Craise, "Commitment and Conformity in the American College," *Journal of Social Issues*, 23 (1967): 10–52.

27. Keniston, *Young Radicals*, p. 118, 133, 254, and 355.

28. Richard Flacks, "The Liberated Generation: An Exploration of the Roots of Students' Protest," *Journal of Social Issues*, 23 (1967): 52–76, especially p. 69.

29. See Chapter 12 and Robert W. White, *Lives in Progress: A Study of the Natural Growth of Personality*, 2d ed. (New York: Holt, Rinehart & Winston, 1966), p. 397.

30. Sanford, *American College*, p. 261. This is Sanford's definition of maturation.

31. Talcott Parsons, "Youth in the Context of American Society," *Daedalus*, 91 (1962): 97–123.

32. Melvin Seeman, "On the Meaning of Alienation," *American Sociological Review*, 24 (1959): 783–91.

33.   Keniston, *Uncommitted*, p. 192.

34.   Ibid., p. 338.

35.   Kenneth Keniston, "Student Activism, Moral Development, and Morality."

36.   Anna Freud, *The Ego and the Mechanisms of Defense* (New York: International Universities Press, 1946).

37.   See, for example "Campus Crisis: Tough Questions over the Rebels," *New York Times*, May 4, 1969, sec. 4, p. 1.

38.   Abraham J. Tannenbaum, "Introduction" to "Alienated Youth," *Journal of Social Issues*, 25 (1969): 2, reviewing Edgar Z. Friedenberg, "Current Patterns of Generational Conflict," pp. 21–38 in the same journal.

39.   Friedenberg, "Current Patterns of Generational Conflict," pp. 22–23.

40.   Keniston, *Uncommitted*, pp. 170–71, 199. Similar family structures have been posited for delinquents and for the predecessors of the "hippies," the "beats" of the 1950s. Paul Goodman, in *Growing up Absurd* (New York: Random House, 1956), p. 164, attributes a similar analysis of "beats" to Talcott Parsons.

41.   Keniston, *Young Radicals*, pp. 51 and 80.

42.   William A. Watts, Steve Lynch, and David Whittaker, "Alienation and Activism in Today's College-Age Youth: Socialization Patterns and Current Family Relationships," *Journal of Counseling Psychology* 16 (1969): 1–7.

43.   Keniston, *Young Radicals*, p. 51.

44.   Ibid., p. 293, Appendix A.

45.   Watts, Lynch, and Whittaker, "Alienation and Activism." See also D. L. Westby and R. G. Braungart, "Class and Politics in the Family Background of Student Political Activists," *American Sociological Review*, 31 (1966): 690–92.

46.   R. William Cowdry, Kenneth Keniston, and Seymour Cabin, "The War and Military Obligation: Private Attitudes and Public Actions," *Journal of Personality*, 38 (1970): 525–49.

47.   Watts, Lynch, and Whittaker, "Alienation and Activism." It should be noted that the alienated in this study differed from Keniston's sample of the Harvard alienated in that they were no longer affiliated with a university.

48.   Keniston, *Young Radicals*, p. 113. William B. Martinson, David G. Jansen, and Bob B. Winborn, "Characteristics Associated with Campus Social-Political Action Leadership," *Journal of Counseling Psychology*, 15 (1968): 552–62.

49.   Keniston, "Notes on Young Radicals." *Change*, 1 (November–December 1969): 28.

50.   Lamar E. Thomas, "Family Congruence of Political Orientations in Politically Active Parents and Their College-Age Children," (Ph.D. diss., University of Chicago, 1968); Haan, Smith, and Block, "Moral Reasoning of Young Adults"; Cowdry, Keniston, and Cabin, "The War and Military Obligation." Thomas compared the children of politically active parents of both the right and the left and found generally higher levels of political activity among the children of left-wing parents but *no* relationship in either group between activism and permissiveness in child rearing. Haan, Smith, and Block conclude, on the basis of data from nearly 1,000 students, that permissiveness is not a determining variable in activism. And Cowdry, Keniston, and Cabin found no relationship between permissiveness and antiwar activism among college seniors.

51.   Keniston, "Notes on Young Radicals."

52.   Herbert J. Cross and Jon G. Allen, "Ego Identity Status, Adjustments, and Academic Achievement," *Journal of Consulting and Clinical Psychology*, 34 (1970):

278–81; and Dianne Jordan, "Parental Antecedents of Ego Identity Formation," Master's thesis, State University of New York at Buffalo, 1970.

53. Dianne Jordan, "Parental Antecedents and Personality Characteristics of Ego Identity Statuses, Ph.D. diss., State University of New York at Buffalo, 1971.

54. Jules M. Riskin and Elain E. Fauncy, "An Evaluative Review of Family Interaction Research," *Family Process*, 11 (1972): 365–56; James L. Framo, "Systematic Research on Family Dynamics," in *Intensive Family Therapy: Theoretical and Practical Aspects*, ed. Ivan Boszormenyi-Nagy and James L. Framo (New York: Harper & Row, Publishers, 1965), pp. 407–62.

55. Matteson, *Alienation vs. Exploration and Commitment*.

56. The system of scoring interpersonal acts used is described in Robert Freed Bales, *Personality and Interpersonal Behavior* (New York: Holt, Rinehart & Winston, 1970), pp. 91–135. The Bales system was slightly modified in this research. A detailed explanation of the system used is contained in Matteson, *A Supplement to Report from Project for Youth Research* (Copenhagen, 1974).

57. Herbert J. Cross and Jon G. Allen, "Ego Identity Status, Adjustment, and Academic Achievement," *Journal of Consulting and Clinical Psychology*, 34 (1970): 278–81.

58. James E. Marcia, work in process, citing Jordan, "Parental Antecedents and Personality."

59. Keniston, *Uncommitted*, p. 301.

60. Patricia Cayo Sexton, *The Feminized Male: Classrooms, White Collars, and the Decline of Manliness* (New York: Vintage Press, 1969).

61. Keniston, *Uncommitted*, p. 148.

62. Matteson, *Alienation vs. Exploration and Commitment*.

63. Jordan, "Parental Antecedents and Personality Characteristics." The study in a group situation was reported in Chapter 14: James Donavan, "A Study of Ego Identity Formation," unpublished doctoral diss., University of Michigan, 1970.

64. Cross and Allen, "Ego Identity Status, Adjustment, and Academic Achievement."

65. Jordan, "Parental Antecedents and Personality Characteristics."

66. Matteson, *Alienation vs. Exploration and Commitment*.

67. Jordan, "Parental Antecedents and Personality Characteristics."

68. This conjecture is based on the assumption that the great majority of non-college youth share the attributes of Marcia's foreclosure subjects. Research on acceptance of authority and of intellectual complexity lend some support to this assumption. See, for example, David R. Matteson, "Changes in Attitude Toward Authority Figures with the Move to College: Three Experiments," *Developmental Psychology*, 4 (1974): 340–47; and David Whittaker and William A. Watts, "Personality Characteristics of a Nonconformist Youth Subculture: A Study of the Berkeley Non-Student," *Journal of Social Issues* 25 (1969): 77.

69. Louis Banks and editors of Fortune Magazine, *Youth in Turmoil* (New York: Time-Life, Inc., 1969).

70. Friedenberg, "Current Patterns of Generational Conflict."

71. Talcott Parsons, "Age and Sex in the Social Structure of the United States," *American Sociological Review*, 7 (1942): 604–16.

72. Peter Blos, *On Adolescence: A Psychoanalytic Interpretation* (New York: Free Press, 1962), pp. 117–18. Blos refers to this as "uniformism."

73. Martin Gold, "Juvenile Delinquency as a Symptom of Alienation," *Journal of Social Issues,* 24 (1969): 133.

74. Abraham J. Tannenbaum, "Introduction" to "Alienated Youth," p. 4.

75. David Gottlieb, "Poor Youth: A Study in Forced Alienation," *Journal of Social Issues,* 24 (1969): 91–120.

76. Tannenbaum, "Introduction" to "Alienated Youth."

77. Keniston, *Young Radicals.*

78. L. Murphey and E. Raushenbush, *Achievement in the College Years* (New York: Harper & Row, Publishers, 1960).

79. J. S. Nevid et al., "Sex Differences in Resolution of Sexual Identity Crisis" (Paper presented at the annual convention of the Eastern Psychological Association, Philadelphia, April 1974.

80. Matteson, *Alienation vs. Exploration and Commitment;* Murphey and Raushenbush, *Achievement in the College Years.*

81. Alfred B. Heilbrun, Jr., "Conformity to Masculinity-Femininity Stereotypes and Ego Identity in Adolescents," *Psychological Reports,* 14 (1964): 351–57; James Marcia, work in process.

82. Keniston, *The Uncommitted,* p. 263.

83. Robert Frost, "The Road Not Taken," *The Poetry of Robert Frost,* edited by Edward Connery Latham. Copyright 1916, © 1969 by Holt, Rinehart and Winston, Inc. Copyright 1944 by Robert Frost. Reprinted by permission of Holt, Rinehart & Winston, Inc.

# 16

## New directions for the family

THIS BOOK BEGAN with a discussion of the family and the development of the sex roles. The effects of these sex roles upon identity formation were examined, along with some of the variables associated with the different personality styles that emerge from the identity process. Now the circle will be completed by exploring the relationships between changes taking place in the American family and the possible consequences of these changes for identity formation.

I have argued that the split in the sex roles and the resulting incongruity between an expressive child rearing and the expectations of an instrumental society work against the development of a mature identity. Are the changes occurring in the family likely to mend the split in

321

sex roles and redress the incongruity between child rearing and society? In this chapter I shall attempt to answer this question. First I shall survey the empirical data regarding the changes occurring in the family. Then I will assess the effects of these changes on the young adults who marry and form new families and upon the children who grow up in these families.

## What's happening to the American family?

Much has been written in the popular press suggesting that the nuclear family is disintegrating. Usually, these obituaries for the family are based on a misinterpretation of divorce statistics, a point to which I shall return. Despite this popular impression, all the demographic data point to the conclusion that the nuclear family is very much intact and will continue to be a primary social institution in our society. According to A. Ferris, "The overwhelming majority of Americans seek and contract marriages, desire and have children, and live in independent households of their own."[1] Alice Rossi, noting that the institution of marriage is more popular today than ever before, cites the following data:

> The proportion of the American population who marry has increased over the past half century. Since 1959, there has been a slight decline of 0.3% per year in the proportion married in the population, but this is largely attributable to increasing numbers of elderly widows in the population, and increasing numbers of unmarried young women as educational attainment has risen to higher levels. In 1967, among young women in their late twenties, 87% were married, an increase for this age group of 13% since 1940.[2]

This is not to say that there have been no changes in the family picture. Two important long-range trends in family life are clear: the change in the timing of family events (a short span of child rearing, with smaller, planned families), and the increasing participation of mothers in the work force.[3] There is some evidence of a third change: an increased willingness to delay marriage until a sound commitment can be made.

### Child rearing is not the only function of families

The shape of the family life cycle has changed markedly in this century. Rossi notes that in the past, an adult woman could expect to become a widow before she had the pleasure of seeing her last child married. A shorter span of life, larger families, erratic timing of births, less adequate health care, and higher occupational risks in men's work contributed to a modal profile 50 years ago which centered women's lives upon child rearing. Two factors, increased longevity and birth control, have changed this profile. A modal young woman today can anticipate three characteristics of her adult life which will be strikingly different from the life of adult women earlier in the century:

(1) she will actually spend almost twice as many years with neither husband nor dependent children as she will with preschool children (23 vs. 13 percent); (2) almost two-thirds of her adult years will be spent either alone or living with a husband but no children under 18 years of age; and (3) of the remaining 36 percent of her adulthood, 25 percent will be largely part-time mothering of post-kindergarten-age children. For a two-child family, only seven of the woman's 56 adult years will go to rearing preschool children.[4]

### More married women are working

Women now make up more than a third of the national work force; 43.8 percent of all working-age women are now employed.[5] And women are no longer restricted to a few vocations; at least a few women have now entered nearly every type of occupation.[6] In 1955, the great majority of women, once they were married, depended upon their husbands for support. Only 31 percent of married women between 20 and 24 years of age were employed. By 1967, the figure had jumped to 43 percent.[7] The reasons for working appear to have changed during the last decades. A study of high school girls in 1959 indicated the main reasons they would work after marriage were in order to help buy a house or because the husband was disabled. A similar study in 1966 showed a decrease in justifying work because the husband was disabled and an increase in emphasis upon working because a woman would be frustrated by restricting herself to homemaking.[8]

Since 1940, increasing proportions of older women have been returning to the labor force.[9] The clearest trend is that more and more married women go to work before and after the period of child rearing. While the vast majority of American women continue to stay at home during the childbearing and early child-rearing years, mothers of young children are entering the work force at a sharply increasing rate. Twenty years ago, a large proportion of mothers of high-school-age children went back to work. Today, there is an equally large proportion of mothers of elementary-school-age children returning to the labor force.[10] Employment may be an increasingly accepted pattern, even for mothers of preschool children.

### Decisions to marry are being delayed

In addition to the changes noted above, a comparison of relevant 1970 and 1960 census data indicates three additional changes:

1. Youth are waiting longer before marrying. (The median age has climbed by half a year and now stands at 20.8 for women and 23.2 for men.)
2. The proportion of divorced or separated women has increased.
3. More women are living alone, particularly women in the 20–34 age bracket.[11]

The significance of these changes is not altogether clear. However, they do suggest that there is an increased willingness, both on the part of youth and on the part of divorced women, to evaluate other options and to delay marriage or remarriage until a sound commitment can be made.

### The family is alive and changing

Nothing in the available data suggests that either marriage or the nuclear family has diminished in popularity. Although the divorce rate continues to be high, the great majority of divorcees remarry. They appear to be disenchanted with individual spouses, but not with the institution of marriage itself.

The data do suggest important changes in the structure of the family. More care is taken before entering marriage, yet there appears to be more freedom to end marriages. The wives need not center their lives so much upon children; working outside the home is increasing, even among mothers of small children.

## Marriage and identity

Turning from hard data to some attempts at interpretation, it can be said that the key to understanding the changes occurring in the American family today may lie in a gradual shift in values in our society. Marriage is less revered as an institution of value in and of itself. Instead, it is judged in terms of its effectiveness or ineffectiveness in fulfilling the needs of the individuals involved. Individuals appear to be demanding more in the way of personal gratification from marriage and are not willing to "save face" by perpetuating bad or outgrown marriages.[12]

### Intimacy: The basic function of marriage

The need for genuine intimacy and sharing with another human being is one of the strongest factors in preserving the nuclear family, in spite of the many forces working against personal relations in our culture. In fact, some of the cultural changes which at first seemed to be destructive to the family, such as increased mobility, have proved in many cases to strengthen the ties that hold the family together.[13] This social dynamic, whereby changes in one direction are compensated for by other changes, makes it extremely difficult to predict the future of social institutions. If the culture as a whole grows more impersonal, those institutions within the culture that are personal and intimate could actually be strengthened.

Looking more closely at the effects of mobility on the family, there is some evidence that the marriage unit takes on increased importance in highly mobile families; it provides a close-knit personal unit, a portable island of intimacy in a sea of changes and transient relationships. Marriage has been called "our last stronghold of intimacy."[14] In contrast to many predictions, it is the most sociable families who move, and the presence of school-age children in the family seems to be an advantage in integrating the family into the new community.[15] The women in mobile families do not generally feel rootless; rather, they feel they have become more flexible and adaptable and "express the conviction that they have grown in their skills to meet people and form friendships."[16] Not surprisingly, the wife's happiness in the new community is related to the degree to which she felt involved in the planning of the move. Self-perceptions of mental health reveal the highest scores for persons who choose to move (as opposed to those who move, but prefer not to)—even higher than those who choose to stay where they are.[17] Transience and mobility appear to increase the need for an intimate family life; the "very impermanence of so many relationships heightens the need for some relationships which are dependable."[18]

Connected with the need for intimacy in our society is the increased emphasis on communication in marriage. An interview study of young married couples noted increasing concern with communication between spouses and the belief that marriage can last "because we can discuss our problems together."[19] Though attempts have been made to demonstrate experimentally the relationship between communication and adjustment in marriage, they must be read critically. Sometimes those couples who are working most vigorously to improve their marital communication and reassess their roles appear on objective measures very much like the most conflicted and disturbed couples. Later ratings of videotaped interviews have borne out clinical assessments that they are engaged in constructive conflict.[20] At present, available measurements of interpersonal interaction are too crude to elicit trust in research data on the relationships between intimacy and healthy conflict resolution.

## Autonomy, for husbands and wives

I have suggested that a change in values in our society has shifted the focus away from holding a particular marriage together and toward assessing whether that marriage is satisfying the needs of those involved.

What sort of marriage can sustain a deep intimacy between the partners and also encourage each to develop a degree of autonomy?

The changes occurring in marriage and the family can be viewed as part of a historical trend away from ascribed roles toward achieved roles.[21] In the days of monarchy, the role of king was an ascribed role, passed down as a birth right from father to son. The development of Western democracy was, in part, an attempt to place governing authority in the hands of those who demonstrated themselves worthy of governing. Similarly, occupational roles have shifted from ascribed roles, passed down through the family, to achieved roles. The institution of marriage has been associated historically with the conferring upon the couple of certain ascribed roles. It was presumed to define the personal, sexual, economic, and child-rearing responsibilities of the two persons. Increasingly, these prescriptions are not being accepted; instead, the couple recognizes that each must work out his and her own role definitions. They must achieve their own type of "contract" which satisfies the needs of two autonomous individuals.

Much of what is popularly seen as the instability of the institution of marriage has to do with this move from ascribed to achieved roles. The loss of a clear and defined social prescription does take its toll in increased anxiety and confusion. This loss fosters uncertainty and insecurity in the individual and intensifies fluidity and change in the society. The move to achieved roles brings positive gain in that it allows for greater individuation. Respect for the other's autonomy permits a deeper interdependency to develop between the partners.

In the past, the institution of the family served a number of functions. Today, education, religious training, the development of work skills, and many other functions previously carried out in the home are delegated to other social institutions. Perhaps, as the family has been freed from fulfilling these functions, its justification more and more depends upon its ability to fulfill the needs of its members for intimacy and autonomy.

### Intimacy, autonomy, and the sex roles

The orientation toward interpersonal needs has been associated with femininity. Intimacy appears to have higher priority in the formation of identity for women than for men. Conversely, in our culture men receive greater support in developing autonomy. My own position is that mature adulthood depends upon an integration of the instrumental and expressive orientations. The mature adult needs both sensitivity and strength, both an openness to the variety of human experience and the courage to make commitments and become involved in the real world.

Changes in family structure which allow women greater autonomy would appear to be positive changes in terms of mending the split in sex roles. Changes which open up the possibility of men becoming more expressive, and more involved in child-rearing, would likewise aid in bridging the chasm between home and world. The point is that a move away from sex-typed ascriptions of family roles and toward the achievement of roles on the basis of individual competence and individual needs seems desirable. Of course, in some families, the autonomous choice of roles will lead to a pattern which on the surface is identical with the stereotypic pattern. It should be possible for parents who have chosen traditional roles after having experienced alternatives to teach their children to explore real alternatives. That is, the negative effects of maternal child rearing need not occur if the traditional roles genuinely express the individual needs. The couple, as parents, can train the children to fulfill their own individual needs, rather than to pattern themselves according to sex roles. It is only when the traditional roles are chosen without awareness of alternatives, and the parents demand traditionally sex-typed children, that negative training in sex roles appears inevitable.

In what follows I shall examine the changes occurring in the American family in order to assess implications for changes in sex roles. The phenomena which have classically been termed "role-reversals," wherein members of one sex assume the roles traditionally assigned to the opposite one, will be interpreted as positive signs of increased flexibility and individuation. The assumption is that as marriage and family roles are assigned in terms of individual needs and competence, group statistics will show fewer sex differences. It is not assumed, I repeat, that all couples should move toward reversing roles; only that group statistics will move this way as choices are made individually rather than stereotypically.

## Factors which may increase women's autonomy

### Women working in the outside world

There is little doubt that many more women are now working outside the home than was previously the case. However, woman is still not treated as man's equal in the working world. Women who want jobs have a harder time finding them than men do; their unemployment rate has been persistently much higher than that for men. Though a few women succeed in entering the highest levels of employment, the great majority are still clustered in relatively low-paying, low-status jobs.[22] Women are less likely than men to be satisfied with their jobs.[23] In many jobs, the working woman does not get equal pay for equal work; the gap between male and female earnings has not narrowed,[24] and median earnings of women have actually declined relative to those of men.[25] And in a recession, women, like blacks, are likely to be fired first. Even in colleges and universities, women have made little progress; they make up about the same proportion of the faculty today, 28 percent, as they did 40 years ago.[26]

Former President Nixon's Council of Economic Advisors suggested that the inequality is not so much due to overt discrimination as to women's acceptance of the traditionally assigned cultural role. One sociologist notes that the proportion of women seeking high-level professional and semiprofessional careers is actually declining and argues that women want "a job requiring relatively little training, which can be fitted into their free hours, and which can be dropped without serious loss of seniority, fringe benefits, etc."[27]

Probably the majority of working women have not radically broken with the cultural sex-role ideology. It is useful to distinguish three viewpoints regarding work and women's roles:

1. The view that there is only one appropriate role for women; "woman's place is in the home."
2. The two-role position, which allows women to add the working role to their traditional responsibilities of caring for children and home.
3. The position that women should have full equality, with men and women sharing both expressive and instrumental roles.[28]

One of the few studies which traced career patterns for women showed that married women in their late thirties through midforties at the time of the study (1961) usually had one of three career patterns. The largest group (45 percent) worked before marriage but quit at the time of marriage or pregnancy, in some cases returning to work years later when the children were older. A smaller group (21 percent) allowed domestic responsibilities to interrupt their work only for short periods and returned to work as soon as possible. A third group of the married women (10 percent) had maintained both the work and the homemaking roles continuously throughout the years since marriage. Data collected in this study suggest that the "work role is more central to woman's existence and more internalized than many writers would contend."[29]

It is striking, however, that despite the importance of work for these women, in all three patterns they continue to assume the main responsibility for the household. Despite talk about more egalitarian division of labor in the household, in actuality women still do most of the house-hold chores, even if they work full time. Rossi notes that:

> When couples are both working full time, the total amount of time devoted to house maintenance drops, but there is relatively little change in the amount of time children or husbands contribute to maintenance chores. . . . Other family members contribute an average of only seven hours a week to ease the task of an employed mother.[30]

There is little doubt that, despite the increase in working mothers, woman's responsibility for domestic tasks has not substantially decreased. In general, the traditional division of roles has not changed although more women have entered the work force. The husband continues to be the primary income-earning member, and it is his occupation that determines the family status. The wife's principal role is still that of wife and homemaker, and her work is either an unwelcome necessity to maintain the standard of living or a "hobby." Seldom is it truly a career involving a high degree of commitment and having a develop-mental sequence.[31]

It has been hypothesized that if a mother goes to work, even if only for economic reasons, it will increase her decision-making power vis-à-vis her husband. Instead, it appears from a carefully controlled study that working mothers actually decrease their role in making decisions, appar-ently to maintain stability in the marriage and to compensate for the threat of their taking over the man's role. The experimenter concluded that "the male dominance ideal is so deeply imbedded in American culture and personality structure that unless strongly rejected, it operates as a counter-force to the pressure from mother's working."[32]

Surprisingly, even in families in which both husband and wife are professionals, the wife is still expected to run the home and care for the children. A study of 53 dual-career couples found nearly half (25) still fit the traditional pattern of roles, with the wife's career treated as a hobby. The majority, 27 couples, did consider the wife's professional activity in making such decisions as where to move, but even in these cases, the husband did not assume much responsibility for the home. Only 1 couple of the 53 studied could be considered an egalitarian family in which child-rearing functions and economic responsibilities were truly shared and the woman's career had equal importance to the man's.[33]

Most working women appear to have accepted the two-role position, simply adding the working role to the traditional domestic responsibili-ties. Even professionally employed women focus on jobs, not careers,[34] and "seem oriented to adapting to men, rather than to themselves."[35] The differences in male and female career statistics may reflect not only discrimination but the effectiveness of our cultural indoctrination of male superiority. Women seem to have learned a "tolerance for domestication."[36]

Certainly the romantic view of marriage discourages girls from taking career planning seriously at both the high school and college levels.[37] Some school counselors perpetuate the view that women should have a "different orientation" than men to working.[38] In opposition to this, data on emotional adjustment from a study of career patterns for women point up "the folly of too early commitment to marriage without full exploration of career."[39] This result is supported by the general data on the increase in women's envy of men's roles as they grow older.[40]

These data suggest that a large percentage of women find the traditional home-centered role unsatisfactory. Yet the nontraditional role is no bed of roses. Women, much more frequently than men, favor the wife's accepting a job outside the home.[41] Men still generally prefer the "old-fashioned" girl when it comes to sex roles, and girls recognize this.[42] If the woman chooses to work and is satisfied with her job, it does not usually affect her interaction with her husband. Even if she becomes dissatisfied with the work, it seldom hurts the marriage, *provided* her job doesn't mean much to her. But the woman who seeks to combine motherhood with a fulfilling vocation and really invests herself in her work can seldom depend upon either her husband or the larger society for emotional support when she becomes dissatisfied at work.[43] Once again it appears that women are only permitted to take on occupational roles as extras, on top of their feminine roles. They are not encouraged to view their work as important to their identity.

### The feminist movement: A source of strength

Whether the traditional sex roles can be successfully challenged may well depend upon whether a new consciousness can emerge among women which not only sensitizes them to their own compliance in being domesticated but provides a support group which can weather the anxieties and pressures that accompany all social change. A new self-consciousness and pride does seem to be emerging among a portion of America's "oppressed majority."

A woman's entrance into the working world does not, in itself, liberate her from the traditional feminine self-concepts. The important aspect of work is her search for her own identity rather than a vicarious one. What the woman does (homemaking, working, both, or neither) is not of central importance, but rather that she affirm her right to choose what she will do in accord with her abilities and interests, and that she not feel restricted to the home.[44]

The discussion of youth identity styles in Chapter 15 distinguished two basic revolutionary attitudes toward the adult world: wanting a piece of the adult action, and seeking to change and reform the adult world. This same distinction can be applied to the goals of women's liberation. One of the goals is to allow women a more equal role in the male-dominated society. This goal has received the most attention, and perhaps it must be achieved first before women can turn to the second (and, to my mind, more crucial) goal of reforming the masculine, instrumental, world. It is one thing to let women into the work force with equal standing. It is another to allow the personal values that have become associated with femininity and the expressive role to begin to affect the masculine world. Erik Erikson believes that:

> Woman may, in new areas of activity, balance man's indiscriminate endeavor to perfect his dominion over the outer spaces of national and technological expansion (at the cost of hazarding the annihilation of the species) with the determination to emphasize such varieties of caring and caretaking as would take responsibility for each individual child born in a planned humanity. There will be many difficulties in a new joint adjustment of the sexes to changing conditions, but they do not justify prejudices which keep half of mankind from participating in planning and decision making, especially at a time when the other half, by its competitive escalation and acceleration of technological progress, has brought us and our children to the gigantic brink on which we live, with all our affluence.[45]

## Factors which may increase male sensitivity

### Role definitions: A reciprocal process

Up to now I have affirmed the ability of some contemporary men to accept their feminine identifications but have attributed it largely to forces in their child rearing and prolonged adolescence. Now the role of their female peers in their development deserves note: The woman's revolution is changing the way men view themselves. It is true, of course, that as women become more assertive in communicating themselves to men, many men are becoming defensive. But others are beginning to see women more clearly and to define themselves in more personal terms. The breakdown of sex-role stereotypes is a reciprocal process.

The normal solution to the separation of home and work for American man, well summarized by Kenneth Keniston, is to compartmentalize his life:

> He expresses his feelings in family and fun, and satisfies his needs for achievement and cognitive performance in the job. . . . When it works, this compartmentalization almost literally permits psychic sur-

vival; a man can tolerate the cold unemotionality of his work because
he can "live for the weekends," and—though it is less obvious—he
can put up with the sometimes vacuous round of family feeling and
fun because his work—however meaningless in ultimate terms—permits
him to use his highly developed cognitive skills.[46]

But psychic compartmentalization is hard to maintain and threatens
to break down into a primary investment in one or the other area (which
Keniston terms "familism" and "careerism"), or a feeling of
fragmentation.[47]

Though technology has in part produced the division between work
and home, it has also eliminated the necessity that the nursing and
child-rearing functions be carried out by the female. The baby bottle
is just one example of why the biological determination of roles is no
longer relevant. One of the few studies that have investigated the father's
role in the family directly, by interviewing the fathers, found that they
did see their family role as important. They valued companionship with
their children and regretted that their economic activities limited the
time they could spend with them.[48] Perhaps when men's values become
more humanized, and their wives become more insistent, men will take
time to involve themselves more deeply with their families.

Just as the importance placed upon individuation in our culture argues
well for women's liberation, the need of man for intimacy suggests that
the family, in some form, will survive. Confrontation within the context
of intimacy, as women redefine their roles vis-à-vis their husbands, may
allow personal growth to occur in both partners.

### From a machine age to a service society

Another hopeful sign is that we are now moving beyond the Industrial
Revolution to the technocratic society. As machines and automation
handle much of the work in the realm of production, man's training
and efforts can go into distribution and services. The technocratic society
is becoming a "service society." Already nearly 65 percent of the civilian
work force is employed in service-producing occupations, as compared
to 35 percent in goods production.[49] Thus the direction of job training
may become more and more integrative and personal, decreasing the
gap between profession and parenting.

It is a fortunate accident of history that new styles of vocation which
emphasize human service are emerging at precisely the time that young
men are rejecting as hypocrisy the split between the world of pleasure
and consumption and the world of work and delayed gratification. Perhaps the demands of the industrial society for "aggressive, disciplined,
competitive pursuit of definite goals" will succumb to the need for men
who integrate the expressive identifications of childhood into their adult
identity.[50]

# But what about the children?

## Children should be wanted, not expected

American society has been among the world's most monolithic in its insistence upon heterosexual love, monogamous marriage, and child rearing as the only acceptable lifestyle for adulthood. We have pictured marriage and child rearing as necessities for personal fulfillment and have looked askance at individuals who remain single, viewing them as eccentric if not downright sick. Similarly, when a married couple remains childless, we have assumed they could not have children or wondered what's wrong. Though these attitudes still prevail, some youths are beginning to recognize that the monogamous marriage is only one style of life. When these youths do marry, they are more likely to do so as a conscious choice rather than in unquestioned compliance to social custom. Further, they recognize that the intimacy and commitment of marriage need not imply raising a family. Young couples may wisely delay children until they have found themselves and discovered each other. Often, by then, they have become too accustomed to the freedom and flexibility of childlessness to surrender it easily. They may well decide not to have children.

If they should decide to have children, they have the advantage of having lived together long enough to learn to communicate with each other and solve problems together, making the inevitable mistakes of such learning before they complicate their relationship with children. Secondly, they have the opportunity to conscientiously prepare for parenthood. As one scholar has noted, "In general, rearing children is the most demanding, the most important, the most rewarding, and the most disappointing of occupations, and yet is virtually the only occupation for which the practitioner has had no training. This is, of course, idiotic."[51] Many youths recognize this lack and seek to learn what they can to prepare for parenthood. For most, preparation is limited to reading the current paperbacks on child rearing: Spock, Ginot, and so on.[52] But many young couples recognize that reading is not the best approach and seek out opportunities for personal growth. A frequent motivation for students taking child psychology courses (if my classes are typical) is "to prepare myself to be a better parent"—a reason given by male students as well as female. Unfortunately most students pass through such courses never having seen a child; they are given little opportunity to integrate their newly acquired information except at a verbal level.[53]

It may be that on-the-job training is more fruitful than advanced academic preparation. Many young parents are surprisingly open in expressing their frustrations and uncertainties about child rearing to other young couples; they do indeed learn from each other. And, at long last, practical seminars and programs for parenting are now being offered.[54]

## The next generation

If couples cease defining their relationship in terms of the ascribed sex roles and seek to work out mutually satisfying divisions of responsibility, it is likely that many children will be raised with less mothering and more fathering. What consequences would this have for their personalities and their identity development?

I have presented evidence that child rearing as it is presently carried out in the American home centers around mother, and this makes the transition into the world during adolescence a difficult one. If the family that emerges from the changes described is one that is less confined by traditional sex roles and one in which father plays a larger role in child rearing, I would predict an easier move into adulthood for the next generation of adolescents. It is too early to test that prediction. There is, however, preliminary evidence on the effects upon children of some of the current changes in the family.

*If parents change roles.* There is no reason to assume that a change or reversal of roles would be bad for the children. One of the best controlled studies showed that girls who strongly identified with highly feminine mothers had the poorest adjustment, as a group; the better adjusted girls tended to identify with masculine mothers.[55]

A later study showed that girls with masculine identifications tended to be both goal-oriented (instrumental) and socially sensitive (expressive), whereas feminine girls tended to be socially sensitive but lacked goal orientation.[56] Parsons would seem to be right in theory: the male who can accept and use both his prior expressive identification with his mother and his later learned instrumental orientation could make a very rich contribution to his children's development.[57] It is this integrated man who is best equipped to become a father in today's world. What goes unrecognized in Parson's theory is that the same integration of expressive and instrumental roles would make better mothers as well.

*If mother steps out.* If parents increasingly share responsibilities for child rearing and bread-winning, it is likely that mothers will spend less time confined to the home. What effect will this have upon the children? The psychological studies most frequently cited to answer this question are the studies of extreme maternal deprivation. The pathological consequences of extreme deprivation have been well documented,[58] but they should not be construed to argue against mothers' working. The problem in the American home is not the absence of mother but her overwhelming presence.

Research on the effects of maternal employment upon children provides information about the consequences of diminished involvement of mothers in child rearing. Unfortunately, there are not sufficient data on the effects of maternal employment upon infants to permit conclusions.[59] Empirical studies of the effects on school-age children yield no evidence for the view that harmful deprivation results from mothers accepting employment. Certainly the absence of consistency in child care can have harmful results. Studies that have included those children for whom no consistent child care has been provided not surprisingly report more behavioral problems in the children of working mothers than in those of nonworking mothers.[60] On the other hand, studies in which class and educational differences were controlled (which roughly approximates a control for consistent child care) suggest that children of working mothers are not harmed by the child-rearing pattern that results, and in some cases actually benefit from it.[61]

Deprivation does not appear to be the cause of whatever effects occur due to maternal employment. A more likely hypothesis is that the effects depend upon the emotional state of the employed mother. For many bright, educated women, some continuation of professional life, at least on a part-time basis, is beneficial to their own well-being. It improves their emotional state, which may mean that they do a better job of mothering when they are with the children.[62] Studies supporting that hypothesis have been reviewed by Lois Hoffman, who concludes:

> The working mother who obtains satisfaction from her work, who has adequate arrangements so that her dual role does not involve undue strain, and who does not feel so guilty that she overcompensates, is likely to do quite well and, under certain conditions, better [in rearing children] than does the nonworking mother.[63]

Because they are more involved in the world, working mothers can interact with children as competent models as well as nurturing persons. They can demonstrate strength and objectivity as well as warmth and concern. Hoffman's review of studies of the effects of maternal employment gives concrete evidence that mothers who work provide more positive role models for their daughters. These mothers are also more likely to stress independence training in their children. Children of mothers who work have less traditional sex-role concepts and a more positive evaluation of the competence of women.[64] Interestingly enough, sons of working women feel more positively toward their fathers as well and attribute to them some positive traits usually associated with mothers; they see their fathers as warm and expressive. Possibly these fathers are more involved with the children.[65]

*If father helps rear children.* A reassignment of family roles in terms of individual needs and personalities will frequently result in greater participation of fathers in child rearing. When fathers are really involved with children in a personal way, the children have an opportunity to identify with masculine strengths, without viewing them as impersonal and coercive. If the father can share his own emotions and can express the warmth and concern he feels, his children may recognize that the subjective world is not antithetical to the outer world; they will be less likely to desecrate the expressive aspects of their own personalities in their attempts to develop competence.[66] Such personal involvement on the part of the male figure, rather than feminizing sons, helps them to move to stronger and healthier independence.[67]

It seems likely that greater paternal involvement with child rearing would decrease the children's dependence upon mother. Robert Sears, Eleanore Maccoby, and H. Levin found high dependency upon mother to be positively correlated with low involvement with father. On the other hand, boys with stronger identifications with their fathers exhibited lower dependency upon mother.[68] It can be inferred from these studies that greater involvement of fathers in child rearing would lead to stronger, more independent youth.[69]

The negative effects of father absence in childhood have been detailed earlier and need not be repeated here. Some research results indicate that the lack of contact with father continues to be common when the child reaches adolescence. Though fathers are generally unaware of it, the teen-ager frequently believes that father considers his own status as far superior to the youth's. Further, teen-agers often feel their fathers fail to recognize the youth's personal achievements.[70] In short, youths frequently experience father as an impersonal authority. Perhaps greater involvement of fathers with adolescents would decrease alienation in youth.

*Mixing the roles: Other effects.* Children raised in homes in which both parents work are likely to have more peer experience earlier in life than other children. During the time parents are working, the children may take part in a day-care center, nursery school, pooled babysitting, or some other form of child care which brings him into contact with peers. There is some evidence that where peer interaction in early childhood has been minimal, alienation or an authoritarian personality is more likely to develop.[71] The suggestion is that early experience with peers leads the child to develop greater empathy with others: "Others may . . . be perceived as 'part of the same family' and thus sharing a common fate."[72] When early experience is limited to authorities, this sense of unity with others is less likely to develop.

The parents' marriage can also benefit from the mixing of roles, which may aid communication between husband and wife. Because real talk can exist only between equals, to the degree that a woman envies the man's involvement in the world and feels inferior to him real talk between them is handicapped. Similarly, if the male feels inferior to the woman and is uncertain about her "mysterious and awesome" inwardness and apprehensive about her expressive style, his communication to her is hindered.[73] Equality need not mean sameness, but it is questionable whether the severe split between expressive and instrumental orientations fostered by traditional sex roles gives the couple much common ground for communication—or much to communicate about. As a veteran marriage counselor notes:

> [Some] argue that marriage fails because the relationship is too close and demanding—bonds must be slackened to provide variety as a remedy for boredom. My conclusion . . . is exactly the opposite. Marriage fails because the relationship is so attenuated and superficial that it fails to meet our human needs for intimacy, involvement and the emotional security that comes from being deeply understood and loved.[74]

It is easy for a relationship to become superficial if either or both members feel "in a rut" and stagnated. Life together is far more interesting if, when they come together intimately, each partner experiences that the other has grown, has become in some way a new person. For this to happen, both husband and wife need involvement beyond the nuclear family. If a woman's only place is in her home, she becomes a rather boring woman to live with.

It bears repeating that there are real difficulties in managing a home with children and two working parents, and each couple will have to work out its own way of sharing responsibilities. One pattern which has recently gained attention among researchers is the professional couple.[75] Husbands and wives with the same profession sometimes find they can work out joint job assignments which allow greater flexibility with the family roles. A couple who are both medical doctors may work out a private practice together, carrying only a joint load of the size either might handle alone and splitting parental duties. Another striking illustration is provided by a professional couple of my acquaintance who are both elementary school teachers. When they decided to raise a family, the wife took a few years off from teaching but then wished to go back to work part time. The husband, on the other hand, longed for more involvement with the children. In a creative attempt at problem solving, they proposed to their school board that they be hired together for one teaching position.

*Bridging the gap between home and world.* Whatever alternatives couples choose to work out their individual and complementary roles, the shared responsibilities of work and child rearing are likely to have two important results. First, and very important, both parents are more likely to bring the world into the home. The recognition in early childhood of the wider world of public affairs, the reader may recall, was one of the features which marked the histories of Keniston's committed youth. If both parents are involved in the outside world, father will no longer be the sole representative of that world to the child. Rather than seeing the world as a threatening place, a perception commonly promoted by the protective mother,[76] the child will have two personal models of movement into the world.

Secondly, shared parenthood should increase the child's ability to take the benefits of home into the world. Recall that the young radicals showed greater continuity of values than the alienated; they sought to implement family values in the world.[77] The emotional learning of the home may carry over into the world with greater strength where both parents are involved in the child rearing; then neither parent is likely to consistently push his expressive orientation into the background, and emotional training is less likely to be sex typed. Training for citizenship in the world needs to include learning how to develop new friendships and how to be intimate. Since both parents are involved in a wider world and are regularly developing relationships outside the nuclear family, they are better equipped to provide examples which teach the child to develop intimate relationships. The expressive mode is less likely to be linked with passivity; relationships are less likely to be seen as events which "just happen." Rather, the children can emulate models who actively seek and develop relationships.

Today's society is a mobile one in which the family cannot continue to be the main source of support after adolescence. Today's youth must learn to seek care and concern in the larger world. Further, today's society is a changing one. The older generation is too tied to the past to provide the creative changes needed, and today's youth must learn to care deeply for the world beyond their homes. The family of tomorrow, the family of shared responsibility for home and world, is one which can train children to seek and to give care in the world.

## Summary

Though some of the educational and economic functions of the family have been taken over by other institutions, the nuclear family shows no evidence of going out of existence. Individuals appear to be demanding more personal gratification from marriage; the family must provide an island of intimacy and stability in a fast-flowing world and yet allow for individual autonomy. Ascribed sex roles handicap the fulfillment of autonomy and intimacy in both partners. Though resistance to sex-role change is strong, women are increasingly entering the work world, even during the years of child rearing. Possibly the feminist movement will provide the support and strength for women not only to enter the masculine world but to reform it. As women redefine their roles, men are forced into a reciprocal redefinition. Further, the move toward service-oriented jobs rather than jobs of production may force men to reintegrate the expressive aspects of their development.

As married couples feel free to decide for or against children and to divide responsibilities for child rearing and bread-winning in terms of personal needs and talents rather than along sexual lines, it should prove easier for children to develop their own potentials without experiencing as deep a split between the expressive and instrumental orientations. The move into the world should become a more gradual, continuous process.

## Notes

1. A. Ferris, *Indicators of Change in the American Family* (New York: Russell Sage Foundation, 1970).

2. Alice S. Rossi, "Changing Sex Roles and Family Development," a paper read at the 124th annual meeting of the American Psychological Association, Washington D.C., August, 1971. A revision of this paper was published as "Family Development in a Changing World," *American Journal of Psychiatry*, 128 (1972): 1057–66. Rossi cited Ferris, *Indicators of Change in the American Family*, for her statistics.

3. Rossi, "Family Development in Changing World," p. 1058.

4. Ibid.

5. *Time*, March 20, 1972, p. 28.

6. Joan Joesting and Robert Joesting, "Future Problems of Gifted Girls" Paper presented to the 17th annual meeting of the National Association for Gifted Girls.

7. Rossi, "Family Development in Changing World," p. 1060.

8. Helen Y. Nelson and Phyllis R. Goldman, "Attitudes of High School Students and Young Adults toward the Gainful Employment of Married Women," *The Family Coordinator*, 18 (July 1969): 251–55.

9. Rossi, "Family Development in Changing World," p. 1059.

10. Ibid.

11. Rossi, "Changing Sex Roles."

12. Ferris, *Indicators of Change in the American Family*.

13. This pertains to the nuclear family, as opposed to the extended family.

14. John Charles Wynn, "The American Family—Surviving through Change," *The Episcopalian*, March 1970, p. 30, citing Gibson Winter.

15. Ronald J. McAllister, Edgar W. Butler, Edward J. Kaiser, "The Adaptation of Women to Residential Mobility," *Journal of Marriage and the Family*, 34 (1973): 197–204, especially pp. 197 and 201.

16. Stella B. Jones, "Geographic Mobility as Seen by the Wife and Mother," *Journal of Marriage and the Family*, 35 (1973): 210–18, especially pp. 213–14.

17. Edgar W. Butler, Ronald J. McAllister, and Edward Kaiser, "The Effects of Voluntary and Involuntary Residential Mobility in Females and Males," *Journal of Marriage and the Family*, 35 (1973): 219–27, especially p. 225.

18. C. W. Hobart, "Commitment, Value Conflict and the Future of the American Family," *Marriage and Family Living*, 25 (1963): 405–14.

19. Paul Hilsdale, "Marriage as a Personal Existential Commitment," *Marriage and Family Living*, 24 (1962): 143.

20. Donald C. Murphy and Lloyd A. Mendelson, "Communication and Adjustment in Marriage: Investigating the Relationship," *Family Process*, 12 (1973): 324.

21. Carle C. Zimmerman, "The Future of the Family in America," *Journal of Marriage and the Family*, 34 (1972): 323–33.

22. "A Long Road for Women," *Time*, February 12, 1973, p. 69.

23. 1973 data from *Social Indicators, 1973*, U.S. government document, reported in Robert Reinhold, "Study of Social Temperature in U.S.," *International Herald Tribune*, February 18, 1974, p. 1.

24. *Social Indicators, 1973*, comparing 1956 and 1971 data. An alternate interpretation is that the decline in proportion is an artifact of the later entry of nonprofessional women into the work force.

25. *Time*, March 20, 1972, p. 28.

26. "A Long Road for Women," p. 69.

27. Edward Gross, "A Sociological Approach to the Analysis of Preparation for Work Life," *Personnel and Guidance Journal*, 45 (1967): 416–23.

28. Jessie Bernard, cited in Gunella Anderman and Steven Anderman, trans., and Edmund Dahlstrom, ed., *The Changing Social Roles of Men and Women* (Boston: Beacon Press, 1971).

29. Mary Crowley Mulvey, "Psychological and Sociological Factors in Predication of Career Patterns of Women," *Genetic Psychology Monographs*, 68 (1963): 309–86, especially pp. 332 and 381.

30. Rossi, "Changing Sex Roles." Part of the problem lies in a self-defeating syndrome supported by our consumer economy. Women appear to give in to the temptation to buy and then are stuck with maintenance chores they dislike. Rossi, "Family Development in a Changing World," p. 1059.

31. Margaret M. Poloma and T. Neal Garland, "The Married Professional Women: A Study in the Tolerance of Domestication," *Journal of Marriage and the Family*, 33 (1971): 531; Rhona Rapaport and Robert Rapaport, "The Dual-Career Family," *Human Relations*, 22 (1969): 3–30.

32. Lois W. Hoffman, "Effects of the Employment of Mothers on Parental Power Relations and the Division of Household Tasks," *Marriage and Family Living*, 22 (1960): 27–35.

33. Poloma and Garland, "Married Professional Woman."

34. Ibid. See the reference to Margaret Poloma and T. Neal Garland, "Jobs or Careers? The Case of the Professionally Employed Married Woman," in *Family Issues of Employed Women*, ed. A. Michel (London: E. S. Brill, forthcoming).

35. Raymond J. Ademek, "College Major, Work Commitment, and Female Perceptions of Self, Ideal Women, and Men's Ideal Woman," *Social Forces*, 3 (1970): 97–112, especially p. 98.

36. The phrase comes from Pierre L. Van den Berghe, "The Two Roles of Women," *The American Sociologist*, 5 (1970): 376.

37. Elizabeth M. Almquist and Shirley Angrist, "Career Salience and Atypicality of Occupational Choice among College Women," *Journal of Marriage and the Family*, 32 (1970): 242–49; Ademek, "College Major, Work Commitment, and Female Perceptions."

38. Gross, "Analysis of Preparation for Work Life."

39. Mulvey, "Predication of Career Patterns of Women," p. 382.

40. See Chapter 5.

41. Nelson and Goldman, "Gainful Employment of Women."

42. Ademek, "College Major, Work Commitment, and Female Perceptions."

43. Carl A. Ridley, "Exploring the Impact of Work Satisfaction and Involvement in Marital Interaction When Both Partners Are Employed," *Journal of Marriage and the Family*, 35 (1973): 229–37. Note especially p. 223.

44. Dr. Vivian P. Makowsky (Department of Psychology, St. Lawrence University, Canton, N.Y.), personal communication, November 1972.

45. Reprinted from *Identity: Youth and Crisis*, p. 292, by Erik H. Erikson. By permission of W. W. Norton & Company, Inc. Copyright © 1968 by W. W. Norton & Company, Inc. Austen Riggs Monograph No. 7.

46. Kenneth Keniston, *The Uncommitted: Alienated Youth in American Society* (New York: Harcourt Brace & World, 1965), p. 295. Copyright © 1962, 1965, by Kenneth Keniston. Reprinted by permission of Harcourt Brace Jovanovich, Inc.

47. Ibid., pp. 296–300.

48. R. J. Tasch, "The Role of Father in the Family," *Journal of Experimental Education*, 20 (1952): 319–61. Tasch used fathers from a wide range of socioeconomic settings in his sample. Like women's housework, man's work away from home seems to "expand so as to fill the time available for its completion"—C. Northcote Parkinson, *Parkinson's Law and Other Studies in Administration* (Boston: Houghton Mifflin Co., 1957), p. 2. Increased time in commuting to and from work partially balances shorter working hours. But in men, as in women, there may also be a failure to make conscious value commitments and set priorities.

49. Alan Gartner and Frank Riessman, *The Service Society* (New York: Harper & Row, Publishers, in press).

50. Charles Reich, *The Greening of America* (New York: Random House, 1970), pp. 208 and 258.

51. George Henry Moulds, "The Generation Gap: Causes and Cures," in *Faculty Forum: A Continuing Conversation among Faculty Regarding the Christian Faith*, January 1971.

52. Benjamin M. Spock, *Baby and Child Care*, rev. ed. (New York: Hawthorn Books, 1968); Haim Ginot, *Between Parent and Child* (New York: Macmillan Co., 1965).

53. One suggestion for home care assistance for working mothers could be of mutual benefit to students:

> There could be a registry at junior and senior high schools to which a local family could apply for pairs of students to be assigned to their families on a regular basis. A mixed-sex pair would add social interest to the assignment for the students, provide them with useful experience in sharing the care of very young infants and preschool children, and assure home coverage for the mother in case one of the students was ill.

Rossi, "Family Development in Changing World," p. 1061.

54. The Parent Effectiveness Training program is one example. See Thomas Gordon, *Parent Effectiveness Training* (New York: Peter H. Wyden, 1970).

55. A. B. Heilbrun and D. K. Fromme, "Parental Identification of Late Adolescents and Level of Adjustment: The Importance of Parent-Model Attributes, Ordinal Position, and Sex of the Child," *Journal of Genetic Psychology*, 107 (1965): 49–59.

56. A. B. Heilbrun, "Sex Role, Instrumental-Expressive Behavior, and Psychopathology in Females," *Journal of Abnormal Psychology*, 73 (1968): 131–36.

57. See Alfred B. Heilbrun, Jr., "An Empirical Test of the Modeling Theory of Sex-role Learning," *Child Development*, 36 (1965): 789–99.

58. Robert D. Singer and Anne Singer, *Psychological Development in Children* (Philadelphia: W. B. Saunders Co., 1969): 65–70.

59. Lois W. Hoffman, "Effects of Maternal Employment on the Child—A Review of the Research," *Developmental Psychology*, 10 (1974): 204–28; see especially p. 204.

60. John A. Rose, "Child Development and the Part Time Mother," *Children*, 6 (1959): 213.

61. Marian Radke Yarrow et al., "Child-Rearing in Families of Working and Non-Working Mothers," *Sociometry*, 25 (1962): 122–40.

62. Judith Bardwich, interview in *CAPS Capsule* (Council for the Advancement of the Psychological Professions and Sciences), Spring 1971, and personal communication July 10, 1974.

63. Hoffman, "Effects of Maternal Employment," p. 213.

64. Ibid., pp. 207 and 224.

65. Ibid., p. 208; Paul Rosenkrantz et al., "Sex-Role Stereotypes and Self-Concepts in College Students," *Journal of Consulting and Clinical Psychology*, 32 (1968): 287–95.

66. Paul Rosenkrantz et al., "Sex-Role Stereotypes and Self-Concepts in College Students;" Hoffman, "Maternal Employment."

67. See Chapter 5 for a review of the supportive data.

68. Robert R. Sears, Eleanore Maccoby and H. Levin, *Patterns of Child Rearing* (Evanston, Ill.: Row Peterson, 1957).

69. Hoffman, "Effects of Maternal Employment," p. 211; Diana Baumrind, "Authoritarian vs. Authoritative Parental Control," *Adolescence*, 3 (1968): 255–72; David R. Matteson, *Alienation vs. Exploration and Commitment: Personality and Family Correlaries of Adolescent Identity Statuses*, Report from the Project for Youth Research (Copenhagen, 1974). See also the discussion of the comparison of Danish and American youth in Chapter 7.

70. Robert D. Hess and Irene Goldblatt, "The Status of Adolescents in American Society: A Problem in Social Identity," *Child Development*, 28 (1957): 459–68.

71. Elizabeth Bing, "Effects of Childrearing Practices on Development of Differential Cognitive Abilities," *Child Development*, 34 (1963): 631–48.

72. E. Stotland and J. Walsch, "Birth Order and an Experimental Study of Empathy," *Journal of Abnormal and Social Psychology*, 66 (1963): 610–14.

73. Leslie H. Farber, "He Said, She Said," *Commentary*, March, 1972, pp. 53, 56–57.

74. David R. Mace, "Marry Go Round," an interchurch feature in *United Church Herald, The Lutheran*, and *Presbyterian Life*.

75. Jessie Bernard, *Academic Women* (University Park: Pennsylvania State University Press, 1964), and T. Neal Garland, "The Better Half? The Male in the Dual Profession Family."

76. Elizabeth Bing, "Effects of Childrearing Practices."

77. Charles Derber and Richard Flacks, "An Exploration of the Value System of Radical Students and Their Parents" (Paper presented at the annual meeting of the American Sociological Association, San Francisco, August 28–31, 1967). Reviewed in Chapter 15.

# 17

## Can many be one?
## Some concluding thoughts
## on identity

THE DATA which have been presented in this book suggest the need for a revised image of adolescence.[1] There is little support for thinking of this as a period of rebellion against parents. What turmoil is present centers around a series of identity issues. This struggle typically reaches its peak in late adolescence, at least among those individuals who consciously struggle with establishing an autonomous identity. Late adolescence is the critical period—in both senses of the phrase. Not only is late adolescence the important period of value decisions essential to the move into mature adulthood, but late adolescents are highly critical of the world into which they are expected to move.

Although only a minority of adolescents presently enjoy the luxury of a prolonged identity quest, the cultural factors which have lengthened adolescence for this minority show no signs of abatement. We can project, then, a decline in the percentage of youth who close off the search for identity prematurely, and an increase in the number of youth likely to experience a period of prolonged adolescence. Whether this will lead to more differentiated personalities, capable of human commitment, or, instead, to increased alienation depends upon cultural forces that are

343

difficult to predict. The factors that lead to alienation appear to be related to the transition from home to world. Alienation should decrease if the dichotomy of instrumental and expressive roles is diminished—if child rearing becomes less protective and indulgent on the one hand, and the world becomes more humanized on the other. There are grounds for cautious optimism on both points. The move from an industrial to a technocratic society and from a production-oriented to a service-oriented economy provides forces which could result in a humanizing of man's (and woman's) work. The increasing influence of women in the work world could tip the balance in that direction—particularly if women's liberation progresses to a second goal of reform: not merely wanting a piece of the action, but seeking to change the goals and shape the action. Certainly, as committed youth move into the work force, they will be pushing for change in that direction.

If changes in the American family lead to a breakdown of the stereotypic sex roles, we can hope that our homes will become more related to the wider world. The traditional sex-typing of the instrumental and the expressive roles has constricted women to feeling without power and encouraged men to wield power without feeling—thus ensuring the shattering of social community.[2] As mothers extend their involvement in the world, as fathers increase their participation in the home, and as society (through provisions for parental training, child care, and so on) assumes a larger responsibility in child rearing, the discontinuity between inner and outer spaces may diminish and the possibilities of community may be reestablished. These changes should increase the possibilities that prolonged adolescence will lead to commitment rather than alienation.

I draw hope, then, from the changing sex roles within the home and the movement toward technocracy outside the home. However, my hope is tempered on two counts. First, the resistance to changes in the sex roles makes me wonder how easily progress will come. Secondly, and somewhat ironically, I am worried by the speed of unsystematic change. Will social cohesion and personal identity be destroyed in the acceleration of change upon change, without planning or foresight?

## Identity and transience

Even if family change is secured in the expected direction, the movement toward technocracy may not prove as unambiguously humane as it is portrayed in the dreams of Marshall McLuhan and Charles Reich.[3] The speed of social change already has left "cultural lags" which threaten to rip apart the fabric of human society; unless the acceleration of change can be checked, we can predict ever-widening gaps between generations and an increase in age segregation as a cushion against "future shock."[4] Men can be trained to tolerate more change than they are presently prepared for, but there is a limit beyond which society disintegrates and individual identity becomes too fragmented to function.

One of the tasks which lies ahead for adolescent psychology is to study the relationship between the speed of cultural change and identity. We live in a period of history in which, within any individual's lifetime, very little remains constant. I know of no empirical data on the effects of accelerating cultural change upon individual stability. It is necessary to examine the concepts being used to determine whether they are based on outdated assumptions about continuity in life.

Traditionally, the concept of identity has been linked to the stability of an individual personality. Identity, in whatever historic context it occurred, has tended to emphasize the elements of constancy, the static elements, in a personality. In classical psychoanalytic theory the personality was thought of as more or less fixed for life once the oedipal strivings had emerged and been handled. Later psychoanalytic theorists (Ernst Jones, Peter Blos, and others) placed increasing emphasis on the adolescent period for the formation of identity.[5] They saw adolescence as ending when the various identity possibilities were consolidated into a stable personality.

Erik Erikson brought the identity issue into focus, labeling adolescence the period of the "crisis of identity."[6] The emphasis in psychoanalytic theory upon stability in defining healthy personality had been countered by numerous clinical theorists who stressed that the self is always in process.[7] Though Erikson continued to base his work on the psychoanalytic framework, he sought to get away from the principles of fixity in his concept of identity: "Identity is never 'established' as an 'achievement' in the form of a personality armor, or of anything static and unchangeable."[8] Nonetheless, Erikson seemed to equate identity diffusion with pathology. And he clearly viewed the identity issue as one which should be resolved; a firm identity was necessary before intimacy could be achieved. Though identity was not fixed for life, Erikson believed, the issue of identity formation belongs primarily to adolescence. Perhaps Erikson can be characterized as steering a middle road on the issue of stability in identity; certainly he was alert to the problem of defining identity without making it synonomous with a fixed, unchanging self.

## Open-ended commitments

My own position on the relationship of change and stability in modern identity is reflected in the discussions of criteria for mature identity in each of the content areas (Chapters 8–12). A review of these criteria may be clarifying.

## The crisis of the body

Adolescence brings change in the body. Establishment of mature identity involves the acceptance of a new adult body and a development of trust in that body. This may be facilitated by the fact that growth and change stabilize for a period. Yet the sudden changes which occur in adolescence, and the sexual awakening, are vivid experiences which may bring about the realization that change is inevitable. Thus the adolescent learns not only to accept his present body but to affirm change itself. Perhaps one of the most significant discoveries of adolescence is this awareness that "I change"; identity is not static.

## The crisis of sexuality

Since the beginning of adolescence is marked by the emergence of adult sexuality, traditionally the closure of adolescence has been described as the establishment of heterosexual commitment. It would seem more appropriate today to describe the adolescent quest as reaching fulfillment when the individual is able to affirm his individuality and yet "lose himself" in intimacy. Today's youth seem to be sensing, in the experimentation of new styles, that genuine caring is not an absorption in the other and does not deny one's separateness and individuality. Mature love is not a bond.

## The search for vocational identity

When a person can confidently enter into interaction with the environment, both with care and with competence, we can consider his vocational identity to be established. The resolution of the crisis of identity in the area of work is poorly defined in terms of some final choice of a particular job; our society is too fluid for that. Rather, vocational identity involves a realistic awareness of one's values and one's areas of competence, with an openness to be changed as well as to change. A mutual respect for self and environment and a commitment to interaction (rather than coercive domination) define the achievement motive appropriate to a humane society. Thus, maturity is reached not when some absolute and final choice is made, but when the individual knows himself well enough and has enough confidence to enter genuinely mutual interactions.

## The crisis in values

Among the most difficult of the identity issues is the attempt to establish one's own value system. Value decisions are not fully integrated as part of the identity until "there is a clear effort to define moral values . . . apart from . . . authority."[9] The fall of the gods and a confrontation with the relativity of values appears a necessary step. The humanizing of values, when it is actually achieved, involves uniting the feminine and masculine identifications. A deep subjectivity, identifying with the feelings of others, must be combined with the strength to make commitments. As a student phrased it, "Firm identity would imply acceptance of both expressive and goal-directed orientations; both are necessary for a true comprehension of what is valuable."[10]

### The quest for independence and the confrontation with authority[11]

Adolescents resolve the dependency issue as they begin to take responsibility for their lives with others. The distinction between authorities and peers begins to break down; youth stops expecting older people to be certain, to have answers for the future. This growth is aided, it seems to me, by the physical move away from home, which can help the adolescent break away from his dependence on the family and provide him with new models for identification and new possibilities for taking initiative in creating community. These new experiences introduce him to a wider world than he has known before.

Not all interactions in the wider world allow interpersonal exploration and understanding to develop. In the crisis of confrontation with impersonal authority, criteria cannot be centered wholly upon individual development. In my judgment, the issue will not be truly resolved until our society is changed. The most mature state of identity I can envision in our present society is not one which becomes resigned to impersonal authority but one which learns to cope with it.

In these criteria I have suggested not a final commitment and closing off of the process of growth but an affirmation of self in interaction with others. Functional identity formation does not require the same degree of personal closure (versus continued openness) in each of the content areas. Further, the process of change is not seen as unilateral; in the area of impersonal authority, social change, rather than passive adjustment, seems indicated. The style of identity suggested in these criteria involves continued growth; yet certain learnings do become established, and centeredness develops within a person.

## Modern man as Proteus

The most direct attack on the static view of identity has been made by Robert Lifton, who claims "that certain contemporary historical trends . . . have become sufficiently powerful and novel to create a new kind of man."[12] Lifton calls this modern form of identity "protean man," after Proteus in Greek mythology. A description of Lifton's position on the issue of change in identity provides an extreme point which is clarifying. In the Greek myth, Proteus

> . . . was able to change his shape with relative ease—from wild boar to lion to dragon to fire to flood. But what he did find difficult, and would not do unless seized and chained, was to commit himself to a single form, a form most his own, and carry out his function of prophecy. We can say the same of protean man, but we must keep in mind his possibilities as well as his difficulties.
>
> The protean style of self-process, then, is characterized by an interminable series of experiments and explorations—some shallow, some profound—each of which may be readily abandoned in favor of still new psychological quests. The pattern in many ways resembles what Erik Erikson has called "identity diffusion" or "identity confusion," and the impaired psychological functioning which those terms suggest can be very much present. But I would stress that protean style is by no means pathological as such, and in fact may well be one of the functional patterns of our day. It extends to all areas of human experience—to political as well as sexual behavior, to the holding and promulgating of ideas, and to the general organization of lives.[13]

Two cultural phenomena are invoked by Lifton to explain the emergence of protean man: "Historical dislocation, the break in the sense of connection which men have long felt with the vital and nourishing symbols of their cultural tradition" and the "flooding of imagery," the mass communication of pluralistic and "post-modern cultural influences."[14] Lifton believes the influence of historical normlessness is so profound that the individual personality must do without any permanent integration. We live in a world with no absolutes, no overarching integrative truths. Instead of one profound, soul-searching period of conflict and identity formation, one major ideological shift in a lifetime, the protean man may experience a number of such shifts. His change in ideological viewpoints is almost constant.[15]

By asserting that a protean lifestyle, somewhat like identity diffusion, is appropriate and functional in our day of fluidity and transience, Lifton alludes to "what is revolutionary in this modern man": precisely "his break with the idea of identity as we have known it."[16] Not only is modern man bereft of any physical home or any ideological certainty to which he can return, the protean man Lifton describes has no "home" in himself—indeed it is almost accurate to say he has no self, no identity. Lifton illustrates by quoting a gifted teacher:

> I have an extraordinary number of masks I can put on or take off. The question is: Is there, or should there be, one face which should

be authentic? I'm not sure that there is one for me. I can think of other parallels to this, especially in literature. There are representations of every kind of crime, every kind of sin. For me, there is not a single act I cannot imagine myself committing.[17]

We are reminded here of the deeper empathy which allows one to say with Adelphi Terence, "I am a man: nothing human is alien to me."[18] Such empathy depends upon a highly differentiated personality. But Lifton goes further than that:

Which is the real person, so far as an actor is concerned? Is he more real when performing on the stage—or when he is at home? I tend to think that for people who have these many, many masks, there is no home. Is it a futile gesture for the actor to try to find his real face?[19]

## Flexibility at what price?

Such a person, who simply assumes various masks with no sense of a self behind the masks, as in a disintegrated series of modules, is strikingly similar to the character disorder described in Robert Crichton's *The Great Impostor*.[20] This clever man was able to feign being a surgeon, a school teacher, even a priest; yet he experienced no inner conflict; he seemingly had no internalized self. His "identity" was whatever he pretended to be at that moment. It was as if he had no identity; he had only his acts, the roles he played. Some clinicians call such persons "as-if" personalities. I am led to ask whether the protean man who has no home also experiences no limits and feels no sense of integrity. Is he merely a sensor, a radar screen which is continually registering the environmental influences around him but has no private or autonomous responses? Is he the modern man whom Riesman has termed "other-directed man"?[21]

In his description of the protean man, Lifton is not simply stating that a loss of integration is occurring in some modern men; he seems also to be suggesting that this type of personality, this man without permanent identity, is the type that can function best in a modern society. Lifton forces us to ask not only whether identity, in the previous sense, is possible for modern man, but whether it is even desirable. We are thus engaged in the important process of defining the type of identity which is most valid for our time—a process which, of course, involves our own value judgments.

Throughout this book I have spoken of adolescence as the move into the world. The image of movement suggests both process and participation. The protean image, while appropriately emphasizing the fluidity of the self, may fail to emphasize the mutuality of the interaction between person and environment. The concept of identity still serves us well, I submit, if it conveys a level of active participation in the environment. The healthy person is not just "open"; he can risk sustained contact and active participation.

I have chosen an active image. Moving into the world is not simply being in the world. The youth who moves into the world makes a commitment; he intends to take a place in that world. Words fail here; phrases such as "one's place" and "one's stance" seem too static. What I wish to convey is that this committed youth does not simply submit to the world but *enters* it, taking up space in it. He intends to *participate* in what history brings, to involve himself with history, not just be carried along by it.

## Man and society

The issue of static versus fluid models of modern identity leads to a critical value concern which can be sharply stated in the question: Should society change to fit man? In Lifton's prototype of the protean man, the value of openness, a willingness to receive and be changed by new experiences, becomes preeminent. I share Lifton's concern that we describe personality in a manner appropriate for a fast-changing, transient society. I am concerned, however, that we not repeat the errors of early clinical psychology, which emphasized adjustment to society as the main criterion of mental health. Does the protean style amount to adjustment in the worst sense of the term? Is protean man totally formed by his environment, taking no responsibility for changing and shaping it? If so, in abandoning a concept of identity, Lifton has collapsed the dialectic between individual and society.

The two negative examples of modern men given above, the Great Impostor and the other-directed man, bring to the fore dimensions which may be overlooked when the discussion of identity pivots around the issue of stability and change. Though the Great Impostor was incredibly flexible, he lacked any depth of concern for others.

I would include the capacity to care as a central element in a definition of healthy identity. Identity and intimacy seem more closely interrelated than is generally recognized. A capacity to become deeply involved with others is crucial to personal growth. The Imposter, in his lack of interpersonal concern, was adapting only in the masculine sense. He succeeded, but he did not *care*.

In my judgment, identity cannot be defined apart from intimacy and involvement. The self is nothing if it is not in contact with the other. And the initial question, "Should man change to fit society, or society change to fit man?" is naive if it appears to define humanity in terms of the isolated individual. The point is that man exists in relation to others, and any description which places all the power either inside the individual or outside him in others destroys the mutuality of the relationship.

Stated another way, the illustration of the other-directed man signals the issue of locus of control.[22] I would define healthy identity as including not only the ability to grow and be changed by new experience, but also the possibility of acting upon the environment, to change it as well as be changed by it. Identity is an act, and the modern man is an actor—both in the sense of playing roles and in the sense of one who takes action, one who meets the environment and is not simply shaped by it. In this respect, the other-directed person has not integrated the instrumental role. He remains a passive receiver. By way of contrast, the committed youth takes a stand, and this action gives him an integrity which is alien to the impostor. He is open to possibilities, he is free to change, but he also has the capacity to make commitments and a centeredness from which to make them. He meets the "other," and in the meeting, both may be changed.

In certain respects, the Protean image is an appropriate one for modern identity. More than in previous times, contemporary man must keep the adolescent quest open. There is a real wisdom in the humorous assertion that "adolescence begins with puberty and ends with death." The identity of modern man must include, to quote Kenneth Keniston, a concept of

> . . . a lifetime of personal change, of an adulthood of continual self-transformation, or an adaptability and openness to the revolutionary modern world that will enable the individual to remain with it—psychologically youthful and on top of the present.[23]

However, the elements of centeredness and contact are overlooked in the Protean prototype. The courage to make deep, sustained contact with others and with society—to change the other and to be changed by the other and to truly involve oneself in life rather than withdrawing from it or floating through it—seems central to what I value as psychologically healthy.

Healthy 20th-century identity, I submit, involves constant change and intense involvement. Like Proteus, we cannot pledge to stay in the same form forever; commitments in that sense may be impossible for us. But we dare not shy away from particularity; the amorphous clinging to all possibilities (so typical of identity diffusion) results in attaining none. For what does it profit a man if he gain the whole world, but lose his own soul?[24] In contemporary terms, what does it profit a man to cling to every possibility but to actualize none?

## *Close contact with others, and fragmentation*

The effects of accelerated change and mobility upon identity have been discussed, in popular form, by Alvin Toffler. While Lifton speaks of modern identity as formless, Toffler describes it in terms of fragmentation. Toffler argues that accelerated change and mobility have already produced the "modular man." Human relations are increasingly characterized by "temporariness," for "just as things and places flow through our lives at a faster clip, so, too, do people." Accordingly, Toffler says:

> Rather than becoming deeply involved with the total personality of every individual we meet . . . we necessarily maintain superficial and partial contact with some. We are interested only in the effect of the shoe salesman in meeting our needs: we couldn't care less that his wife is an alcoholic.
>
> What this means is that we form limited involvement relationships with most people around us. Consciously or not, we define our relationships with most people in functional terms. So long as we do not become involved with the shoe salesman's problems at home, or his more general hopes, dreams and frustrations, he is, for us, fully interchangeable with any other salesman of equal competence. In effect, we have applied the modular principle to human relationships. Rather than entangling ourselves with the whole man, we plug into a module of his personality. . . .[25]

Toffler's concept of human modules raises some important issues for the description of modern identity. First, the concept is similar to the sociological concept of roles, and like the term "roles" there is a danger that the concept will be misunderstood to suggest a phony or superficial relationship. However, as Elizabeth Janeway notes: "In its origins, a role is not false, nor does it oppose or misrepresent the activity which it surrounds.[26] The criterion of authenticity is not whether or not a person "plays roles" but whether he assumes roles that fit him. A person may express himself in a role, and the role may help him to communicate publicly what he knows, privately, to be himself. A role "makes actions or situations or attitudes public and communal by tying them into a known and recognizable pattern of events and emotions. Consequently, like all means of communication, it must use terms that are common and recognizable to the public."[27]

The existence of many partial roles or "modules" within a personality does not, in itself, suggest a lack of integrity. It may, in fact, suggest a highly differentiated personality. Furthermore, a healthy personality may include some very diverse roles; totally opposite feelings and opinions may be experienced at different times. Each of these can be authentic in the particular context in which it occurs. I suspect that attempts to define health in terms of consistency or holism are inappropriate in our fluid time. Fragmentation needs to be distinguished from disintegration. One can accept a variety of "fragments" within oneself. Disintegration occurs when one portion of the self rejects another portion, and denial or dissociation emerges. The test of healthy identity, I submit, is not consistency but communication. The existence of many partial roles or modules within a personality need not be destructive if these different aspects of the self can speak to one another. A person can learn to accept and enjoy considerable variety within himself.[28]

The second issue has to do with intimacy. There is no need for every interaction to be an intimate one. The fact that at a particular time we relate only to one module of a person has its advantages. It frees any one person from the expectation that he should fill all our needs. Toffler notes that "To a certain point, fragmentation and freedom go together." At least fragmentation guarantees a degree of autonomy. On the other hand, Toffler says, "all of us seem to need some totalistic relationships in our lives."[29] The concern is that we may become so accustomed to partial relationships that we end up with *no* totalistic, intimate relationships.

To illustrate, will a person accustomed to fragmentary relationships strive to relate intimately to a spouse? Or will he not, instead, dispose of one spouse and seek a new one as he enters each new phase of his life and finds he has different needs? Not that breaking of marital ties is necessarily wrong, but might we not become so adapted to changing relationships that we forsake all encounters that might really affect our identities? Avoiding sustained contact and continuing relationships, we may never see beyond our own needs. Though in one sense we may satisfy ourselves, we may lose the capacity to care, to give, and to receive.

## Summary: Orestes and healthy identity

To summarize, it seems to me that identity cannot be usefully defined apart from intimacy and involvement with society. A healthy modern identity includes (1) the capacity to adapt to a fast-changing society. This demands (2) a high degree of personality differentiation; multiple roles may be experienced within the same person. Yet there is (3) a centeredness to the person; the various aspects of the personality are in communication with one another; each expression is authentic, without denying the others. Communication is not limited to the self; there is (4) an openness to others, a capacity to care and to sustain involvement, to affect others and to be affected by them. This contact with one's own and others' humanness leads to (5) active participation in the environment; a willingness to make contact that will change as well as be changed, to take some responsibility for the social structures which permit or hamper human development.

At the beginning of this book the myth of Oedipus was presented. Freud used this myth to express the adolescent conflict of his Victorian period. The myth of Proteus has been useful in this chapter to express the fluidity and adaptability of modern identity. Proteus represents for us an openness both to the changes occurring around us and to change in ourselves. However, the Proteus myth is onesided; it fails to express a strength which allows one to move into the world, to change it. I shall bring this book to a close by reminding the reader of still a third figure in Greek mythology, Orestes.[30]

Orestes is the heir in a long line of successors to the throne of the family of Atreus. For generation after generation they have been condemned to working out a cruel pattern of fate. But the story of Orestes is not the working out of blind fate but the tale of a man who made commitments. Orestes made a vow to the god Apollo to take up his adult responsibility as son and heir.[31] In his attempt to move toward adult responsibility, Orestes recognized that he had to break from his mother, who represented security, warmth, and authority. He chose to kill his mother, because she had "become corrupt and an evil bearer of all that she [was] supposed to represent."[32] Thus Orestes freed himself, physically, from the past generation. But still he was not free; he was haunted by fantasies and guilt. After much suffering, he returned confidently to Athens, to his people. He placed himself in judgment, refusing even his dependence upon Apollo, and took upon himself full responsibility for his actions. And thus the curse on the family of Atreus was lifted.

The story of Orestes can be contrasted to the Oedipal myth in several important ways. The struggle of Oedipus (and of earlier generations) was the struggle against the father, whom Oedipus inadvertently killed. Orestes, like today's youth, must struggle against mother. Unlike Oedipus, who remained in psychological bondage with mother and inadvertently entered an incestuous relationship with her, Orestes forcefully broke from mother. The break is expressed in the myth as the murder of the mother. (It conveys an active rejection of that which cripples and corrupts.) The Oedipus myth ends with the hero guilty, grief-stricken by the truth, and blinded. In fact, Oedipus had been blind throughout, for the myth is a tragedy of blind fate. Orestes, however, was not blind, but had a sense of direction. He performed his acts not out of fate but out of commitment and, finally, out of his own centeredness.[33]

Orestes serves as the mythical paradigm of healthy identity today.[34]

He is the prototype of the man who, despite the urge to return to the womb, has the strength to enter the world and live out his commitment. He lives through conflict, accepts responsibility, and returns to sensitive and active participation in life.

## Notes

1. This chapter is a review, in essay form. It is a personal synthesis, not a scientific analysis.

2. John Fantuzzo, student, Marietta College, Marietta Ohio, personal communication, December 1972.

3. Marshall McLuhan and Quentin Fiore, *The Medium is the Message* (New York: Random House, 1970); Charles Reich, *The Greening of America: The Coming of a New Consciousness and the Rebirth of a Future* (New York: Random House, 1970).

4. See Alvin Toffler, *Future Shock* (New York: Random House, 1970).

5. Ernest Jones, "Some Problems of Adolescence," in *Papers on Psychoanalysis* (Boston: Beacon Press, 1961); Peter Blos, *On Adolescence: A Psychoanalytic Interpretation* (New York: Free Press, 1962).

6. Erik H. Erikson, *Identity: Youth and Crisis* (New York: W. W. Norton & Company, 1968), pp. 15–19.

7. Carl R. Rogers, *Client Centered Therapy* (Boston: Houghton Mifflin Co., 1951).

8. Erikson, *Identity: Youth and Crisis*, p. 24.

9. Lawrence Kohlberg, "Development of Moral Character and Moral Ideology," in Martin L. Hoffman and Lois W. Hoffman, eds., *Review of Child Development Research* (New York: Russell Sage Foundation, 1964), vol. 1, pp. 383–432.

10. Brian Caterino, student, Marietta College, Marietta, Ohio, unpublished paper, 1972.

11. Issues from Chapters 7 and 12 have been combined here.

12. Robert Jay Lifton, *History and Human Survival* (New York: Random House, 1961), p. 312.

13. Ibid., pp. 318–19.

14. Ibid., p. 318.

15. Ibid., p. 324.

16. Ibid., p. 314.

17. Ibid., p. 319.

18. Adelphi Terence, *Self-Tormentor*, trans. Frank O. Copley (New York: Bobbs-Merrill Co., 1963).

19. Lifton, *History and Human Survival*, p. 320.

20. Robert Crichton, *The Great Impostor* (New York: Random House, 1959).

21. David Riesman, Reuel Denney, and Nathan Glazer, *The Lonely Crowd: A Study of the Changing American Character*, rev. ed. (New Haven, Conn.: Yale University Press, 1969).

22. Julian B. Rotter, "Generalized Expectancies for Internal Versus External Control of Reinforcement," *Psychological Monographs: General and Applied*, 80 (1966): 1–28.

23.  Kenneth Keniston, "You Have to Have Grown Up in Scarsdale to Know How Bad Things Really Are," *New York Times Magazine*, April 27, 1969, p. 27.

24.  Matthew 16:26, Mark 8:36; Luke 9:25.

25.  Toffler, *Future Shock*, pp. 96–97.

26.  Elizabeth Janeway, *Man's World, Woman's Place: A Study in Social Mythology* (New York: William Morrow & Co., 1971), chap. 19.

27.  Ibid., p. 79.

28.  There is, of course, a limit to the number of roles a person can handle at one time without feeling out of touch with himself. But this is more a question of levels of tolerance and limits of communication within the self than an issue of internal consistency.

29.  Toffler, *Future Shock*, p. 99.

30.  See William Hamilton, "The Death of God Theologies Today," in *Radical Theology and the Death of God*, ed. Thomas J. Altizer and William Hamilton (New York: Bobbs-Merrill Co., 1966). I am indebted to Hamilton, my former teacher, for much of this summary.

31.  Edith Hamilton, *Mythology* (Boston: Little, Brown & Co., 1942), p. 357.

32.  William Hamilton, "The Death of God Theologies Today," p. 43.

33.  Ibid.

34.  Herbert Fingaretta, "Orestes: Paradigm Hero and Central Motif of Contemporary Ego Psychology," *Psychoanalytic Review*, 50(1963):87–111. Though the Orestean myth approximates the view of committed youth presented in Chapters 13 and 15, it is weak as a myth in that it fails to provide a clear value orientation.

# Conclusions to part three

*The search for identity is best pursued through active involvement with others. Three styles of identity process have been compared: the foreclosure of the identity process, prolonged identity leading to alienation, and prolonged identity leading to commitment. Social and developmental factors influencing each of these types have been examined.*

*The first part of this book focused upon the childhood years and the development of sex roles. In Part three consideration of the generational cycle was completed with an examination of the kinds of marriage and child-rearing patterns that are emerging today and the effects they are likely to have on the identity process in tomorrow's adolescents. Modern identity cannot be defined primarily in terms of stability. Yet survival in a fast-changing, pluralistic world demands not only that man adapt to change but that he be able to direct change out of his own human values.*

# Bibliography

## Part one: Preparations for conflict

Andry, R. G. "Faulty Paternal and Maternal Child Relationships, *British Journal of Delinquency,* 97 (1960): 329–40.

Annastasi, Anne. *Individual Differences.* New York: John Wiley & Sons, 1965.

Armentrout, James A., and Burger, Gary K. "Children's Reports of Parental Child-Rearing Behavior at Five Grade Levels." *Developmental Psychology,* 7 (1972): 44–48.

Bach, G. R. "Father-Fantasies and Father-Typing in Father-Separated Children." *Child Development,* 17 (1946): 63–80.

Bandura, Albert. "Influence of Model's Reinforcement Contingencies on the Acquisition of Imitative Responses." *Journal of Personality and Social Psychology,* 1 (1965): 589–95.

Bandura, Albert. "Relationships of Family Patterns to Child Behavior Disorders." Progress report, U.S. Public Health Service Research Grant M-1734, Stanford University, 1960.

Bandura, Albert, and Huston, A. C. "Identification as a Process of Incidental Learning." *Journal of Abnormal Sociology and Psychology,* 63 (1961): 311–18.

Bandura, Albert, and Walters, R. H. *Social Learning and Personality Development.* New York: Holt, Rinehart & Winston, 1963.

Becker, Wesley C. "Consequences of Different Kinds of Parental Discipline." In *Review of Child Development Research,* edited by Martin L. Hoffman and Lois W. Hoffman, vol. 1, New York: Russell Sage Foundation, 1964.

Bennett, E. M., and Cohen, L. R. "Men and Women: Personality Patterns and Contrasts." *Genetic Psychology Monographs,* 60 (1959): 101–53.

Berger, E. Manuel. "The Relation between Expressed Acceptance of Self and Expressed Acceptance of Others." *Journal of Abnormal Psychology,* 47 (1952): 778–82.

Bergman, P., and Escalona, S. "Unusual Sensitivities in Very Young Children." In *Psychoanalytic Study of the Child,* vols. 3–4. New York: International Universities Press, 1949.

Berry, J. L., and Martin, B. "GSR Reactivity as a Function of Anxiety, Instructions and Sex." *Journal of Abnormal and Social Psychology,* 54 (1957): 9–12.

Bieri, James. "Parental Identification, Acceptance of Authority, and Within-Sex Differences in

Cognitive Behavior." *Journal of Abnormal and Social Psychology*, 60 (1960): 69–79.

Bieri, James, and Lobeck, Robin. "Acceptance of Authority and Parental Identification." *Journal of Personality*, 27 (1959): 76–79.

Bowlby, J. *Maternal Care and Mental Health.* Geneva: World Health Organization, 1951.

Brown, D. G. "The Development of Sex-Role Inversion and Homosexuality." *American Journal of Orthopsychiatry*, 50 (1957): 613–19.

Brown, D. G. "Sex-Role Development in a Changing Culture." *Psychological Bulletin*, 55 (1958): 232–42.

Burton, Roger V. "Cross-Sex Identity in Barbados." *Developmental Psychology*, 6 (1972): 365–74.

Chinn, W. L. "A Brief Survey of Nearly 1000 Delinquents." *British Journal of Educational Psychology*, 8 (1938): 78–85.

Clautour, Sibylla E., and Moore, T. W. "Attitudes of Twelve-Year-Old Children to Present and Future Life Roles." *Human Development*, 12 (1969): 221–38.

Colley, Thomas. "The Nature and Origins of Psychological Sexual Identity." *Psychological Review*, 66 (1959): 165–77.

DeLucia, Lenore A. "Some Determinants of Sex-Role Identification in Young Children." Master's thesis, Brown University, 1961.

Devore, I., and Jay, Phyllis. "Mother-Infant Relations in Baboons and Langurs." In *Ma-ternal Behavior in Mammals*, edited by Harriet L. Rheingold. New York: John Wiley & Sons, 1963.

Dornbusch, Sanford M. "After-word." In *The Development of Sex Differences*, edited by Eleanor E. Maccoby. Stanford, Calif.: Stanford University Press, 1966.

Elkin H. "Aggressive and Erotic Tendencies in Army Life." *American Journal of Sociology*, 51 (1946): 408–13.

Emmerich, W. "Young Children's Discriminations of Parent and Child Roles." *Child Development*, 30 (1959): 403–19.

Epstein, R., and Leverant, S. "Verbal Conditioning and Sex-Role Identification in Children." *Child Development*, 34 (1963): 99–106.

Erikson, Erik H. *Identity: Youth and Crisis.* New York: W. W. Norton, 1968.

Faris, R. E. L. *Social Psychology.* New York: Ronald Press Co., 1952.

Ford, Clellan S., and Beach, Frank A. *Patterns of Sexual Behavior.* New York: Harper & Row, Publishers, 1951.

Garai, Josef E., and Scheinfeld, Amram. "Sex Differences in Mental and Behavioral Traits." *Genetic Psychology Monographs*, 77 (1968): 169–299.

Gardner, L. P. "Analysis of Children's Attitudes to Fathers." *Journal of Genetic Psychology*, 70 (1947): 3–38.

Gardner, L. P. "A Survey of the Attitudes and Activities of Fathers." *Journal of Genetic Psychology*, 63 (1943): 15–53.

Gesell, Arnold. *The First Five Years of Life: A Guide to the Study of the Preschool Child.* New York: Harper Bros., 1940.

Gold, Alice R., and St. Ange, M. Carol. "Development of Sex Role Stereotypes in Black and White Elementary School Girls," *Developmental Psychology,* 10 (1974): 461.

Goodenough, F. L *Anger in Young Children.* Institute of Child Welfare Monograph Ser. 9. Minneapolis: University of Minnesota Press, 1931.

Gray, Susan W. "Masculinity and Femininity in Relation to Anxiety and Social Acceptance." *Child Development,* 28 (1957): 203–14.

Gray, Susan W., and Klaus, Rupert. "The Assessment of Parental Identification." *Genetic Psychology Monographs,* 54 (1956): 87–114.

Grayson, Henry T. "Psychosexual Conflict in Adolescent Girls Who Experience Early Parental Loss by Death." Ph.D. dissertation, Boston University, 1967. *Dissertation Abstracts* No. 67-13, 327.

Gronsetti, E. "The Impact of Father-Absence in Sailor Families upon the Personality Structure and Social Adjustment of Adult Sailor Sons," Part I. In *Studies of the Family,* edited by N. Anderson. Gottingen, Norway: Vanderhoeck and Ruprecht, 1957.

Hamburg, D. A., and Lunde, D. T. "Sex Hormones in the Development of Sex Differences in Human Behavior." In *The Development of Sex Differences,* edited by Eleanor E. Maccoby. Stanford, Calif.: Stanford University Press, 1966.

Harlow, Harry F. "The Nature of Love." *American Psychologist,* 13 (1958): 673–85.

Harlow, Harry, and Zimmerman, R. R. "Affectional Responses in the Infant Monkey." *Science,* 130 (1959): 431–32.

Harrington, Charles C. *Errors in Sex-Role Behavior in Teen-Age Boys.* New York: Teachers College Press, 1970.

Hartley, Ruth E. "Sex-Role Pressure and the Socialization of the Male Child." *Psychological Reports,* 5 (1959): 457–68.

Hartley, R. E.; Frank, L. K.; and Goldenson, R. M. *Understanding Children's Play.* New York: Columbia University Press, 1952.

Hartley, R. E., and Hardesty, F. "Children's Perception and Expression of Sex Preferences." *Child Development,* 33 (1962): 221–27.

Hebb, D. O. "Behavioral Differences between Male and Female Chimpanzees." *Bulletin of the Canadian Psychological Association,* 6 (1946): 56–68.

Heilbrun, Alfred B. "An Empirical Test of the Modeling Theory of Sex-Role Learning." *Child Development,* 36 (1965): 789–99.

Hetheringon, E. Mavis. "The Effects of Father Absence on Personality Development in Adolescent Daughters." *Developmental Psychology,* 7 (1972): 313–26.

Hetherington, E. Mavis. "Girls without Fathers." *Psychology*

*Today,* February 1973, pp. 46–52.

Hilgard, Ernest, and Atkinson, Richard C. *Introduction to Psychology.* 4th ed. New York: Harcourt, Brace & World, 1967.

Hoffman, L. L. "Father Absence and Conscience Development." *Developmental Psychology,* 4 (1971): 400–406.

Hoffman, Martin L., and Hoffman, Lois W., eds. *Review of Child Development Research,* vol. 1. New York: Russell Sage Foundation, 1964.

Holman, Portia. "The Etiology of Maladjustment in Children." *Journal of Mental Science,* 99 (1959): 654–88.

Jackson, P. W. "Verbal Solutions to Parent-Child Problems." *Child Development,* 27 (1956): 339–51.

Janeway, Elizabeth. *Man's World, Woman's Place: A Study in Social Mythology.* New York: William Morrow & Co., 1971.

Johnson, M. M. "Sex Role Learning in the Nuclear Family." *Child Development,* 34 (1963): 320–32.

Josselyn, Irene M. "Cultural Forces, Motherliness and Fatherliness," *American Journal of Orthopsychiatry,* 26 (1956): 264–71.

Kagan, Jerome. "Acquisition and Significance of Sex Typing and Sex Role Identity." In *Review of Child Development Research,* edited by Martin L. Hoffman and Lois W. Hoffman, vol. 1. New York: Russell Sage Foundation, 1964.

Kagan, Jerome. "The Child's Perception of the Parent." *Journal*

*of Abnormal and Social Psychology,* 53 (1956): 257–58.

Kagan, Jerome. *Understanding Children: Behavior, Motives, Thoughts.* New York: Harcourt Brace Jovanovich, 1971.

Kagan, Jerome; Hosken, B.; and Watson, S. "Child's Symbolic Conceptualization of Parents." *Child Development,* 32 (1961): 625–36.

Kagan, Jerome, and Lemkin, Judith. "The Child's Differential Perception of Parental Attributes." *Journal of Abnormal and Social Psychology,* 61 (1960): 446–47.

Kagan, Jerome, and Moss, H. A. "The Stability of Passive and Dependent Behavior from Childhood through Adulthood." *Child Development,* 31 (1960): 577–91.

Kagan, Jerome; Moss, H. A.; and Sigel, I. E. "The Psychological Significance of Styles of Conceptualization." *Monographs of the Society for Research in Child Development,* 28 (1963): 73–111.

Klausmeier, J. H., and Wiersma, William. "Relationship of Sex, Grade Level, and Locale to Performance of High I.Q. Students on Divergent Thinking Tests." *Journal of Educational Psychology,* 55 (1964): 114–19.

Kohlberg, Lawrence. "A Cognitive-Developmental Analysis of Children's Sex-Role Concepts and Attitudes." In *The Development of Sex Differences,* edited by Eleanor E. Maccoby. Stanford, Calif.: Stanford University Press, 1966.

Kohlberg, Lawrence. "Moral Development and Identification." In *Child Psychology: Sixty-second Yearbook of the National Society for the Study of Education*, edited by H. W. Stevenson. Chicago: Univeristy of Chicago Press, 1963.

Lasowick, Lionel W. "On the Nature of Identification." *Journal of Abnormal and Social Psychology*, 51 (1955): 175–83.

Leifer, Aimee Dorr. "The Relationship between Cognitive Awareness in Selected Areas and Differential Imitation of a Same-Sex Model." Master's thesis, Stanford University, 1966.

Levinger, George. "Task and Social Behavior in Marriage." *Sociometry*, 27 (1964): 443–48.

Lindskoog, D. "Children's Differentiation of Instrumental and Expressive Parent Roles." Master's thesis, University of Chicago, 1964.

Lynn, D. B. "Divergent Feedback and Sex-Role Identification in Boys and Men." *Merrill-Palmer Quarterly*, 10 (1964): 17–23.

Lynn, D. B. "The Process of Learning Parental and Sex-Role Identification." *Journal of Marriage and the Family*, 18 (1966): 466–70.

Lynn, D. B. "Sex Differences in Identification Development." *Sociometry*, 24 (1961): 372–84.

Maccoby, Eleanor E. "Sex Differences in Intellectual Functioning." In *The Development of Sex Differences*, edited by Eleanore E. Maccoby. Stanford, Calif.: Stanford University Press, 1966.

Maccoby, Eleanore E., ed. *The Development of Sex Differences*. Stanford, Calif.: Stanford University Press, 1966.

Maccoby, Eleanor; Dowley, Edith M.; Degerman, J. W., and Degerman, R. "Activity Level and Intellectual Functioning in Normal Preschool Children." *Child Development*, 36 (1965): 761–70.

Malinowski, Bronislaw, *Argonauts of the Western Pacific*. New York: E. P. Dutton & Co., 1961; originally published, 1922.

May, Rollo. *Existence*. New York: Basic Books, 1958.

McCandless, Boyd R.; Bilous, C. B.; and Bennett, H. D. "Peer Popularity and Dependence on Adults in Pre-school Age Socialization." *Child Development*, 32 (1961): 511–18.

Mead, Margaret. *Sex and Temperament in Three Primitive Societies*. New York: William Morrow, 1935.

Medinnus, Gene R., and Johnson, Ronald C. *Child and Adolescent Psychology: Behavior and Development*. New York: John Wiley & Sons, 1969.

Meili, R. "A Longitudinal Study of Personality Development." In *Dynamic Pschopathology of Childhood*, edited by L. Jessner and E. Pavenstedt. New York: Grune & Stratton, 1959.

Miller, Walter B. "Lower Class Culture as a Generating Milieu of Gang Delinquency." *Journal of Social Issues*, 143 (1958).

Millon, Theodore. *Modern Psychopathology*. Philadelphia: W. B. Saunders & Co., 1969.

Minuchin, Patricia. "Children's Sex-Role Concepts as a Function of School and Home Environments." Paper presented at the American Orthopsychiatric Association Meeting, March 1964.

Mischel, Walter. "A Social-Learning View of Sex Differences in Behavior." In *The Development of Sex Differences,* edited by Eleanor E. Maccoby. Stanford, Calif.: Stanford University Press, 1966.

Mogey, J. M. "A Century of Declining Paternal Authority." *Marriage and Family Living,* 1957, p. 238.

Money, J.; Hampson, Joan G.; and Hampson, J. L. "Imprinting and the Establishment of Gender Role." *Archives of Neurology and Psychiatry,* 77 (1957): 333–36.

Murdock, G. P. "Comparative Data on the Division of Labor by Sex." *Social Forces,* 15 (1937): 551–53.

Mussen, P. H. "Some Antecedents and Consequences of Masculine Sex-Typing in Adolescent Boys." *Psychological Monographs* No. 2, 75 (1961).

Mussen, P. H., and Distler, L. M. "Child-Rearing Antecedents of Masculine Identification in Kindergarten Boys." *Child Development,* 31 (1960): 89–100.

Nadelman, Lorraine. "Sex Identity in American Children: Memory, Knowledge, and Preference Tests." *Developmental Psychology,* 10 (1974): 413–17.

Nash, John. "The Father in Contemporary Culture and Current Psychological Literature." *Child Development,* 36 (1965): 261–97.

Nawas, M. M. "Changes in Efficiency of Ego Functioning and Complexity from Adolescence to Young Adulthood." *Developmental Psychology,* 4 (1971): 412–15.

Oetzel, Roberta M. "Annotated Bibliography." In *The Development of Sex Differences,* edited by Eleanor E. Maccoby. Stanford, Calif.: Stanford University Press, 1966.

Omwake, K. "The Relation between Acceptance of Self and Acceptance of Others Shown by Three Personality Inventories." *Journal of Consulting Psychology,* 18 (1954): 443.

Pace, Robert C. "College Environments." In *Encyclopedia of Educational Research.* Toronto: Macmillan Publishing Co., 1969.

Parsons, Talcott. *Social Structure and Personality.* London: Free Press, 1964.

Plank, Emma H., and Plank, R. "Emotional Components in Arithmetic Learning as Seen through Autobiographies." In *The Psychoanalytic Study of the Child,* edited by R. S. Eissler et al., vol. 9, New York: International Universities Press, 1954.

Pomeroy, Wardell B. *Boys and Sex.* New York: Delacorte Press, 1968.

Rainwater, Lee. "Crucible of Identity: The Negro Lower-Class Family." *Daedalus,* 95 (1966): 1.

Rogers, Dorothy. *Issues in Adolescent Psychology.* 2d ed. New

York: Appleton-Century-Crofts, 1972.

Rosenberg, B. G., and Sutton-Smith, Brian. *Sex and Identity.* New York: Holt, Rinehart & Winston, 1972.

Rosenkrantz, Paul; Bee, Helen; Vogel, Susan; Broverman, Inge; and Broverman, Donald. "Sex-Role Stereotypes and Self-Concepts in College Students." *Journal of Counseling and Clinical Psychology,* 32 (1968): 287–95.

Rossi, Alice. "Transition to Parenthood." *Journal of Marriage and Family,* 30 (1968): 26–39.

Rubenstein, B. O., and Levitt, "Some Observations Regarding the Role of Fathers in Child Psychotherapy." *Bulletin of the Menninger Clinic,* 21 (1957): 16–27.

Rudy, Arthur J. "Sex-Role Perceptions in Early Adolescence." *Adolescence,* 3 (1968): 453–70.

Sears, Pauline. "Child Rearing Factors Related to the Playing of Sex-Typed Roles." *American Psychologist,* 8 (1953): 431.

Sears, Pauline S. "Doll Play Aggression in Normal Young Children: Influence of Sex, Age. Sibling Status, Father's Absence." *Psychological Monographs* No. 6, 65 (1951).

Sebald, Hans. "Parent-Peer Control and Masculine-Marital Role Perceptions of Adolescent Boys." *Social Science Quarterly,* 49 (1968): 229–36.

Seigman, A. W. "Father Absence during Early Childhood and Antisocial Behavior." *Journal of Abnormal Psychology,* 71 (1966): 71–74.

Sexton, Patricia. *The Feminized Male: Classrooms, White Collars, and the Decline of Manliness.* New York: Vintage Press, 1969.

Sheerer, E. "An Analysis of the Relationship between Acceptance of and Respect for Self and Acceptance and Respect for Others in Ten Counseling Cases." *Journal of Consulting Psychology,* 13 (1949): 169.

Sheriffs, A. C., and McKee, J. P. "Quantitative Aspects of Beliefs about Men and Women." *Journal of Consulting Psychology,* 13 (1957): 169.

Skolnick, Arlene. "Stability and Interrelations of Thematic Test Imagery over Twenty Years." *Child Development,* 37 (1966): 389–96.

Smith, Charles E. "The Effect of Father-Absence in the Development of Sex-Role Attitudes in Boys." Ph.D. dissertation, University of Chicago, 1969.

Smith, S. "Age and Sex Differences in Children's Opinions Concerning Sex Differences." *Journal of Genetic Psychology,* 54 (1939): 17–25.

Sontag, L. W. "Physiological Factors and Personality in Children." *Child Development* 18 (1947): 185–89.

Souerwine, Andrew H. "Relationships between Parents and Sons in Authoritarianism." *Dissertation Abstracts,* 15 (1955): 157.

Stephens, W. N. "Judgments by Social Workers of Boys and Mothers in Fatherless Families." *Journal of Genetic Psychology,* 99 (1961): 53–64.

Stevenson, H. W. "Social Reinforcement of Children's Behavior." In *Advances in Child Development*, edited by C. C. Spiker, and Lipsitt, L. P. New York: Academic Press, 1965, vol. 2.

Stolz, Lois M., et al. *Father Relations of War-Born Children.* Stanford, Calif.: Stanford University Press, 1954.

Walter, G. "Electroencephalographic Development of Children." in *Discussions on Child Development*, edited by J. M. Tanner and Barbel Inhelder. New York: International Universities Press, 1953.

Warren, W. "Conduct Disorders in Children." *British Journal of Delinquency*, 1 (1957): 164.

Whiting, J. W.; Kluckhohn, R.; and Anthony, A. "The Function of Male Initiation Ceremonies at Puberty." In *Readings in Social*

*Psychology,* edited by Eleanore Maccoby, T. M. Newcomb, and E. L. Hartley. New York: Holt, Rinehart & Winston, 1958.

Wylie, Ruth. *The Self Concept.* Lincoln: University of Nebraska Press, 1961.

Winch, Robert "Some Data Bearing on the Oedipal Hypothesis." *Journal of Abnormal and Social Psychology*, 45 (1950): 481–89.

Yarrow, Leon J. "Separation from Parents during Early Childhood." In *Review of Child Development Research*, edited by Martin L. Hoffman and Lois Hoffman, vol. 1. New York: Russell Sage Foundation, 1964.

Yerkes, R. M., and Elder, J. H. "Oestrus, Receptivity, and Mating in the Chimpanzee." *Comparative Psychological Monographs*, 13 (1936): 1–39.

## Part two: *Where the battle is waged*

Adorno, T. W.; Frenkel-Brunswik, Else; Levinson, D. J., and Sanford, R. Nevitt. *The Authoritarian Personality.* New York: Harper & Row, Publishers, 1950.

Angelio, H., and Mech, E. V. "Fears and Worries Concerning Physical Changes: A Preliminary Survey of 32 Females. *Journal of Psychology*, 39 (1955): 195–98.

Angrist, Shirley S. "Role Constellation as a Variable in Women's Leisure Activities." *Social Forces*, 45 (1967): 423–31.

Angrist, Shirley S. "The Study of

Sex Roles." *Journal of Social Issues*, 25 (1969): 215–32.

Astin, Alexander W., and Nichols, Robert C. "Life Goals and Vocational Choice." *Journal of Applied Psychology*, 48 (1964): 50–58.

Bandura, Albert. "The Stormy Decade: Fact or Fiction?" *Psychology in the School*, 1 (1964): 224–31.

Bandura, Albert, and Walters, Richard H. *Adolescent Aggression.* New York: Ronald Press Co., 1959.

Bayley, Nancy. "Some Psychological Correlates of Somatic Androgyny." *Child Development,* 22 (1959): 47–60.

Bealer, R. C.; Willits, F. K.; and Maida, P. R. "The Rebellious Youth Subculture—A Myth," *Children,* 11 (1964): 43–48.

Becker, Wesley C. "Consequences of Different Kinds of Parental Discipline." In *Review of Child Development Research,* edited by Martin L. Hoffman and Lois W. Hoffman, vol. 1. New York: Russell Sage Foundation, 1964.

Bell, Robert R. "Parent-Child Conflict in Sexual Values." *Journal of Social Issues,* 22 (1966): 34–44.

Bell, Robert R., and Chaskes, J. B. "Premarital Sexual Experience among Coeds, 1958 and 1968." *Journal of Marriage and the Family,* 32 (1970): 81–84.

Bernard, Harold W. *Adolescent Development.* Scranton, Pa.: Intext Educational Publishers, 1971.

Bernard, Jessie, ed. *Teen-age Culture.* Philadelphia: American Academy of Political and Social Sciences, 1961.

Birnbaum, Morton P. "Anxiety and Moral Judgement in Early Adolescence." *Journal of Genetic Psychology,* 120 (1972): 13–26.

Blos, Peter. *On Adolescence: A Psychoanalytic Interpretation.* New York: Free Press, 1962.

Blos, Peter. "The Second Individuation Process of Adolescence." *Psychoanalytic Study of the Child,* 22 (1967): 162–87.

Borow, Henry. "Development of Occupational Motives and Roles." In *Review of Child Development Research,* vol. 2,

edited by Lois W. Hoffman and Martin L. Hoffman. New York: Russell Sage Foundation, 1966.

Borup, J. H., and Elliot, W. F. "College Students' Attitudes toward Laws, Courts and Enforcers." *College Student Survey,* 4 (1970): 24–27.

Bowerman, Charles E., and Kinch, John W. "Changes in Family and Peer Orientations of Children between the Fourth and Tenth Grades." *Social Forces,* 37 (1959): 206–11.

Brittain, Clay V. "Adolescent Choices and Parent-Peer Cross-Pressures." *American Sociological Review,* 28 (1963): 385–91.

Broderick, Carlfred B. "Going Steady: The Beginning of the End." In *Teen-Age Marriage and Divorce,* edited by Seymour Farber and R. H. L. Wilson. San Francisco: Diablo Press, 1967.

Broderick, Carlfred B., and Flower, Stanley E. "New Patterns of Relationships between the Sexes among Preadolescents." *Marriage and Family Living,* 23 (1961): 27–30.

Brodsky, C. M. *A Study of Norms for Body Form Behavior Relationships.* Washington: Catholic University of America Press, 1954.

Bronfenbrenner, Urie. "Toward a Theoretical Model for the Analysis of Parent-Child Relationships in a Social Context." In *Parental Attitudes and Child Behavior,* edited by J. C. Glidewell. Springfield, Ill.: Charles C Thomas, 1961.

Bullen, B. A.; Monello, L. F.; Cohen, H.; and Mayer, Jean.

"Attitudes toward Physical Activity, Food, and Family in Obese and Nonobese Adolescent Girls." *American Journal of Clinical Nutrition,* 12 (1963): 1–11.

Burchinal, Lee G. "Adolescent Dating, Attitudes, and Behavior." In H. T. Christensen, ed., *Handbook of Marriage and the Family.* Chicago: Rand McNally, 1964.

Burchinal, Lee G. "Trends and Prospects for Young Marriages in the United States." *Journal of Marriage and the Family,* 27 (1965): 243–54.

Burchinal, L. G.; Haller, A. O., and Taves, M. *Career Choices of Rural Youth in a Changing Society.* Bulletin no. 458, Agricultural Experimentation Station, University of Minnesota. Rosemount, 1962.

Burwen, LeRoy S., and Campbell, Donald T. "The Generality of Attitudes toward Authority and Non-authority Figures." *Journal of Abnormal and Social Psychology,* 54 (1957): 24–31.

Calden, G.; Lundy, R. M., and Schlafer, R. J. "Sex Differences in Body Concepts." *Journal of Consulting Psychology,* 23 (1959): 378.

"Campus '65." *Newsweek,* March 22, 1965, pp. 43–54.

Caplan, H. "Some Considerations of the Body-Image Concept in Child Development," *Quarterly Journal of Child Behavior,* 4 (1952): 382.

Carter, H. D. "The Development of Vocational Attitudes." *Journal of Counseling Psychology,* 4 (1940): 185–91.

Cavior, Norman, and Dokecki, Paul R. "Physical Attractiveness, Perceived Attitude Similarity, and Academic Achievement as Contributors to Interpersonal Attraction among Adolescents." *Developmental Psychology,* 9, 1973: 44–54.

Christensen, H. T. "Scandinavian and American Sex Norms: Some Comparisons with Sociological Implications," *Journal of Social Issues,* 22 (1966): 60–75.

Christie, Richard, and Jahoda, Marie, eds. *Studies in the Scope and Method of "The Authoritarian Personality."* New York: Free Press, 1954.

Cobb, H. V. "Role-Wishes and General Wishes of Children and Adolescents." *Child Development,* 25 (1954): 161–71.

Coleman, James S. *The Adolescent Society: The Social Life of the Teenager and Its Impact on Education.* New York: Free Press, 1961.

Connor, R.; Johannes, T.; and Walters, J. "Parent-Adolescent Relationships: I. Parent-Adolescent Conflicts." *Journal of Home Economics,* 46 (1964): 183–86.

Constantinople, Anne. "An Eriksonian Measure of Personality Development in College Students." *Developmental Psychology,* 1 (1969): 357–72.

Dansereau, H. Kirk. "Work and the Teenager." In *Annals of the American Academy of Political and Social Science,* vol. 338, November 1961.

Davis, Kingsley. "The Sociology of Parent-Youth Conflict." *Ameri-*

can Sociological Review, 5 (1940): 523–35.

Dolger, L., and Ginandes, J. "Children's Attitudes toward Discipline as Related to Socio-economic Status." *Journal of Experimental Education*, 15 (1946): 161–65.

Douvan, Elizabeth. "Sex Differences in Adolescent Character Processes." *Merrill-Palmer Quarterly*, 6 (1960): 203–11.

Douvan, Elizabeth, and Adelson, Joseph. *The Adolescent Experience.* New York: John Wiley & Sons, 1966.

Dubbe, M. C. "What Teen-Agers Can't Tell Parents and Why," *Family Coordinator*, 4 (1956): 3–7.

Duncan, O. D., and Hodge, R. W. "Education and Occupational Mobility: A Regression Analysis." *American Journal of Sociology*, 68 (1963): 629–44.

Dunphy, Dexter C. "The Social Structure of Urban Adolescent Peer Groups." *Sociometry*, 26 (1963): 230–46.

Dwyer, Johanna T.; Feldman, J. J.; and Mayer, Jean. "Adolescent Dieters: Who Are They? Physical Characteristics, Attitudes, and Dieting Practices of Adolescent Girls." *American Journal of Clinical Nutrition*, 20 (1967): 1045–56.

Dwyer, Johanna, and Mayer, Jean. "Psychological Effects of Variations in Physical Appearance during Adolescence." *Adolescence*, 3 (1968–69): 353–80.

Ehrmann, Winston W. *Premarital Dating Behavior.* New York: Holt, Rinehart & Winston, 1959.

Eisenman, Russell. "Values and Attitudes in Adolescence." In *Understanding Adolescence,* edited by James F. Adams. Boston: Allyn & Bacon, 1968.

Elder, Glen H., Jr. "Democratic Parent-Youth Relations in Cross-National Perspective." *Social Science Quarterly,* 49 (1968): 216–28.

Elder, Glen H., Jr. "Parental Power Legitimation and Its Effect on the Adolescent." *Sociometry,* 26 (1963): 50–65.

Elkin, Frederick, and Westley, William A. "The Myth of Adolescent Culture." *American Sociological Review,* 20 (1955): 680–84.

Elkind, David. *Children and Adolescents.* New York: Oxford University Press, 1970.

Epperson, D. C. "A Reassessment of Indices of Parental Influence in the Adolescent Society." *American Sociological Review,* 29 (1964): 93–96.

Erikson, Erik. *Identity and the Life Cycle.* New York: International Universities Press, 1959.

Erikson, Erik H. *Identity: Youth and Crisis.* New York: W. W. Norton & Co., 1966.

Espenschade, A. "Motor Performance in Adolescence." *Monographs of the Society for Research in Child Development,* 5 (1940): no. 1.

Farnsworth, Dana L. "Sexual Morality and the Dilemma of the Colleges." *American Journal of Orthopsychiatry,* 35 (1965).

Faust, Margaret Siler. "Developmental Maturity as a Determinant in Prestige of Adolescent

Girls." *Child Development,* 31 (1960): 173–84.

Ford, Clellan S., and Beach, Frank A. *Patterns of Sexual Behavior.* New York: Harper & Row, Publishers, 1951.

Frantz, Thomas T. "Student and Non-student Change." *Journal of College Student Personnel,* January 1971, pp. 49–53.

Frazier, Alexander, and Lisonbee, Lorenzo K. "Adolescent Concerns with Physique." In *Adolescent Behavior and Society: A Book of Readings,"* edited by Rolf E. Muuss. New York: Random House, 1971.

Freedman, Mervin B. "The Sexual Behavior of American College Women: An Empirical Study and an Historical Survey." *Merrill-Palmer Quarterly of Behavior and Development,* 11 (1965): 33–39.

Freud, Anna. "Adolescence." *Psychoanalytic Study of the Child,* 15 (1960): 98.

Freud, Anna. *The Ego and the Mechanisms of Defense.* New York: International Universities Press, 1946.

Garai, Josef E., and Scheinfeld, Amram. "Sex Differences in Mental and Behavioral Traits." *Genetic Psychology Monographs,* 77 (1968): 169–299.

Ginzberg, Eli. *Occupational Choice.* New York: Columbia University Press, 1951.

Gold, Martin, and Douvan, Elizabeths, eds. *Adolescent Development: Readings in Research and Theory.* Boston: Allyn & Bacon, 1969.

Goodman, Paul. *Growing up Absurd.* New York: Random House, 1956.

Greenbank, R. K. "Are Medical Students Learning Psychiatry?" *Pennsylvania Medical Journal,* 64 (1961): 989–92.

Gribbons, Warren D., and Lohnes, Paul R. "Shifts in Adolescents' Vocational Values." *Personnel and Guidance Journal,* 44 (1965): 248–52.

Gronlund, Norman E., and Anderson, Loren. "Personality Characteristics of Socially Accepted, Socially Neglected, and Socially Rejected Junior High School Pupils." *Educational Administration and Supervision,* 43 (1957): 329–38.

Gross, Edward. "A Sociological Approach to the Analysis of Preparation for Work Life." *Personnel and Guidance Journal,* 45 (1967): 416–23.

Gross, Edward. "The Worker and Society." In *Man in a World at Work,* edited by Henry Borow. Boston: Houghton Mifflin Co., 1964.

Group for the Advancement of Psychiatry. *Normal Adolescence.* New York: Charles Scribner & Sons, 1968.

Haan, Norma; Smith, M. Brewster; and Block, Jeanne H. "Moral Reasoning of Young Adults: Political-Social Behavior, Family Background and Personality Correlates." *Journal of Personality and Social Psychology,* 10 (1968): 183–201.

Halleck, Seymour L. "Sex and Mental Health on the Campus." *Journal of the American Medical Association,* 200 (1967): 684–90.

Haller, A. O., and Wolff, Carole Ellis. "Personality Orientations of Farm, Village, and Urban Boys," *Rural Sociology,* 27 (1962): 275–93.

Harlow, R. G. "Masculine Inadequacy and Compensatory Development of Physique." *Journal of Personality,* 19 (1951): 312–33.

Harmon, Lenore W. "Anatomy of Career Commitment in Women." *Journal of Counseling Psychology,* 17 (1970): 77–80.

Harris, D. B. "Sex Differences in the Life Problems and Interests of Adolescents." *Child Development,* 30 (1959): 453–59.

Harris, D. B., and Tseng, Sing Chu. "Children's Attitudes toward Peers and Parents as Revealed by Sentence Completions." *Child Development,* 28 (1957): 401–11.

Hawley, Peggy. "Perceptions of Male Models of Femininity Related to Career Choice." *Journal of Counseling Psychology,* 19 (1972): 308–13.

Hawley, Peggy. "What Women Think Men Think: Does It Affect Their Career Choices?" *Journal of Counseling Psychology,* 18 (1971): 193–99.

Hershenson, David B. "Life-Stage Vocational Development System." *Journal of Counseling Psychology,* 15 (1968): 23–30.

Hershenson, David B., and Langbauer, William R. "Sequencing of Intrapsychic Stages of Vocational Development." *Journal of Counseling Psychology,* 20 (1973): 519–21.

Herzog, Elizabeth, and Sudia, Cecelia E. "The Generation Gap in the Eyes of Youth." *Children,* 17 (1970): 53–58.

Hoffman, Martin L., and Saltzstein, Herbert D. "Parent Discipline and the Child's Moral Development." *Journal of Personality* (1967): 45–57.

Holstein, Constance E. "The Relation of Children's Moral Judgment Level to That of Their Parents and to Communication Patterns in the Family." In *Adolescents: Development and Relationships,* edited by Mollie S. Smart and Russell C. Smart. New York: Macmillan Publishing Co., 1973.

Horrocks, John E. *The Psychology of Adolescence: Behavior and Development.* 3rd ed. Boston: Houghton Mifflin Co., 1969.

Houts, P. S., and Entwisle, D. R. "Academic Achievement Effort among Females: Achievement Attitudes and Sex Role Orientation." *Journal of Counseling Psychology,* 15 (1968): 284–86.

Huenemann, R. L.,; Shaping, L. R.; Hampton, M. C.; and Mitchell, B. W. "A Longitudinal Study of Gross Body Composition and Body Confirmation and Association with Food and Activity in a Teen-Age Population: Views of Teen-age Subjects on Body Conformation, Food, and Activity." *American Journal of Clinical Nutrition,* 18 (1966): 323–38.

Jacob, Philip E. *Changing Values in College.* New York: Harper Bros., 1957.

Joesting, Joan, and Joesting, Robert. "Future Problems of Gifted Girls." Paper presented at the 17th Annual Meeting of the

National Association for Gifted Girls, New Orleans, November 1969.

Jones, H. E. "Adolescence in Our Society." In *The Family in a Democratic Society,* Anniversary Papers of the Community Service Society of New York (New York: Columbia University Press, 1949).

Jones, M. C. "The Later Careers of Boys Who Were Early- or Late Maturing." *Child Development,* 28 (1957): 113–28.

Jones, M. C. "Psychological Correlates of Somatic Development." *Child Development,* 36 (1965): 899–916.

Jones, M. C., and Bayley, Nancy. "Physical Maturing among Boys as Related to Behavior." *Journal of Educational Psychology,* 41 (1950): 129–48.

Jones, M. C., and Mussen, P. H. "Self-Conceptions, Motivations, and Interpersonal Attitudes of Early- and Late-Maturing Girls." *Child Development,* 29 (1958): 491–501.

Jones, Vernon. "Attitudes of College Students and Their Changes: A 37-Year Study." *Genetic Psychology Monographs,* 81 (1970): 3–80.

Kaczkowski, Henry. "Sex and Age Differences in the Life Problems of Adolescents." *Journal of Psychological Studies,* 13 (1962): 165–69.

Kagan, Jerome. *Understanding Children: Behavior, Motives, and Thought.* New York: Harcourt Brace Jovanovich, 1971.

Kagan, Jerome, and Moss, H. A. "The Stability of Passive and Dependent Behavior from Childhood through Adulthood."

*Child Development,* 31 (1960): 577–91.

Kandel, Denise, and Lesser, Gerald. "Parent-Adolescent Relationships and Adolescent Independence in the U.S. and Denmark." *Journal of Marriage and the Family,* 31 (1962): 348–58.

Kandel, Denise, and Lesser, Gerald S. *Youth in Two Worlds: United States and Denmark.* San Francisco: Jossey-Bass, Publishers, 1972.

Kanin, Eugene J. "An Examination of Sexual Aggression as a Response to Sexual Frustration." *Journal of Marriage and the Family,* 29 (1967): 428–33.

Katz, Joseph and Associates. *No Time for Youth: Growth and Constraint in College Students.* San Francisco: Jossey-Bass Publishers, 1968.

Katz, Joseph. "Four Years of Growth, Conflict and Compliance," pp. 3–73. In *No Time For Youth,* edited by Joseph Katz. San Francisco: Jossey-Bass, Publishers, 1968.

Keniston, Kenneth. *The Uncommitted: Alienated Youth in American Society.* New York: Harcourt, Brace & World, 1965.

Kinloch, Graham C. "Parent-Youth Conflict at Home: An Investigation among University Freshmen." *American Journal of Orthopsychiatry,* 40 (1970): 658–64.

Kinsey, Alfred C.; Pomeroy, Wardell B.; and Martin, Clyde E. *Sexual Behavior in the Human Male.* Philadelphia: W. B. Saunders Co., 1948.

Kinsey, A. C.; Pomeroy, W. B.; Martin, C. E.; and Gebhard, P. H. *Sexual Behavior in the*

*Human Male.* Philadelphia: W. B. Saunders Co., 1953.

Kluckhohn, Clyde, and Kluckhohn, Florence. "American Culture: Generalized Orientation and Class Patterns." In L. Bryson et al., *Conflict of Power in Modern Culture.* New York: Harper Bros., 1947.

Kohlberg, Lawrence. "The Child as Moral Philosopher." *Psychology Today,* September 1968, pp. 24–30.

Kohlberg, Lawrence. "Development of Moral Character and Moral Ideology." In *Review of Child Development Research,* vol. 1, edited by Martin L. Hoffman and Lois W. Hoffman. New York: Russell Sage Foundation, 1964.

Kohlberg, Lawrence. "Moral Development and Identification." In *Child Psychology: Sixty-second Yearbook of the National Society for the Study of Education,* edited by H. W. Stevenson. Chicago: University of Chicago Press, 1963.

Kohlberg, Lawrence. "Stage and Sequence: The Cognitive-Developmental Approach to Socialization." In *Handbook of Socialization Theory and Research,* edited by David A. Goslin. Chicago: Rand McNally & Co., 1969.

Kohlberg, Lawrence, and Kramer, R. "Continuities and Discontinuities in Childhood and Adult Moral Development." *Human Development,* 12 (1969): 93–120.

Kohrs, E. V. "The Disadvantaged and Lower Class Adolescent." In *Understanding Adolescence: Current Developments in Ado-*

*lescent Psychology,* edited by James F. Adams. Boston: Allyn & Bacon, 1968.

Korn, Harold A. "Personality Scale Changes from the Freshman Year to the Senior Year." In *No Time for Youth,* Joseph Katz and Associates, San Francisco: Jossey-Bass, Publishers, 1968.

Kramer, R. "Moral Development in Young Adulthood." Ph.D. dissertation, University of Chicago, 1968.

Krieger, Leslie H., and Wells, William D. "The Criteria for Friendship." *Journal of Social Psychology,* 78 (1969): 109–12.

Krippner, S. "Sex, Ability and Interest: A Test of Tyler's Hypothesis." *Gifted Child Quarterly,* 6 (1962): 105–10.

Kuhlen, Raymond G., and Arnold, M. "Age Differences in Religious Beliefs and Problems during Adolescence." *Journal of Genetic Psychology,* 65 (1944): 291–300.

Kuhlen, Raymond G., and Houlihan, Nancy B. "Adolescent Heterosexual Interest in 1942 and 1963." *Child Development,* 36 (1965): 1049–52.

Lample-de-Groot, J. "On Adolescence." *Psychoanalytic Study of the Child,* 15 (1960): 98.

Landis, P. H. "Research on Teen-Age Marriage." *Marriage and Family Living,* 22 (1960): 266-67.

Latham, A. J. "The Relationship between Pubertal Status and Leadership in Junior High School Boys." *Journal of Genetic Psychology,* 78 (1951): 185–94.

Lerner, Richard M. "The Development of Stereotyped Expectancies of Body Build-Behavior Relations." *Child Development,* 40 (1969): 137–41.

Lesser, Gerald S.; Krawitz, Rhoda N., and Packard, Rita. "Experimental Arousal of Achievement Motivation in Adolescent Girls." *Journal of Abnormal and Social Psychology,* 66 (1963): 59–66.

Lessing, Elise E. "Extension of Personal Future, Time Perspective, Age, and Life Satisfaction of Children and Adolescents." *Developmental Psychology,* 6 (1972): 457–68.

Lewis, Robert A. "A Longitudinal Test of a Developmental Framework for Premarital Dyad Formation." *Journal of Marriage and the Family,* 35 (1973): 16–25.

Liccione, John V. "The Changing Family Relationship of Adolescent Girls." *Journal of Abnormal and Social Psychology.* 51 (1955): 421–26.

Lostia, Marcello. *"Atteggiamento dei Geovani nei Confronti della Autorita"* ["Attitudes of Adolescents when Confronted with Authority"], *Rivista di Psicologia Sociale, e Archivio Italian di Psicologia Generale, e Del Lavoro,* April–September 1966, pp. 217–64.

Luckey, E. B., and Nass, G. D. "A Comparison of Sexual Attitudes and Behavior in an International Sample." *Journal of Marriage and the Family,* 31 (1969): 364–79.

Maas, H. S. "Some Social Class Differences in the Family Systems and Group Relations of Pre- and Early Adolescents." *Child Development,* 22 (1951): 145–52.

Makowsky, Vivian P. "Fear of Success, Sex-Role Orientation of the Task, and Competitive Condition as Variables Affecting Women's Performance in Achievement-Oriented Situations." Paper presented to the 44th Annual Meeting, Midwestern Psychological Association, Cleveland, May 1972.

Marcus, Irwin M. "From School to Work: Certain Aspects of Psychosocial Interaction." *Adolescence: Psychosocial Perspectives,* edited by Gerald Caplan and Serge Lebovici. New York: Basic Books, 1969.

Masters, William H., and Johnson, Virginia E. *Human Sexual Inadequacy.* Boston: Little, Brown & Co., 1970.

Matteson, David D. *Alienation vs. Exploration and Commitment: Personality and Family Correlaries of Adolescent Identity Statuses.* Report from the Project for Youth Research. Copenhagen: Royal Danish School of Educational Studies, 1974.

Matteson, David R. "Changes in Attitudes toward Authority Figures in Selected College Freshmen." Ph.D. dissertation, Boston University, 1968.

Matteson, David R. "Changes in Attitudes toward Authority Figures with the Move to College: Three Experiments." *Developmental Psychology,* 4 (1974): 340–47.

McCandless, Boyd M. "The Socialization Process." In *Children: Behavior and Development,* 2d ed. New York: Holt, Rinehart & Winston, 1967.

McCreary-Juhasz, A. "How Accurate Are Student Evaluations of the Extent of Their Knowledge of Human Sexuality?" *The Journal of School Health,* 37 (1967): 409–12.

McNeil, J. "Changes in Ethnic Reaction Tendencies during High School." *Journal of Educational Research Archives,* 53 (1960): 199–200.

McNeil, J. "Rebellion, Conformity and Parental Religious Ideologies." *Sociometry,* 24 (1961): 125–35.

Medinnus, Gene R. "Moral Development in Childhood." In *Selected Readings in Child Psychology,* edited by Joseph Duffy and George Giuliani. Berkeley, Calif.: McCutchan Publishing Corp., 1970.

Medinnus, Gene R., and Johnson, Ronald C. *Child and Adolescent Psychology: Behavior and Development.* New York: John Wiley & Sons, 1969.

Meredith, Howard V. "A Synopsis of Pubertal Changes in Youth." *Journal of School Health,* 37 (1967): 171–76.

Middleton, Russell, and Putney, Snell. "Political Expression of Adolescent Rebellion." *American Journal of Sociology,* 67 (1963): 527–37.

Miller, Walter B. "Lower Class Culture as a Generating Milieu of Gang Delinquency." *Journal of Social Issues,* 143 (1958).

Montgomery, Jason. "Toward an Understanding of Cohabitation." Ph.D. diss., University of Massachusetts, 1972.

Moss, H. A., and Kagan, Jerome. "Stability of Achievement and Recognition Seeking Behavior from Early Childhood through Adulthood." *Journal of Abnormal and Social Psychology,* 63 (1961): 504–13.

Murphy, Elizabeth B., and Silber, Earle. "Development of Autonomy in Parent-Child Interaction in Late Adolescence." *American Journal of Orthopsychiatry,* 33 (1963): 643.

Mussen, Paul H. "Long-Term Consequences of Masculinity of Interests in Adolescence." *Journal of Consulting Psychology,* 26 (1962): 435–40.

Mussen, Paul H., and Boutourline-Young, H. "Relationships between Rate of Physical Maturing and Personality among Boys of Italian Descent." *Vita Humana,* 7 (1964): 186–200.

Mussen, Paul H.; Conger, John J.; and Kagan, Jerome. *Child Development and Personality,* 3rd ed. New York: Harper & Row, Publishers, 1969.

Mussen, Paul H., and Jones, Mary Cover. "Self-Conceptions, Motivations, and Interpersonal Attitudes of Late- and Early-Maturing Boys." *Child Development,* 28 (1957): 243–56.

Muuss, Rolf E. "Adolescent Development and the Secular Trend." *Adolescence,* 5 (1970): 267–84.

Muuss, Rolf E. "Puberty Rites in Primitive and Modern Societies." *Adolescence,* 5 (1970): 109–28.

Muuss, Rolf E. *Theories of Adolescence.* 2d ed. New York: Random House, 1968.

Newcomb, Theodore M. "Student Peer-Group Influence." In *The American College: A Psychological and Social Interpretation of the Higher Learning*, edited by Nevitt Sanford. New York: John Wiley & Sons, 1962.

Nixon, Robert E. *The Art of Growing*. New York: Random House, 1962.

Nye, F. Ivan. "Child Adjustment in Broken and in Unhappy Homes," *Marriage and Family Living*, 19 (1957): 356–61.

Offer, Daniel; Marcus, David; and Offer, Judith L. "A Longitudinal Study of Normal Adolescent Boys." *American Journal of Psychiatry*, 126 (1970): 917–24.

Offer, Daniel; Sabshin, M.; and Marcus, David. "Clinical Evaluation of Normal Adolescence." *American Journal of Psychiatry*, 121 (1965): 864–72.

O'Hara, Robert P. "The Roots of Careers." *Elementary School Journal*, 62 (1962): 277–80.

O'Hara, Robert P., and Tiedman, David V. "Vocational Self-Concept in Adolescence." *Journal of Consulting Psychology*, 6 (1959): 292–301.

Ostlund, Leonard A. "Environment-Personality Relationships." *Rural Sociology*, 22, (1957): 31–39.

Parsons, Talcott. "Age and Sex in the Social Structure of the United States." In *Essays in Sociological Theory, Pure and Applied*. Glencoe, Ill.: Free Press, 1949.

Parsons, Talcott. "Youth in the Context of American Society." *Daedalus*, 91 (1962): 97–123.

Perls, Frederick; Hefferline, Ralph E.; and Goodman, Paul. *Gestalt Therapy: Excitement and Growth in Personality*. New York: Julian Press, 1951.

Peskin, H. "Pubertal Onset and Ego Functioning." *Journal of Abnormal Psychology*, 72 (1967): 1–15.

Phelps, H., and Horrocks, J. E. "Factors Influencing Informal Groups of Adolescents." *Child Development*, 29 (1958): 69–86.

Piaget, Jean. *The Moral Judgment of the Child*, translated by M. Gabain. New York: Harcourt, Brace & World, 1932.

Plant, Walter T. "Changes in Ethnocentrism Associated with a Two-Year College Experience." *Journal of Genetic Psychology*, 92 (1958): 189–97.

Plant, Walter T. *Personality Changes Associated with a College Education*. USOE Cooperative Research Project 348, San Jose State College, 1962.

Pomeroy, Wardell B. *Boys and Sex*. New York: Delacorte Press, 1968.

Pomeroy, Wardell B. *Girls and Sex*. New York: Delacorte Press, 1970.

Putnam, Barbara A., and Hansen, James C. "Relationship of Self-Concept and Feminine Role Concept to Vocational Maturity in Young Women." *Journal of Counseling Psychology*, 19 (1972): 436–40.

Quigley, Carol. "Youth's Heros Have No Halos." *Today's Education*, February 1971, pp. 28–29.

Reich, Charles A. *The Greening*

*of America: The Coming of a New Consciousness and the Rebirth of the Future.* New York: Random House, 1970.

Reiss, Ira L. *The Family System in America.* New York: Holt, Rinehart & Winston, 1971.

Reiss, Ira L. *Premarital Sexual Standards in America: A Sociological Investigation of the Relative Social and Cultural Integration of American Sexual Standards.* New York: Free Press, 1960.

Reiss, Ira L. "Sexual Codes in Teen-Age Culture," *Annals of the American Academy of Political and Social Sciences,* 338 (1961): 53–62.

Reiss, Ira L. *The Social Contest of Premarital Permissiveness.* New York: Holt, Rinehart & Winston, 1967.

Remmers, H. H., and Radler, D. H. *The American Teenager.* Indianapolis: Bobbs-Merrill Co., 1962.

Reynolds, E. L., and Wines, J. V. "Physical Changes Associated with Adolescence in Boys." *American Journal of Diseases of Children,* 82 (1951): 529–47.

Rezler, Agnes G. "Characteristics of High School Girls Choosing Traditional or Pioneer Vocations." *Personnel and Guidance Journal,* 45 (1967): 659–65.

Rogers, Dorothy. *Adolescence: A Psychological Perspective.* Monterey, Calif.: Brooks/Cole Publishing Co., 1972.

Rose, Arnold. "The Adequacy of Women's Expectations for Adult Roles." *Social Forces,* 30 (1951): 69–77.

Rose, Arnold M. "Reference Groups of Rural High School Youth." *Child Development,* 27 (1956): 351–63.

Rosenberg, Morris. "Occupational Orientation." In *Society and the Adolescent Self-Image.* Princeton, N.J.: Princeton University Press, 1955.

Rosenberg, Morris. "Personality and Career Choice." In *Occupations and Values* (Glencoe, Ill.: Free Press, 1957).

Rossi, Alice. "Changing Sex Roles and Family Development." Paper presented at the meeting of the American Psychological Association, Washington, D.C., September 1971.

Rubin, Isadore. "Changing College Sex: New Kinsey Report." Sexology Magazine, 1968, 780–81.

Schmuck, Richard. "Concerns of Contemporary Adolescents." *Bulletin of the National Association of Secondary School Principals,* 49 (1965): 19–28.

Schonfeld, William A. "The Body and Body-Image in Adolescents." In *Adolescence: Psychosocial Perspectives,* edited by Gerald Caplan and Serge Lebovici. New York: Basic Books, 1969.

Seward, G. H., and Williamson, R. C. "A Cross-National Study of Adolescent Professional Goals." *Human Development,* 12 (1969): 248–54.

Sheldon, W. H.; Stevens, S. S.; and Tucker, W. B. *The Varieties of Human Physique.* New York: Harper & Row, Publishers, 1940.

Shepherd, J. "The *Look* Youth

Survey." *Look,* September 20, 1966, pp. 44–49.

Shipman, Gordon. "The Psychodynamics of Sex Education." In *Adolescent Behavior and Society: A Book of Readings,* edited by Rolf E. Muuss. New York: Random House, 1971.

Silber, Earle, et al. "Adaptive Behavior in Competent Adolescents: Coping with the Anticipation of College." *Archives of General Psychiatry,* 5 (1961): 354–65.

Simon, William, and Gagnon, John. "Psychosexual Development." *Transaction,* 6 (1969): 15–16.

Slocum, W. L., and Empey, L. T. *Occupational Planning by Young Women.* Bulletin no. 568, Agricultural Experimental Station, State College of Washington. Pullman, 1956.

Smart, Mollie S., and Smart, Russell C. *Adolescents: Development and Relationships.* New York: Macmillan Publishing Co., 1973.

Smith, Ernest A. "The Date." In *American Youth Culture.* Glencoe, Ill.: Free Press, 1956.

Smith, W. D., and Lebo, D. "Some Changing Aspects of the Self-Concept of Pubescent Males." *Journal of Genetic Psychology,* 88 (1956): 61–75.

Stagner, Ross. "Attitudes toward Authority: An Exploratory Study." *Journal of Social Psychology,* 11 (1954): 197–210.

Stagner, Ross. "The Role of Parents in the Development of Emotional Instability." *Psychological Bulletin,* 30 (1933): 696–97.

Stolz, H. R., and Stolz, L. M. "Adolescent Problems Related to Somatic Variations." In *Adolescence: 43rd Yearbook of the National Society for the Study of Education,* edited by N. B. Henry. Chicago: University of Chicago Press, 1944.

Stone, C. P., and Barker, R. G. "The Attitudes and Interests of Pre-menarchial and Post-menarchial Girls." *Journal of Genetic Psychology,* 54 (1939): 27–71.

Stone, Lawrence, and Church, Joseph. *Childhood and Adolescence,* 2d ed. New York: Random House, 1968.

Sullivan, Henry Stack. *The Interpersonal Theory of Psychiatry.* New York: W. W. Norton & Co., 1953.

Super, Donald E. "Consistency and Wisdom of Vocational Preference as Indices of Vocational Maturity in the Ninth Grade." *Journal of Educational Psychology,* 52 (1961): 35–43.

Super, D. E., et al. *Career Development: Self-Concept Theory.* New York: College Entrance Examination Board, Research Monograph No. 4, 1963.

Super, Donald E., et al. "Some Generalizations Regarding Vocational Development." In *Selected Readings in Adolescent Psychology,* edited by Joseph Duffy and George Giulani. Berkeley, Calif.: McCutchan Publishing Corp., 1970.

Survey Research Center. *A Study of Adolescent Boys.* Ann Arbor: University of Michigan Press, 1956.

Sutton-Smith, Brian; Rosenberg, B. G.; and Morgan, E. F. "Development of Sex Differences in Play Choices during Preadolescence." *Child Development*, 34 (1963): 119–26.

Tanner, J. M. "The Adolescent Growth-Spurt and Developmental Age." In *Human Biology: An Introduction to Human Evolution, Variation, and Growth*, edited by G. T. Harrison, J. S. Weiner, J. M. Tanner, and N. A. Barnicot. Oxford: Clarendon Press, 1964.

Tanner, J. M. *Growth at Adolescence*. 2d ed. Blackwell Scientific Publishers, 1962.

Taylor, Harold. "Freedom and Authority on the Campus." In *The American College: A Psychological and Social Interpretation of the Higher Learning*, edited by Nevitt Sanford. New York: John Wiley & Sons, 1967.

Thompson, George C., and Gardner, Eric F. "Adolescents' Perceptions of Happy-Successful Living." *Journal of Genetic Psychology*, 115 (1969): 107–20.

Thompson, O. E. "Student Values in Transition." *California Journal of Educational Research*, 19 (1968): 77–86.

Tierney, Roger J., and Herman, Al. "Self-Estimate Ability in Adolescence." *Journal of Counseling Psychology*, 20 (1973): 298–302.

Troll, Lillian E.; Neugarten, Bernice L., and Kraines, Ruth J. "Similarities in Values and Other Personality Characteristics in College Students and Their Parents." *Merrill-Palmer Quarterly*, 15 (1969): 323–36.

Tuma, Elias, and Livson, Norman. "Family Socioeconomic Status and Adolescent Attitudes toward Authority." *Child Development*, 31 (1960): 387–99.

Turiel, Elliot. "Conflict and Transition in Adolescent Moral Development." *Child Development*, 45 (1974): 14–29.

Turiel, Elliot. "Developmental Processes in the Child's Moral Thinking." In *New Directions in Developmental Psychology*, edited by Paul H. Mussen, Jonas Langer, and M. Covington. New York: Holt, Rinehart & Winston, 1969.

Turiel, Elliot, and Rothman, Golda R. "The Influence of Reasoning on Behavioral Choices at Different Stages of Moral Development." *Child Development*, 43 (1972): 741–56.

Tyler, Leona E. "The Antecedents of Two Varieties of Vocational Interests." *Genetic Psychology Monographs*, 70 (1964): 177–227.

Walster, Elaine: Aronson, Vera; Abraham, Darcy; and Roltman, Leon. "The Importance of Physical Attractiveness in Dating Behavior." *Journal of Personality and Social Psychology*, 4 (1966): 508–16.

Waterman, Alan S.; Geary, Patricia S.; and Waterman, Caroline K. "Longitudinal Study of Changes in Ego Identity Status from the Freshman to the Senior Year at College." *Developmental Psychology*, 10 (1974): 387–92.

Weatherly, D. "Self-Perceived Rate of Physical Maturation and Personality in Late Adolescence."

*Child Development*, 35 (1964): 1197–210.

Webster, Harold; Freedman, Mervin; and Heist, Paul. "Personality Changes in College Students." In *The American College: A Psychological and Social Interpretation of the Higher Learning*, edited by Nevitt Sanford. New York: John Wiley & Sons, 1967.

White, Robert W. *Lives in Progress: A Study of the Natural Growth of Personality*. 2d ed. New York: Holt, Rinehart & Winston, 1966.

White, Robert W. "Motivation Reconsidered: The Concept of Competence." *Psychological Review*, 66 (1959): 297–333.

Wright, Derek, and Cox, Edwin. "Religious Belief and Co-education in a Sample of Sixth-Form Boys and Girls." *British Journal of Social and Clinical Psychology*, 6 (1967): 23–31.

Yahoda, A., and Kuse, T. "The Psychological Study of Parent-Adolescent Relationships." *Bulletin of Faculty Education, Nagaya University*, 3 (1957): 100–127.

Yinger, J. M. "Contraculture and Subculture." *American Sociological Review*, 25 (1960): 625–35.

## Part three: Victories and losses

Abramowitz, Stephen I., and Abramowitz, Christine V. "A Tale of Serendipity: Political Ideology, Sex Role Prescriptions and Students' Psychological Adjustment." *Developmental Psychology*, 1 (1974): 299.

Ademek, Raymond J. "College Major, Work Commitment, and Female Perceptions of Self, Ideal Women, and Man's Ideal Woman." *Social Forces*, 3 (1970): 97–112.

Almquist, Elizabeth M., and Angrist, Shirley. "Career Salience and Atypicality of Occupational Choice among College Women." *Journal of Marriage and the Family*, 32 (1970): 242–49.

Banks, Louis, and editors of Fortune Magazine. *Youth in Turmoil*. New York: Time-Life, Inc., 1969.

Baumrind, Diana. "Authoritarian vs. Authoritative Parental Control." *Adolescence*, 3 (1968): 255–72.

Bay, Christian. "Political and Apolitical Students: Facts in Search of a Theory." *Journal of Social Issues*, 23 (1967): 77–91.

Bing, Elizabeth. "Effects of Child-rearing Practices on Development of Differential Cognitive Abilities." *Child Development*, 34 (1963): 631–48.

Block, Jeanne H.; Haan, Norma; and Smith, M. Brewster. "Activism and Apathy in Contemporary Adolescents." In *Understanding Adolescence*, edited by James F. Adams. Boston: Allyn & Bacon, 1968.

Blos, Peter. *On Adolescence: A Psychoanalytic Interpretation*. New York: Free Press, 1962.

Blos, Peter. "Prolonged Adolescence: The Formulation of a Syndrome and Its Therapeutic Implications." *American Journal of Orthopsychiatry,* 24 (1954): 733.

Bob, Sheila R. "An Investigation of the Relationship between Identity Status, Cognitive Style, and Stress." Ph.D. dissertation, State University of New York at Buffalo, 1968.

Bob, Sheila R., and Marcia, James. "Ego Identity Status and Two Cognitive Controls." Report, National Institutes of Mental Health, Grant MH13103-01. Bethesda, Md., 1967.

Butler, Edgar W.; McAllister, Ronald J.; and Kaiser, Edward. "The Effects of Voluntary and Involuntary Residential Mobility in Females and Males." *Journal of Marriage and the Family,* 35 (1973):) 219–27.

"Campus Crisis: Tough Questions over the Rebels." *New York Times,* May 4, 1969, sec. 4, p. 1.

Cowdry, R. William; Keniston, Kenneth; and Cabin, Seymour. "The War and Military Obligation: Private Attitudes and Public Actions." *Journal of Personality,* 38 (1970): 525–49.

Cross, Herbert J., and Allen, Jon G. "Ego Identity Status, Adjustment, and Academic Achievement." *Journal of Consulting and Clinical Psychology,* 34 (1970): 278–81.

Derber, Charles, and Flacks, Richard. "An Exploration of the Value System of Radical Students and Their Parents." Paper presented at the annual meeting of the American Sociologi-

cal Association, San Francisco, August 28–31, 1967.

Donovan, James. "A Study of Ego Identity Formation." Ph.D. dissertation, University of Michigan, 1970.

Dufresne, J., and Cross, Herbert. "Personality Variables in Student Drug Use." Master's thesis, University of Connecticut, 1972.

Erikson, Erik. *Identity and the Life Cycle.* New York: International Universities Press, 1959.

Erikson, Erik. *Identity: Youth and Crisis.* New York: W. W. Norton & Co., 1968.

Farber, Leslie H. "He Said, She Said." *Commentary,* March 1972, pp. 53–57.

Ferris, A. *Indicators of Change in the American Family.* New York: Russell Sage Foundation, 1970.

Fingaretta, Herbert. "Orestes: Paradigm Hero and Central Motif of Contemporary Ego Psychology," *Psycholanalytic Review,* 50 (Fall 1963): 87–111.

Flacks, Richard. "The Liberated Generation: An Exploration of the Roots of Students' Protest." *Journal of Social Issues,* 23 (1967): 52–76.

Friedenberg, Edgar Z. "Current Patterns of Generational Conflict." *Journal of Social Issues,* 25 (1967): 21–38.

Gold, Martin. "Juvenile Delinquency as a Symptom of Alienation." *Journal of Social Issues,* 24 (1969): 133.

Gordon, Thomas. *Parent Effectiveness Training* (New York: Peter H. Wyden, 1970).

Gottlieb, David. "Poor Youth: A Study in Forced Alienation." *Journal of Social Issues,* 24 (1969): 91–120.

Gould, Laurence J. "Conformity and Marginality: Two Faces of Alienation." *Journal of Social Issues,* 25 (1969): 39–64.

Greason, A. L. "Protests and Reaction: Students and Society in Conflict." *North American Review,* 6 (1961): 48–53.

Haan, Norma; Smith, M. Brewster; and Block, Jeanne. "Moral Reasoning of Young Adults: Political-Social Behavior, Family Background, and Personality Correlates." *Journal of Personality and Social Psychology,* 10 (1968): 183–201.

Hamilton, William. "The Death of God Theologies Today." In *Radical Theology and the Death of God,* edited by Thomas J. Altizer and William Hamilton. New York: Bobbs-Merrill Co., 1966.

Heilbrun, A. B., Jr. "Conformity to Masculinity-Feminity Stereotypes and Ego Identity in Adolescents." *Psychological Reports,* 14 (1964): 351–57.

Heilbrun, A. B. "Sex Role, Instrumental-Expressive Behavior and Psychopathology in Females." *Journal of Abnormal Psychology,* 73 (1968): 131–36.

Heilbrun, A. B., and Fromme, D. K. "Parental Identification of Late Adolescents and Level of Adjustment: The Importance of Parent-Model Attributes, Ordinal Position, and Sex of the Child." *Journal of Genetic Psychology,* 107 (1965): 49–59.

Heist, Paul. "The Dynamics of Student Discontent and Protest." Paper presented at annual meeting of the American Psychological Association, New York, September 1966.

Hess, Robert D., and Goldblatt, Irene. "The Status of Adolescents in American Society: A Problem in Social Identity." *Child Development,* 28 (1957): 459–68.

Hillsdale, Paul. "Marriage as a Personal Existential Commitment." *Marriage and Family Living,* 24 (1962): 143.

Hobart, C. W. "Commitment, Value Conflict, and the Future of the American Family." *Marriage and Family Living,* 25 (1963): 405–14.

Hoffman, Lois W. "Effects of the Employment of Mothers on Parental Power Relations and the Division of Household Tasks." *Marriage and Family Living,* 22 (1960): 27–35.

Hoffman, Lois W. "Effects of Maternal Employment on the Child—A Review of the Research." *Developmental Psychology,* 10 (1974): 204–28.

Janeway, Elizabeth. *Man's World, Woman's Place: A Study in Social Mythology* (New York: William Morrow & Co., 1971.

Jones, Stella B. "Geographic Mobility as Seen by the Wife and Mother." *Journal of Marriage and the Family,* 35 (1973): 210–18.

Jordan, Dianne. "Parental Antecedents and Personality Characteristics of Ego Identity Statuses." Ph.D. dissertation,

State University of New York at Buffalo, 1971.

Jordan, Dianne. "Parental Antecedents of Ego Identity Formation." Master's thesis, State University of New York at Buffalo, 1970.

Josselson, Ruthellen. "Identity Formation in College Women." Ph.D. dissertation, University of Michigan, 1972.

Josselson, Ruthellen. "Psychodynamic Aspects of Identity Formation in College Women." *Journal of Youth and Adolescence*, 2 (1973): 3–52.

Keniston, Kenneth. "Notes on Young Radicals." *Change*, 1 (November–December 1969): 28.

Keniston, Kenneth. "Student Activism, Moral Development, and Morality." *American Journal of Orthopsychiatry*, 40 (1970): 577–92.

Keniston, Kenneth. *The Uncommitted: Alienated Youth in American Society*. New York: Harcourt, Brace & World, 1965.

Keniston, Kenneth. "You Have to Have Grown up in Scarsdale to Know How Bad Things Really Are." *New York Times Magazine*, April 27, 1969, p. 27 ff.

Keniston, Kenneth. *Young Radicals*. New York: Harcourt, Brace & World, 1968.

Kerpelman, Larry C. *Activists and Nonactivists: A Psychological Study of American College Students*. New York: Behavioral Publications, 1972.

Kerpelman, Larry C. "Student Political Activism and Ideol-

ogy: Comparative Characteristics." *Journal of Counseling Psychology*, 16 (1969): 8–13.

Kinsler, Philip. "Ego Identity Status and Intimacy." Ph.D. dissertation, State University of New York at Buffalo, 1972.

Kohlberg, Lawrence. "The Development of Modes of Moral Thinking and Choice in the Years Ten to Sixteen," Ph.D dissertation, University of Chicago, 1958.

Kohlberg, Lawrence. "Relationship between the Development of Moral Judgement and Moral Conduct." Paper presented at the Symposium on Behavioral and Cognitive Concepts in Child Development, Minneapolis, March 1965.

Kohlberg, Lawrence, and Kramer, R. "Continuities and Discontinuities in Childhood and Adult Moral Development." *Human Development*, 12 (1969): 93–120.

Lifton, Robert Jay. *History and Human Survival*. New York: Random House, 1961.

"A Long Road for Women," *Time*, February 12, 1973, p. 69.

Mahler, C. "The Assessment and Evaluation of the Coping Styles of Two Ego Identity Status Groups: Moratorium and Foreclosure, to Identify Conflict Arousing Stimuli." Master's thesis, State University of New York at Buffalo, 1969.

Marcia, James E. "Development and Validation of Ego Identity Status." *Journal of Personality and Social Psychology*, 3 (1966): 551–58.

Marcia, James. "Ego Identity

Status: Relationship to Change in Self-Esteem, 'General Maladjustment,' and Authoritarianism," *Journal of Personality,* 1 (1967): 118–34.

Marcia, James E., and Friedman, M. L. "Ego Identity Status in College Women," *Journal of Personality,* 38 (1970): 249–63.

Martinson, W. D.; Jansen, D. G.; and Winborn, B. B. "Characteristics Associated with Campus Social-Political Action Leadership." *Journal of Counseling Psychology,* 15 (1968): 552–62.

Matteson, David R. *Alienation vs. Exploration and Commitment: Personality and Family Correlaries of Adolescent Identity Statuses.* Report from the Project for Youth Research. Copenhagen: Royal Danish School of Educational Studies, 1974.

McAllister, Ronald J.; Butler, Edgar W.; and Kaiser, Edward J. "The Adaptation of Women to Residential Mobility." *Journal of Marriage and the Family,* 34 (1973): 197–204.

Mulvey, Mary Carol. "Psychological and Sociological Factors in Predication of Career Patterns of Women." *Genetic Psychology Monographs,* 68 (1963): 309–86.

Murphey, L., and Raushenbush, E. *Achievement in the College lege Years.* New York: Harper & Row, Publishers, 1960.

Murphy, Donald C., and Mendelsohn, Lloyd A. "Communication and Adjustment in Marriage: Investigating the Relationship." *Family Process,* 12 (1973): 324.

Nelson, Helen Y., and Goldman, Phyllis R. "Attitudes of High School Students and Young Adults toward the Gainful Employment of Married Women." *The Family Coordinator,* (July 1969): 251–55.

Nevid, J. S.; Nevid, A. S.; O'Neill, M., and Waterman, C. M. "Sex Differences in Resolution of Sexual Identity Crisis." Paper presented at the convention of the Eastern Psychologcial Association, Philadelphia, April 1974.

Orlofsky, J. L.; Marcia, James; and Lesser, Ira M. "Ego Identity Status and the Intimacy versus Isolation Crisis of Young Adulthood." *Journal of Personality and Social Psychology,* 27 (1973): 211–19.

Perry, William G., Jr., et al. "Patterns in Development in Thought and Values of Students in a Liberal Arts College: A Validation of a Schema." Bureau of Study Counsel, Harvard University, April 1968.

Peterson, Richard E. "The Student Left in Higher Education." *Daedalus,* 97 (1968): 293–317.

Podd, Marvin. "An Investigation of the Relationship between Ego Identity Status and Level of Moral Development." Ph.D. dissertation, State University of New York at Buffalo, 1969.

Podd, Marvin H.; Marcia, James E.; and Rubin, Barry M. "The Effects of Ego Identity and Partner Perception on a Prisoner's Dilemma Game. *Journal of Social Psychology,* 82 (1970): 117–26.

Poloma, Margaret M., and Garland,

T. Neal. "The Married Professional Woman: A Study in the Tolerance of Domestication." *Journal of Marriage and the Family,* 33 (1971): 531–40.

Rapaport, Rhona, and Rapaport, Robert. "The Dual-Career Family." *Human Relations,* 22 (1969): 3–30.

Reichart, Sandford. "A Greater Space in Which to Breathe: What Art and Drama Tell Us about Alienation." *Journal of Social Issues,* 25 (1969): 137–46.

Ridley, Carl A. "Exploring the Impact of Work Satisfaction and Involvement in Marital Interaction When Both Partners Are Employed." *Journal of Marriage and the Family,* 35 (1973): 229–37.

Rose, John A. "Child Development and the Part Time Mother." *Children,* 6 (1959): 213.

Rossi, Alice S. "Family Development in a Changing World." *American Journal of Psychiatry,* 128 (1972): 1057–66.

Rotter, Julian B. "Generalized Expectancies for Internal versus External Control of Reinforcement." *Psychological Monographs: General and Applied,* 80, no. 609 (1966): 1–28.

Schenkel, Susi, and Marcia, James. "Attitudes toward Premarital Intercourse in Determining Ego Identity Status in College Women." *Journal of Personality,* 3 (1972): 472–82.

Seeman, Melvin. "On the Meaning of Alienation." *American Sociological Review,* 24 (1959): 783–91.

Tannenbaum, Abraham J. "Introduction" to "Alienated Youth." *Journal of Social Issues,* 25 (1969): 1–6.

Tasch, R. J. "The Role of Father in the Family." *Journal of Experimental Education,* 20 (1952): 319–61.

Thomas, Lamar E. "Family Congruence of Political Orientations in Politically Active Parents and Their College-Age Children." Ph.D. diss., University of Chicago, 1968.

Toder, Nancy L., and Marcia, James E. "Ego Identity Status and Response to Conformity Pressure in College Women." *Journal of Personal and Social Psychology,* 26 (1973): 287–94.

Toffler, Alvin. *Future Shock.* New York: Random House, 1970.

Trent, James W., and Craise, Judith L. "Commitment and Conformity in the American College." *Journal of Social Issues,* 23 (1967): 10–52.

Waterman, Alan S.; Geary, Patricia S.; and Waterman, Caroline K. "Longitudinal Study of Changes in Ego Identity Status from the Freshman to the Senior Year at College." *Developmental Psychology,* 10 (1974): 387–92.

Waterman, Alan S., and Waterman, Caroline K. "A Longitudinal Study of Changes in Ego Identity Status during the Freshman Year at College." *Developmental Psychology,* 5 (1971): 167–73.

Waterman, Alan S., and Waterman, Caroline K. "The Relationship between Ego Identity Status and Satisfaction with College." *Journal of Educational Research,* 64 (1970): 165–68.

Waterman, Alan S., and Waterman, Caroline K. "The Relationship between Freshman Ego Identity Status and Subsequent Academic Behavior: A Test of the Predictive Validity of Marcia's Categorization System for Identity Status." *Developmental Psychology,* 6 (1972): 179.

Waterman, C. K.; Buebel, M. E.; and Waterman, A. S. "Relationship between Resolution of the Identity Crisis and Outcomes of Previous Psychological Crises." In *Proceedings of the 78th Annual Convention of the American Psychological Association* (1970), vol. 5, pp. 467–68 (summary).

Watts, William A.; Lynch, Steve; and Whittaker, David. "Alienation and Activism in Today's College-Age Youth: Socialization Patterns and Current Family Relationships." *Journal of Counseling Psychology,* 16 (1969): 1–7.

Westby, D. L., and Braungart, R. G. "Class and Politics in the Family Background of Student Political Activists." *American Sociological Review,* 31 (1966): 690–92.

Whittaker, David, and Watts, William A. "Personality Characteristics of a Nonconformist Youth Subculture: A Study of the Berkeley Non-student." *Journal of Social Issues,* 25 (1969): 65–90.

Winborn, B. B., and Jansen, D. G. "Personality Characteristics of Campus Social-Political Action Leaders." *Journal of Counseling Psychology,* 14 (1967): 509–13.

Wynn, John Charles. "The American Family—Surviving through Change." *The Episcopalian,* March 1970, p. 30.

Yarrow, Marian Radke; Scott, Phyllis; DeLeeuw, Louise; and Heinig, Christine. "Child-Rearing in Families of Working and Non-Working Mothers," *Sociometry,* 25 (1962): 122–40.

Zimmerman, Carle C. "The Future of the Family in America." *Journal of Marriage and the Family,* 34 (1972): 323–33.

# Indexes

# Author index

## A

Abramowitz, Christine, V., *288, 289*
Abramowitz, Stephen I., *288, 289*
Adelson, Joseph, 98, *104, 171, 172,* 177, 196, *199, 202, 228*
Ademek, Raymond J., *340, 341*
Adler, Alfred, 6
Adorno, T. W., 234, *245, 285*
Allen, Jon G., *285, 286, 318, 319*
Almquist, Elizabeth M., *340*
Anastasi, Anne, *48*
Anderson, Loren, *141*
Andersson, Bengt-Erik, *122*
Andry, R. G., 66, *74*
Angelino, H., *143*
Angrist, Shirley S., *200, 340*
Anthony, A., *86*
Arkoff, Abe, *142*
Armentraut, James A., *28*
Arnold, M., *228*
Asch, Solomon E., *288*
Astin, Alexander W., *202*
Atkinson, Richard C., *49, 123, 141*

## B

Bach, G. R., *73*
Baer, Donald M., *13*
Bain, R. K., *289*
Bales, Robert F., *245, 319*
Bandura, Albert, 45–46, *50, 70, 74, 85, 86,* 94–95, 99, *102*
Bardwich, Judith, *342*
Barker, R. G., *171*
Baumrind, Diana, *342*
Bay, Christian, *264*
Bayley, Nancy, *143, 144*
Beach, Frank A., 43, 44, *50, 172*
Bealer, R. C., 94, 99, *102*

Becker, Wesley C., 28, 30, *122, 123*
Bell, Robert R., 164, *173, 174*
Bennett, E. M., 28, *31*
Bennett, H. D., *86*
Berger, E., 29
Bergman, P., *48*
Bernard, Harold W., *141, 173*
Bernard, J., *144*
Bernard, Jessie, *340, 342*
Bernfeld, S., *263*
Berry, J. L., *49*
Bieber, Irving, *31*
Bieri, James, 71, *87*
Bijou, Sidney, W., *13*
Bilous, C. B., *86*
Bing, Elizabeth, *342*
Birnbaum, Morton P., 212, 213, *228*
Block, J., *143*
Block, Jeanne H., *229, 230, 265, 317, 318*
Blos, Peter, *101, 121, 144, 171, 245,* 252–56, *263, 264,* 267, 269, *285,* 310, *319,* 345, *355*
Bob, Sheila R., *286*
Bohn, Martin J., Jr., *200*
Bonhoeffer, Deitrich, *230*
Borow, Henry, *199, 200, 202*
Borup, J. H., *244*
Boutourline-Young, H., *144*
Bowerman, Charles E., *103, 171*
Bowlby, John, *73*
Braungart, R. G., *318*
Brittain, Clay V., 93–94, 98, *102, 104, 171, 227*
Broderick, Carlfred B., *173*
Brodsky, C. M., *142*
Bronfenbrenner, Uri, *123*
Brown, D. G., *73*
Brown, D. S., *86*
Brown, Roger, *200, 245*
Buebel, M. E., *285, 286*

*Italic numbers indicate pages for end-of-chapter notes.*

389

# Subject index

*Italic numbers indicate pages for end-of-chapter notes.*

This book has been set in 10 and 9 point
Caledonia, leaded 2 points. Part numbers are
24 point Scotch Roman italic and part titles
are 24 point Scotch Roman. Chapter numbers
are 30 point Scotch Roman italic and chapter
titles are 18 point Scotch Roman italic. The
size of the type page is 27 × 45½ picas.